NUCLEAR FOLLY

NUCLEAR
FOLLY

A HISTORY OF
THE CUBAN MISSILE CRISIS

Serhii Plokhy

W. W. NORTON & COMPANY
Independent Publishers Since 1923

For information about permission to reproduce selections from this book, write to
Permissions, W. W. Norton & Company, Inc., 500 Fifth Avenue, New York, NY 10110

For information about special discounts for bulk purchases, please contact
W. W. Norton Special Sales at specialsales@wwnorton.com or 800-233-4830

Manufacturing by LSC Communications, Harrisonburg
Production manager: Beth Steidle

Library of Congress Cataloging-in-Publication Data

Names: Plokhy, Serhii, 1957– author.
Title: Nuclear folly : a history of the Cuban Missile Crisis / Serhii Plokhy.
Description: First edition. | New York, N.Y. : W. W. Norton & Company,
[2021] | Includes bibliographical references and index.
Identifiers: LCCN 2020033221 | ISBN 9780393540819 (hardcover) |
ISBN 9780393540826 (epub)
Subjects: LCSH: Cuban Missile Crisis, 1962. | Cold War. | Nuclear crisis
control—History—20th century. | International relations—History—20th century. |
United States—Foreign relations—1961–1963. | Cuba—Foreign
relations—1959–1990. | Soviet Union—Foreign relations—1953–1975.
Classification: LCC E841 .P55 2021 | DDC 972.9106/4—dc23
LC record available at https://lccn.loc.gov/2020033221

W. W. Norton & Company, Inc., 500 Fifth Avenue, New York, N.Y. 10110
www.wwnorton.com

W. W. Norton & Company Ltd., 15 Carlisle Street, London W1D 3BS

1 2 3 4 5 6 7 8 9 0

To those who had the courage to step back

Today, every inhabitant of this planet must contemplate the day when this planet may no longer be habitable. Every man, woman and child lives under a nuclear sword of Damocles, hanging by the slenderest of threads, capable of being cut at any moment by accident or miscalculation or by madness.

—JOHN F. KENNEDY, SEPTEMBER 1961[1]

Of course, I was scared. It would have been insane not to be scared, I was frightened about what could happen to my country and all the countries that would be devastated by a nuclear war. If being frightened meant that I helped avert such insanity, then I'm glad I was frightened. One of the problems in the world today is that not enough people are sufficiently frightened by danger of nuclear war.

—NIKITA KHRUSHCHEV, DECEMBER 1962[2]

CONTENTS

IV. MOMENT OF TRUTH

V. BLACK SATURDAY

VI. RISING FROM THE DEAD

VII. SETTLEMENT

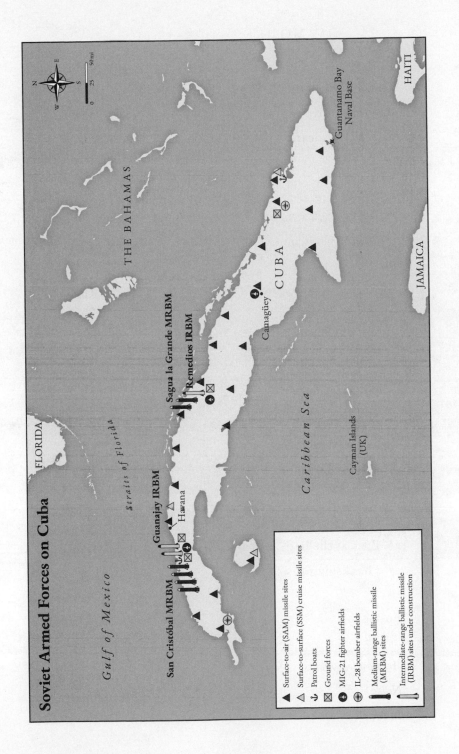

Soviet Armed Forces on Cuba

FLORIDA

Gulf of Mexico

Straits of Florida

San Cristóbal MRBM

Guanajay IRBM

Hawana

Sagua la Grande MRBM

Remedios IRBM

THE BAHAMAS

Caribbean Sea

Cayman Islands (UK)

Camagüey

CUBA

Guantanamo Bay Naval Base

JAMAICA

HAITI

▲ Surface-to-air (SAM) missile sites
△ Surface-to-surface (SSM) cruise missile sites
⚓ Patrol boats
⊠ Ground forces
⊕ MIG-21 fighter airfields
⊕ IL-28 bomber airfields
▮ Medium-range ballistic missile (MRBM) sites
▮ Intermediate-range ballistic missile (IRBM) sites under construction

N
W E
S

0 25 50 mi

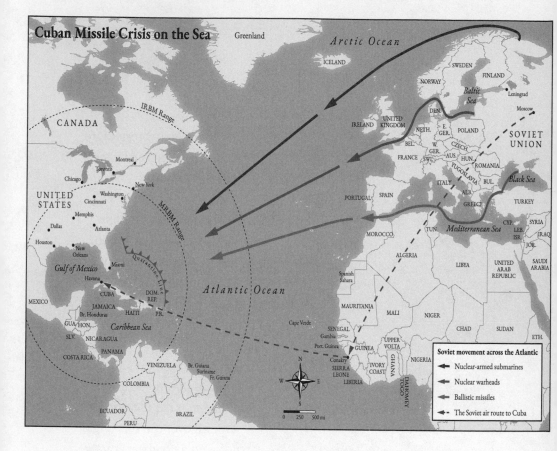

Cuban Missile Crisis on the Sea

Soviet movement across the Atlantic

→ Nuclear-armed submarines
→ Nuclear warheads
→ Ballistic missiles
←-→ The Soviet air route to Cuba

PREFACE

"Ballistic missile threat inbound to Hawaii. Seek immediate shelter. This is not a drill," said a text message received by tens of thousands of Hawaii residents on the morning of January 13, 2018. "First instinct was to jump out of bed and figure out what was going on," recalled Luke Clements, a twenty-one-year-old college sophomore and football player at the University of Hawaii at Manoa. The basement classroom where Clements found temporary refuge was soon full of people. Some were screaming, demanding that the door be closed. "For a good 10 minutes, there were no rules. Everyone was trying to survive together," recalled Clements. "It was a calm chaos."

The message turned out to be a false alarm. As the authorities would later say, someone had pushed the "wrong button." In fact, the story was more complicated. The official who made the mistake was a ten-year veteran of the emergency agency and had to push not one but two buttons to activate the alert that caused panic all over the state. The missile alert that sent Clements, his classmates, and a good part of the population of Hawaii in search of nonexistent shelters and eventually into the basements of buildings did not come completely out of the blue. The Hawaii authorities began to test their sirens in December 2017 for the first time in thirty years; the previous test had been back in 1987.[1]

In 2017 Kim Jong-un, the secretive thirty-four-year-old leader of North Korea, defied the United States and the international community by choosing July 4, America's Independence Day, to launch an intercontinental ballistic missile capable of reaching Alaska. Later that year he declared his country a "full-fledged nuclear power" whose missiles could hit targets around the globe. In October 2017, when the North Korean media announced the test of a hydrogen bomb, President Donald Trump threatened to "totally destroy North Korea." He declared that "Rocket Man [Kim Jong-un] is on a suicide mission for himself and for his regime." Kim shot back, calling Trump a "mentally deranged old lunatic." In May 2018, President Trump withdrew from the multilateral agreement with Iran that precluded that country from developing nuclear weapons. In January 2020, Iran declared its own withdrawal from the agreement, raising fears of the rapid development of its nuclear capabilities.[2]

As the United States was experiencing the worst nuclear crises since the end of the Cold War, history suddenly became the present. In August 2017, two influential commentators, one a Republican, the future national security adviser to President Trump, John Bolton, the other a Democrat, the former White House chief of staff under President Clinton and CIA director and secretary of defense under President Obama, Leon Panetta, suggested in unison that the US–North Korean standoff over the development of Kim Jong-un's nuclear and missile program was the worst nuclear crisis to hit the world since the standoff over Cuba. In February 2019, Vladimir Putin joined the fray, declaring that he was prepared for a new Cuban-type missile crisis and threatened the United States with supersonic rockets to be installed on ships and submarines off the American coast. He repeated the same statement in February 2020. One month earlier, in January 2020, after the US assassination of Iran's architect of clandestine warfare Qasem Suleimani and Tehran's announcement of Iran's complete withdrawal from the nuclear deal, the US media compared President Trump's nuclear gamble with President Kennedy's actions in the Cuban missile crisis.[3]

The references to the Cuban missile crisis have shown no tendency of disappearing from the world political scene and media any time soon. The return of nuclear weapons to the center stage of international politics inevitably brought back memories of the nuclear stand over Cuba. Can we prevent the emergence of a new nuclear showdown, or at least resolve it without a nuclear war, by reexamining the history of the crisis? In this book I argue that there is indeed much to be learned from the experience of those who created and then resolved the crisis. There is an additional reason to revisit that history. With the world sliding back into the nuclear brinkmanship that characterized the 1950s and early 1960s, it is essential to educate new generations about the dramatic events of that era in a way that addresses the uncertainties of today's world.

◊◊◊

THE BODY OF LITERATURE ON THE HISTORY OF THE CUBAN MISsile crisis is truly enormous, but as I show below there are major gaps both in the coverage of the crisis and in understanding it as an international rather than a solely American affair. The deep dive into the history of the crisis began in the 1960s with Robert Kennedy's *Thirteen Days: A Memoir of the Cuban Missile Crisis*. It remains very popular with readers. But the appearance in the public domain of tapes of the ExCom* debates, made secretly by President Kennedy and apparently available to his brother when he was working on his book, challenged many established "truths" about the process of decision-making. Later research showed that his account was often self-serving and inaccurate with regard to the role played in the crisis by Robert Kennedy's nemeses and rivals, such as Secretary of State Dean Rusk and then vice president Lyndon Johnson.[4]

Major progress has been made by historians, political scientists, and journalists since the publication of Robert Kennedy's book in 1971. The classic work of the Harvard historian Graham Allison (later joined by Philip Zelikow) on decision-making during the crisis became a must-read for generations of international relations students through-

---

* An acronym for the Executive Committee of the National Security Council convened during the Cuban missile crisis.

out the world. The work done in the 1990s by the American historian Timothy Naftali and his Russian colleague Aleksandr Fursenko contributed enormously to our understanding of the decision-making process in Moscow, while an excellent journalistic investigation by Michael Dobbs presented the bottom-up story of the crisis, which involved dozens if not hundreds of thousands of people in the three belligerent countries. The Cuban side of the story, long unavailable, has become known in recent decades with the publication and eventual translation into English of works by Cuban historians.[5]

But no matter how many academic and popular studies have been written and published in recent years and decades about the Cuban missile crisis, the dominant narrative remains the same: John Kennedy refused to budge and, thanks to the decision-making process involving his closest advisers, managed to make the right assumptions and draw the right conclusions about Soviet intentions and capabilities, thereby resolving the crisis. I challenge that established narrative by taking a road toward the reconstruction and understanding of the Cuban missile crisis rarely traveled before. Instead of identifying moments in the crisis when key figures and rank-and-file participants got things right and determining how they reached those correct decisions, I consider the myriad situations in which they got things wrong.

John Kennedy, highly alert to the possibility of starting a war by misreading the adversary, was particularly impressed by Barbara Tuchman's Pulitzer Prize–winning history of the "accidental" outbreak of World War I, *The Guns of August*, published in the spring of 1962. He not only gave copies to close allies but also had the book sent to American military commanders throughout the world. But the story of the crisis, as I see it, might be well summarized by the title of another award-winning book by Tuchman, *The March of Folly*. As I show in this book, both Kennedy and Khrushchev marched from one mistake to another. They were caused by a variety of factors, from ideological hubris and overriding political agendas to misreading the other side's geostrategic objectives and intentions, poor judgment often due to the lack of good intelligence, and cultural misunderstandings.[6]

Kennedy found it difficult to understand Khrushchev's motives and was consumed with worry about a nuclear crisis over Berlin. He proposed a strike against the Soviet missiles in Cuba without knowing either the number of Soviet troops on the island or their nuclear capabilities. Khrushchev, never expecting such a determined response from Kennedy, panicked at first and then had difficulty communicating his desire to resolve the crisis as soon as possible. He lost the initiative and, ultimately, control over his troops in Cuba to Fidel Castro, who was himself prone to panic and eager to fight the Americans.[7]

As I examined my sources, which included recently released KGB files, for errors committed by Kennedy, Khrushchev, and their advisers and subordinates, I could not help posing the question of what prevented nuclear war from breaking out. A great deal—too much, one might say—depended on the decisions of the leaders, so different in background, political trajectory, ideological views, and managerial styles. But as I argue in this book, they had one thing in common that proved decisive—fear of nuclear war. The crisis did not develop into a shooting war because Kennedy and Khrushchev both feared nuclear weapons and dreaded the very idea of their use.

Kennedy, who wanted to strike at the Soviet missiles on Cuba, turned to a blockade once he understood that the missiles were ready to fire. Khrushchev, initially willing to prevent a possible US attack on Cuba by using nuclear missiles, ordered his ships to turn back once he learned of the blockade and brought Soviet missiles out of Cuba when nuclear-armed American strategic bombers went on high alert. The two leaders hastened to compromise on American missiles in Turkey when they realized that they were losing control on the ground and in the air, as demonstrated by the Soviet downing of an American U-2 plane over Cuba without authorization from Moscow. Later, Khrushchev removed even undetected nuclear weapons from the island to avoid causing another crisis and, potentially, war.

Kennedy, Khrushchev, and their generation of world leaders and the citizens of their countries came of age in the shadow of the atomic bombing of Hiroshima and Nagasaki, as well as the mind-boggling destructive power demonstrated by the hydrogen bomb tests of Castle Bravo by the Americans in 1954 and the Tsar Bomba (Emperor Bomb) by the Soviets in 1961. That generation was keenly aware of the destruction that atomic and especially hydrogen bombs could wreak on their countries and humankind as a whole. Every move of the two leaders described in this book was dictated by their fear of the use of nuclear weapons. There is little doubt that today there are world leaders prepared to take a more cavalier attitude toward nuclear weapons and nuclear war than Kennedy and Khrushchev had in 1962.

Unbeknownst to most of its inhabitants, the world entered a new and dangerous era on August 2, 2019. On that day the planet's strongest nuclear powers, the United States and Russia, with thirty thousand warheads between them, declared their withdrawal from the Intermediate-Range Nuclear Forces Treaty signed by Ronald Reagan and Mikhail Gorbachev in 1987. Until that day the treaty was the last Cold War–era arms-control agreement still remaining in place. We are now officially at the start of an uncontrolled nuclear arms race. What it might bring became clear on August 8, less than a week after the Reagan-Gorbachev agreement was abandoned. The reactor of a nuclear-powered and nuclear-armed Russian cruise missile, codenamed Skyfall, exploded in the Barents Sea, killing five Russian scientists and naval officers and contaminating the atmosphere and waters in the Arkhangelsk region of Russia. The ultimate target of Skyfall, as President Putin demonstrated in a public video a year earlier, was the United States.[8]

What we are witnessing today has been characterized by some authors as the arrival of the "second nuclear age." But we are in a more dangerous and unpredictable world today than we were during the Cold War because more powers are prepared to threaten adversaries with nuclear weapons, and the fear of such weapons acquired in the first decades of the Cold War has been considerably dulled. We unlearned the lessons of the past. To survive in the current nuclear age, we must learn them anew.[9]

NUCLEAR FOLLY

PROLOGUE

obert McNamara could not believe what he had just heard. According to a witness, he "had to hold on to a table to steady himself" after he absorbed the news. It was January 9, 1992, and McNamara, the seventy-five-year-old former secretary of defense under John F. Kennedy and Lyndon B. Johnson, was now in Havana attending a conference on its history, in which he had been a key participant.

In attendance were Fidel Castro and some other prominent participants in the events from the United States, Cuba, and the recently defunct Soviet Union. At the podium was General Anatoly Gribkov, the former commander of the Warsaw Pact military forces and, before that, one of the key planners of the Soviet deployment in Cuba in 1962. What shocked McNamara was Gribkov's matter-of-fact remark that the Soviets had managed to deploy forty-three thousand men on the island in the summer and fall of 1962. McNamara and his military experts had been sure that there could be no more than ten thousand Soviet troops in Cuba. That was the number on which they were basing their decision whether to strike the Soviet installations and invade the island.

But that was only the first shocking revelation. Gribkov also calmly stated that apart from their huge troop concentration, antiaircraft weapons, bombers, and medium-range missiles capable of striking the United States with nuclear warheads, the Soviets had on the island tactical nuclear weapons that the Americans knew nothing about. There were six Luna (US designation "Frog") missile launchers with nine missiles and nuclear warheads. These were short-range missiles that could not reach Florida but could have been used against an American invasion force with devastating consequences. Each nuclear warhead had an explosive power of 6 to 12 kilotons of TNT, only slightly less than the 15-kiloton nuclear bomb dropped on Hiroshima in August 1945. On top of that, as McNamara learned, at one stage of the crisis it was up to the Soviet commander in the field to decide whether to use the Luna missiles or not.[1]

"We didn't believe there were nuclear warheads in Cuba," commented McNamara a few days later. "There was no evidence of nuclear warheads." Arthur M. Schlesinger Jr., a former special assistant to President Kennedy and McNamara's fellow participant at the conference, was equally taken aback. He recalled that Gribkov's revelations had startled and appalled the Americans. "Incredible," wrote Schlesinger, remembering his own reaction to the news. "I had earlier believed that we had overestimated the dangers of the crisis—that Khrushchev, well aware of US overall nuclear superiority as well as of US conventional superiority in the Caribbean, would never have risked war. But Soviet forces, we are now told, were ready to fire tactical nuclear missiles at an invading force."[2]

A few hours earlier McNamara told the conference that the actions of the three main actors in the Cuban missile crisis "had been distorted by misinformation, miscalculation, and misperceptions." But even he had not realized the depth of those misunderstandings and misperceptions. "That was horrifying. It meant that had a U.S. invasion been carried out, if the missiles had not been pulled out, there was a 99 percent probability that nuclear war would have been initiated," McNamara told a reporter.[3]

I

NEMESES

1

APPRENTICE

John Fitzgerald Kennedy cut an impressive figure on the cold Washington day of his inauguration, January 20, 1961. Tall and erect, despite his back problems, dressed in a tailcoat as everyone around him wore a winter coat, he projected youth, energy, optimism, and determination. The youngest person ever elected president of the United States—he was only forty-three years old—left no doubt by his looks and words that he was ready to chart a new course for his country and the world, not just for the duration of his presidency but for decades ahead.[1]

Leadership was passing from one generation to another, the transition captured by cameras as the gray, balding, and warmly dressed outgoing president, Dwight Eisenhower, accompanied his young successor to the ceremony in the same automobile and then shook his hand after the swearing-in. Eisenhower, a war hero and one of the most successful presidents in American history, was seventy at the time. But he was not the oldest man in attendance. To greet the new president and pass the torch of moral leadership came the eighty-six-year-old dean of

American literature, Robert Frost. Kennedy wanted him to take part in the ceremony, and Frost accepted the invitation: "If you can bear at your age the honor of being made president of the United States, I ought to be able at my age to bear the honor of taking some part in your inauguration."[2]

Frost appreciated the challenges that Kennedy would face as president but counted on his youth as an asset, envisioning a glorious age for his country modeled on the era of the first Roman emperor, Augustus. It would be an age of peace, tranquility, and an alliance of power with culture. In a dedicatory poem he wrote specifically for the inauguration but never read, as he was blinded by light reflected from the snow that had fallen on Washington the previous night, Frost heralded "The glory of a next Augustan age / Of a power leading from its strength and pride / Of young ambition eager to be tried / Firm in our free beliefs without dismay / In any game the nations want to play."[3]

If Frost had a bold vision but lacked good eyesight, the much younger Kennedy possessed both. His inauguration speech became one of the best known texts in American political history, making its way into elementary school classrooms all over the country. According to the website of the JFK Presidential Library and Museum, the most memorable line of the speech, "ask not what your country can do for you—ask what you can do for your country," "inspired children and adults to see the importance of civic action and public service." Indeed, it did. But public service at home was not at the center of Kennedy's attention. Sacrifice abroad in the pursuit of Robert Frost's Augustan age was. "[W]e shall pay any price, bear any burden, meet any hardship, support any friend, oppose any foe to assure the survival and success of liberty," declared Kennedy. His speech was largely dedicated to world politics. The great social turmoil of the 1960s was still ahead; the current preoccupation was the scare caused by the Soviet Sputnik and communist advances in Asia, Africa, and, most recently, in Latin America.[4]

Kennedy warned his fellow citizens and the world at large of the possibility of what he called "mankind's final war." The nuclear arms race and its consequences were on his mind. A key part of the speech was addressed to the Soviet leader, Nikita Khrushchev, though neither his name nor that of his country was mentioned. Kennedy referred instead to "those nations who would make themselves our adversaries." He called on his unnamed adversary to "begin anew the quest for peace, before the dark powers of destruction unleashed by science engulf all humanity in planned or accidental self-destruction." Borrowing a phrase from the Harvard economist John Kenneth Galbraith, who advised him on the speech, Kennedy declared: "Let us never negotiate out of fear. But let us never fear to negotiate."

Kennedy was promising the rise of a new America in a new world. It would be based on liberty and brought into being through the dedication and sacrifice of American citizens. He promised Latin American countries—"sister republics," as he called them—to "convert our good words into good deeds" and form a "new alliance for progress" against poverty. "But this peaceful revolution of hope cannot become the prey of hostile powers," continued Kennedy. "Let all our neighbors know that we shall join with them to oppose aggression or subversion anywhere in the Americas. And let every other power know that this Hemisphere intends to remain the master of its own house."[5]

The Pax Romana inaugurated by Augustus at the turn of the common era was to be emulated by Kennedy's Pax Americana. But was that vision achievable? And could it be implemented by a young, inexperienced president? Robert Frost believed it could. The test of his vision and Kennedy's talents and determination still lay ahead. It came sooner than anyone expected and closer to American shores than could have been predicted. The name of the test was Cuba.

◊◊◊

IN THE TWENTIETH CENTURY, CUBA BECAME A SYMBOL OF America's failure to live up to the high standards of its own anti-imperial calling and the expectations raised by anticolonial revolutions around the world. A former Spanish colony, Cuba had played a catch-up game with the rest of the region when it came to liberation from colonial rule.

Neighboring Haiti freed itself from French overlordship in 1804, and Mexico declared its independence from Spain in 1821, the year in which Simón Bolívar won independence for Venezuela in a bloody war with the Spaniards. Cuba, though, remained loyal to Madrid throughout the first half of the nineteenth century. The Cubans first rebelled against their Spanish rulers in 1868, but the revolt was crushed after a ten-year struggle. They rebelled again in 1879, and yet again in 1895. This time they had a powerful ally, the United States of America.[6]

American troops landed on the beaches of Cuba in June 1898. The US government entered the conflict partly in response to public demand to stop Spanish atrocities against the Cubans, widely covered and often exaggerated in the American media. But behind the move was also the implementation of the decades-old Monroe Doctrine. Back in 1823, in the midst of Latin American revolutions, President James Monroe had declared that his country would treat any European interference in the region intended to establish control over newly independent states as a "manifestation of an unfriendly disposition toward the United States." The Monroe Doctrine was born. In 1898 it acquired a new meaning: the Americans were ready not only to protect the independence of Latin American countries but also to bring it about. The Spaniards found themselves obliged to withdraw and renounce their claims to Cuba. Cuban independence—received, unlike most sovereignties in the region, from American hands—was proclaimed in 1902.

In 1820 Thomas Jefferson had regarded Cuba as a potential new US state. In 1902, there was no appetite in Washington to extend American borders to include Cuba, but neither was there much desire to make it fully independent. The Platt Amendment to the US Army Appropriations Act of 1901, named after its principal author, Senator Orville H. Platt, limited Cuban sovereignty by giving the US government the right to have military bases on the island and intervene in Cuba's internal affairs for the sake of "good governance." The amendment established Cuba as a de facto American protectorate and served as a rallying point for Cuban rebels and revolutionaries, of whom there would be no shortage in the decades to come. The new masters against whom the Cubans rebelled were American, not Spanish.[7]

In all but name Cuba became a colony of the United States in the Caribbean. Most of the assets in the agricultural sector, mining, utilities, and financial services ended up in American hands. To safeguard American strategic and economic interests on the island, the United States made alliances with the local landowning elite and the military. By far the most trusted American ally in the presidential office in Havana became General Fulgencio Batista, who served as president of Cuba between 1940 and 1944, returning to power in 1952 as a result of a military coup. He developed close ties with the two most powerful American economic forces on the island, the agricultural corporations and the Mafia clans. Gambling and prostitution catering to American tourists became thriving industries.[8]

Upon his return to Cuba, Batista canceled the impending presidential elections. His corrupt rule antagonized not only the poor but also the middle class. With elections canceled and democracy under attack, dissatisfied young people took up arms. On July 23, 1953, a group of young revolutionaries staged an attack on the Moncada Barracks in Santiago. The assault was repelled and its leaders arrested. Among the latter was a twenty-six-year-old lawyer and descendant of a wealthy landowning family, Fidel Castro, who was sentenced to a fifteen-year term. His younger brother, Raúl, and twenty-four more participants in the attack were also imprisoned.

Luckily for the Castro brothers and their coconspirators, they were released in May 1955 as Batista sought to improve his international image. Fearing a new arrest, the Castro brothers left Cuba for Mexico. The Moncada Barracks story seemed to be over. Batista had survived the assault, conducted fraudulent elections, and got the rebels out of the country, all to the satisfaction of his American allies, who wanted to safeguard their assets without turning American and world public opinion against themselves. To the surprise of many, the Castro brothers were back in Cuba by November 1956, with Fidel leading a group of

Cuban and Latin American revolutionaries. They arrived illegally on a leaky yacht, the *Granma*, to start a new revolt.

The guerrilla warfare that would eventually bring down Batista began with a major setback. Government troops attacked the *Granma* rebels soon after their landing, forcing them to seek refuge in the Sierra Maestra mountains of Oriente province, in southeastern Cuba. Of the initial group of eighty-one rebels only nineteen, including Fidel and Raúl Castro and their close ally, the Argentinian doctor Ernesto "Che" Guevara, made it to the safety of the mountains. It was a difficult beginning, but the small group began to grow in ranks, recruiting new members among dissatisfied Cuban urban youth and local peasants.

Batista's regime used ever more brutal tactics to suppress the rebels, but that only increased the number of fighters. Those measures also tarnished the image of the regime abroad, turning US public opinion against the Cuban dictator. The US government was obliged to recall its ambassador to Havana and impose a trade embargo on Cuba, which stopped the sale of arms to Batista and gave a huge boost to the rebels. The year 1958, when arms sales ceased, became a turning point in the Castro-led revolution. After suffering a major defeat at the hands of government forces in the summer, Castro managed to regroup and launch his own offensive. On December 31, the diverse rebel groups came together in a battle for Santa Clara, taking the city and causing enough panic in Havana to make Batista flee the country.

With the dictator gone, resistance to the revolutionary forces, which had been all but wiped out only half a year earlier, collapsed. Castro staged a victory march on Havana, already in rebel hands, and entered the city on January 8, 1959. He was not about to repeat the mistakes of Batista, who had released him from prison under international pressure. Enemies of the regime would be punished mercilessly, whatever the world might say about it. Hundreds of old-regime officials were dismissed and put on trial, and close to two hundred were executed by firing squad. Leading figures of the new regime, Raúl Castro and Che Guevara conducted purges and persecuted enemies. A corrupt and highly unpopular dictator was gone, replaced by a presumably incorruptible and charismatic new one.

The Cuban revolution had succeeded, but what that meant was not yet clear either to its leaders or to its supporters and opponents, both in Cuba and abroad. Direct American investment increased during the first year of Castro's rule, but that changed quickly as the government embarked on badly needed agrarian reform. In May 1959 Castro limited the size of agricultural estates to one thousand acres; the rest were to be confiscated and redistributed by the government without compensation to the landowners. In July 1960 the government nationalized all US-owned businesses and properties: since the revolutionary government needed resources and lacked money, no compensation was offered for the confiscated properties. In response President Eisenhower closed American markets to Cuban sugar, by far the island's main export.[9]

The United States found itself in a situation akin to the one that the old imperial powers, Britain and France, had faced in their Asian and African colonies and dependencies. There was also the prospect of rising communist and pro-communist movements in Cuba and direct Soviet involvement in the region—a pattern that repeated itself throughout the former colonial world. In April 1959, on a visit to the United States at the invitation of the American Society of Newspaper Editors, Castro made a statement distancing himself from communism. "I know the world thinks of us, we are Communists, and of course I have said very clear that we are not Communists; very clear." But things were changing rapidly. In February 1960, Cuba was visited by one of the top advisers to Nikita Khrushchev, the old Bolshevik and seasoned politician Anastas Mikoyan. He urged his boss in Moscow to provide economic assistance to the young revolutionary regime. In May, Khrushchev made a public statement threatening the United States with nuclear arms over Cuban independence. It was the Monroe Doctrine in reverse. The Soviet Union was prepared to protect the independence of Latin American countries from the United States.

As far as Eisenhower was concerned, American interests were at stake, and communism was on the march in Cuba, whether Castro was a communist or not. Luckily, the president's advisers had a plan to deal with the crisis. Only a few years earlier, in June 1954, the CIA had executed a successful coup in Guatemala, where land reform threatened the interests of the United Fruit Company. In March 1960, with agrarian reform in Cuba already underway but confiscation of American commercial properties not yet announced, Eisenhower decided to bring about regime change in Cuba. Castro was to be removed from power in the same way he had acquired it: through a popular uprising initiated by political exiles returning to Cuba. The CIA prepared a plan, but Eisenhower did not have time to carry out the project. It was passed on instead to the new president, John Kennedy.[10]

◊◊◊

ALLEN DULLES WAS A GRAY-HAIRED, PIPE-SMOKING VETERAN of US espionage and a holdover from the Eisenhower administration. Director of the CIA, he first presented his plan for the invasion of Cuba to Kennedy on January 28, one week after the inauguration.

The CIA deputy director for plans, Richard M. Bissell, the former administrator of the Marshall Plan in postwar Germany, was the principal author of the plan, which proposed to land on Cuba hundreds of guerrilla fighters recruited from the ranks of Cuban exiles and trained in CIA camps in Guatemala. Bissell recommended the establishment of a beachhead on Cuban territory with access to the sea and an airstrip that could serve as a base of operations for the future Cuban government. He hoped that the invasion would inspire a popular uprising against Castro's regime but did not count on that. Bissell envisioned the next stage of the operation as "an overt, open US initiative to institute a military occupation of the island by a composite OAS [Organization of American States] force in order to put a stop to the civil war."[11]

The last part of the plan made some of Kennedy's advisers nervous. General Lyman Lemnitzer, the chairman of the Joint Chiefs of Staff, suggested that the force of some six to eight thousand men currently in training was inadequate to achieve the goal, given the Castro government's continuing military buildup. He suggested that "final planning will have to include agreed plans for providing additional support for the Cuban force—presumably such support to be US." Lemnitzer knew that the American military would have to intervene and wanted clarity on the matter. Secretary of State Dean Rusk had different concerns, predicting an international backlash against the invasion. His people foresaw "grave political dangers to our position throughout the Western hemisphere in any overt military action not authorized and supported by the Organization of American States."

Kennedy sent his advisers back to the drawing board. The Defense Department was ordered to make a military assessment of the operation and the State Department to work on getting the Latin American countries on board. It was "agreed that the United States must make entirely clear that its position with respect to the Cuban Government is currently governed by its firm opposition to Communist penetration of the American Republics, and not by any hostility to democratic social revolution and economic reform." How to distinguish support for democratic social revolution from opposition to communism in the Cuban situation was not entirely clear.[12]

Kennedy continued to meet with his advisers in the course of February and March 1961, trying to figure out whether the invasion plan submitted by the CIA was indeed the best way to deal with the problem. The president was caught between a number of conflicting agendas. He was determined to stop the spread of communism to the Western Hemisphere, but he was also eager to present a new face to the "sister republics" in Latin America, staying away from the use of American military might. Also at stake were US-Soviet relations, which Kennedy wanted to improve. He was told that time was running out, that he had to act, and he probably felt that the only way to reconcile his conflicting agendas was to take clandestine action in Cuba.

At a meeting with his advisers on February 8, 1961, Kennedy suggested the infiltration of the task force in small groups, with their first big operation to be conducted from Cuban bases, not "as an invasion force sent by the Yankees." Neither the CIA nor the military liked that idea. On March 11, the CIA's Bissell presented a memorandum that effectively rejected Kennedy's idea of infiltration of small groups, arguing that without air support and tanks guerrilla groups had little chance of making it from the beaches to the mountains. Bissell recommended instead "landing in full force." Kennedy was not pleased. Once again, he sent the CIA back to the drawing board, asking for a plan that would make the US involvement "less obvious."[13]

Four days later, on March 15, Bissell proposed an alternative plan. He still insisted on air support but suggested that the planes to be used in the operation be camouflaged as Cuban rather than American. To make the claim work, an airstrip on Cuban territory would be needed to serve as the base of operations for alleged anti-Castro rebels in the Cuban Air Force. Thus, suggested Bissell, the invasion force would immediately have to take over an area with a landing strip. Besides, given that deployment would take place in an "endocuticular manner," the territory captured by the landing force would have to be suitable for prolonged defense. Bissell proposed the beaches of the Bahía de Cochinos (Bay of Pigs), which were surrounded by marshes. The location was far from the mountains but had two airstrips suitable for landing B-26 bombers and could be defended effectively by a relatively small task force. Kennedy approved the new plan with one caveat. To ensure deniability he wanted a night landing on the island, with the ships carrying the task force to be removed from the area by dawn.

Kennedy decided to approve the invasion during the Easter break, following discussions with his father and his decision to accept Khrushchev's offer of a summit meeting at Kennedy's earliest convenience. With the invasion planned for Sunday, April 16, Kennedy decided to spend that weekend away from the White House at his family retreat in Glen Ora, Virginia. Since the media knew his whereabouts, this was one more ploy to deny involvement in the planned invasion not only on the part of American forces but also on that of the president. Far from relaxing at his hideaway, Kennedy would be on and off the phone again and again, following with growing anxiety the launch of the operation, which was codenamed "Zapata."[14]

◊◊◊

THE SHIPS CARRYING BRIGADE 2506, A FORCE OF CLOSE TO 1,400 Cuban exiles, left the shores of Nicaragua and headed for Cuba on the night of April 14. At 6:00 a.m. on April 15, eight B-26 bombers painted in the colors of the Cuban air force and piloted by Cuban exiles took off from airstrips in Nicaragua and headed for Cuban airfields with the task of destroying Castro's air force while it was still on the ground. The raid was declared a success, with the attackers unaware that quite a few of Castro's planes had remained undamaged.[15]

Fidel Castro fought back in the court of public opinion. That day Raúl Roa, the Cuban foreign minister, who happened to be in New York, managed to convince the UN leadership to convene an emergency meeting of the Political and Security Committee to discuss the airstrikes, which he characterized as a prelude to an American-backed invasion of the island. The American representative in the UN, Adlai Stevenson, repeated assurances given by President Kennedy three days earlier that there would be no involvement by the American military or American citizens in the Cuban crisis. Countering Roa's claims that it was US planes that bombed Cuba, Stevenson produced a photograph of a plane that had landed earlier that day at Miami airport in Florida. It was a B-26 bomber painted in the colors of the Cuban air force, and its pilot had told reporters that he had taken part in a bombing raid organized and executed by anti-Castro officers in his country's air force. Unbeknownst to Stevenson, the landing of the plane was part of a CIA operation aimed at misleading international public opinion.[16]

With ships in the water and planes in the air, the CIA-trained teams still needed a final go-ahead from President Kennedy. His deadline for that decision was noon on Sunday, April 16. The day began on a sour note. Articles published that morning in some of the leading US newspapers exposed the CIA operation involving the plane landing at Miami as a cover-up of a US-backed attack on Cuba. Reporters noticed that the gun on the B-26 had not been fired and that the airplane was a different model from those used by the Cubans. Kennedy was vacillating. He and his wife, Jacqueline, went to Mass at the local Catholic church and then had lunch with family members. After that, the president went off to play golf. The noon deadline for his decision had long passed, but he could not make up his mind. Finally, he returned to his house around 1:45 p.m. and called Bissell at the CIA: the invasion could go ahead.

Late on the night of April 16, the landing of Brigade 2506 began at multiple locations on the island. In the early hours of April 17 four transport ships approached Playa Girón in the Bay of Pigs. It was an isolated place and, with no Cuban military units around, the exiles easily overwhelmed the local militia fighters. But they were in for a major surprise: the remote location of the landing failed to ensure its secrecy. A Cuban radio operator managed to broadcast news of the invasion before his unit was overtaken by the brigade. When Castro was alerted, he ordered the airplanes that had survived the initial attack (including Lockheed T-33 fighter jets and B-26 bombers) into action.

The invaders had little air cover: the surviving Cuban planes outnumbered the six aircraft provided by the CIA to support Brigade 2506. They would soon lose two ships, the USS *Houston* and the USS *Rio Escondido*, which carried their supplies of fuel, ammunition, and medicine. Besides, the coral reefs that CIA scouts had mistaken for seaweed prevented the rest of the transport ships from reaching the beaches, and the exiles had to use boats to get there, losing some of their weapons and ammunition in the high water. What they managed to save was wet and often inoperable. Short of weapons, supplies, and ammunition, they were also outnumbered and outgunned once Castro's reinforcements began to arrive at the Bay of Pigs—altogether close to twenty thousand police officers, soldiers, and members of local militias. They were assisted by crews in Soviet-made T-34 tanks.[17]

The CIA asked Kennedy to authorize the use of US airplanes to help the invasion force, but he refused. Dean Rusk of the State Department was furious that by withholding information about the alleged Cuban plane that had landed in Miami, the CIA had put Adlai Stevenson in the position of lying to a world audience. Rusk was now determined to kill CIA plans for any airstrikes that could not be credibly attributed to the planes taking off from airstrips in Cuba. Kennedy, with whom Rusk had spoken by phone after 9:00 p.m. on April 16, was of the same opinion. As far as he was concerned, he had never authorized such strikes and now gave an order to cancel those already planned by the CIA. The CIA had to accept the president's verdict, but, as the landing began in the early hours of April 17, General Charles Cabell of the CIA called Rusk at home and asked him to reconsider. He made the same plea to the president. But the order remained in force: invasion—yes, air support—no. The invaders floundered on the beaches of the Bay of Pigs, fighting now for their lives, not for a chance to break out and launch a nationwide uprising.[18]

On Monday, April 17, Kennedy was back at the White House, keeping his regular schedule of official meetings and meals while trying to figure out what to do next. Bruised politically but not yet militarily, he refused a CIA request to use now camouflaged American bombers to support the struggling troops on the Cuban beaches. But in the early hours of April 19, with things going from bad to worse, he yielded, allowing the use of camouflaged planes piloted by Americans in support of the invaders, but the pilots were not allowed to fight enemy aircraft, and their mission was limited to a few hours. The military commanders seized the opportunity but failed to take advantage of it. Because of the time difference between Nicaragua and Cuba, the planes arrived later than expected. Two of them were shot down, and four American pilots went missing. Radio Havana declared that the Cubans had recovered the body of one of the Americans. By now the venture had turned into a complete disaster.[19]

Kennedy would never again authorize even limited use of the US Air Force. By Thursday, April 20, it was all over. The invaders had spent two and a half days resisting the inevitable. Lacking air support, low on ammunition, outnumbered, outgunned, and increasingly demoralized, they surrendered. The casualties included more than 100 dead and more than 360 wounded; close to 1,200 were taken prisoner. Castro's losses were greater, but it did not matter: neither he nor his armed forces surrendered. It was a stunning victory for Castro and his regime and an astounding defeat for Kennedy.[20]

Kennedy had lost on both fronts, militarily and politically. Political victory turned out to be impossible without a military one. In the days and months that followed, analyzing what had gone wrong with the Bay of Pigs invasion, Kennedy blamed himself first, but then went on to blame the CIA and the military, not the State Department and those who had advised him against an overt US military operation. As far as Kennedy was concerned, the CIA and the military had promised him something they could not deliver and set a trap to force him into a military operation that he did not want to authorize. "In a parliamentary government, I'd have to resign. But in this government, I can't, so you and Allen [Dulles] have to go," he told Bissell.[21]

◊◊◊

BEFORE THE END OF THE YEAR, BOTH BISSELL AND DULLES were gone. The chairman of the Joint Chiefs of Staff, General Lemnitzer, who had kept insisting on an invasion of Cuba, was removed from his post in September 1962. Even though some of the key participants in the Bay of Pigs debacle left the scene, mistrust and suspicion between the president and the generals remained. Each side blamed the other for the disaster. If the generals wanted to go back to Cuba and carry out the invasion properly, rectifying their humiliating defeat, the president did his best to deny them that opportunity. There was one key beneficiary of the American blame game: Nikita Khrushchev.

2

MASTER OF THE GAME

No world leader watched John Kennedy's handling of the Cuban invasion more carefully and was prepared to draw from it more far-reaching conclusions than the sixty-seven-year-old leader of the Soviet Union, Nikita Khrushchev.

Fat, bold, full of energy, prone to bravado, theatrics, and often bluff, Khrushchev cut a very different figure from that of the young American president. Born to poverty and low social status, he was also Kennedy's complete opposite in upbringing, career trajectory, and political ideology. If the young Kennedy's ambitions were driven by a desire to live up to the expectations of his strong-willed father, Khrushchev's were inspired by his mother's desire to see her son succeed in life, unlike her weak husband, considered to be the failure in the family. If Kennedy received the best education his country could provide, Khrushchev never graduated from college. If Kennedy's only experience of managing people was limited to his command of PT-109, the patrol torpedo boat during the war, Khrushchev had spent most of his life overseeing big projects and huge numbers of people. If Kennedy had prepared himself his entire life for involvement in international politics, Khrushchev was first exposed to high-level diplomacy after he turned sixty. There was also a great age difference between the two men. The Russian Revolution of 1917 was the turning point of Khrushchev's life and career. Kennedy, twenty-three years younger than his Soviet counterpart, was just born in that year.[1]

Khrushchev and his advisers, who were unhappy with the secret U-2 overflights of Soviet territory ordered by Dwight Eisenhower and his administration, first noticed John Kennedy in July 1960, when the young senator from Massachusetts won his party's nomination for president of the United States. To many in Moscow he seemed less tough than Richard Nixon, whom Khrushchev had had a chance to size up during his visit to Moscow the previous year, and more susceptible to Khrushchev's subterfuge and intimidation. Kennedy appeared to believe in a missile gap between the Soviet Union and the United States favoring the former—a notion fed not only by the Soviet success with Sputnik but also by Khrushchev's own fiery rhetoric, and one that Eisenhower's U-2 spy flights were threatening to debunk.

Khrushchev wanted to help Kennedy win the election and ordered his KGB aides to do all they could to achieve that goal. The KGB complied, setting up a number of meetings that in today's parlance would qualify as nothing less than "collusion" between Kennedy's presidential campaign and the Kremlin. Soon after Kennedy had won his party's presidential nomination, Yurii Barsukov, a KGB officer posing as a reporter for the Soviet newspaper *Izvestiia*, knocked on the office door of no less a figure than Robert Kennedy, who was running his brother's electoral campaign. He asked Robert what Moscow could do to help his brother. According to the memoirs of the chief of the KGB station in Washington, Aleksandr Feklisov, Robert drew aside the curtain covering the map of the United States with projected numbers of potential Democratic and Republican votes in every state. He invited Barsukov to write down the numbers, which the KGB officer did. Robert then suggested that the best strategy for Moscow was neutrality: once his brother won the election, better relations could be established.[2]

Throughout the summer of 1960, Nikita Khrushchev and the Soviet propaganda machine followed Robert Kennedy's advice, doing nothing to voice support for John Kennedy. Khrushchev lambasted the Eisenhower administration instead, suggesting that the missile gap Kennedy was talking about really existed. In September 1960, in the middle of the presidential campaign, Khrushchev popped up in the United States to speak at the UN General Assembly. Going on the attack as always, he asked: "Do you want to make us turn the arms race into a competition? We do not want that, but we are not afraid of it. We will beat you! Our missile production is on a conveyor belt." If any American thought that Kennedy was mistaken in speaking of a missile gap, there was the leader of the Soviet state himself confirming the words of the junior senator from Massachusetts.[3] The missile gap rhetoric helped Kennedy win the presidential race.

At 10:00 a.m. on December 1, 1960, less than a month after Kennedy's election, the KGB agent Yurii Barsukov once again knocked on the door of Robert Kennedy's office. "Mr. B, *Izvestiia* Daily, coming in," read Robert's calendar that day. In his report on the meeting, which went all the way to Khrushchev, Barsukov noted that Robert was ready to speak on behalf of his brother, not just himself. "Kennedy expects," read the report, "to sign a nuclear test-ban treaty as early as 1961 if both sides take a number of steps to accommodate each other." Robert Kennedy also assured the Kremlin emissary that the president "would do all he could to reach agreement on the Berlin problem." Kennedy ended the meeting by hinting at the possibility of American-Soviet cooperation with regard to common concerns about China, telling Barsukov that "in the next few years the fundamental problem would not be Soviet-American relations but Washington's relations with China."[4]

Khrushchev could not fail to be pleased by what he read in Barsukov's report. On January 21, 1961, the day after Kennedy's inauguration, he ordered the publication of the young president's inaugural address in the Soviet media. He also did something that he had refused to do for Eisenhower, releasing two American pilots then in Soviet custody. Captains Freeman Bruce Olmstead and John McCone had been piloting an RB-47H Stratojet full of electronic surveillance equipment off the Kola Peninsula in the Barents Sea when they were shot down by a Soviet MiG-19 (NATO designation "Farmer") jet on July 1, 1960. Now they were free. Kennedy announced the release of the pilots on January 25 at the first presidential press conference ever to be televised. He basked in national attention and approval when on January 27 he greeted the returning pilots with their happy wives on their arrival at Andrews Air Force Base.[5]

Khrushchev believed that the young president owed him his victory and expected something in return. "We helped elect Kennedy," he declared in the summer of 1961 to a group of Soviet political leaders and scientists. "It can be said that we elected him." Khrushchev wanted a summit meeting as soon as possible in order to assess his opposite number in Washington. Instead of toppling any hopes of a high-level summit, the Cuban debacle only whetted Khrushchev's appetite for it. An inexperienced president unsure of himself was the best counterpart he could imagine with whom to discuss world affairs. Bruised by the Cuban debacle and seeking to recover his standing in the international arena, John Kennedy stepped into a trap: the two leaders agreed to meet as soon as possible.[6]

◊◊◊

KHRUSHCHEV AND KENNEDY HAD THE FIRST CHANCE TO SIZE each other up on June 3, 1961. The venue was the US embassy in Vienna. But it was Khrushchev rather than Kennedy who felt fully at home, presenting himself as a senior statesman meeting his younger and thus inferior counterpart. He reminded Kennedy that he had arrived late for their first brief meeting in the course of Khrushchev's visit to the United States at Eisenhower's invitation back in 1959. They then moved on to discuss Kennedy's young age. Khrushchev remarked that he would be happy to "share his years with the president." It was a friendly beginning, but Khrushchev had already established his position of authority.[7]

Back in April the Cuban debacle had seemed to have eliminated any chance of a summit meeting, but Khrushchev had surprised Kennedy by reviving the idea in early May. On May 4, 1961, the Soviet foreign minister, Andrei Gromyko, summoned the American ambassador to the Soviet Union, Llewellyn Thompson, to his office and told him that the Soviet leader was prepared to go ahead with the summit. The Cuban crisis, argued Gromyko, had shown the need to build bridges between the two countries. On May 16 Khrushchev wrote to Kennedy, welcoming what he suggested was the president's idea for a personal meeting to ease tensions between the two countries and resolve international disagreements peacefully. He agreed to Kennedy's proposal on the place and time of the meeting: Vienna, June 3, 1961.[8]

Khrushchev proposed a discussion of the peace settlement in Laos, nuclear disarmament, and the situation in West Berlin. Kennedy, badly needing an achievement in the international arena, was receptive. He hoped to obtain an agreement on Laos, where the two countries were backing different sides in a civil war, and regarded a discussion on disarmament as a possible stepping-stone toward a nuclear test-ban treaty, which he had wanted all along. West Berlin seemed a more problematic issue, but there Kennedy decided to limit himself to a mere discussion. That proved to be wishful thinking, since it turned out that all Khrushchev wanted to talk about was Berlin. He wanted the Americans out and, to that end, was preparing a psychological attack on the young president, who was shaken and demoralized by the Cuban debacle. Khrushchev intended to bully him into submission.[9]

◊◊◊

WEST BERLIN, AN ISLAND OF CAPITALISM IN THE EAST GERman socialist sea, was a legacy inherited by Khrushchev and Kennedy from Stalin and Truman. The agreement that placed American, British, and French military units in the western part of Berlin, one hundred miles deep in the Soviet-controlled part of Germany, was a product of the Potsdam Conference. It was there, in 1945, that the occupation zones in Germany were delineated. The city of Berlin was divided into four zones: Soviet, American, British, and French, one for each of the Allies who had won the war against Nazi Germany. Superficially, the division indicated concordant Allied policy, but the actual disunity and animosity between the USSR and the Western allies soon led to an effective bisection of Berlin into an eastern Soviet-controlled zone and a western zone controlled by the rest of the Allies.

In June 1948, with the Cold War becoming acute, the Soviets blocked the railway and highway transportation corridors leading from the western parts of Germany to Berlin, thereby blockading the western part of the city. They wanted to force the Americans and their allies out of West Berlin, leaving the eastern part of Germany under total Soviet control. The agreements signed in conjunction with the Potsdam Conference established three air corridors for flights to West Berlin and back. The Americans took advantage of that provision to break the blockade from the air. The US Air Force performed something of a miracle for the two and a quarter million people of West Berlin, flying in thirteen-thousand tons of food supplies daily and conducting more than two hundred thousand sorties over a twelve-month period.

The Soviets eventually gave up and lifted the land blockade in May 1949. In the same month the Western allies ended the occupation of their part of the country, declaring the creation of the Federal Republic of Germany. The Soviets followed suit in October, announcing the creation of the German Democratic Republic in their sphere of occupation. Sovereign rights were restored to the two German governments with the exception of Berlin, which remained under four-power occupation. The main problem that the Soviets faced, given the continuing Western presence in Berlin, was not military, political, or even ideological but economic. The United States offered the Marshall Plan, a $17 billion revitalization package, to war-ravaged Western Europe, resulting in an economic miracle in West Germany. As the Soviets lacked resources to revive the economy of mainly agricultural East Germany, West Berlin soon became an attraction to East Germans and an escape route for those who wanted to leave the socialist "paradise" for the capitalist "inferno" in the West.[10]

The burgeoning crisis over Berlin played an important role in Khrushchev's rise to supreme power in the USSR. In June 1953, a workers' strike in East Berlin grew into a popular uprising against the regime of the East German communist strongman Walter Ulbricht, only to be crushed by Soviet tanks. At the same time, Khrushchev executed his coup in the Kremlin by arresting Lavrentii Beria, thereby making himself first among equals of the post-Stalin leadership group. One of the accusations against Beria was his supposed readiness to capitulate to the West in Germany by abandoning the socialist experiment in East Germany and permitting the creation of a united, ostensibly capitalist but neutral German state.[11]

Khrushchev's second crucial step toward the consolidation of supreme power, a showdown in July 1957 with the majority of the party Presidium, was also closely linked to the German problem. The opposition, led by the diehard Stalinists, was critical of Khrushchev's proposal to provide the flagging East German economy with credits worth three billion rubles. Khrushchev stood his ground. The defeat of the "anti-party" group and the removal of his opponents from leadership positions cemented Khrushchev's hold on power in the Kremlin and his determination to save East Germany from economic collapse at almost any price.[12]

Khrushchev unveiled his own plans for Berlin in a speech he delivered in November 1958 to a delegation of Polish communists. The Soviet leader proposed declaring West Berlin a free city, which would mean the withdrawal of American, British, and French troops. Khrushchev's speech amounted to an ultimatum: if the West did not accept his proposal, he was ready to sign a separate treaty with East Germany, withdrawing from the four-party agreements of 1945 and handing over control of Western access routes to Berlin to his East German minions. That might easily lead to armed conflict between the Allies and the East Germans, and many feared further escalation into a global military crisis and even nuclear war. While preparing for the Vienna summit with Kennedy, he put Berlin at the top of his agenda. His plan was to scare Kennedy out of the city.[13]

◊◊◊

KHRUSHCHEV BEGAN HIS ATTACK ON KENNEDY ON JUNE 3, 1961, with a Marxism-for-dummies analysis of American imperialism and a declaration of his conviction that the future belonged to communism. Although Kennedy allowed himself to be dragged into an ideological debate, he was focused on realpolitik. Referring to "modern weapons," he warned Khrushchev: "if our two countries should miscalculate, they would lose for a long time to come." His objective, said the president, was peace. Khrushchev was anything but appreciative. "Miscalculation," declared the Soviet leader, was a very vague term. The United States "wanted the USSR to sit like a schoolboy with his hands on his desk." Khrushchev, for his part, was ready to misbehave.[14]

On June 4, the second day of the summit, Khrushchev used the president's concern over "miscalculation" to threaten Kennedy. Bilateral relations would be greatly affected "if the US were to misunderstand the Soviet position," he told the president. He wanted a comprehensive peace treaty to formally end the war, recognizing the existence of two German states and making West Berlin a free city. The Soviet Union was prepared to guarantee the city's free contact with the rest of the world and promised not to interfere in its internal affairs. There would be no more blockades, suggested Khrushchev. The Americans could even leave their troops there, but in that case the Soviet Union would also station its troops in the western part of the city. He expressed his desire for an agreement with Kennedy, but if it did not materialize, he was ready to sign a separate agreement with East Germany. Khrushchev made a moral argument to support his case: the Soviet Union had lost twenty million citizens in World War II, that war had to come to an end, and there was no reason to postpone the conclusion of a treaty sixteen years after the end of hostilities.

Kennedy's defense was rooted in nothing but the right of the conqueror and the importance of great-power prestige. "We are in Berlin not because of someone's sufferance. We fought our way there, although our casualties may not have been as high as the USSR's," said Kennedy. He did not specify the US losses, which stood at approximately 420,000, and were well below the Soviet numbers. "If we were expelled from that area and if we accepted the loss of our rights, no one would have any confidence in US commitments and pledges," continued the president, ignoring Khrushchev's suggestion that American troops could stay in the free city of West Berlin. "If we were to leave West Berlin, Europe would be abandoned as well," Kennedy argued. "Our leaving West Berlin would result in the US becoming isolated."

Khrushchev was furious. Returning to the issue of Soviet war losses and recapitulating his earlier argument, he put forward another ultimatum: "The USSR will sign a peace treaty and the sovereignty of the GDR will be observed. Any violation of that sovereignty will be regarded by the USSR as an act of open aggression against a peace-loving country, with all the consequences ensuing therefrom." When Kennedy asked whether a Soviet–East German treaty would affect US rights of access to West Berlin, Khrushchev responded in the affirmative. As the unpleasant debate continued, he declared that the Soviet Union could not wait and would sign a treaty by the end of the year giving East Germany control over access rights to West Berlin.

The tensions grew, the two leaders soon began to talk war instead of peace. When Kennedy responded to Khrushchev's mention of Soviet World War II losses that the United States wanted to avoid another war precisely to avoid such losses, Khrushchev responded angrily. "[I]f the US should start a war over Berlin, there is nothing the USSR could do about it," exploded the Soviet leader. He turned again to the miscalculation theme: "ours is a joint account and each of us must see that there is no miscalculation." He could not get off the topic of war: "If the US wants to start a war over Germany, let it be so; perhaps the USSR should sign a peace treaty right away and get it over with. . . . If there is any madman who wants war, he should be put in a straitjacket." Kennedy was taken aback: Khrushchev was threatening the president with war.[15]

Kennedy's attempt to return to the question of Berlin in private conversation with Khrushchev later that day brought no results. Khrushchev was adamant: "force will be met with force." Kennedy ended the discussion with the words, "it will be a cold winter."[16]

◊◊◊

KENNEDY RETURNED TO THE UNITED STATES WITH WHAT HE believed was his second major defeat on the international stage in less than two months. He felt beaten up. "Pretty rough?" asked James Reston of the *New York Times*, immediately after his last meeting with Khrushchev. "Roughest thing in my life," came Kennedy's candid response. He assumed that he had been treated that way because of the Bay of Pigs debacle. Khrushchev "thought that anyone who was so young and inexperienced as to get into that mess could be taken," speculated Kennedy. "And anyone who got into it and didn't see it through had no guts. So he just beat the hell out of me." Khrushchev did not boast about "beating the hell" out of Kennedy in private or public, but he told one of his advisers: "This man is very inexperienced, even immature. Compared to him, Eisenhower was a man of intelligence and vision."[17]

Kennedy felt destroyed both physically and emotionally. He had gone into the summit with excruciating pain in his back, which he had reinjured a few weeks earlier, and relied on a cocktail of drugs and hot baths to keep functioning. Now his back pain was worse, and he had to rely on crutches to move even a few feet. Although he tried to smile for the cameras, there was no way to hide his chagrin. On June 6, Kennedy admitted in front of a television audience that the negotiations had not produced the results he hoped for and that there had been no progress on the German front—the subject, as he said, of "our most somber talks."

Khrushchev returned from Vienna without the decisive victory he had hoped for, but in a much better mood than Kennedy. He called the summit a good beginning, and his Central Committee colleagues commended him on his diplomatic skills and "aggressive spirit." Khrushchev followed up on June 11 with a public release of the memorandum he had handed to Kennedy in Vienna, threatening to sign a peace treaty with East Germany in six months. It was another embarrassment for Kennedy, who did not mention the memorandum in his own address on the summit. On June 15, Khrushchev publicly attacked the "capitalist monopolists" for the lack of progress on negotiations concerning Berlin and once again alluded to war. "Surely, it is clear that a Cold War is a period of preparation, accumulating forces for war," asserted the Soviet leader.[18]

The possibility of war was very much on Kennedy's mind, and it frightened him. When Kennedy asked his military advisers about estimated losses in case of a nuclear war with the Soviet Union, he was given a number of 70 million people. Since the country's total population as of 1960 had been slightly more than 180 million, that meant every second or third American could die. One nuclear missile striking a major city would mean 600,000 victims. That number was comparable to total losses during the Civil War, remarked Kennedy when presented with the estimate. He then added: "And we have not gotten over that in a hundred years."[19]

Kennedy had to respond to Khrushchev's challenge without increasing tensions that might produce all-out war, to which the Soviet leader had said the Cold War was only a prelude. So far, he had failed to carry through the invasion of Cuba planned by President Eisenhower, signaled readiness to compromise with the Soviets on Laos against his predecessor's advice, and suffered public humiliation in Vienna. Kennedy had to do something to change both Khrushchev's perception and, more important, that of his opponents at home, who saw him as a weak president, potentially disastrous for the country. Resorting to the lessons he had drawn from his Harvard thesis on Britain's lack of preparedness for World War II, the president made a public show of getting ready for war.

On July 25, Kennedy made his way on crutches to the White House to deliver a speech about the growing Berlin crisis. He told the television audience that he was prepared to stand up to the Soviet bully. Four days earlier, Congress had authorized more than $12 billion for new aircraft, missiles, and ships that Kennedy had requested earlier. Now he called for additional defense spending of $3.25 billion and 90,000 more recruits for the navy and air force. It was a drastic increase in military spending and a dramatic departure from the Eisenhower years. Kennedy's message was that America was not going to sleep, as Britain had done before the war. It was going to arm itself to the teeth.

"We do not want to fight," declared the president, "but we have fought before. And others in earlier times have made the same dangerous mistake of assuming that the West was too selfish and too soft and too divided to resist invasions of freedom in other lands. Those who threaten to unleash the forces of war on a dispute over West Berlin should recall the words of the ancient philosopher: 'A man who causes fear cannot be free from fear.' "[20]

◊◊◊

KHRUSHCHEV WAS "REALLY MAD," RECALLED JOHN J. MCCLOY, Kennedy's chief negotiator on disarmament, who visited Khrushchev in late July 1961 at the Black Sea resort of Pitsunda. Khrushchev called Kennedy's speech a "preliminary declaration of war." He threatened to sign his peace treaty with Germany no matter what and warned that there would be no small war—it would be nuclear.[21]

For Khrushchev, Kennedy's bellicose speech and the military buildup he had just announced suggested that his psychological attack on Kennedy in Vienna had not produced the desired results. It looked as if a weak president intimidated at a summit submitted to manipulation by his advisers upon his return home. For Khrushchev, who prided himself on having helped to elect Kennedy, that was quite a disappointment. "Look, we helped elect Kennedy last year," Khrushchev told a group of officials and scientists on July 10, 1961. "Then we met with him in Vienna, a meeting that could have been a turning point. But what does he say? 'Don't ask for too much. Don't put me in a bind. If I make too many concessions, I'll be turned out of office.' Quite a guy! He comes to a meeting but can't perform. What the hell do we need a guy like that for? Why waste time talking to him?" If that was Khrushchev's

view on July 10, then Kennedy's speech of July 25 could only have deep-
ened his pessimism.[22]

Khrushchev needed a solution to the Berlin crisis that would not
involve the threatened peace treaty with East Germany, the loss of
American access rights, and a possible military confrontation. Such
a scenario might lead to thermonuclear war, perhaps more easily with
a weak president than with a strong one. Khrushchev knew that he
had nothing with which to counter Kennedy: the "missile gap" actually favored the United States, and he had no additional funds for his
military to match Kennedy's unprecedented buildup. Nor could he wait
any longer to solve his Berlin problem, as East Germans, attracted by
higher living standards in the West, were leaving the German socialist
paradise in ever greater numbers. They could easily do so through West
Berlin, since there was free movement between the Allied and Soviet
sectors of the city. In June 1961, 19,000 people used the Berlin loophole
in the Iron Curtain to go west; in July, 30,000 did so. The total for the
seven months of that year alone was 130,000.

The East German leader, Walter Ulbricht, had a solution: surrounding West Berlin with a wall. That, however, was a difficult proposition.
First, East and West Berlin constituted a joint railway hub without which
the East German economy would grind to a halt. Second, the Soviet
leaders and their allies in Czechoslovakia and Hungary were concerned
that the construction of a wall would be followed by an economic blockade of the whole Eastern bloc, making their economic situation worse
and necessitating greater Soviet subsidies. Ulbricht did not care, and
by May 1961 he had another argument in his favor: his work crews had
completed the construction of an outer ring railroad. West Berlin could
now be cut off from the eastern part of the city without hurting the East
German economy. All he needed now was Khrushchev's go-ahead. But
Khrushchev vacillated, hoping to browbeat Kennedy into submission.[23]

On August 1, six days after Kennedy's speech, Khrushchev told
Ulbricht that he could start building the wall. Less than two weeks
later, in the early morning of Sunday, August 13, the East German army
and border police sealed off West Berlin and, with the help of construc-

tion crews, began to surround it with barbed wire. Khrushchev had proposed making West Berlin a free city: now it was turning into a big concentration camp. He had visited both East and West Berlin before construction began, thinking about the possible American reaction. Kennedy had insisted in Vienna on maintaining American access rights, and Khrushchev had no plans to interfere with them. He also all but buried his plans to sign a peace agreement with East Germany—the wall was supposed to solve his main problem without a treaty. But he remained nervous.[24]

◊◊◊

KENNEDY'S FIRST REACTION TO THE WALL WAS SHOCK, FOL-lowed by a sigh of relief. He had not seen the wall coming, nor had his spies in West Berlin, who missed the preparations for construction. But he soon realized that the wall was not a challenge to the American access rights that he had promised to defend by force. Kennedy approved a State Department announcement that described the construction of the wall as a violation of the four-power agreement on Berlin while noting that "the measures undertaken so far are directed against the residents of East Berlin and East Germany and not against the Allied position in West Berlin or the access routes to West Berlin."

The president's sanguine view was not shared by the people of West Berlin. They felt that the construction of the wall was aimed against them and demanded American help. Once again, Kennedy was looking weak. Once again, he had to do something drastic without being irresponsible and raising tensions even further. Another request for military funding and calling in reservists would not do the trick. Kennedy rose to the challenge when the mayor of West Berlin, Willy Brandt, asked for the reinforcement of the American garrison. On August 20, one week after the sealing of West Berlin, 1,500 US troops marched on Kennedy's orders toward the city along the only highway linking it with West Germany in order to reaffirm American access rights, reinforce the garrison, and reassure the West Berliners. Both Kennedy and

Khrushchev hoped that the march would go off without a hitch and that there would be no accident. None took place.[25]

What the Berlin Wall really meant was anything but clear at the time. It did not result in an immediate conflict, but could it lead to a new one in the future? Khrushchev reached out to Kennedy in late September 1961, still arguing in favor of a peace treaty. Kennedy rejected the idea. "I do not see the need for a change in the situation of West Berlin, for today its people are free to choose their own way of life and their own guarantees of that freedom," he wrote on October 17. He accepted the wall, but that was the limit of his flexibility. Khrushchev received Kennedy's letter on October 19. Three days later, on October 21, speaking to the Twenty-Second Party Congress in Moscow, he removed the end-of-year deadline from his ultimatum threatening to sign a peace treaty with East Germany. Ulbricht, who had seen the wall as a stepping-stone to a future peace agreement with the Soviets, as well as to the establishment of his government's sovereignty over East Berlin and access routes to West Berlin, was anything but pleased. He wrote to Khrushchev indicating his dissatisfaction with the Soviet leader's declaration.[26]

If Khrushchev had difficulty controlling Ulbricht, Kennedy had his own rebel to deal with. This was General Lucius Clay. The successor to Eisenhower as the American military governor of Germany and the hero of the 1948–49 Berlin airlift, Clay was sent by Kennedy to West Berlin in August 1961 as his adviser and representative to calm the city's residents. Clay achieved that goal but made everyone very nervous on October 27 when he sent American tanks to Checkpoint Charlie on the border between the eastern and western sectors to enforce American rights to move freely through the entire city, including its eastern part, as guaranteed by the four-power agreements of the immediate postwar era. The Soviets responded by moving their own tanks to the area.

By early evening the two columns of tanks faced each other at Checkpoint Charlie, each less than one hundred meters from the demarcation line. The tanks had live ammunition, and their crews had orders to respond if fired upon. Clay, in charge of the US troops, was prepared to use his tanks to crush parts of the newly constructed Berlin Wall. Darkness fell with no resolution to the crisis. Not until morning did the tanks begin to draw back from the demarcation line. First the Soviet tanks moved five meters back; the Americans followed suit. Then came another five meters from both sides, then another. The standoff, which had begun at 5:00 p.m. on October 27, was over by 11:00 a.m. on October 28. The orders came from the very top—the White House and the Kremlin. Neither Kennedy nor Khrushchev wanted the situation to escalate into war.[27]

The danger of immediate military confrontation was removed as a result of the secret deal between Kennedy and Khrushchev. Its parameters were defined during the two conversations between the president's brother Robert Kennedy and Colonel Georgii Bolshakov of Soviet military intelligence, who was stationed in Washington. The Soviets were asked to avoid any aggressive actions and were assured that the Americans would respond in kind. Khrushchev was first to order his tanks to begin withdrawing. The Americans followed suit. The price exacted from the Americans included an end to civilian travel across sectoral lines. The Soviets won that point, but the world, seeing the Soviet tanks withdrawing first, assumed otherwise. Unbeknownst to both sides, it would be a model for the solution of a later and much more serious crisis.[28]

II

RED GAMBLE

3

TRIUMPH OF COMMUNISM

Nikita Khrushchev's inauguration as the world leader of communism took place in October 1961, just as American and Soviet tanks confronted each other at Checkpoint Charlie in divided Berlin. What amounted to induction into the communist hall of fame took place in Moscow, where a congress of the Communist Party of the Soviet Union was held from October 17 to 31.

Numbered twenty-second in the party's history, it entered the annals as the congress of the "builders of communism." At that assembly, the party of Lenin, Stalin, and now Khrushchev adopted its third and final program. The first party program, adopted in 1902, had announced the goal of toppling Russian authoritarianism; the second, approved in 1919, had put the party in charge of building a socialist state; and the third was to announce the construction of communism. To celebrate the impending victory of communism, Khrushchev had invited Vasilii Shulgin, a member of the Russian imperial parliament, or Duma, who had attended the abdication of the last Russian tsar, Nicholas II, to attend the congress and help usher in the triumph of the new era.[1]

Unbeknownst to most of the delegates attending the congress—close to five thousand in all—the event was accompanied by the largest "fireworks" in world history. On October 30, three days after the Berlin confrontation and one day before the end of the congress, American airplanes collecting air samples around the North Pole detected a major nuclear explosion in the Soviet north. A hydrogen bomb, referred to by the Soviets as either "Big Ivan" or "Tsar Bomba," went off at the Novaia Zemlia Archipelago in the Arctic Ocean. It yielded the explosive power of 58 megatons, compared to the 15 megatons of the Castle Bravo test conducted by the United States at Bikini Atoll in 1954. The largest nuclear explosion in history, it sent an eight-kilometer-wide fireball 60 kilometers into the atmosphere and was visible 1,000 kilometers away. Doctors registered third-degree burns 100 kilometers from the epicenter of the explosion, and houses were completely destroyed at 400 kilometers.[2]

"The test at Novaia Zemlia took place successfully. The safety of those in charge of the test and inhabitants of the region was guaranteed. The proving ground and all those taking part fulfilled the task set by the Motherland," went a telegram sent to Moscow from the test site by two key Soviet officials, Yefim Slavsky, the minister of medium machine-building—the Soviet nuclear superministry—and Marshal Kirill Moskalenko, Khrushchev's key military ally who had helped him arrest Beria in 1953 and was now in charge of the Soviet strategic missile forces. "We are returning to the congress," concluded the telegram. The two Soviet officials, who were delegates to the congress, had skipped the party leaders' speeches to travel to Novaia Zemlia and oversee the test of the new weapon. The explosion of the world's most powerful nuclear device was the Soviet nuclear industry's "gift" to the congress.[3]

On the day the Tsar Bomba was set off, the congress delegates voted to remove the corpse of Joseph Stalin from the mausoleum where it had lain next to Lenin's embalmed remains since Stalin's death in 1953. Khrushchev was now the unquestioned leader of the Soviet Union, having emerged fully from the shadow of his predecessor both at home and abroad. But his rise to the pinnacle of world communism did not go uncontested. The challengers were right there in the congress hall, led by Zhou Enlai, the long-serving head of the Chinese communist government. A few days before the removal of Stalin's corpse from the mausoleum, Zhou had placed a wreath at his coffin. The inscription referred to Stalin as "the great Marxist-Leninist." The two communist countries were in a growing conflict over Khrushchev's de-Stalinization policy and his attack on Stalin's "cult of personality," which was interpreted by China's communist leader and Khrushchev's challenger, Mao Zedong, as an attack on him and his regime.

At the congress Zhou Enlai criticized the Soviets for being soft on the West, while Khrushchev argued that his policy of "peaceful coexistence," adopted a few years earlier, was working and could be criticized only by "hopeless dogmatists." A CIA study of Soviet-Chinese relations that focused intensely on the party congress in Moscow summarized the tensions between Moscow and Beijing (called Peiping in the paper) as follows. "Although these differences had not usually been stated polemically in 1961, the Soviet party had continued to favor an opportunistic strategy of softening Western resistance by peaceful gestures while exploiting indigenous political movements in non-Communist countries primarily by non-military means, whereas the Chinese party had continued to advocate a more militant revolutionary program for the world movement on all fronts, particularly in the underdeveloped areas. Moscow contended that the bloc should not accept serious risks of world war, while Peiping argued that a more militant program would not increase the existing risk."[4]

The two communist leaders, Khrushchev and Mao Zedong, also competed for leadership of the world communist movement and influence in the Third World. No Third World country received more attention at the Moscow congress than Fidel Castro's Cuba, which half a year earlier had repelled the American-backed invasion and was represented at the congress by a delegation of Cuban communists. "Under the leadership of the courageous patriot and revolutionary Fidel Castro, the Cubans quickly routed the American hirelings, driving them into the Bahía de Cochinos, which means 'Bay of Pigs' in Russian. That's where they belong!" declared Khrushchev. The congress of the "builders of communism" exploded in laughter and applause. Khrushchev spared no effort to praise the "anti-imperialist" struggle of the Cuban people. At the same time, not unnoticed by the Chinese and Cubans alike, he was more than reluctant to recognize the Cuban revolution as socialist, accept Castro as a Marxist, or commit himself ideologically to the defense of Cuba and put his country on a collision course with the United States. Even when the long-serving head of the Cuban Communist Party, Blas Roca, presented Khrushchev with the Cuban national banner as a symbol of the continuation of the Bolshevik Revolution, he responded by praising Cuba rather than socialism.[5]

Faced with the task of balancing Soviet relations between Washington and Beijing, Khrushchev had to figure out how to deal with Cuba in a way that would consolidate his claim to lead the world communist movement while avoiding a direct confrontation with the United States. Unexpectedly to Khrushchev and his aides, Castro's survival of the Bay of Pigs invasion and his public embrace of socialism presented a major challenge not only to Washington but also to Moscow. Khrushchev's cautious approach to the Cuban revolution was at odds with public pronouncements by Fidel Castro himself and his communist aides that associated their revolution as closely as possible not only with the Soviet Union but also with Marxism and socialism.

◊◊◊

FIDEL CASTRO'S "NEAR DEATH" EXPERIENCE AT THE BAY OF Pigs produced a dramatic shift in the regime's official rhetoric. In a speech given in Havana on May 1, International Workers' Day, adopted by communists throughout the world as their emblematic holiday, Castro declared that his revolution was socialist and asked lawyers to produce a new socialist constitution for Cuba. He also firmly positioned himself and his country on the socialist side of the world divide. "If Mr. Kennedy does not like socialism, well, we do not like imperialism!"

declared Castro. "We do not like capitalism! We have as much right to protest over the existence of an imperialist-capitalist regime 90 miles from our coast as he feels he has to protest the existence of a socialist regime 90 miles from his coast." If anyone doubted his intentions, Castro had a column of children parade through the streets of Havana in a formation that read, "Long Live Our Socialist Revolution."[6]

Scarred by the Bay of Pigs invasion and expecting a much more powerful invasion in the near future, Castro apparently believed that to save his revolution he had to turn it into a socialist one. He badly needed socialist solidarity and wanted it to come not only in the form of Soviet purchases of sugar, trade credits for Soviet equipment, and supplies of oil. He also wanted weapons, missiles in particular. In his letter of September 4, 1961, Castro asked Moscow for 388 surface-to-air missiles like the one that had shot down the American U-2 airplane in May 1960 over the Soviet Union. His overall request for military assistance amounted to US $200 million. The Soviets were open to the idea but reduced the aid package to approximately $150 million. They also dragged their feet on delivery. Khrushchev was taking his time.[7]

Before the end of the year, the desperate Castro had declared himself a Marxist and a Leninist. On December 2, 1961, he delivered a speech that directly engaged some of the statements made by Khrushchev at the "builders of communism" congress a month earlier. Castro referred to Khrushchev's report to the congress as evidence that Marxism was a living and developing ideology. He pointed out that Marx did not leave a blueprint for building a socialist society. In Castro's reading of Marx, every anti-imperial revolution was a socialist one. "There could have been only one anti-imperialist and socialist Revolution, because there is but one revolution," he declared.[8]

The speech raised the ideological stakes in relations between the Soviet Union and Cuba. Castro declared himself a Marxist-Leninist, or a Marxist of the Soviet type—someone who had read Marx and Lenin in his student days but had come to a full appreciation of their works only recently. While American newspapers had a field day commenting on Castro's declaration of his Marxist beliefs, claiming to have known all along that Castro was a communist, the Soviet media were much more reserved.

In Moscow Castro was still regarded as part of a broad group of Third World leaders who opposed imperialism. "Statesmen as different as the popular hero of Cuba, Fidel Castro, and President Sukarno of Indonesia, Prime Minister Nehru of India and President Nkrumah of Ghana turn to the ideas of the Twenty-Second Congress of the CPSU, to Marxism-Leninism—each, of course, in his own way," wrote the leading Soviet newspaper *Izvestiia* in December 1961. "Not even the American Federal Bureau of Investigation would venture to declare them all communists. If Fidel Castro proclaims himself a Marxist, Sukarno is not about to do so."[9]

As one could guess from the tone of the newspaper edited by his son-in-law, Nikita Khrushchev was anything but pleased by the self-outing of the alleged closet Marxist Castro. Privately Khrushchev welcomed the development but believed it premature on Castro's part to declare his socialist agenda and communist goals in public. He wrote in his memoirs: "We had trouble understanding the timing of that statement. Castro's declaration had the immediate effect of widening the gap between himself and the people who were against socialism, and it narrowed the circle of those he could count on for support against the invasion." He continued: "As far as Castro's personal courage was concerned, his position was admirable and correct. But from a tactical standpoint, it did not make much sense."[10]

If the statement made little tactical sense from Khrushchev's point of view, it made a great deal from Castro's. He needed weapons as soon as possible. By declaring his revolution socialist and himself a Marxist, he was putting Khrushchev on the spot: could the leader of the world communist movement say no to a Marxist leading a socialist revolution almost within sight of an imperialist monster? There was still no word from Moscow on the military assistance requested by Castro. On December 17, two weeks after his "I Am a Marxist" speech, Castro and his aides approached a man they believed to have a direct line to the Kremlin—the head of the KGB station in Cuba, Aleksandr

Shitov, known to the outside world as Alekseev. The KGB man sensed the Cubans' unhappiness. They complained to him about unfulfilled promises on the part of Soviet officials to deliver missiles and warned of the "expected US aggression against Cuba." Alekseev filed a report to Moscow, but Khrushchev gave no response.[11]

◊◊◊

THE YEAR 1962 BROUGHT UNPRECEDENTED ECONOMIC HARD-ship to Cuba. In February, President Kennedy introduced new economic sanctions against the island, closing the American market not only to Cuban sugar but also to Cuban cigars. Soviet and Chinese purchases of sugar from Castro could not fill the widening gap in the Cuban state budget. Everything was now in short supply. To deal with food short-ages, Castro was forced to introduce rationing. "Cuba is now faced with an economic crisis attributable in large part to an acute shortage of the convertible foreign exchange required to finance greatly needed imports of foodstuffs and of replacement parts for machinery and equipment of US origin," stated a CIA memorandum compiled in early April.[12]

Feeling increasingly insecure and ever more frustrated with Mos-cow's procrastination about supplying weapons, Castro was prepared to reverse tactics and turn on the Marxists in his own country—the members of the Cuban Communist Party. This was meant to solidify his political control over the regime and send a signal of frustration to the communist world at large. On March 25, Castro delivered a long television address accusing the Cuban communists of sectarianism. "What sectarianism?" asked Castro, and answered the question him-self: "Well, the sectarianism of believing that the only revolutionists, that the only *compañeros* who could hold positions of trust, that the only ones who could hold a post on a people's farm, on a cooperative, in the government, anywhere, had to be old Marxist militants."[13]

The main target of Castro's attack was Aníbal Escalante, a long-time communist activist and editor of the party's leading newspaper. A year earlier, Castro had appointed him secretary of the Integrated Revolutionary Organizations, a political body to which Castro brought not only Cuban communists but also his own supporters from the July 26 Movement and the student-based Revolutionary Directory. Escalante managed to turn that post into one of the most important positions in the state hierarchy, challenging the authority if not the popularity of no less a figure than Castro's key ally, Che Guevara. If Guevara was known for his desire to spread revolution throughout Latin America and was suspected of sympathy toward the Chinese, Escalante was known as a strong supporter of Moscow. In defiance of Moscow, Castro sacked Escalante from his all-important position. Castro also managed to turn the communist old guard into scapegoats at a time when popular support for his regime was declining and discontent caused by the worsening economic situation was on the rise.[14]

The brewing Cuban crisis was brought urgently home to the Kremlin when Escalante came to Moscow to tell his side of the story. Chinese influences were on the rise in Havana, he claimed: he had tried to curtail them, only to lose his position. Escalante submitted his report to the Central Committee on April 3, 1962. Prospects looked grim, and Khrushchev had to act. Eight days after Escalante filed his report, the Central Committee's mouthpiece, the newspaper *Pravda,* published a long article on the situation in the Cuban leadership. To Escalante's disappointment and, probably, shock, the Central Committee decided to renounce him and back his nemesis, Fidel Castro, whose actions Escalante had tried to explain as a result of growing Chinese influence. *Pravda* stressed the need for unity against imperialist aggression.[15]

Forced to choose between the old communist Escalante and the brand-new Marxist Castro, Khrushchev had decided to back the latter, in whose leadership he saw the best guarantee of keeping Cuba in the Soviet camp. The KGB informed him that the Chinese threat in Havana was being exaggerated, and he believed that the threat of American invasion was real. On March 12, Aleksei Adzhubei, the editor of *Izvestiia* and Khrushchev's son-in-law, sent the Central Committee a report on his conversations with President Kennedy earlier that year. Among other things, they had discussed Cuba. "From a psychological point of view, it is very hard for the American people to agree with what is going on in Cuba," Kennedy told Adzhubei. "After all, it is only 90 miles from our coast. It is very hard." He compared favorably the decisive measures taken by the USSR in Hungary in 1956 with the CIA's inability to handle Cuba. The impression conveyed by the memo was that Kennedy had not given up on Cuba, and that military intervention was coming.[16]

◊◊◊

ON APRIL 12, 1962, THE DAY AFTER THE PUBLICATION OF THE *Pravda* editorial, the Presidium of the Central Committee, the USSR's governing body under the leadership of Nikita Khrushchev, approved a set of urgent measures to help Fidel Castro and his government. The Presidium decreed to expedite delivery to Cuba of 180 antiaircraft surface-to-air missiles requested by Castro in September 1961. He was also to get Sopka air-to-surface cruise missiles developed on the basis of the Soviet MiG-15 fighter for use as an anti-ship weapon. Some of the missiles that the Presidium decided to send to Cuba were taken from the quota already promised to another Soviet client in the Third World, Prime Minister Gamal Abdel Nasser of Egypt. Cuba was given priority over Egypt in the Soviet pecking order.

When it came to missiles, Moscow was still sending fewer than Castro had asked for, but he was also offered something he had not requested: ten Ilyushin-28 medium bombers and four R-15 cruise-missile launchers. By cutting back on some of Castro's requests while offering other weapons and equipment instead, the Presidium was not trying to save money. It wanted to better prepare Cuba to repel a possible invasion; to that end, bombers were no less important than missiles. Besides arms, members of the Soviet military would be coming to Cuba: 650 officers, sergeants, and soldiers to operate the launchers, pilot the planes, and teach the Cubans how to do both.[17]

The cost of the missiles and other equipment to be sent to Cuba on the basis of the Presidium's decision of April 12 was 23 million rubles. That was coming on the top of an already impressive military aid package. The USSR had begun to supply arms to Cuba back in 1960, and by May 1962 agreements worth 228 million rubles had been signed. Armaments worth 142 million rubles had already been delivered to Havana. Some were donated, others offered at a discount, and still others sold at their regular price by means of a line of credit extended to Cuba. In 1962 Cuba was expected to pay the USSR up to 50 million rubles for armaments already received, but the crisis-stricken country had no money to do so, let alone to afford new shipments.

Khrushchev decided not only to write off Cuba's debt for the armaments supplied earlier but also to supply new armaments free of charge for the next two years, regardless of quantity and cost. The USSR also agreed to cover the expenses of its own personnel, except for housing and transportation, to be provided by the Cuban army. That army in turn would be supplied with all its requirements free of charge by the Soviet Union for the next two years. The calculations were based on a figure of 100,000 soldiers in the Cuban armed forces. A proposal to make a formal decision in that regard was sent to the Central Committee on May 7.[18]

That same day Khrushchev met with the new Soviet ambassador to Havana, Aleksandr Alekseev, who had previously headed the KGB station in the Cuban capital and, unlike his predecessor career diplomat Sergei Kudriavtsev, was highly regarded by Castro. "I do not want diarchy any longer," Khrushchev told him. "We recognize one ambassador, and the Cubans recognize another." Khrushchev clearly wanted an ambassador who enjoyed a good rapport with Castro. Alekseev's suggestion that he was not up to the task because he lacked economic expertise was dismissed. Khrushchev wanted a new man in the job to help turn the page on an unhappy period in Soviet-Cuban relations. He sent Alekseev to the Central Committee to help draft a letter to Castro that would spell out the new aid package offered him by Moscow.[19]

By May 11, 1962, the letter that Alekseev had worked on was ready for the Presidium's approval and was accepted without delay. Apart from forgiving Cuba's debt for armaments and offering a free supply of new weapons, the letter proposed economic and managerial assistance.

The Soviets committed themselves to building an underground radio center and supplying five Soviet fishing vessels, to be transferred to the Cubans if they so desired. The Soviets were also prepared to help with irrigation: the head of the Soviet delegation to be dispatched to Cuba with the good news was Sharof Rashidov, the party boss of the Soviet republic of Uzbekistan, who was considered an expert in the field. He was described to Alekseev as someone who had experience in growing sugar cane and could therefore help the Cubans with their problems. Overlooked in the excitement and chaos of putting together the new "save Cuba" economic package was the fact that the Cubans had problems with selling, not producing, their sugar.[20]

The Soviet Union was making unprecedented military and financial commitments to Cuba, and the stakes were growing higher. The same letter invited Castro to visit the USSR before the end of the year. Castro's pledge to lead his country to socialism, previously ignored, had finally paid off, but only after his unexpected attack on Moscow's allies in Havana. Khrushchev's hitherto cautious approach to Castro and Cuba was completely abandoned on April 18, when he sent a letter to "Comrade Fidel Castro" commemorating the first anniversary of the Cuban victory at the Bay of Pigs. Castro had finally gotten Khrushchev on an ideological leash, but Khrushchev was willing to be caught. His motive was not purely ideological. Great-power rivalry and the nuclear arms race with the United States, which Khrushchev knew he was losing, were among the factors that attracted him to Cuba.[21]

4

ROCKET MAN

On May 14, 1962, Nikita Khrushchev left Moscow for a long-planned visit to Bulgaria, one of the most reliable Soviet satellites in Eastern Europe. It was linked to Russia by culture, religion, and common struggle against the Ottoman Turks during the tsarist era. In fact, both countries had previously been ruled by tsars; now they were headed by first secretaries. Khrushchev was going to Bulgaria to sign a cooperation agreement and celebrate Soviet-Bulgarian friendship with his client and counterpart, Todor Zhivkov.

Zhivkov, who became first secretary of the Bulgarian Communist Party in 1954, after Stalin's death, and held that office until the fall of the communist regime in 1989, mobilized hundreds of thousands of citizens and shepherded them to rallies organized in Khrushchev's honor. A quarter of a million people gathered in the main square and adjoining streets of Sofia on May 19 to greet the visitor from Moscow. For a country with a population below eight million whose capital had fewer than eight hundred thousand residents, that was quite a feat— every fourth inhabitant of Sofia was there to see the mayor present

Khrushchev with the symbolic gift of a key to the city gates. Sofia, Varna, and Pleven bestowed the title of honorary citizen on the Soviet guest.

No member of the Soviet party Presidium accompanied him on the trip, making Khrushchev the sole object of attention and adulation. One of the photos taken during the five-day visit showed Khrushchev in a light-colored suit standing out against Soviet and Bulgarian officials in dark suits, for all the world like a white-robed communist pope surrounded by a throng of black-clad bishops. And Khrushchev's visit had all the trappings of a religious ritual, not unlike a papal visit to a heavily Catholic country. It was a celebration of communism, Slavic brotherhood, and, more than anything else, the personal power and infallibility of the man at the center of it all—Nikita Khrushchev, the high priest of the world communist movement.[1]

"And where is communism now?" asked Khrushchev rhetorically, addressing festively clad crowds of peasants in the village of Obnova (meaning "Renovation"), a showcase of socialist agriculture in northern Bulgaria. And he answered in grandiose fashion: "Communism has broadened its boundaries. And if, not long ago, the Soviet Union was the only socialist country, the socialist camp has now broadly expanded its boundaries, uniting in one fraternal family many socialist countries of Europe, the Chinese People's Republic, the Korean People's Democratic Republic, and the Democratic Republic of Vietnam. Postwar Europe found itself missing many states that had gone socialist. Now the banner of socialism waves proudly over Cuba."[2]

Cuba was constantly on Khrushchev's mind throughout his Bulgarian trip. For all the ritual atmosphere of triumph, he felt deeply insecure. "While I was on the official visit to Bulgaria," recalled Khrushchev later, "one thought kept hammering away at my brain: 'what will happen if we lose Cuba?'" The possibility of another American-backed invasion gave him no rest. "We had to think up some way of confronting America with more than words," remembered Khrushchev. "We had to establish a tangible and effective deterrent to American interference in the Caribbean, but what exactly?"[3]

◊◊◊

IN APRIL 1962 KHRUSHCHEV FOUND HIMSELF SIMULTA-
neously besieged by a number of foreign policy crises. First there was
Castro's sudden turn against the communists in his government and
threat of a new invasion of the island. Then came news that Kennedy had
resumed atmospheric nuclear testing—a nuclear bomb was exploded at
Christmas Island in the Pacific on April 25. It was a response to Soviet
tests conducted in the fall of the previous year. That month Khrushchev
fired the commander in chief of the Soviet Strategic Missile Forces,
Marshal Kirill Moskalenko, who was blamed for allowing the real missile gap between the US and the USSR to increase.[4]

Marshal Moskalenko became the first victim of the American
missile called "Minuteman." This was a new type of land-based intercontinental ballistic missile, powered by solid fuel and, unlike earlier
liquid-fueled missiles that needed hours of fueling before a strike,
could be ready at any minute—hence the name. Moreover, the Minuteman could be housed in silos hard for the enemy to destroy, making them almost impregnable. The USSR had nothing comparable to
the Minuteman, because its missiles ran on liquid fuel and needed
hours of prestrike fueling on open pads, making them vulnerable to
enemy attack.[5]

Work on rockets powered by solid fuel began in the United States
before 1957, but it was Sputnik that alerted Congress to the need to
speed up the project. In 1958 the Minuteman development budget was
almost quadrupled from $40 million to $150 million, and in 1959 it was
further increased by $2 billion. By 1960 twelve thousand engineers and
workers had been employed by Boeing alone to work on the Minuteman
construction line in northern Utah. The first successful test of the new
missile was conducted at Cape Canaveral, Florida, in February 1961.
Construction of the first Minuteman missile field began in Montana in
March. The Kennedy administration favored the Minuteman over other
missile projects: expensive to design, it was relatively cheap to produce.

By March 1962 American newspapers were writing about new rockets capable of delivering "one megaton of death and destruction."[6]

Khrushchev was alerted to the imminent American deployment of the Minuteman and Soviet inability to respond effectively at a meeting of his Defense Council held at the Pitsunda resort on the Black Sea in February 1962. According to Khrushchev's son Sergei, a young missile engineer who attended the meeting, the bad news was delivered to the first secretary by Marshal Moskalenko. Khrushchev trusted the marshal, a native of the Donbas region of Ukraine, where Khrushchev had long lived and worked. In June 1953 Moskalenko had shown his loyalty to Khrushchev by leading the group of officers who arrested Khrushchev's archenemy Lavrentii Beria. Four years later, in July 1957, when the party Presidium tried to oust Khrushchev, Moskalenko had helped to convene a plenum of the Central Committee, which exonerated Khrushchev and removed his opponents from leadership positions. It was on Moskalenko's watch that the Soviets put Yurii Gagarin into orbit in April 1961 and exploded the Tsar Bomba in October of the same year. But with the Americans ready to deploy the Minuteman, Moskalenko ran out of luck.[7]

Moskalenko began his report on a positive note: starting that year, the army would get a new intercontinental ballistic missile, the R-16 (SS-7 Sadler in US classification). A 30-meter-long missile weighing 140 metric tons, it could deliver a 5-megaton nuclear warhead at a distance of up to 11,000 kilometers, well in excess of the 8,000 kilometers that separated Moscow from Washington. The news that the R-16 missiles were ready for deployment had special meaning for Moskalenko and all those in the room. In October 1960, one of the earlier versions of that missile had exploded on the launchpad at the Baikonur test range in Kazakhstan, killing ninety-two people, including Moskalenko's predecessor, the first commander of the Soviet Strategic Missile Forces, Marshal Mitrofan Nedelin. The first successful launch of the R-16 from a silo took place in January 1962. The missile was now ready for deployment.[8]

But that was all the good news Moskalenko could deliver. He had to admit that the long-awaited R-16 was no match for the Minuteman. It was the first Soviet rocket to use storable liquid fuel, which reduced the preparation time for launching, but even so, fueling the two stages took hours—up to six hours, according to Moskalenko. Preparation time for the Minuteman, he reported, was only a few minutes. "While we bring it out and put it in place, there won't be a wet spot left of any of us," theatrically declared Moskalenko, known among the troops by his nickname, "General Panic." There was yet another problem with the R-16: the fuel had to be drained from the rocket's tanks if it was not launched, as its unstable components were too corrosive to remain there longer than a couple of days. "According to American experts," said Moskalenko, "the solid-fueled Minutemen can remain constantly ready for years."[9]

The chief designer of the R-16 missile, Mikhail Yangel, who had survived the catastrophic explosion of his rocket in October 1960, was now working hard to improve its design but could not promise quick results. When Yangel went to the podium, he told Khrushchev that the R-16 was the last missile of the generation that began with Sputnik. The Minuteman had changed the game. The Soviet Union needed a new generation of missiles that could stay ready for launch at any minute. Disturbing news was coming not only from Yangel and his design bureau in Dnipropetrovsk, where Khrushchev had boasted that missiles were being mass-produced like sausages. Yangel's competitor Sergei Korolev, the father of the Sputnik, was struggling with his own problems. His rocket, the R-9, also used liquid fuel—a mix of kerosene and oxygen stored at low temperature. Loss of oxygen from the fuel tanks required constant refueling of the missile. If the R-16 had already been tested and was ready for deployment, the R-9 was still undergoing tests, each of them uncovering new problems with Korolev's rocket.[10]

A further problem was the virtual absence of battle-ready long-range missiles. Very few of the missiles that Khrushchev had at his disposal were intercontinental ones capable of reaching the United States. Korolev's R-7A rockets could do so, but there were only four of them, and they were unreliable and badly outdated, requiring twenty hours for fueling, which made them a perfect target for US bombers. Yangel's R-16 was much better but had just entered the deployment phase, and tests of the silo-based models had just begun. Altogether the Soviets had only a few dozen R-16s, vulnerable, as Moskalenko had explained, to enemy missile attack and incapable of being launched as part of a second strike. The Soviets thus had little to deter a possible attack from the United States.[11]

All that was bad news not only for the Soviet missile program but also for Khrushchev personally. He had gambled on missiles, cutting all other branches of his military significantly. But he had no solid-fuel rocket engines, which meant that his rockets had to spend hours on launchpads to be filled with liquid fuel, making them vulnerable to American strikes. They could be used as first-strike weapons but were useless for retaliation. "Father looked around the room gloomily. The result he wanted had once again proved impossible to achieve," remembered Sergei Khrushchev. "He asked those present to think about what could be done to reduce to a minimum the amount of time it would take to catch up with the Americans." The Soviets were behind not just in quantity of missiles but also in their quality, which meant that the missile gap long known to Khrushchev had just become wider.

The Soviet leader demanded new ideas and projects. He was eager to fill the gap as soon as possible. On April 16, a few days after Khrushchev and his colleagues in the party Presidium authorized a major military aid package for Cuba, they approved a new program to build intercontinental ballistic missiles capable of delivering nuclear warheads (euphemistically called a "special charge" in the party and government resolution) to the United States. Khrushchev's new favorite, the missile designer Vladimir Chelomei, was authorized to develop two new missiles—the Universal Rocket 500, capable of delivering a 50-megaton charge equivalent to the Tsar Bomba, and the Universal Rocket 200, capable of carrying a 7,000-pound payload a distance of up to 12,000 kilometers. Mikhail Yangel in Dnipropetrovsk was charged with building a new rocket, the R-36, with a range of 16,000 kilometers. It would become known in the West as the SS-18 Satan, the first Soviet MIRV, or multiple independently targetable reentry vehicle missile. It could take a warhead into orbit and keep it there, reducing the time required to execute a strike to a few minutes.[12]

But all that would come later, with Satan being deployed only in 1974. Meanwhile, Khrushchev needed a solution. He started with a shakeup at the top of the Soviet missile establishment. Marshal Moskalenko, who had failed to keep the missile designers in line, had to go. At the Pitsunda meeting Sergei Korolev and the designer of the rocket engines, Valentin Glushko, got into a nasty fight over the type of fuel they wanted to use for a Soviet missile capable of reaching the moon, leaving it to Khrushchev, who wanted to reach the United States, not the moon, to stop the fight. Loyal but ineffective, Moskalenko had to go. Khrushchev later recalled that in his opinion there were three Moskalenkos: a brave and energetic general; a rude administrator insensitive to his subordinates and prone to hysterics; and, finally, a careerist. He decided to fire all three Moskalenkos: on April 24, 1962, his former protégé was shifted to the post of inspector in chief of the Ministry of Defense and replaced in his former office by the commander of the Soviet Air Defense Forces, Marshal Sergei Biriuzov.[13]

With Moskalenko gone, Biriuzov appointed, and plans for new missiles in the works, Khrushchev still needed a quick solution to his missile-gap problem. Surprisingly, he found it on his trip to Bulgaria, where Cuba and missiles were much on his mind. The solution he came up with involved both.

◊◊◊

ON MAY 12, TWO DAYS BEFORE LEAVING MOSCOW FOR SOFIA, Khrushchev met with a visiting American, someone as close to President Kennedy as could be—the White House press secretary, Pierre Salinger. He found time to take Salinger on a boat ride on the Moscow River, spending a total of fourteen hours with him. Khrushchev lashed out at Kennedy's recent remark to the effect that he did not exclude a nuclear strike against the Soviet Union. "Of course, in some circumstances we must be prepared to use nuclear weapon at the start, come what may—a clear attack on Western Europe, for example," the president had said, trying to explain that the appearance of Soviet intercontinental missiles had shifted the balance of power and made the Eisenhower administration's plan to strike without possibility of retaliation obsolete. Kennedy had soon retracted his remark, but that did not satisfy Khrushchev, who responded furiously both in his private conversations with Salinger and in public.[14]

Speaking to the extremely friendly crowd in Sofia, Khrushchev said that Kennedy "had not hesitated even to declare that under certain circumstances the United States might take 'the initiative in a nuclear conflict with the Soviet Union.' Doesn't that statement mean that the president of the United States wants to incite me, as head of the Soviet government, to compete with him as to who will 'push the button' first?" Khrushchev said that he was opposed to such a competition. He then added: "The president of the United States of America made an ill-advised statement. Is it wise to threaten someone who is at least as strong as you? Pushing the button and taking 'the initiative in a nuclear conflict with the Soviet Union' would actually mean committing suicide."[15]

As Khrushchev knew better than anyone, the American and Soviet nuclear missile arsenals were unequal. He had virtually no rockets capable of reaching the United States to serve as a deterrent. That bothered him a lot, and he would speak of missiles more than once on his Bulgarian trip. At the Black Sea port of Varna, he asked his audience: "Is it not time for the ruling circles of Turkey and neighboring countries to realize the fruitlessness of their course of isolation from their neighbors, a course that subordinates national interests to those of foreign monopolies and senseless preparations for war? Is it not better to turn the shores on which NATO military bases and launchpads for missiles with atomic payloads are located into places of peaceful endeavor and prosperity?"[16]

Khrushchev was referring to the PGM-19 Jupiter medium-range ballistic missiles with 1.44-megaton nuclear warheads that had been deployed by the United States in Italy and Turkey. In February 1961 the Soviet Union had issued a public statement protesting the deployment, to no effect. In June the United States Air Force deployed fifteen Jupiters in Turkey. "The missile base (five launchpads with 15 installations) should be completely ready by March 1962," said a report from the Soviet embassy in Ankara to Moscow in early 1962. "By the end of the year the number of American military and civilian personnel, including family members, had reached a record figure—120,000 persons." Given that the Jupiter had a range of 2,400 kilometers, and the distance from the environs of Izmir in Turkey, where the missiles were placed, to Moscow was 2,080 kilometers, the Americans could now easily strike Moscow.[17]

Khrushchev had little expectation that the Turks would follow his advice and return the American missiles. Instead, as claimed by his son Sergei, while walking in a Varna seaside park he had a eureka moment: he would do to the Americans what they had done to the Soviet Union and place his nuclear missiles on the shores of Cuba. "It was during my visit to Bulgaria that I had the idea of installing missiles with nuclear warheads in Cuba," wrote Khrushchev in his memoirs. This looked like a solution to both of his problems, protecting Cuba and bridging the missile gap with the United States. "Khrushchev had a rich imagination, and when some idea took hold of him, he was inclined to see in its implementation an easy solution to a particular problem, a sort of cure-all," recalled the Soviet leader's assistant, Oleg Troianovsky.[18]

Khrushchev had found the "cure-all" on the shores of the Black Sea. While he lacked long-range ballistic missiles, he had plenty of short- and medium-range ones, designed and produced by Mikhail Yangel at the Dnipropetrovsk works that Khrushchev had visited in the summer of 1959. The missiles that he bragged the Soviets could allegedly produce like sausages were R-12 or SS-4 Sandals, capable of reaching targets within a 2,000-kilometer range. In 1962 the army had begun the deployment of R-14 or SS-5 Skean intermediate missiles with an operational range of 3,700 kilometers. By installing those short- and medium-range missiles in Cuba, Khrushchev could reach American targets. It looked like the perfect solution.[19]

On the flight back to Moscow, Khrushchev approached his foreign minister, Andrei Gromyko, for a private conversation. "The situation that has now developed around Cuba is dangerous," Khrushchev told his surprised colleague. "To save it as an independent state we must install a number of our nuclear rockets there. I think that's the only thing that can save the country. Washington will not be deterred by last year's failed intervention at Playa Girón." Khrushchev asked Gromyko for his opinion. The foreign minister was less than enthusiastic, but not yet having become a member of the Presidium and thus of the high Soviet leadership, was more than cautious in expressing his concern. "I should say frankly," wrote Gromyko, recalling his words, "that bringing our nuclear missiles to Cuba will cause a political explosion in the United States." Khrushchev was not pleased but did not rebuke his foreign minister. After a pause, he told Gromyko: "We don't need a nuclear war, and we are not about to fight." Gromyko was relieved.[20]

Khrushchev was not going to start a nuclear war, but what he had in mind was extremely dangerous nuclear brinkmanship. And yet it looked like the only solution to the two foreign policy imperatives facing him—the need to support Cuba's newfound communism and overcome American superiority in nuclear missiles. Khrushchev had presented himself publicly as the defender of world communism and leader of a country that was outdoing the Americans in missile technology. Now he had to deliver.

5

GOING NUCLEAR

Now that he knew what had to be done, Khrushchev was unstoppable. On May 21, 1962, the day after his return to Moscow from Bulgaria, Khrushchev called a meeting of the Defense Council, which consisted of members of the party and government leadership. Also present was the new chief of the Soviet Strategic Rocket Forces, Marshal Sergei Biriuzov.

Khrushchev began a report on his trip and then turned to Cuba. "I said that it would be foolish to expect the inevitable second invasion to be as badly planned and as badly executed as the first," recalled Khrushchev. "I warned that Fidel would be crushed if another invasion were launched against Cuba and said that we were the only ones who could prevent such a disaster from occurring." He then presented his case for placing medium- and intermediate-range ballistic missiles on Cuban soil: "In addition to protecting Cuba, our missiles would equalize what the West likes to call the 'balance of power,'" recalled Khrushchev years later.[1]

Brief minutes of that day's meeting identified the topic of discussion as "On Assistance to Cuba," suggesting that Khrushchev framed the discussion as one about saving Cuba rather than addressing the lack of parity in the Soviet and American nuclear arsenals and missile capabilities. Vladimir Malin, the head of the Central Committee's General Department, who kept an informal record of the meeting, scribbled in his notes: "How to help Cuba so that it holds out." Judging by Malin's notes, no one objected to Khrushchev's solution to the problem. But according to another notetaker, the secretary of the Defense Council, Colonel General Semen Ivanov, there was at least one dissenter, Khrushchev's first deputy in the Council of Ministers, Anastas Mikoyan, who voiced his objections to the idea of "placing our missiles and troops on Cuba."[2]

Khrushchev spoke with Mikoyan before the meeting and knew about his objections to the missile plan. Mikoyan was anxious that once the Americans learned about the missiles, they would not tolerate such a proximate threat of nuclear attack and would strike the missile sites, killing Soviet troops there. "What are we supposed to do in such a case—respond with a strike on US soil?" asked Mikoyan. Khrushchev did not disagree. "I had expressed the same idea as well," recalled Khrushchev of one of his discussions with Mikoyan. "I even said that such a step, roughly speaking, was on the verge of being reckless. The recklessness of the plan was that our desire to defend Cuba could lead to an unprecedented nuclear war. We needed to find ways to avoid it by any means, because a deliberate initiation of such a war would definitely be reckless adventurism." Khrushchev knew that he was risking war, and nuclear war at that, but believed that he could get away with his reckless step.

Khrushchev tried to get Mikoyan on his side but failed. "What if we send our missiles there and deploy them quickly and unnoticeably?" he asked Mikoyan at a private meeting after his return from Bulgaria. "Then we will notify the Americans about it, first through diplomatic channels and then publicly. That will put them in their place. They will be put in a position of the same balance of forces as with our country. Any aggression against Cuba will mean a strike on American territory. They will have to give up any plans of an invasion of Cuba." Mikoyan

was unconvinced by what he heard. "I told him that it was dangerous," he recalled later. "Such things are hard to hide—what if they are
detected?" he asked Khrushchev. There was no satisfactory answer.[3]

Still, on May 21, Khrushchev's argument carried the day. With
the rest of the leadership either silent or expressing support for Khrushchev's proposal, he was able to brush off Mikoyan's dissent with little
difficulty. Mikoyan remained in the minority, recalling later that he was
the only one who opposed Khrushchev on the issue. The Defense Council, whose meeting doubled as a meeting of the Presidium, decided
to authorize preparations for placing nuclear-armed missiles in Cuba.
The terse notes on specific measures discussed and approved by the
leadership read as follows: "Install nuclear rocket weapons. Transport
them secretly. Disclose later. Rockets under our command. This will
be an offensive policy." Those present also decided to initiate talks with
Castro about signing a mutual defense treaty.[4]

Ever since he crushed the old-guard opposition to his rule in the
summer of 1957 and made himself head of both party and government
in the spring of 1958, Khrushchev had had little if any opposition to
his leadership of the party and the state. Mikoyan, who had begun his
party career under Lenin and survived Stalin, was the only old-timer
in government still in a position to ask Khrushchev questions and con-
tradict him in open discussion. The rest were Khrushchev's appointees
who, like Andrei Gromyko, preferred not to voice their thoughts and,
in particular, their criticism of Khrushchev's ideas and increasingly
adventurous behavior at home and abroad. One-man rule gave Khrushchev enormous latitude to be quick, decisive, and flexible in crisis
situations, but it also gave him opportunities to create crises at will.
One could only hope that he would be as good at resolving such crises
as he was at creating them.

◊◊◊

KHRUSHCHEV CHARGED THE MINISTER OF DEFENSE, MAR-
shal Rodion Malinovsky, and the commander in chief of the Strategic

Missile Forces, Marshal Biriuzov, with assessing the scope and time frame of the operation required to deliver the missiles and nuclear warheads to Cuba.

Khrushchev knew that he could count on the sixty-three-year-old Malinovsky, a round-faced, burly, outspoken officer who had fought against Francisco Franco during the Spanish Civil War and whom he had met during World War II. Malinovsky had distinguished himself at Stalingrad, led the Soviet army groups liberating his native Ukraine, and ended his service in Europe by capturing Vienna. Khrushchev had chosen Malinovsky to replace the independent-minded Georgii Zhukov as minister of defense in 1957, and thereafter Malinovsky had become his closest ally in the painful reform of the armed forces. They were significantly reduced in numbers, with funds redirected from the traditional services to the newborn missile forces.[5]

Malinovsky ordered Colonel General Ivanov, the secretary of the Defense Council and chief of the Main Operations Directorate of the General Staff, who had attended the May 21 meeting with Khrushchev, to prepare the proposal for execution. When Ivanov returned to his headquarters after the meeting of the Defense Council, one of his subordinates, the forty-three-year-old curly-haired Major General Anatoly Gribkov, realized right away that something extraordinary had happened. "I had long known my direct superior, but this was the first time that I saw him so agitated," recalled Gribkov. Ivanov gave Gribkov the notes he had made at the meeting. He wanted the young general to turn them into a draft proposal for the deployment operation. The assignment was so secret that only two others would work on the plan under Gribkov's command. Clerical support was ruled out as well. "No typist is to be involved," ordered Ivanov. "Except for you three, no one is to know of the document."[6]

The task was not only secret but urgent. "Forgetting all about time, we set to work," recalled Gribkov years later. The seven-page draft was ready in two days. Gribkov and his subordinates proposed sending to Cuba a total of 44,000 officers and soldiers, as well as 1,300 civilians—an impressive number of people, to be accompanied by an equally impressive amount of weaponry, equipment, and supplies. According to Gribkov's estimate, some seventy or eighty cargo and passenger ships would be required to take them to Cuba. The Group of Soviet Forces in Cuba, as the new task force was officially called, was to be drawn from all branches of the armed forces—navy, air force, air defense, and army. Their main task was to enable the deployment and ensure the protection of four missile regiments, two equipped with twenty-four launchers of R-12 medium-range missiles and two with sixteen launchers of R-14 intermediate-range missiles. The forty launchers were to be provided with sixty missiles and sixty warheads.

When it came to time requirements for such an operation—another question addressed to Malinovsky and Biriuzov by the Defense Council—Gribkov suggested that the missiles could be sent to Cuba in two shipments, starting in early July. The concentration of the entire task force in Cuba could be completed by September. Gribkov and his assistants estimated that the R-12 missiles with prefabricated launch-pads could be rendered operational within ten days after arrival at the designated location. The construction of launch facilities for the R-14s, however, would take about four months. Thus the R-12s could become operational in September and the R-14s by the end of December 1962. Apart from detailed enumeration of the weaponry, equipment, and units needed for the operation, the draft document suggested a name for the supersecret operation—Anadyr.[7]

Gribkov never revealed whose idea it was to name the Soviet deployment in tropical Cuba after a Siberian river in the Chukotka Peninsula, separated by a narrow stretch of water from Alaska, but the choice of name left no doubt that the planners took the secrecy of the operation seriously. They also showed tremendous daring: delivering to Cuba and then secretly deploying forty missile launchers, sixty missiles, and sixty nuclear warheads along with forty-five thousand personnel and escort was a task bordering on the impossible. Nevertheless, Minister of Defense Malinovsky duly signed the document prepared by Gribkov. Khrushchev's half-baked idea had taken on the specifics of a military plan. The military were going for the kill: they were about to create a full-fledged military base in Cuba, and the proposed name of the task force, the Group of Soviet Armed Forces in Cuba, mirrored the name of the Soviet forces in East Germany, suggesting a dramatic extension of the Soviet western military frontier all the way to the Caribbean.[8]

On May 24, Marshal Malinovsky presented Gribkov's proposal to the Central Committee Presidium, largely the same group of Soviet plenipotentiaries as the one that constituted the Defense Council. Those taking part in the discussion of the document, apart from Khrushchev himself, included government heavyweights: Frol Kozlov, the de facto second man in the party after Khrushchev; Leonid Brezhnev, the future Soviet leader, who then held the largely ceremonial office of chairman of the Supreme Soviet, the rubber-stamp parliament; Aleksei Kosygin, the future prime minister under Brezhnev and Khrushchev's first deputy in the government at the time; and Anastas Mikoyan, another first deputy of Khrushchev and the only member of the leadership who had voiced reservations about the plan. Once again, he was polite and respectful but critical of the idea concocted by Khrushchev and the proposal resulting from it.[9]

Faced with Mikoyan's continuing opposition, Khrushchev called on his ally Marshal Malinovsky, asking how long it would take him to overrun an island such as Cuba. What Khrushchev had in mind was not the speed with which Malinovsky could take the island under control so as to prevent an American invasion but the speed with which the Americans could capture the island. Malinovsky knew what was expected of him and suggested that it would take him roughly four days, perhaps a week. "Do you see?" Khrushchev told Mikoyan. "We have no other option." Khrushchev was expecting an American invasion and using the threat of it to cow the only dissident in the party and government leadership into submission. Still Mikoyan disagreed.

Mikoyan, who had visited Cuba a few years earlier, did not think that the operation could be kept secret and that the missiles, once deployed, could escape American detection. "I told him," recalled Mikoyan, "what I saw with my own eyes in 1960: no woods to hide missile launchers, just some palm trees too far away from each other." The palm trees were in fact "naked trees" with leaves only on top, continued Mikoyan. The members of the Presidium had visited the Black Sea resort of Sochi in the Soviet subtropics and knew what palm trees looked like. They had nothing to say in response. "I told them," said Mikoyan, "that the consequences could be dangerous or even catastrophic. The Americans could launch a strike on our missiles and destroy them in several minutes." He suggested that the leaders had to think about their next steps: "What would we have to do then? Just swallow that, look disgraced in front of the entire world and possibly lose Cuba, for whose sake we are doing everything? Or retaliate with a nuclear strike, which would mean the initiation of the war?"[10]

Mikoyan received support from an unexpected quarter when Khrushchev asked the newly appointed ambassador to Havana, Aleksandr Alekseev, to join the meeting. "Comrade Alekseev, in order to help Cuba and save the Cuban revolution, we have decided to place rockets on the island," said Khrushchev, surprising the government's leading expert on Cuba. "What do you think of this? How will Fidel react? Will he give his agreement?" Alekseev, a KGB officer who was about to become a diplomat, summoned all his diplomatic skills and responded that Castro was spearheading campaigns all over Latin America against foreign military bases and trying to force the Americans to leave Guantánamo, so for him to accept a Soviet military base in Cuba would go against his own policies.

Khrushchev remained silent, but Marshal Malinovsky, whose Anadyr plan suddenly appeared to be in jeopardy, went on the offensive, trying to intimidate Alekseev. "What sort of revolution is it if, as you say, they do not agree?" yelled Malinovsky. "I fought in Spain, there was a bourgeois revolution there, but they accepted help from us even so. . . . And socialist Cuba has far more reason to do so!" If the Soviets were trying to rescue Cuba in order to save socialism, as Khrushchev had suggested, then, according to Malinovsky's logic, how could socialist Cuba refuse Soviet missiles? Faced with the ideological argument, Alekseev fell silent. But Kozlov, Khrushchev's chief deputy in the party, defended Alekseev: Castro's support of Khrushchev's bold initiative could not be taken for granted. Khrushchev, for his part, wanted Alekseev to help the Soviet political and military delegation that was going to Havana convince Castro to accept the nuclear missiles.[11]

Khrushchev proposed a compromise of sorts. He suggested pushing ahead with preparations while delaying a final decision on the launch of the mission. He told Mikoyan: "Let's not talk about it anymore. We will ask Fidel Castro and then we will decide. We will send [Marshal Sergei] Biriuzov with his specialists to check if there are spots to hide missile launchers to make them invisible to the aircraft." Ivanov scribbled in his notes: "The Presidium members and those who spoke agreed and approved the decision. Decision: approve Operation Anadyr completely and unanimously. Keep the document in the Defense Ministry. Ratify it after receiving F[idel] Castro's consent." Mikoyan's criticism had had some impact. He now hoped that Castro would refuse and that Biriuzov would find the Cuban terrain unsuitable for concealing missiles.[12]

Before the meeting was adjourned and the participants went their separate ways, Khrushchev delivered his concluding remarks, summarizing his argument for placing nuclear missiles in Cuba. Alekseev recalled Khrushchev's words decades later: "To avenge their defeat at Playa Girón, the Americans will undertake an intervention in Cuba not with the help of mercenaries but with their own armed forces: we have reliable information to that effect." He continued: "They must be given to understand that, in attacking Cuba, they will be dealing not only with one stubborn country but also with the nuclear might of the Soviet Union. The price of a military venture against Cuba must be raised to the maximum, and in some measure the threat to Cuba must be made comparable to the threat to the United States. Logic suggests . . . that only the installation of our rockets with nuclear warheads on Cuban territory can be such a means."[13]

According to Alekseev, Khrushchev did not stop with the "save Cuba" argument but went on to address the disparity of Soviet and American nuclear arsenals, maintaining that the installation of Soviet missiles in Cuba would redress the balance of nuclear terror. "Since the

Americans have already surrounded the Soviet Union with a ring of their military bases and multipurpose missile installations, we should pay them back in their own coin and give them a taste of their own medicine so that they find out for themselves how it feels to live as a target of nuclear arms," argued Khrushchev. He specifically mentioned the American missiles in Europe and Turkey. The Jupiter missiles in Turkey were of special concern to Marshal Malinovsky, who had warned Khrushchev earlier that they could reach Soviet territory within ten minutes. While a Soviet ballistic missile response to the American Minuteman was years away, the Jupiter could be countered immediately by placing Soviet missiles in Cuba. Khrushchev clearly did not want to lose the opportunity.[14]

Furthermore, Khrushchev considered that such a response to the American nuclear threat was unlikely to provoke a nuclear war: after all, the Soviets had accepted the installation of American missiles in Turkey without a murmur. Concluding his remarks at the Presidium meeting, Khrushchev expressed confidence that "the pragmatic Americans would not venture on a senseless risk, just as we cannot now undertake anything against the American missiles aimed at the Soviet Union in Turkey, Italy, and the FRG." He added: "After all, sensible politicians in the USA should think just as we are thinking today." The cool-headed politicians Khrushchev had in mind were President Kennedy and his supporters in the Democratic Party. He did not want the Soviet missile deployment to hurt their chances in the November 1962 congressional elections, which gave him a further reason to insist on the secrecy of the operation. "It is especially important to avoid publicity at a time when political passions are reaching their peak in the USA—the Congressional election campaign," he said.[15]

Khrushchev's speech served as a formulation of the position to be taken by the senior delegation, headed by the Uzbek communist party secretary Sharof Rashidov, that was scheduled to depart for Cuba in a few days. At the top of its official agenda was economic, not military, assistance to Cuba. The nuclear missiles were the responsibility of Marshal Biriuzov, who was to join the group, as was the ambassador-designate Alekseev. Before the delegates departed, Khrushchev hosted them at a state country house near Moscow. Alekseev remembered that among the members of the Central Committee Presidium there was an atmosphere of relaxation and "complete unanimity." The leader who had effectively silenced the opposition gave a farewell speech. Off they went.[16]

◊◊◊

ON MAY 28 RASHIDOV, BIRIUZOV, AND ALEKSEEV, ALONG with the rest of the delegation, left for Guinea, a West African nation that had gained independence from France in 1962 and was now allied with the Soviets. From there they departed for Havana: as there were no direct flights between the Soviet Union and Cuba, Conakry, the capital of Guinea, would become a stopover for dozens if not hundreds of Soviet military officers on their way to the "island of freedom." The day after leaving Moscow, Rashidov and his team were already in Havana. Alekseev asked Raúl Castro for an urgent meeting with his brother, and the very same evening Fidel met with his guests of honor. Events were moving at ever increasing speed.[17]

Missiles, not economic aid, now topped the agenda of the Soviet-Cuban meeting. Rashidov, the head of the delegation, spoke little, and most of the talking on the Soviet side was done by Biriuzov. The Cubans were taking notes—the first time that Alekseev, who now doubled as an interpreter, had ever seen them do so. Biriuzov began by expressing Soviet concern over the growing threat of an American invasion and asked Castro what could be done to avert it. Castro, knowing that something big was being considered, did not ask for additional military support but went directly for the ultimate prize: he had long wanted an agreement with the USSR that would give Cuba a guarantee of Soviet protection in the event of an American invasion. He had brought Cuba into the socialist camp and wanted an agreement like the one concluded by the Soviets with the Warsaw Pact in Eastern Europe, or the equivalent of article 5 of the NATO Charter—an attack on one member meant an attack on all. "Well," Castro recalled having said many years later, "if the United States were to understand that an invasion of Cuba would mean war with the Soviet Union, that would be the best way to keep it from invading Cuba."[18]

Biriuzov either did not understand the hint or decided not to take it. He made use of Castro's comment to sell his own solution to the problem—missiles. "But specifically how?" asked Biriuzov with reference to Castro's suggestion that the United States should be given to understand that an attack on Cuba would mean war with the Soviet Union. "Something concrete must be done to indicate that," continued Biriuzov. According to Alekseev, Biriuzov declared that "the government of the USSR is prepared to help Cuba strengthen its defensive capability by all possible means, up to considering the question of installing intermediate-range missiles on its territory if our Cuban friends should find such a means of intimidating a potential aggressor useful."[19]

As Castro remained silent, Alekseev sensed nervousness on the part of Biriuzov. "[H]e had been assigned the mission of proposing that the strategic missiles be installed, and he may have been afraid that we wouldn't agree to it," recalled Castro years later. The ball was now in his court, but the idea was absolutely new to him. It indicated a profound shift in the Soviet attitude. Earlier in the month Castro had complained that the Soviets were not willing to give him enough Sopka coastal defense antiship missiles to fight off a possible invasion, offering only one missile complex instead of three. All of a sudden they were offering nuclear missiles. Besides, as Alekseev had suggested to Khrushchev, the proposal was politically problematic, given Castro's campaign against foreign military bases in Latin America. There was a great deal to take in and consider all at once.[20]

Castro decided to take his time. He promised to discuss the proposal with his colleagues in the Cuban leadership and come back soon with an official response. It seems, however, that he was favorably disposed to the idea. He quickly came up with a way of dealing with his aversion to foreign bases: the missiles could help defend socialism worldwide, not just in Cuba. He told the Soviet delegation that "this idea seems very interesting because, besides defending the Cuban revolution, it will serve the interests of world socialism and oppressed peoples in their struggle against brazen American imperialism, which seeks to dictate its will throughout the world." Castro asked his guests about the number of missiles intended for Cuba and their capabilities.[21]

The leadership of the Integrated Revolutionary Organization, Castro's own Communist Party in the making, met the next day, May 30. Present were Che Guevara and the leader of the "old" Communist Party, Blas Roca, who had attended the Soviet party congress back in October 1961 and handed Khrushchev the symbolic banner of the Cuban revolution. Convinced by now that he had to take the missiles to save his regime, Fidel presented the case for accepting them to the gathering. "We didn't really like the missiles," recalled Castro later. "We viewed the matter from the standpoint of our moral, political and internationalist duty, as we understood it." After some deliberation they decided to take the missiles. Castro met with Biriuzov the same day. "If this will strengthen the socialist camp and also—and this is in the second place—contribute to the defense of Cuba, we are willing to accept all of the missiles that may be necessary—even 1,000, if you want to send us so many," he told the marshal.[22]

Biriuzov had accomplished the first part of his task, getting Castro on board. The other part of his mission was to determine whether the missiles could be deployed in Cuba without being detected by the Americans. On May 31, the day after receiving Fidel's approval, Biriuzov joined Raúl Castro, who served as the Cuban minister of defense, to survey sites for possible missile deployment. Raúl now learned that the missiles to be delivered to Cuba were to be 20 meters long (the R-12 was in fact more than 22 meters long, and the length of the R-14 exceeded 24 meters). He later shared his doubts with Fidel that they could be hidden effectively from American view. But Biriuzov, who saw plainly that Cuban palms could not possibly hide missile installations covering hundreds of square meters, seemed unconcerned.[23]

General Gribkov, one of the key planners of Operation Anadyr who came to Cuba in the fall of 1962, saw the lack of natural cover for himself and later lamented "the conclusion, striking in its strategic illiteracy, that missiles could easily and secretly be deployed in Cuba, as there were . . . many palm groves there." As it did not behoove Gribkov to criticize his military superior, Biriuzov, he blamed the "specialists" from the Rashidov group instead. Khrushchev had sent Biriuzov to Cuba to make sure that Operation Anadyr would go ahead. He might have considered raising the camouflage problem had Castro refused Khrushchev's proposal, but the Cuban leader accepted it, and Biriuzov probably felt that he had no choice. He returned to Moscow to report good news on both counts: Castro's agreement and the suitability of Cuban terrain for concealing the missiles.[24]

Biriuzov spoke to the Central Committee Presidium on June 10. After he finished his report, Khrushchev took the podium. The terse notes of the meeting record the gist of his remarks as follows: "Proceed to deciding the question. I think that we will win this operation." It was a victory for Khrushchev and a setback for his main opponent on the issue, Anastas Mikoyan. "Castro gave his consent, and the Cuban landscape was found to be suitable for camouflaging the missiles," he recalled later. "I did not believe that conclusion." Meanwhile, the jubilant Khrushchev wrote to Castro expressing his satisfaction with the results of the delegation's visit and Castro's acceptance of the missiles. This would "mean a further fortification of the victory of the Cuban revolution and of the greater success of our general affairs," asserted Khrushchev. While Castro stressed the benefit to world socialism, and Khrushchev put Cuba first, their political posturing was of secondary importance. They had agreed on the main thing—deployment of the missiles. Operation Anadyr could now begin in earnest.[25]

6

OPERATION ANADYR

On July 7, 1962, Nikita Khrushchev invited to the Kremlin a group of generals chosen to lead the Soviet deployment in Cuba. They would leave for the "island of freedom" in three days, on July 10. It was Khrushchev's chance to give final instructions, inspire confidence, and bid farewell to those on whose actions the success of his nuclear gamble would depend.

Khrushchev was full of energy, and his rhetoric was accompanied by active gesticulation, recalled the forty-three-year-old Major General Leonid Garbuz, a deputy commander of the 43rd Missile Army headquartered in Vinnytsia, Ukraine. He had now been appointed deputy commander of the Soviet task force in Cuba. As usual, Khrushchev joked, spoke in metaphors, and told stories to convey his thoughts. "We in the Central Committee decided to toss America a 'hedgehog' by placing our rockets in Cuba so that America would be unable to swallow the Island of Freedom," declared Khrushchev. He had earlier told Marshal Malinovsky, who was in attendance, that the hedgehog was supposed to go down Uncle Sam's pants. The hedgehog metaphor went down well with the commanders: Garbuz would remember it decades later.

"This operation has a single goal: to help the Cuban revolution withstand aggression from the USA," continued Khrushchev. "The political and military leadership of our country, having weighed all the circumstances, sees no other way to prevent an attack by America, which, according to our intelligence, is making intensive preparations for it. Once the rockets are in place, America will grasp that if it wants to make short work of Cuba, it will have to deal with us." Khrushchev was giving the generals an already well-established narrative about Soviet motives for deploying missiles in Cuba. But he also wanted to assure them that he had no intention of provoking war. "If we manage to gain a foothold in Cuba, then the Americans will have to reconcile themselves to what has happened," said Khrushchev. He added that an agreement would be signed with the Cubans, and that he was in constant touch with President Kennedy, hinting that a potential crisis could be resolved peacefully through diplomatic channels.

General Garbuz appreciated what he heard. An experienced commander, he believed that Khrushchev had made his presentation with psychological skill: "On the eve of a difficult and dangerous undertaking, he wanted to instill confidence in the rightness of the idea and serenity in those who would be called upon to carry out extraordinary tasks on the ground," wrote Garbuz later. But Khrushchev was there not only to assure others but also to get assurances himself. "What do you think: can the deployment of our rockets in Cuba be kept secret?" he asked the chief Soviet military adviser in Cuba, General Aleksei Dementiev. "No, Nikita Sergeevich, that is impossible," responded the general after some hesitation. "There's no place there to hide a chicken, let alone a rocket," continued Dementiev in the down-to-earth tone of Khrushchev's comment about the hedgehog. Judging by Garbuz's memoirs, Khrushchev had no ready comeback. If Khrushchev was to stuff a nuclear hedgehog down America's pants, he would have to find a way of hiding chickens more than twenty meters long in the

Cuban barnyard or, rather, prevent the Americans from noticing them in plain sight.[1]

Concerns about the secrecy of the planned operation were expressed not only by Soviet commanders such as Dementiev but also by the Cubans. Raúl Castro, who came to Moscow in early July to negotiate an agreement on the deployment of the missiles, was just as uneasy about the prospect. Fidel Castro wanted an official and public agreement with the Soviets. "What precautions have you taken in case the operation is discovered by the United States before it is made public?" Raúl asked Khrushchev. "Don't worry, I'll grab Kennedy by the balls and make him negotiate," responded the Soviet leader. It seems to have escaped him that grabbing someone by the balls if he already had a hedgehog down his pants was a highly dangerous undertaking.[2]

◊◊◊

THE COMMANDER OF THE STRATEGIC MISSILE FORCES, MAR-shal Biriuzov, approved the plans for what was officially called "Anadyr Maneuvers" on June 13, 1962, three days after Khrushchev and the Presidium gave their official approval for the operation. The Soviet rocket men learned of their secret assignment a few days later, when Biriuzov's first deputy, Colonel General Vladimir Tolubko, arrived at the headquarters of the 43rd Missile Division of the 43rd Missile Army in the Ukrainian city of Romny, an old Cossack town more than two hundred kilometers east of the republic's capital, Kyiv. A former commander of a tank army in Dresden, East Germany, Tolubko had been transferred to the newly formed Strategic Missile Forces in 1960 and was now responsible for the transportation of the missile troops to Cuba. He called in the divisional commanding officers for a meeting.[3]

"The meeting took place under conditions of extraordinary secrecy: serious guard posts were placed, doors closed, and blinds drawn—counterintelligence officers had been at work," remembered First Lieutenant and Young Communist League organizer Igor Kurennoi. "In a half-whisper Colonel General Tolubko announced: 'Comrade officers, the party and government are showing great confidence in you. Your division will be obliged to undertake a highly responsible mission. It will be beyond the borders of the Soviet Union.'" Tolubko was in no hurry to disclose the place of service to the officers, implying that he himself did not know it. But he added: "When you return, your names will be inscribed in golden letters on marble plaques."[4]

Tolubko honored Romny with his presence for a reason. The 43rd Division located in that city had already been chosen as the main missile unit to be sent to Cuba in the first draft of the Operation Anadyr planning proposal, approved by Khrushchev and his party colleagues on May 24. The document read: "To send to Cuba the 43rd Missile Division (commander of the division Major General Statsenko), comprising five missile regiments." Igor Statsenko was a forty-three-year-old graduate of the General Staff Academy who had received his general's epaulettes in April 1962, a few weeks before his name appeared in the proposal. A native of the town of Chornobyl, where a devastating nuclear disaster would take place in 1986, he fought in air defense units during the Second World War and stayed with them afterward.[5]

Tall and lean, with a full head of black hair, Statsenko was well regarded by superiors and subordinates alike. "Always looking smart, in irreproachable form on the parade ground and in daily activity, a lover of poetry who wrote verse himself and sang in his circle of friends and, most important, unforgettably devoted to military life, Igor Demianovich [Statsenko] was for me personally a model officer, general and citizen," wrote one of his subordinates later. General Gribkov, who entered Statsenko's name in the very first planning document, had an equally high opinion of him: effective, energetic, and always in good humor. Some considered Statsenko too ambitious, but others believed that he had just the right amount of drive and ambition. How otherwise could a native of a small Ukrainian town in the middle of nowhere have risen to become commander of a missile division at the age of forty-two and a general at the age of forty-three?[6]

The Strategic Missile Forces were only a year and a half old when

Statsenko joined them in the summer of 1961. The division (which began as a brigade) was formed only a year before Statsenko's arrival in Romny, and he literally had to build it from scratch: most of his time was taken up with overseeing the construction of launchpads for missiles. The job would take a year to a year and a half, and the launchpads would not be fully ready until early 1963. There were also problems with the missiles and accompanying equipment that Statsenko and his fellow division commanders were getting from the rocket builders. To meet installation deadlines, the commanders reported to Moscow that they had put the missiles on combat alert, when in fact, because of problems with new, untested, and often malfunctioning equipment, they needed another six months to prepare the launchpads and missiles for firing. The KGB reported that this was the case in the units headed by General Dmitrii Kobzar, who commanded a missile division in the same missile army as Statsenko. It appears to have been a common problem at the time.[7]

There were four missile regiments under Statsenko's command, two armed with Mikhail Yangel's R-12 missiles and two with his R-14s. The R-12s had an operational range of 2,080 kilometers: from the launchpads of one of Statsenko's regiments, located in Okhtyrka, they could reach Vienna, located 1,711 kilometers away, but not the next major Western city, Munich, at a distance of 2,162 kilometers. Missiles from the two R-14 regiments could hit targets at a distance of 3,700 kilometers. From their launchpads in the towns of Lebedyn and Hlukhiv they could reach Paris but would fall short of Madrid—two European capitals located, respectively, 2,710 and 3,994 kilometers from Hlukhiv, a former Cossack capital near the Russo-Ukrainian border and only 58 kilometers northeast of the village of Kalinovka, the birthplace of Nikita Khrushchev.

Statsenko's 43rd Division was part of the 43rd Missile Army, headquartered in the central Ukrainian city of Vinnytsia and commanded by General Pavel Dankevich. Statsenko's other superior there was Dankevich's deputy, General Leonid Garbuz—both Dankevich and Garbuz would be sent to Cuba along with Statsenko. Units of the missile army were deployed as far west as the Carpathian Mountains. That made Statsenko's division, located in northeastern Ukraine on the border with Russia, the unit farthest removed from targets in Central and Western Europe and thus dispensable when it came to transfer from the East European theater.

The plan for Operation Anadyr suggested that Statsenko move three of his four regiments to Cuba. The westernmost regiment, stationed in the central Ukrainian city of Uman and armed with R-12s, would stay in place, while the two regiments with R-14s and one with R-12s, located farther away from European targets, would be shipped to Cuba. Statsenko was to be "compensated" for the R-12 regiment he would leave in Ukraine with two other R-12 regiments transferred from northern Ukraine and Lithuania. The newly formed unit under Statsenko's command would be renamed the 51st Missile Division. In Cuba it would become known as "the Statsenko outfit" after its commander.[8]

◊◊◊

THE SIXTY-YEAR-OLD COLONEL GENERAL ISSA PLIEV BECAME the commander of the Group of Soviet Troops in Cuba—the official name of the task force—on July 7. This last-minute appointment to the most important and sensitive position in the whole operation came as a surprise to many, most notably Pliev himself. As the main objective of Operation Anadyr was placing missiles in Cuba, it had been assumed that a senior officer from the Strategic Missile Forces would be selected to lead the mission. Many expected the position of commander in chief to go to the forty-three-year-old Lieutenant General Pavel Dankevich, the commander of the 43rd Missile Army and Statsenko's direct superior. Four of the five missile regiments that would comprise Statsenko's division in Cuba came from Dankevich's army.

But Khrushchev decided on a different commander and personally requested Dankevich not to take offense. General Garbuz and others who expected Dankevich to become the supreme commander in Cuba explained the bypassing of Dankevich by the need for secrecy: the appointment of a commander of a missile army as head of the Cuban contingent would give away the main purpose of the operation— installing ballistic missiles on the island. General Garbuz suggested also another interpretation: "We realized that Khrushchev chose a different commander because he knew that there could be some critical moments during the deployment of detachments, when it would be necessary to stand up for ourselves, to defend the right to deploy missiles there."⁹

That was closer to the reality. From the start, the General Staff planners envisioned the operation as one that involved not only the missile troops but also the army, navy, and air force. Khrushchev recalled later: "We considered that if we were indeed to place rockets, then they had to be protected and defended. That required infantry. That is why we decided to send infantry there as well, something like a few thousand men. Antiaircraft equipment was also essential. Then we decided that we also needed artillery to defend the rockets in case the enemy landed parachute troops." Khrushchev had to look for a senior officer with experience of commanding different branches of armed forces. The status of the newly formed task force was equal if not superior to that of the groups of Soviet armed forces in East Germany and other East European countries. Moreover, the title of "commander in chief" was initially suggested for the leader of the group—a step above "commander," the title used in Germany. The suggestion was not implemented, and Pliev served with the title "commander," but the idea that someone be experienced in coordinating different services remained in place. Pliev fit the bill.¹⁰

There was another feature that distinguished Pliev from his competitors: the minister of defense, Marshal Malinovsky, had known him personally for many years and trusted him. A native of North Ossetia on the Russo-Georgian border, Pliev had joined the Red Army in 1922. A cavalryman to boot, he demonstrated the continued effectiveness of large cavalry formations in modern mechanized warfare during World War II. Soviet tank formations reinforced by Pliev's cavalry and under his command would make deep raids into German-held territory after the Battle of Stalingrad. Fighting under Malinovsky in 1944, he carried out a surprise raid on Malinovsky's native city of Odesa and received his first Gold Star of the Soviet Union for liberating that urban center on the Black Sea. He earned his second gold star in the following year when, again under Malinovsky's command, he led a surprise raid through the Gobi Desert of southern Mongolia toward Beijing, forcing the surrender of Japanese forces there.[11]

In April 1962 Pliev was promoted to the highest rank in the Soviet army short of marshal—General of the Army. At that time he was the commander of the North Caucasus Military District, which covered southern Russia and the autonomous republics of the North Caucasus, including his native North Ossetia. In June, Pliev came to the attention not only of his former commander and supporter, Marshal Malinovsky, but of the entire Communist Party Presidium. That month workers in the industrial city of Novocherkassk in the center of the Don Cossack region of southern Russia went on strike to protest an increase in the prices of meat and butter. Khrushchev's government, struggling to make ends meet in the midst of a food crisis caused by bad weather and mismanagement of the agricultural sector, had resorted to that measure. The workers besieged the local party headquarters, driving out the high-level delegation sent to Novocherkassk by Khrushchev himself: among its members was Anastas Mikoyan.

Frol Kozlov, a secretary of the Central Committee and Khrushchev's second in command, ordered not only KGB and police personnel but also soldiers into the streets. Pliev in turn ordered his tanks, armed with live ammunition, to move into the city. The tanks were never used against the rebels, but Interior Ministry troops under Pliev's operational command opened fire on the protesters, killing at least twenty-four and wounding eighty-seven. The revolt was suppressed. Its surviving leaders and activists were put on trial: of those, seven were sentenced to death and shot.[12]

What happened in Novocherkassk on June 2, as well as Pliev's participation in the events, remained a top state secret until the last days of the USSR. But the Russian dissident writer Aleksandr Solzhenitsyn described the Novocherkassk events in his 1968 documentary novel. According to Solzhenitsyn, Pliev, an Ossetian by birth, used non-Russian soldiers to shoot at the Russian protesters, and then, once the shooting was over, replaced them with ethnic Russians to take the blame for what had happened. The debate on Pliev's role in suppressing the Novocherkassk uprising continues to this day. Some suggest that he exercised caution and acted under duress, while others indicate that only the refusal of his subordinates to use live ammunition prevented even greater bloodshed. Whatever the truth of the matter, Pliev's role in suppressing the revolt clearly pleased the higher-ups, and he gained new political capital in the Kremlin. Not only Malinovsky but also Khrushchev now knew that they could count on the general.[13]

Pliev was summoned to Moscow on July 4 in the middle of maneuvers that he was conducting in his district and ordered to take command of the new Cuban task force. Khrushchev recalled the circumstances of Pliev's appointment years later: "Malinovsky, as minister of defense, proposed that General of the Army Pliev, an Ossetian by nationality, be confirmed as leader. General Pliev was summoned, and I spoke with him. He was already of advanced age and ill but knew his business. He had served throughout the Patriotic War, and I believe that he had also taken part in the Civil War. I more or less knew him as commander of a cavalry corps in the Second World War. An intelligent man. Pliev said that if he were confirmed, he would consider it a personal honor to go to Cuba and carry out the task assigned to him." Khrushchev had found in Pliev the kind of experience and loyalty he was looking for. He saw nothing wrong with a cavalry man from the past war taking charge of the nuclear weapons that could start a future one.[14]

Pliev headed a group of missile-force generals and officers who had been personally approved by Khrushchev before Pliev took command of the task force. The favorite of the missile lobby, General Dankevich, was appointed Pliev's first deputy. Dankevich's deputy in the Vinnytsia missile division, General Leonid Garbuz, became Pliev's deputy in charge of battle readiness of troops, while General Aleksei Dementiev, who had told Khrushchev that it would be difficult to hide even a chicken on Cuban terrain, was approved as Pliev's deputy in charge of ground troops. A calm, soft-spoken man with a smile on his lips under a small black mustache, Pliev was good at dealing with people but was ill prepared for the operation he was about to lead.

Having spent most of his military career in the cavalry, he knew little about missiles and, to the ridicule of his subordinates, used the term "squadron," reserved in the Soviet Army exclusively for a cavalry unit, to refer to missile detachments. He also had no diplomatic experience—a liability in his new position, which demanded a good deal of it. On top of that he was ill, suffering from a kidney disease, and the General Staff had to ship a personal doctor to attend to the general with the next reconnaissance group, which left for Cuba on July 18. Old, sickly, and incompetent, Pliev was now surrounded by young and ambitious deputies who had little respect for their commander. Khrushchev and Malinovsky got what they wanted—a man they considered loyal and smart was now in charge of the task force—but his health problems would become more pronounced in the hot and humid climate of Cuba, while his ability to command respect and keep his subordinates in line would be challenged.[15]

◊◊◊

GENERAL PLIEV, WHOSE LAST NAME WAS CHANGED FOR CON- spiracy reasons to Pavlov, and his deputies flew to Havana on July 10 on board a Tupolev 114, the largest and fastest airplane of its time—the same model that Khrushchev had used to fly to the United States in the fall of 1959. They joined a delegation led by the head of the Soviet Civic Aviation Administration, Yevgenii Loginov, posing as Soviet airplane experts. Their flight to Havana was special—the very first Soviet flight to the island, intended as a test run to check the feasibility of regular passenger flights between Moscow and Havana.

The plane had to make a refueling stop, and the new Soviet satellite of Guinea on the west coast of Africa was its first destination. The Soviets had built a new airport in the capital, Conakry, partly as a component of an assistance program and partly to accommodate their own need for transatlantic flights. Accordingly, Pliev and his group first headed for Conakry, where they witnessed the festive opening of the Soviet-built airport, with Loginov presiding, and then continued to Havana, where they were greeted by crowds celebrating the arrival of the first flight from Moscow.[16]

The next airplane for Havana left Moscow on July 18. On board, apart from Pliev's personal doctor, was a group of officers from Statsenko's division in Ukraine. They had been called to Moscow a month earlier, on June 18, and held meetings with Biriuzov, Tolubko, and Gribkov. They had to prepare for their first task—surveying locations for the placement of the missiles, which were going to be shipped by sea. As this would be the first deployment in history of Soviet missiles outside the USSR, there were many issues to be discussed and resolved. For seven days Statsenko's people were advised on how to organize the movement of missiles by land and sea, maintaining the utmost secrecy. Biriuzov also made sure that the missile regiments in Cuba would get the latest model of R-12 missiles.[17]

Major Anatoly Burlov, the deputy commander of the missile regiment located in the town of Okhtyrka, later recalled that in Moscow he and his fellow officers were handed documents suggesting that they were specialists in agricultural melioration. Gribkov remembered that the names of some of the officers were misspelled or mixed up, but there was no time to change the documents, and they were ordered to assume the names that appeared in their new passports. In Burlov's group some protested at being called specialists in melioration, since they knew nothing about it. Those complaints were dismissed, and officers with even the slightest information about the industry they allegedly represented had to share their "knowledge" with the rest.[18]

Burlov's group of "agriculturalists" flew to Havana with numerous stopovers and changes of planes. A tropical storm in the area forced the pilots to make an emergency landing at Nassau airport in the Bahamas. With tropical heat and high humidity penetrating the plane, they were eventually allowed to leave the plane and instantly became objects of interest to hundreds of American tourists who were seeing "Russians" for the first time in their lives. The Americans took numerous photos of Soviet "agriculturalists" suffering from the heat, having no idea that they were in fact documenting the arrival in the Caribbean of one of the first groups of Soviet rocket men. Once the storm was over, Burlov and his fellow officers were allowed to continue their flight to Havana, where their group was welcomed by General Statsenko.[19]

The first thing that the reconnaissance groups grasped on arrival in Cuba was that Marshal Biriuzov, who had visited Havana in early June and later shared his excitement about the wonderful climate with his subordinates, was mistaken not only about the Cuban landscape but also about the weather. He had simply missed the hurricane season that typically begins on the island in June and continues into November. As for the landscape, Biriuzov had little time to travel around the island and simply told Khrushchev what he wanted to hear: there was sufficient natural cover to deploy the missiles so that the Americans would not detect them. Not without sarcasm, Garbuz later recalled Biriuzov's impressions of his visit: "this was a golden country, that you could sleep under every bush, that concealing the missiles would not require much work." Pliev, Statsenko, Garbuz, Burlov, and the others who arrived in July found the heat overwhelming, the humidity debilitating, and the landscape unforgiving.[20]

The reconnaissance teams soon found that small palm groves could not conceal the more than 20-meter-long missiles, while the larger forests impeded the free movement of air: given the heat and humidity, rocket equipment produced for the European theater was prone to malfunction. There were also poisonous plants that the Soviets had never encountered and whose ill effects they could not counteract effectively. The locations mapped by the Biriuzov group simply proved unsuitable. Statsenko later reported on the activities and findings of his group: "The areas where the General Staff had directed the regiments to deploy were surveyed four times by means of helicopter flights. The western and central parts of the island of Cuba were surveyed from helicopters, and it was determined that the areas assigned to the regiments of Comrades Sidorov, Cherkesov, and Bandilovsky had very broken terrain, little vegetation, and a poorly developed road network; hence they are poorly suited for the deployment of rocket regiments."[21]

The Soviet personnel had to start from scratch, looking for new locations. The Cubans put forward their own requirements: no area selected for the deployment of missiles could exceed 1,100 acres in size, and the number of families to be resettled was not to exceed six or eight. With the help of their Cuban hosts, the Soviet teams surveyed more than 150 locations on a territory in excess of 9,000 square kilometers and chose ten areas that more or less met their requirements but still provided no reliable cover from American reconnaissance planes. Each of the five regiments was supposed to be assigned two areas for its launchers. Aided by small engineering detachments, they immediately began preparing positions for the missiles, which were to arrive on the island in early September.

One of the unpleasant discoveries they made right away was that none of the bridges across Cuban rivers was strong enough to support the weight of the Soviet trucks and missiles to be moved to the designated areas. "The division commander often found himself obliged to make nontraditional decisions, especially pouring concrete into riverbeds so that they could be crossed by heavy equipment because of the impossibility of using bridges," recalled a participant in the operation. Other surprises followed. It turned out that the Cuban power stations were generating electricity with a frequency of 60 Hertz, while Soviet equipment was designed for one of 50 Hertz.[22]

News of problems with the chosen locations and the impossibility of hiding missiles and launchers even in the newly surveyed areas soon reached Moscow. Khrushchev would later blame problems involving the secret deployment of missiles on Biriuzov. "And so we sent Biriuzov there with an appropriate crew of staff members of rocket troops so that they could assess how best to deploy the rockets. They returned from there and reported to us that in their opinion the rocket deployment could be concealed. The poor qualities of those scouts became apparent: they naively believed that the palms would mask the disposition of the rockets."[23]

With the realization growing that it would be impossible to hide the missiles from the prying cameras of American U-2 spy planes, the Soviet military commanders decided to adjust their departure timetable for the Soviet missile troops. Instead of dispatching the medium- and intermediate-range missiles right away, the General Staff decided to send antiaircraft missiles ahead of the nuclear warheads and missiles capable of delivering them. The idea was to develop a capability to hit American U-2s before they could discover the deployment of the ballistic missiles. With such missiles in place, the deployment of R-12 and R-14 rockets could begin.

It turned out to be a brilliant move. The delivery of the antiaircraft missiles to Cuba indeed helped to keep secret the subsequent arrival of the nuclear warheads and R-12 missiles capable of carrying nuclear charges, but not in the way imagined by the Soviets. The Americans, alerted to but not greatly disturbed by the arrival of the antiaircraft missiles, assumed that the Soviet military buildup was limited to "defensive" missiles and missed the arrival of much more dangerous weapons. Khrushchev got lucky.[24]

7

HIGH SEAS

Few civilian vessels made such a mark on the history of the Cold War as the Soviet dry cargo ship *Ilia Mechnikov*. Built in France in 1956 and named after the famous Russian immunologist and 1908 Nobel Prize winner, the ship could carry more than 3,000 registered tons of cargo, each registered ton occupying 100 cubic feet. In September 1960 it delivered the first ever shipment of Soviet weapons and ammunition to Cuba, including at least ten Soviet T-34 tanks of World War II fame and one hundred pieces of antiaircraft artillery. Long after its Cuban service, in October 1973, during the Yom Kippur War, the *Ilia Mechnikov* was sunk by rocket fire from Israeli boats while visiting the Syrian port of Tartus.[1]

In 1962 the *Ilia Mechnikov* was as busy as ever, first bringing cattle from India to Bulgaria and then making two trips to Cuba, delivering Soviet weapons and troops. The first trip began on August 8, when the ship left its base in Odesa and stopped at the Crimean port of Feodosia to pick up its cargo. According to its official papers, the ship was delivering 1,260 tons of freight to the French port of Le Havre. In reality, it took on the equipment and personnel of the military communications center to be set up in Cuba and the officers and soldiers who would operate it. The ship left Feodosia on August 11 in utmost secrecy: all shore leaves were canceled, a measure enforced by Captain Zozulia, a KGB officer assigned to the ship.[2]

On August 14, the ship's captain presented its false cargo declaration to the Turkish authorities, and the *Ilia Mechnikov* passed through the Bosporus without incident. But when the ship was already in the Mediterranean, heading toward Gibraltar, an emergency occurred that required the attention not only of the ship's captain but also of the accompanying KGB officer, Captain Zozulia. The emergency concerned the ship's mechanic, whose surname was Mazur. Soon after the *Ilia Mechnikov* left the Black Sea, Mazur began complaining of pain in his abdomen. The ship's doctor, named Zholkevsky, examined Mazur and diagnosed acute inflammation of the appendix. Mazur needed surgery, but Captain Zozulia could not send him ashore. While no one aboard knew the ship's true destination, its military cargo was top secret, and Mazur, like everyone else, knew that there was a discrepancy between the official cargo declaration and the actual freight it was carrying.

Zozulia's task was to make sure that no foreigner, especially the British authorities in Gibraltar, got access to Mazur and discovered through him what was going on. Zholkevsky and three of his colleagues, military doctors accompanying the military personnel, concluded that Mazur would die if he was not operated on. They decided to perform the surgery aboard ship. Zozulia, along with the ship's captain and his deputy, met with Mazur and convinced him to agree to the operation. He gave his consent.

The four doctors spent four hours in the ship's "Lenin room," a special compartment dedicated to the political indoctrination of the crew. The operation did not go well. The doctors failed to remove the inflamed appendix, closed the wound, and declared that Mazur needed another operation in a hospital. His condition was deteriorating, but landing him on shore was still not an option. They cabled Odesa for instructions and were advised to put Mazur on a Soviet ship heading back to the USSR.

Zozulia did as he was told: Mazur was transferred to the tanker *Iziaslav*, which they encountered sixty miles from Gibraltar. It had taken the *Ilia Mechnikov* approximately five days to reach that point, meaning that Mazur would have to wait another five days to get to Odesa and might very well die en route. The captain of the *Iziaslav* was instructed that at worst he could admit Mazur to a hospital in Sicily or in Alexandria, Egypt, but only under escort of a Soviet official who would prevent doctors from asking Mazur any question not directly related to his health condition. Under no circumstances was Mazur to be left in British Gibraltar.

Operation Anadyr had to be conducted in complete secrecy. No one could leave the ship once its cargo had been loaded, especially when it was en route to Cuba. Zozulia, who subsequently filed a report on his trip aboard the *Ilia Mechnikov*, later learned to his horror that Mazur's health had deteriorated so badly that the captain of the *Iziaslav* deemed it necessary to deliver him to a hospital in Gibraltar. Mazur survived against all odds. The sad irony of the situation was that neither Mazur nor Zozulia himself knew the ship's destination at the time. The relevant instructions were in an envelope that the captain could open only after passing through the Strait of Gibraltar. The *Ilia Mechnikov*, as it turned out, was heading for the port town of Nuevitas on the northern shore of Cuba. But when the ship reached its destination, it was redirected to another port, on the southern shore of the island. This was not a deliberate attempt to mislead the Americans but the result of general disorganization. The ship's cargo was eventually unloaded on August 30 and 31 in Santiago de Cuba.[3]

◊◊◊

THE COMMUNICATIONS EQUIPMENT BROUGHT TO CUBA BY the *Ilya Mechnikov* belonged to Colonel Georgii Voronkov's 27th Anti-aircraft Missile Division. It would be used a month and a half later to deliver the order to shoot down an American U-2 plane over Cuba.

Voronkov's division, also known as Antiaircraft Division no. 10, or the Volgograd Division (after its location in the Soviet Union), was the first of two missile divisions dispatched to Cuba on a priority basis once the Soviet General Staff recognized that it would be impossible to conceal the strategic missiles on Cuban territory, and that antiaircraft missiles would be required to stop American overflights. The second antiaircraft division, under the command of Major General Mikhail Tokarenko, came to Cuba from Ukraine. Its Soviet designation was Dnipropetrovsk Antiaircraft Division no. 11—in Cuba it was given the number 12. Both divisions were armed with S-75 Desna (in US terminology, SA 2 Guideline) surface-to-air missiles (SAMs) capable of reaching high altitudes and shooting down U-2 aircraft. The Dnipropetrovsk Division, which took up its position in western Cuba, arrived on the island in July, while the Volgograd Division reached the eastern part of the island in August.[4]

The first medium-range R-12 missiles that the S-75 Desna rockets were supposed to protect from American overflights arrived in Cuba on September 9 aboard the *Omsk*, a Japanese-built cargo ship delivered to the USSR the previous year at a cost of $3.5 million. The *Omsk* was equipped with twelve medium cranes as well as one light and one heavy gibbet, which helped speed up the loading process in the ship's five cargo holds. The *Omsk* brought in six 22-meter-long R-12 missiles and 166 pieces of machinery. Altogether 2,200 tons of missiles and equipment were unloaded from the cargo bay once the ship arrived in Cuba.[5]

The R-12 missiles delivered by the *Omsk* belonged to Missile Regiment no. 637 from the Lithuanian town of Plungė. Its commander, the forty-one-year-old colonel Ivan Sidorov, was a late arrival to Operation Anadyr and was not appointed to his new position until late July, when his predecessor, Colonel V. V. Kolesnichenko, asked the commanders to relieve him of the overseas duty for family reasons. Marshal Biriuzov's deputy, General Tolubko, who was in charge of the selection and shipment of missile regiments to Cuba, sent a special plane to Lithuania to bring both Kolesnichenko and Sidorov, who then commanded a different regiment, to Moscow to attend a meeting of the military council of the Strategic Missile Troops. Kolesnichenko was called in first and dismissed only a few minutes later. By the look on his face, Sidorov realized that he had been demoted. When Tolubko called Sidorov in, he asked whether he would be prepared to embark on a special government assignment. No details were provided, but Sidorov responded in the affirmative, asking only for permission to take his wife along. The request was granted.[6]

Sidorov was given two days to turn over the command of his old regiment to another officer and assume command of the regiment assigned to Cuba. His first task was to move his new regiment to Sevastopol in the Crimea. They began loading their rockets and equipment—some eleven thousand tons of weaponry and supplies—on train platforms on the night of Sidorov's first day in command. Nineteen trains would be required to move the cargo to Sevastopol and six ships, including the *Omsk*, to take it to Cuba. The loading of the *Omsk*, like the other ships headed for Cuba, took place in utmost secrecy. The port was guarded by special troops, and the officers and soldiers on the loading dock were forbidden to leave the area or have any contact with the outside world.

The R-12 rockets were loaded onto carts that were then secured in the cargo holds. It was a risky undertaking, but they had to conceal the missiles from the eyes of American pilots, whom they knew they would encounter in the Atlantic. Another major risk came with placing trucks in the cargo holds loaded with cisterns of hydrogen peroxide used to power the pumps of the missile combustion chambers. They put the trucks in wooden boxes and fixed them on special platforms to avoid accidental collision with the cisterns. Finally, they put their engineering equipment and civilian trucks needed for the construction of missile platforms on deck in full view of anyone who cared to look at it: after all, the *Omsk* was allegedly bringing civilian cargo to Cuba.[7]

To help maintain secrecy, before leaving Lithuania for Sevastopol they loaded the train with a supply of winter clothes—allegedly the troops were heading north. But once the train reached the port of Sevastopol, the officers and men were given summer clothes to wear. To everyone's surprise, these were civilian outfits. According to a participant in the operation, "enlisted men and sergeants" were dressed "in suits, check shirts of various colors and cloth caps, while officers wore suits, white or light-colored shirts, and hats. There were suits even for the enlisted men, also of various colors, and fairly fashionable for the time: single-breasted jackets of middle length in a variety of styles. We looked at one another in bemused surprise, not recognizing ourselves in 'civvies.' "[8]

Colonel Sidorov and some of his men left Sevastopol on August 4 with a load of six R-12 missiles. The ship was designed to carry no more than sixty-one persons: forty-three crew members and eighteen extras—passengers, trainees, and harbor pilots. Now it had to accommodate 250 extras—officers and enlisted men. Since they had to be concealed, for most of the long trip they would be confined to bunks between decks, suffering from immobility and extremely high temperatures beneath decks heated by the sun. Sidorov recalled that when a Turkish harbor pilot came aboard to guide the ship through the Bosporus, the soldiers were ordered to stay between decks, repeatedly watching the 1958 three-part Soviet film epic *And Quiet Flows the Don*. What was also flowing was their sweat. When Sidorov and others who stayed on deck opened the hatches between decks, they saw steam rising. Only when the lights of Istanbul were behind them did they let the soldiers out to breathe some fresh air.[9]

The living or, rather, breathing conditions on the *Omsk* were more the rule than the exception when compared to other ships taking missiles, equipment, and military personnel to Cuba. "The portholes between decks were covered with canvas blinds, and because of poor ventilation the temperature there sometimes reached 50°C and more," wrote Viktor Yesin, deputy chief engineer of one of the missile regiments. A major challenge was to keep the temperature of the hydrogen peroxide below 35 degrees Celsius. Sidorov and his people managed to keep the temperature around 28 degrees—quite an achievement in conditions when the temperature in the tween decks in cargo holds was almost twice as high. There was another problem when they left the Mediterranean and began their journey across the Atlantic, as Lieutenant Valentin Polkovnikov, a financial officer of a missile regiment, recalled: "The rocking motion increased, but people bore it as best they could." According to Yesin, "A great many servicemen (almost 75 percent) were seasick."[10]

◊◊◊

THE THIRTY-SEVEN-YEAR-OLD COLONEL DMITRII YAZOV, WHO would become the last Soviet minister of defense under Mikhail Gorbachev, left the Soviet Union for Cuba on board the German-built ocean liner *Victory*—a subtle reminder that the ship, built in 1928, had been taken from Germany by the Soviets as part of war reparations. Yazov and his men boarded the liner in Kronstadt on August 23. When he came on board, a colonel who was doing the count gave him the number 1,230. The liner's capacity of 330 passengers was being exceeded at least fourfold.[11]

Yazov commanded an infantry regiment and was sent to Cuba with ground troops assigned to protect the missile installations, but he did not initially know his destination. Only after the ship left the Baltic and entered the North Sea did the ship's captain, the obligatory KGB officer, and Yazov, who commanded the military detachment, open the first envelope in the captain's safe. The orders were to head for the English Channel and open another envelope once they had cleared it. By that point they knew what was going on: along with new orders, the envelope contained a twenty-eight-page note on the history of Cuba, probably inserted by mistake. This was the first ocean voyage for most of the infantrymen, who suffered considerably from seasickness. The storms that buffeted the *Victory* for most of the sixteen-day voyage left almost no one willing or even capable of going on deck, lessening the possibility of discovery by surveillance planes and boats. They reached Nipe Bay on the northern coast of Cuba on September 10.[12]

On the long trip to Cuba Yazov befriended the captain of the *Victory*, Ivan Pismenny. Both men were veterans of World War II, dedicated communists and Soviet patriots. Their discussions ranged over political and social issues, and one of them focused on the future. The first generation of revolutionaries was aging, as was the first generation of youth raised by the Soviet regime, to which Yazov and Pismenny had belonged. Many old-timers found the new generation that had come of age during Khrushchev's de-Stalinization campaign insufficiently dedicated to communist ideals, and Pismenny was concerned about the prospects. "We're going to lose the young people, I feel it in my heart—we're going to lose them!" he fretted. Yazov was more optimistic. "You're exaggerating there," he told his new friend. "Look at the new recruits sailing with us. They're village boys, independent, you won't make them stray from the path."[13]

The KGB officers on the Soviet ships bound for Cuba would probably have sided with Pismenny rather than Yazov. Every KGB officer generally had half a dozen informers on board. They were instructed to make sure that the trip remain secret and that there be no defectors. Monitoring the attitudes of officers and men regarding Soviet policy toward Cuba was part of the KGB's job, and what they uncovered was anything but reassuring to Khrushchev and his team. The KGB officers' reports to headquarters after the voyage indicated that unlike Pismenny, who called Cuba "the island of my soul" and was excited about the assignment, many of his fellow sailors as well as military personnel were anything but volunteers and had generally been dispatched to Cuba against their wishes.

"It's offensive that our fate was decided somewhere over a glass of vodka, and we have to pay the bill by heading off to Cuba, which is of no use to anybody," wrote an officer to his wife before departure. Not only had he criticized the government and questioned its policies, but he had also divulged a secret about his destination. The letter was intercepted by the KGB and brought to the attention of the officer's senior commanders, but they decided to send him to Cuba anyway "in the hope that after appropriate explanatory work he will understand the need to help the young Cuban republic." Captain Sizov, who was traveling to Cuba on the *Nikolai Burdenko*, was even more outspoken. "We're being taken for slaughter," he told a fellow officer who turned out to be a KGB informer. "I'm ready to lose my party card as long as I get back to the

Union," continued Sizov, who was deputy head of his unit's party cell. "The best thing to do on encountering Americans is to surrender and be taken prisoner."[14]

More than one thousand soldiers and five hundred officers were found unfit for the assignment for a variety of reasons. Some of the soldiers, once they learned about the forthcoming trip abroad (many suspected that the destination would be Cuba), tried to disqualify themselves by getting into trouble with their superiors, including going AWOL. Especially unhappy were the soldiers whose three-year term of mandatory military service was coming to an end in the summer of 1962: deployment to Cuba meant that their return home was indefinitely postponed. In some cases, commanders tried to ship troublemakers to Cuba. Private Borisov, having ridden drunkenly around Sevastopol on a stolen police bicycle, was arrested and put on a Cuba-bound vessel. Borisov resisted arrest and was probably beaten up by the military police: he would spend ten days, or most of the voyage, in a hospital bed, reported KGB major Verbov.[15]

Private Moiseenko, who was traveling on the dry cargo ship *Orenburg*, told his friends that "he had not taken an oath to serve Fidel Castro and was going to Cuba under duress." He argued that privates such as he had no reason to be afraid of Cuban "counterrevolutionaries," who were allegedly shooting only officers. Moiseenko—a Ukrainian, judging by his surname—probably had in mind popular rumors about the tactics employed by the Ukrainian nationalist underground after World War II. Andzor Somonodzharia, a recruit from Georgia, told his fellow soldiers that in 1956 Russian tanks had crushed the Georgian rebellion, killing old men, women, and children. He hated the Russians and was going to avenge the sufferings of his people. He was referring to riots in the Georgian capital of Tbilisi against Khrushchev's de-Stalinization policies: the protesters had indeed been dispersed by tanks.[16]

There were also nonpolitical discussions among the enlisted men that attracted KGB attention. Some suggested that Cuba was full of monkeys that attacked humans. Others predicted that the United States was going to declare a military blockade of the island. The KGB also picked up signs that as the trip went on, troop morale declined, and more of the men were becoming depressed. Some could not reconcile themselves to the fact that instead of being demobilized and sent home at the end of their three-year term they were being shipped off to Cuba. Others were exhausted by the heat between decks and debilitated by seasickness. Depressed soldiers told KGB informers that they were ready to jump into the sea and end their suffering.[17]

For the KGB, "jumping into the sea" presented a challenge. Those who were thinking of jumping ship might very well survive and reach a foreign shore or a foreign ship and "betray the motherland" by disclosing top-secret information about their units and the ship's cargo. Senior Lieutenant Sennikov, the KGB officer accompanying the *Orenburg*, instructed his informers to look for members of the crew and the military contemplating defection. That might happen when the ship was passing through the narrow waterways of the Black Sea straits, and Sennikov did his best to ensure that no defection would take place there. "During the passage of the Bosporus all passengers, including officers, were shut up in tweendeck 5, and a guard of CPSU members and agents was posted on the stern."[18]

The KGB not only monitored the political views and attitudes of crew members and the military but also kept an eye on their morals. Drinking by officers, who unlike the sergeants and privates were housed in deck compartments rather than in the tween decks and had supplies of alcohol acquired before the departure, appeared to be commonplace aboard ship. Judging by the reports, no KGB officer had more problems with drunkenness than Major Morozov, who traveled on the dry cargo ship *Metallurg Bardin* surveilling the communications unit, headed by Lieutenant Colonel M. T. Zuiek. The unit came from Vinnytsia, the headquarters of the 43rd Missile Army, which formed the core of the Soviet ballistic missile forces dispatched to the island. Zuiek's echelon counted 264 military personnel, including thirty-seven officers and female privates on contract with the army. Morozov reported that Zuiek had set a bad example for his subordinates, as he not only

engaged in drinking parties but also lived with a woman from his echelon, which undermined his ability to maintain discipline.[19]

A special challenge for the KGB were the crewmen of the ships.
The KGB captain Zozulia on board the *Ilia Mechnikov* reported that
crew members were extremely unhappy about the secrecy of the trip
and the cancellation of shore leave. The authorities denied them the
usual hard-currency allowance that they normally used in foreign ports
to buy goods scarce in the Soviet Union and sell them on the black market upon their return. On board *Metallurg Bardin*, the ship's boatswain,
Markovsky, got drunk and locked himself in his compartment with a
woman, refusing to open the door when requested by a senior officer.
The KGB officer Major Morozov largely blamed the women for what
was going on. "Their conduct was extremely negative," he wrote in his
report. "They did not react to the remarks of the echelon commander.
When darkness fell, they had to be rounded up from various places
where they were consorting with military personnel of the echelon."[20]

◊◊◊

ONCE THE SOVIET SHIPS ENTERED THE ATLANTIC AND BEGAN
to approach Cuba, the KGB officers found a new and more important
subject of surveillance and reporting—American airplanes overflying
the Soviet vessels. The senior KGB officers in Moscow to whom the
reports were ultimately addressed found that the later a ship approached
Cuba, the greater the number of overflights to which it was subjected.

Major Morozov reported that the *Metallurg Bardin* was overflown
by a US Navy plane only once on its way to Cuba, on August 18. But on
the way back, on August 31, another US airplane overflew the ship five
times in the course of twenty minutes. Something had changed in the
American attitude toward the Soviet ships. Major Zozulia all but lost
count of the overflights of *Ilia Mechnikov* as it approached Cuban waters
on August 28. "The overflights were conducted at a very low level and
in different directions," wrote Zozulia. "One plane would fly off, only to

be replaced by another after a short time. Every plane carried out two or three overflights of the ship." The Americans were clearly getting more worried about the Soviet ships as August drew to a close.[21]

The continuing American overflights meant one thing: the deal that Nikita Khrushchev had been trying to strike with John Kennedy the previous month was not materializing. In July, with ships en route to Cuba, Khrushchev had decided to enlist the help of President Kennedy himself to get the U-2 and other reconnaissance planes off their back as they transported Soviet missiles to Cuba. John Kennedy seemed open to Khrushchev's idea but wanted something in return—that the Berlin issue be put "on ice." Khrushchev played for time, instructing his secret representative in Washington, Colonel Georgii Bolshakov, to ask Kennedy what putting on ice really meant. It was a mistake. The deal never went into effect.[22]

III

AGONY

of

DECISION

8

PRISONER OF BERLIN

They call it the "Friday news dump"—the practice of releasing bad political news on Friday afternoon to avoid too much attention and media scrutiny. By that time newspaper columns are full of other news and ready to go to print. But the news that reached the White House on the morning of Friday, August 31, which also happened to be the last working day before the Labor Day weekend, could not be concealed or downplayed in that manner. Like a bomb, it would cause devastation no matter when and where dropped. General Marshall S. Carter, the acting director of the CIA, told John Kennedy that the overflight of Cuba by a CIA U-2 spy plane two days earlier had discovered Soviet-made S-75 Desna surface-to-air missiles. They were of the same type that had shot down a U-2 plane over the Soviet Union in May 1960.[1]

CIA analysts looking at the photos taken on August 29 recognized a pattern familiar from other Soviet surface-to-air missile installations: six launchpads connected by makeshift roads, with a command cabin and radar located at the center of the hexagon in an arrangement shaped somewhat like a Star of David. There were eight such sites on the island, each preparing to deploy six missile launchers. Since the U-2 cameras could not discern all the territory of Cuba because of partial cloud cover, that was probably not a complete tally of the missiles deployed there. All the spotted missile sites were in western Cuba, closer to Florida and the mainland United States. Unbeknownst to CIA experts, they belonged to the 12th Dnipropetrovsk Antiaircraft Division, which had begun its deployment on the island back in July.[2]

Kennedy knew that he had a problem on his hands. The most immediate one was political rather than military. The CIA report played right into the hands of Kennedy's Republican opponents, who were ready to turn Cuba into a key election issue in the forthcoming November congressional elections. Media reports about increased Soviet sea traffic to Cuba and the large number of Soviet personnel spotted on the island had already given them enough ammunition to accuse the president of doing nothing about the imminent danger from the island. On the very same day Kennedy received disturbing news from Cuba, Kenneth Keating, a Republican senator from New York, told Congress that "the Soviets are constructing missile bases and sending over technicians and experts to man them." "I am reliably informed—when I say 'reliably informed' I mean that has been checked out from five different sources," declared Keating.[3]

Keating had been on an antimissile crusade against the administration since December 1961, when Admiral E. J. O'Donnell, the commander of the US naval base in Guantánamo, confided to one of Keating's staffers that he believed missile sites were under construction in Cuba. There had been no evidence to back up such claims at the time, but now, with media reports about Soviets spotted on the island by Cuban refugees seeking safe haven in Florida, Keating was back in the spotlight. "More than 20 cargo ships have arrived from Communist ports in the last few weeks," Keating told Congress. "Many have been unloaded under maximum security. Between three and five thousand so called 'technicians' have arrived in the course of the past year." He concluded his presentation with a call to action: "Time is short. The situation is growing worse. I urge upon my Government that prompt action be taken."[4]

Kennedy needed time to think things through. He told the CIA's deputy director, Marshall S. Carter, that he wanted information about the missiles to be put "back in the box and nailed tight." Carter obliged, buying Kennedy some extra time. The president asked Secretary of State Dean Rusk to start working on a public statement. Scarred by his meeting with Khrushchev in Vienna and making no progress with the Soviet leader on nuclear test-ban negotiations or Berlin, Kennedy was coming to distrust Khrushchev as a negotiating partner and had little hope of solving the growing problem in Cuba by appealing to him through diplomatic channels. The only appeal that made sense to him was a public one. It would tell Khrushchev that there were limits to what he could accept regarding the Soviet presence in Cuba.[5]

Later that day Kennedy flew to Rhode Island to spend the long weekend with Jackie, Caroline, and John Jr. He also visited Hyannis Port to see his paralyzed father, Joseph. But the Cuban missiles stayed on his mind. On Saturday, September 1, the first full day of the long weekend, in a telephone conversation with General Carter, Kennedy eased the ban on information about Cuba. Access to it would now be extended to a select group of officials "on a need to know basis for the purpose of preparing a comprehensive hearing for the President Tuesday morning."[6]

Cuba was becoming an absolute priority for Kennedy's foreign policy team, overshadowing its previous object of obsessive concern— West Berlin. The threat of military confrontation was moving dangerously close to the American mainland. But few of those around the president believed that Cuba was simply replacing Berlin in Soviet strategy. For a while it seemed that the Berlin crisis was the bigger and more threatening one. Kennedy and his advisers would judge anything pertaining to Cuba first and foremost with reference to the situation in Berlin.

◊◊◊

WITH HIS HARVARD PEDIGREE AND CONNECTIONS, KENNEDY was able to assemble the most intellectually impressive foreign policy team ever seen in Washington. It included the forty-one-year-old former dean of arts and sciences at Harvard, McGeorge Bundy, who became national security adviser, and the forty-four-year-old Harvard MBA and former president of the Ford Motor Company, Robert McNamara, who became secretary of defense. The president's brother, Robert, also a Harvard graduate, took the position of attorney general and became another key member of Kennedy's foreign policy team. Secretary of State Dean Rusk had gone to Oxford on a Rhodes scholarship. These four were the backbone of the president's foreign policy team, which also included representatives of the CIA and the armed forces, along with top officials from other departments.[7]

The president's foreign policy advisers spent most of the summer trying to deal with the Berlin crisis, analyzing it in terms of the "Poodle Blanket" scenario. It envisioned four phases of escalation over Berlin, the first beginning with Soviet interference with Allied access to West Berlin, the second resulting in a Soviet blockade of the city, the third leading to conventional warfare, and the fourth culminating in a nuclear exchange. The situation was considered to represent phase one, with the expectation that it might rapidly deteriorate. There were signs suggesting that the Soviets were preparing to escalate.

In a letter to Kennedy delivered to the White House on July 5, Khrushchev set forth his new demand for the gradual withdrawal of the Western allies from Berlin, promising a new era in Soviet-American relations if his proposal was accepted and threatening a global crisis if it was not. He wrote: "[F]urther delay in solving the questions connected with a German peace settlement would involve such a threat to peace which must be averted already now when it is not too late." Kennedy responded to Khrushchev's demand by voicing his concern that the situation in Berlin might lead to nuclear war despite the wishes of the leaders themselves. He wrote: "In reading the history of past wars and how they began, we cannot help but be impressed how frequently the failure of communication, misunderstanding and mutual irritation have played an important role in the events leading up to fateful decisions for war." Kennedy was referring to a recently published book by Barbara Tuchman, *The Guns of August*.[8]

Khrushchev unexpectedly signaled a retreat. On July 25 he suggested to the US ambassador in Moscow, Llewellyn Thompson, that he "personally ask President—not through State Department whether it would be better for him if Berlin question brought to a head before or after our Congressional elections. He did not want to make things more difficult for President—and in fact would like to help him." The same message was delivered to Robert Kennedy through the Soviet intelligence officer Georgii Bolshakov, with an additional request: Khrushchev wanted Kennedy to stop American overflights of Soviet ships on their way to Cuba. President Kennedy met with Bolshakov in the White House on July 30 and expressed interest in the deal. At that time, as far as Kennedy was concerned, Cuba barely existed on the Soviet-American agenda, which was fully dominated by Berlin.[9]

Unbeknownst to Kennedy, Khrushchev was playing his Berlin card to distract the president's attention from Cuba. For him, the construction of the Berlin Wall had resolved the crisis, and he did not want to reopen it any time soon. He wrote to the East German leader, Walter Ulbricht, on September 28, a few weeks before the Checkpoint Charlie confrontation between Soviet and American tanks: "Under the present circumstances, since the measures for the safeguarding and control of the GDR borders with West Berlin have been implemented successfully, since the Western powers are tending towards negotiations and contacts between the USSR and the US have already been made in New York, such steps which could exacerbate the situation, especially in Berlin, should be avoided."[10]

The Soviet leader did his best to persuade Ulbricht to abandon the idea of a separate peace treaty with the USSR. "What is pushing us to a peace treaty?" he asked the dissatisfied Ulbricht in February 1962 and responded on his own behalf: "Nothing. Until August 13 [the day the

Berlin Wall went up], we were racking our brains over how to move forward. Now the borders are closed." In June 1962, addressing a Czechoslovak delegation, Khrushchev ridiculed both Ulbricht and the idea of a separate treaty. "The signing of a treaty," argued Khrushchev, "might lead to an economic blockade of the GDR in the first instance. Then Comrade Ulbricht would be the first to come and ask us for gold. . . . The Germans fought a war with us, but now they have a higher standard of living than we do, yet we are supposed to keep giving and giving."[11]

Although Khrushchev did not plan to escalate the Berlin crisis, he was also reluctant to take it off the international agenda. For him it had become a bargaining chip and tool of blackmail too valuable to discard. Khrushchev would compare Berlin to the testicles of the West. "Every time I want to make the West scream, I squeeze on Berlin." And squeeze he did. On August 22, Khrushchev made a move in Berlin that many regarded as another step toward a separate treaty with East Germany. The Soviets abolished the office of Soviet commandant of Berlin, creating a situation in which the American, British, and French commandants would be forced to deal directly with the East Germans and thereby provide the regime with a modicum of international legitimacy.[12]

On August 23, Kennedy and his advisers met to discuss the intensification of the Berlin crisis, which, in the words of the president's national security adviser, McGeorge Bundy, had "warmed up a lot in recent weeks and looks as if it is getting worse." Kennedy believed that the events in Berlin would lead to a major showdown before the end of the year.[13]

◊◊◊

FOR JOHN KENNEDY, CUBA HAD BEEN OF LOW PRIORITY TILL late August 1962. While Robert Kennedy continued to oversee the administration's sabotage and psychological warfare measures against the Castro regime, dubbed Operation Mongoose, no one imagined anything even remotely like Operation Anadyr being unleashed on the island.

On August 1, the CIA issued an intelligence estimate suggesting that while the Soviets had provided arms and military equipment to the Cubans, their military capabilities were "essentially defensive." It was deemed "unlikely that the [Soviet] Bloc will provide Cuba with capability to undertake major independent military operations overseas." Things began to change rapidly less than a week after the CIA issued its estimate. On August 7, a Spanish-language announcer informed the listeners of his Miami-based Cuban radio program that four thousand Soviet soldiers had landed in Cuba in July. Next day the news was in the *New York Times*. The CIA checked the news originating with Cuban exiles in Florida and found it basically correct.[14]

On August 21 John McCone, the sixty-year-old Eisenhower-era chairman of the Atomic Energy Commission, who had replaced Allen Dulles as head of the CIA in November 1961, informed key figures in the Kennedy administration about the CIA's recent findings. According to McCone's memo, twenty-one Soviet ships had reached Cuba in July and seventeen had either already docked or were en route to Cuba in August. Between four thousand and six thousand Soviets had arrived on the island in July alone. They were suspected to be military personnel, but as they were kept isolated from the Cuban population, that was not known for certain. The same applied to the equipment provided by the Soviets: the ships were unloaded in ports and areas cleared of locals. Nevertheless, the crates suggested airplane parts and missiles. Besides, there was clearly identifiable radar equipment. The CIA analysts indicated the possibility that the Soviets were placing surface-to-air missiles in Cuba.[15]

Robert Kennedy, McNamara, Rusk, and Bundy, who gathered on that day to discuss the progress of Operation Mongoose, were now faced with an entirely different situation. They turned the meeting into a brainstorming session on what should be done under the circumstances. The first option that came to mind was to stop the Soviet buildup by establishing a blockade of the island, either complete or limited to Soviet ships and those owned or leased by USSR satellites. That seemed to be a good idea with regard to Cuba, but Bundy, speaking on behalf of the White House, immediately put the brakes on it by point-ing out the possible repercussions worldwide. He was concerned about the situation in Berlin. "It was felt," reads the CIA memorandum of the conversation, "that a blockade of Cuba would automatically bring about a blockade of Berlin."

With Berlin on their minds, the majority turned against the block-ade option. McNamara proposed stepping up covert operations against the Castro regime. Robert Kennedy suggested a provocation including a staged Cuban attack on the Guantánamo base, providing a pretext for US intervention. McCone worried about such suggestions, noting the difficulty of conducting clandestine operations when security on the island was being tightened—the Castro regime was on the lookout for potential spies and saboteurs. But others in the room paid little atten-tion to McCone's concerns. They felt that their hands were tied because of the situation in Berlin. It was agreed that McCone would report to Kennedy in person on the CIA findings.[16]

McCone delivered the disturbing news to the president on August 22. It came as an unpleasant surprise. In fact, a few hours before meet-ing with McCone, Kennedy, speaking at a press conference, had denied the presence of Soviet troops in Cuba. "Troops? We do not have infor-mation, but an increased number of technicians," the president told a reporter. Now McCone suggested that there were not only troops on the island but perhaps missiles as well. The next day McCone told Kennedy that for the time being he could not distinguish surface-to-air missiles from surface-to-surface ones that would endanger US territory. Dis-turbed, Kennedy showered McCone with questions: could the missiles be taken out by an airstrike, ground invasion, or, alternatively, by sabo-tage or local insurgency?[17]

McCone had no answers to all the president's questions, but he had a ready solution to the Cuban problem as a whole. The memo he submit-ted to Kennedy envisioned a three-step operation starting with an inter-national public campaign against the Cuban regime, proceeding to the intensification of sabotage and covert operations on the island, and cul-minating in the "instantaneous commitment of sufficient armed forces to occupy the country, destroy the regime, free the people, and establish in Cuba a peaceful country which will be a member of the community of American states." He hoped that successful implementation of the first two steps might make the third unnecessary but did not count on it. McCone confided to Robert Kennedy that he considered the developments in Cuba "our most serious problem."

But President Kennedy and his advisers were not convinced. "Many in the room," reads the CIA summary of the conversation, "related action in Cuba to Soviet actions in Turkey, Greece, Berlin, Far East and elsewhere." McCone had a suggestion on how to solve the Turkish problem, arguing that the Jupiter medium-range missiles with nuclear warheads in Turkey and Italy presented no strategic advantage. McNamara agreed that they were of no use and undertook to investigate their removal. But there was no solution in sight for the Berlin problem. "President," reads the protocol of the meeting, "raised question of what we should do in Cuba if Soviets precipitated a Berlin crisis. This is the alternative to the proposition of what Soviets would do in Berlin if we moved in Cuba."[18]

On August 29, the day on which CIA overflights located Soviet surface-to-air missiles on the island, Kennedy publicly denied the possible presence of Soviet troops in Cuba and American plans to invade the island. Once again, Berlin was on his mind. He stated: "The United States has obligations all around the world, including West Berlin and other areas, which are very sensitive, and, therefore, I think that in considering what appropriate action we should take, we have to consider the totality of our obligations, and also the responsibilities which we bear in so many different parts of the world." The worst thing that could happen, in Kennedy's view, was that his actions in Cuba might provoke a crisis in West Berlin, leading to a Soviet blockade of the city, a US-Soviet military confrontation, and eventually a nuclear war.[19]

◊◊◊

JOHN KENNEDY RETURNED TO WASHINGTON FROM HIS LABOR Day weekend on the morning of Tuesday, September 4, to confer with his foreign policy team. The key discussion item was a statement that the president had asked Rusk to draft before departing for the holiday. The secretary of state suggested the deployment of offensive weapons as the red line that Khrushchev would be warned not to cross. "Any placing by the Soviets of significant offensive capability in the hands of the self-announced aggressive regime in Cuba would be a direct and major challenge to this hemisphere and would warrant immediate and appropriate action," read the draft statement.

Rusk failed to clarify what constituted "offensive weapons" and what the "appropriate action" might be. On the first issue, McNamara argued that the deployment of Soviet MiG fighters would fit the bill. Bundy suggested instead that "surface to surface missiles are the turning point." Regarding "appropriate action," Bundy argued that, given the consequences of a nuclear exchange to the United States, the Americans would be better off not taking any aggressive action vis-à-vis Cuba. Not only McNamara but also Rusk disagreed with Bundy and considered invasion necessary if nuclear-armed missiles were to be spotted on the island. Rusk believed that if invasion were imminent, the first stage would have to be a blockade of the island.

McNamara proposed blockade as an "appropriate action" in its own right. "If we do it then, why would we not do it today?" he asked the gathering. He had not finished his thought when the president cut him short, saying: "The reason we don't is that, is because we figure that they may try to blockade Berlin and we would then try to blockade Cuba." He wanted to keep the threat of blockading Cuba as leverage against Khrushchev's actions in Berlin. He also thought that a blockade of Cuba "would not do them that much harm for quite a while." Kennedy's intervention shot down the idea of a blockade before it was fully developed and had a chance to gain support in the room.

McNamara would not raise the blockade issue again that day. Instead, he came back with a different strategy, pushing for the mobilization of reserves—a step needed to prepare not only a blockade but also an invasion of Cuba. He also saw it as a means of appeasing and calming Congress: "If the leadership wants to act in relation to Cuba, one of the best actions I can think of is exactly this." Sending a message to Khrushchev while appeasing Congress—Kennedy was sold on McNamara's idea right away. He wanted the statement as soon as possible. "We can't permit somebody to break this story before we do," he told his aides at the start of the meeting.[20]

On the evening of September 4, the White House press secretary, Pierre Salinger, finally released a presidential statement on Cuba to the media. "Information has reached this Government in the last four days from a variety of sources which establishes without doubt that the Soviets have provided the Cuban Government with a number of anti-aircraft defense missiles," read the statement. Its final version included neither Kennedy's pledge not to invade Cuba nor his promises to defend the sanctity of the Monroe Doctrine, which had appeared in the original drafts. Instead it proposed to treat the "Cuban question" as "part of the worldwide challenge posed by Communist threats to peace." The president issued a threat not against the USSR but against Cuba. "It continues to be the policy of the United States that the Castro regime will not be allowed to export its aggressive purposes by force or the threat of force," read the statement. "It will be prevented by whatever means may be necessary from taking action against any part of the Western Hemisphere."[21]

Shortly before issuing the statement, Kennedy had met with congressional leaders. He asked for their consent to call up as many as 150,000 soldiers to deal with Cuba and possibly another international crisis but argued against an immediate invasion of the island. According to him, the missiles spotted on the island were not a threat to the United States: "We are not talking about nuclear warheads." He was also against a blockade, which would constitute an "act of war." In that connection he also mentioned Berlin. "I think Berlin is coming to some kind of climax this fall, one way or another, before Christmas," Kennedy told the congressional leaders. Khrushchev's Berlin bluff had a powerful hold on the president.[22]

9

TIP-OFF

News of the American discovery of the Soviet SAMs on Cuba found Nikita Khrushchev on vacation. He had left Moscow in late July, after General Issa Pliev and the first reconnaissance groups were dispatched to Cuba, and progressed slowly south to the Black Sea—the master surveying his land and people. He checked the state of agriculture in the southern Russian provinces, visited his native village of Kalinovka, and then headed for Dnipropetrovsk to visit Mykhailo Yangel's missile factory, which produced R-12 and R-14 rockets earmarked for shipment to Cuba. He finally made it to the Crimean resort of Yalta on August 1, a few days before Colonel Ivan Sidorov and his regiment of R-12s left the harbor of nearby Sevastopol and set out for Cuba.[1] Khrushchev was sunbathing and swimming but also working—his mercurial personality made it impossible for him to stay still. In mid-August he flew to Moscow for a few days to celebrate another Soviet achievement in outer space, the return of the Soviet astronauts Pavel (Pavlo) Popovych and Adrian Nikolaev from the first dual space flight in history. On the return to the Crimea he dealt with a constant stream of visitors to his mansion. On August 30 Khrushchev welcomed Fidel Castro's emissary Che Guevara to discuss Cuba. Despite continuing pressure from the Cubans, Khrushchev refused to sign a public defense treaty with Havana. His defense minister, Marshal Malinovsky, assured Che that if the Americans discovered the missiles and threatened to invade Cuba, he would send the Soviet Baltic Fleet there. But both Khrushchev and Malinovsky believed that the Americans would accept the new reality. "He said to Che and me, with Malinovsky in the room, 'You don't have to worry; there will be no big reaction from the U.S. And if there is a problem, we will send the Baltic Fleet,'" recalled a participant in the meeting, Emilio Aragonés.[2]

In early September Khrushchev moved to his newly built Pitsunda villa, located on the Abkhazian shore of the Black Sea, for the last stage of his summer vacation. On September 4, as Kennedy and his advisers were busy discussing the discovery of the SAM launching sites in Cuba, Khrushchev signed a letter responding positively to the proposal made by Kennedy and the British prime minister, Harold Macmillan, on August 27 to sign an agreement banning nuclear tests in the atmosphere, under water, and in outer space. Previously Khrushchev had insisted on a comprehensive treaty that would ban underground tests as well, a category in which he believed the Americans were ahead of the Soviets; now he removed that demand. He was trying to be on his best behavior, engaging the Americans in negotiations and making tactical concessions on every front from the nuclear test ban to Berlin— anything to draw their attention away from Cuba and make it more difficult for Kennedy to muster a strong response to Khrushchev's actions there.[3]

News of the American discovery of the antiaircraft missiles in Cuba arrived in Pitsunda on the morning of September 5 like a bolt from the blue. There was no longer any doubt that Khrushchev's Cuban nuclear missile adventure was in jeopardy. Khrushchev had to act without delay. He could still call off the deployment of the ballistic missiles— their unloading in the Cuban ports has not yet begun. The main goal of the American statement was to warn Khrushchev about crossing a red line. His reaction was just the opposite—to cross it as soon as possible. Instead of serving as a warning shot, Kennedy's statement became a tip-off to Khrushchev: he had to complete his secretive game before being fully discovered. Instead of backing off, Khrushchev decided to go on the offensive.

◊◊◊

"PINE FORESTS AND A TEN-FOOT-HIGH CONCRETE WALL SEALED off the huge seafront property from prying eyes," wrote the American journalist Fred Coleman, recalling his visit to Khrushchev's Pitsunda mansion. "Hidden behind the walls were several guesthouses, each too far away to be seen through the trees from its neighbors. The main house, a two-story mansion, contained priceless Oriental rugs, a Japanese garden on the roof and an elevator running up an outside wall. Nearby was a glass-enclosed swimming pool where, in good weather, the roof slid away at the touch of a button to permit bathing in the open air. Telephones were fixed to trees along the garden paths where Nikita Sergeyevich liked to walk."[4]

On September 6, the day after receiving the disturbing news from Washington, Khrushchev welcomed another American, Secretary of the Interior Stewart L. Udall, to Pitsunda. Udall was then completing his tour of Soviet hydroelectric power stations. His unexpected summons to see Khrushchev in his Black Sea villa immediately following Kennedy's statement leaves little doubt that the two events were related. Khrushchev was on the offensive, full of indignation about American actions on the international arena. The thrust of Khrushchev's attack was Berlin. "[H]e reasserted his hard line and indicated the [Soviet-East German] Peace Treaty will be signed," telegraphed Udall on September 7 from the American embassy in Moscow. "He stated flatly he would not allow Western troops [to] remain [in] Berlin and while permitting access for civilian traffic would not allow access for military purposes."[5]

Upon his return to Washington, Udall shared more details about his stormy meeting with Khrushchev. In some ways it was a continuation of the Vienna attack on Kennedy, now conducted through one of his cabinet members. "I know Nixon and Eisenhower, and I must say that Kennedy is better in this respect," began Khrushchev. "As a President he has understanding, but what he does not yet have is courage— courage to solve the German question. If he resolves this problem, he will rise to the heights," pontificated Khrushchev. He then resumed his threats of nuclear war: "We will put him in a situation where it is necessary to solve it. We will give him a choice—to go to war or sign a peace treaty." With his ballistic missiles now targeting Western Europe but not yet America, Khrushchev believed that the Europeans would stop the Americans from starting a war. "War in this day and age means no Paris and no France, all in the space of an hour," declared Khrushchev. "It's been a long time since you could spank us like a little boy—now we can swat your ass."[6]

Khrushchev was trying to use Kennedy's concern about nuclear war not only to "solve" the Berlin problem but also to prevail upon him to show "courage" and not attack Cuba once he learned of the nuclear missiles on the island. "[A]s to Cuba," stated Khrushchev, "here is an area that could really lead to some unexpected consequences." He admitted that the Soviets had provided Castro with modern weapons but stressed that "he needs [them] for defense." "However," continued Khrushchev, "if you attack Cuba, that would create an entirely different situation." A minute later he explained what he meant: "You have surrounded us with military bases. If you attack Cuba, then we will attack one of the countries next to us where you have placed your bases." It was a threat against the American installations in Turkey and Europe. The Cuban leadership would be informed by Moscow that at his meeting with Udall, Khrushchev had warned the American "without any hint of propaganda about all the consequences which could result from its treacherous actions towards Cuba."[7]

The meeting was followed by a dinner attended by Soviet officials, including the leading Soviet Cuba expert, Anastas Mikoyan. A few weeks later he would summarize the Soviet negotiating tactics as follows: "We let the Americans know that we wanted to solve the question of Berlin in the nearest future. This was done in order to distract their attention away from Cuba. So, we used a diversionary maneuver. In reality we had no intention of resolving the Berlin question at that time." Ironically, Mikoyan believed that the Americans were also using Berlin as a decoy in their Cuba game. "When the Americans learned about the transport of strategic weapons to Cuba they themselves began crying a lot about Berlin," argued Mikoyan. "Both sides were talking about the Berlin crisis, but simultaneously believed that at that given moment the essence of their policy was located in Cuba."[8]

Mikoyan was not making things up. The Soviets did indeed fall into the very same trap they had set for Kennedy: if he believed they were serious about Berlin, they believed that he was simply playing them. "Both we and the Americans talked about Berlin—both sides with the same aim, namely, to draw attention away from Cuba; the Americans, in order to attack it; we, in order to make the USA uneasy and postpone attacking Cuba," Khrushchev told a visiting Czechoslovak delegation on October 30.[9]

◊◊◊

KHRUSHCHEV WAS USING THE BERLIN ISSUE TO BUY MORE time to deliver his missiles and nuclear warheads to Cuba, but he was also eager to use the time available to prepare for a possible American invasion of Cuba, which now looked more likely than ever. Instead of backing off, he intensified the pace of missile delivery and added new types of nuclear weapons to the list.

On the day Khrushchev met Udall at Pitsunda, Marshal Malinovsky in Moscow prepared a top-secret document handwritten by one of his top officers. Malinovsky proposed to strengthen the Cuba task force with ten to twelve IL-28 bombers capable of carrying nuclear weapons. They were to be accompanied by six atomic bombs, each with the explosive power of 8 to 12 kilotons, more than one-half of the TNT yield of the Hiroshima bomb. Such bombs were considered tactical and designed to be used in combat. That was not all. Malinovsky pro-

posed to send eighteen "Zemlia" (Earth) cruise missiles armed with
nuclear warheads and two to three divisions of "Luna" (Moon, in NATO
reporting FROG) tactical missiles. That would amount to either eight
or twelve Luna rockets, armed with nuclear warheads. The strategic
nuclear forces were now to be reinforced with tactical ones capable of
protecting the "big guys" in case of attack and ground invasion.

Given the discovery of the SAMs, time was of the essence, and the
fastest way to deliver the nuclear weapons would be by air, but Malinovsky
reported to Khrushchev that while Soviet planes could deliver the missiles and nuclear warheads to Cuba, they could not deliver the much
larger launching pads. Without them, the missiles and warheads would
be useless. Malinovsky proposed to send the bombers, rockets, nuclear
charges, and bombs for them by sea: the nuclear warheads and bombs
would travel together with the nuclear warheads for medium- and
intermediate-range missiles on the dry cargo ship *Indigirka*, scheduled
to depart on September 15, with the tactical missiles to follow in early
October. On September 7 Khrushchev approved the dispatch to Cuba
by sea of six IL-26 bombers with atomic bombs and three divisions of
Luna tactical missiles with nuclear charges for them.[10]

Khrushchev's decision to dispatch tactical nuclear weapons to Cuba
reflected his state of urgency, if not panic, after the release of Kennedy's
statement. It marked a dramatic shift in his thinking about the Cuban
situation from a desire to use nuclear weapons as a deterrent against
an American invasion of Cuba and as a way of redressing the balance
of nuclear forces worldwide to readiness to use them in an actual conflict with the United States. There is nothing in Khrushchev's documents, pronouncements, or comments suggesting that he was trying
to unleash a nuclear war with the United States on either a local or a
global scale, that he preferred the former to the latter, or believed that
it was possible to have the one without the other. But his decision to
send tactical nuclear weapons to Cuba made all those scenarios not just
theoretically but practically possible.[11]

On September 8, the day after Khrushchev approved the transfer
of tactical nuclear weapons to Cuba, Malinovsky and Marshal Matvei

Zakharov, the chief of staff of the Soviet armed forces, ordered the shipment to Cuba of six nuclear bombs for IL-28 bombers and twelve nuclear warheads for the Luna missiles. Malinovsky and Zakharov also signed a new instruction to the commander of the Cuban Task Force, General Issa Pliev, which postulated the use of nuclear weapons to counter an invasion of Cuba. "The task of the Soviet armed forces group on the island of Cuba is not to allow an enemy landing on Cuban territory," read the document. It defined the missile forces as the "backbone for the defense of the Soviet Union and the island of Cuba," and ordered them to be "prepared, upon signal from Moscow, to deal a nuclear missile strike to the most important targets in the United States of America." The American sites were also to be targeted by nuclear submarines to be sent to Cuba as part of the Soviet Navy.[12]

The instruction to Pliev clearly stated that the nuclear weapons, both tactical and strategic, could be used only upon receiving an order from Moscow, meaning from Khrushchev himself. But the General Staff was also considering the possibility of giving Pliev the right to decide on his own whether to use such weapons in case of invasion. On September 8, the day on which the main instruction was signed, someone in the General Staff drafted an additional instruction that would apply if contact between Havana and Moscow became impossible.

The new instruction read: "In a situation of an enemy landing on the island of Cuba and of the concentration of enemy ships with amphibious forces off the coast of Cuba in its territorial waters, when the destruction of the enemy is delaying [further actions] and there is no possibility of receiving instructions from the USSR Ministry of Defense, you are permitted to make your own decision and to use the nuclear means of the 'Luna,' IL-28 or FKR-1 [short-range cruise missiles] as instruments of local warfare for the destruction of the enemy on land and along the coast in order to achieve the complete destruction of the invaders on Cuban territory and to defend the Republic of Cuba."[13]

The instruction on Pliev's discretionary use of nuclear weapons without orders from Moscow remained unsigned by Malinovsky. Khrushchev was not yet prepared to relinquish his personal control of nuclear weapons, even tactical ones. But the instruction to allow Pliev to do so was ready. Only the signature was missing.

◊◊◊

ON SEPTEMBER 8, THE SAME DAY THAT KHRUSHCHEV APPROVED the new shipment of nuclear arms to Cuba, the White House announced that Kennedy was asking Congress for authorization to call up 150,000 reservists if the need arose. For Khrushchev, obsessed with the prospect of an American invasion of Cuba, that could mean only one thing—the Americans were coming. By now he had all but run out of his nuclear ammunition, sending to Cuba almost every type of nuclear weapon in his possession. What was left was the power of bluster, which Khrushchev had in unlimited quantity.

To Kennedy's terse statement of September 5, Khrushchev responded with his own on September 11. It was more than ten times as long as Kennedy's: 4,600 words to Kennedy's 377. Khrushchev used the statement to declare that in response to Kennedy's decision to ask for a possible mobilization of reserves, he was putting his own troops on high alert.

Khrushchev claimed that while there were indeed Soviet military instructors on Cuba, they were fewer in number than the civilian advisers sent to the island. He was lying. He was also bluffing: "Our nuclear weapons are so powerful in their explosive force, and the Soviet Union has such powerful rockets to carry these nuclear warheads, that there is no need to search for sites for them beyond the boundaries of the Soviet Union." To the whole world that sounded like an assurance, if not a guarantee, that Khrushchev was not sending nuclear weapons to Cuba. At the same time he warned Washington against invading Cuba: "[O]ne cannot now attack Cuba and expect that the aggressor will be free from punishment for this attack. If this attack is made, this will be the beginning of the unleashing of war." He had in mind "a universal world war with the use of thermonuclear weapons."[14]

Kennedy refused to answer Khrushchev with a statement of his own, and on September 28, Khrushchev fired off one of his longest letters yet. Totaling close to 4,500 words, it was almost as long as the TASS statement of September 11 on Cuba. The immediate trigger was the resolution, passed by Congress on September 20, giving Kennedy a free hand to invade Cuba. Once again Khrushchev threatened nuclear war. He complained bitterly about American ships following and harassing Soviet vessels on their way to Cuba: "I said then and I repeat—let them try to stop and sink our ships—this will be the beginning of war because we will answer in kind." He also protested overflights of the same Soviet ships: "I can tell you: in August there were 140 cases of such buzzing."

Khrushchev wanted to distract Kennedy's attention from Cuba and discourage him from invading the island. Once again, he was trying to use a carrot and a stick to achieve his goal. The carrot was the nuclear test-ban treaty. "Well, I can say quite definitely that we will not make you wait," wrote Khrushchev in response to Kennedy's proposal to make major progress on the treaty before the end of the year. The stick, as always, was Berlin. Khrushchev ended his long letter by promising to do nothing about Berlin before the elections and threatening drastic actions after that. "After the elections, apparently in the second half of November, it would be necessary in our opinion to continue the dialogue," he wrote. It was more a threat than an invitation to dialogue.[15]

On the following day, Kennedy summoned two of his most experienced Russia hands, the former ambassador to Moscow Charles "Chip" Bohlen and the serving ambassador, Llewellyn Thompson. When asked why they thought Khrushchev had ordered the buildup in Cuba, both raised the ideological component of his decision: "[W]ithin the bloc, the Communist bloc, this is a good step for him." Bohlen wanted Kennedy to issue a strong rebuke to Khrushchev in order to counter his assertions that the United States was too liberal and soft to fight over the issues at hand. "But the thing he's interested in, which is the only thing you worry about, is a nuclear war," Bohlen told the president, suggesting that Khrushchev was exploiting Kennedy's concern about triggering a nuclear confrontation by pushing him on Berlin. He added: "And this is cockeyed, I think."

Bohlen tried to decouple Berlin from Cuba in Kennedy's mind. When the president suggested that an invasion of Cuba might lead to a Soviet seizure of Berlin, Bohlen admitted such a possibility but added: "[T]here are so many places, there are many instances where if we take certain kinds of forcible actions, the Russians can retaliate. I think we tend . . . to let the Berlin situation dominate our whole action." Kennedy did not heed Bohlen's advice and decided not to push back on Berlin. His response to Khrushchev's letter, which he sent to Moscow on October 8, also did not touch on Cuba. The president decided to focus on the nuclear test-ban treaty alone, where Khrushchev seemed open to cooperation and possibly compromise. "I believe we should try to work out such an agreement in time to meet the target day of January 1, 1963," wrote Kennedy.[16]

Between the carrot of the test-ban treaty and the stick of Berlin, Kennedy reached for the carrot, but the stick would remain on his mind for weeks to come. Khrushchev would not respond. This turned out to be their last exchange before the American discovery of the surface-to-surface missiles, to which Kennedy had referred in his statement of September 4 as "offensive weapons." Unbeknownst to Kennedy, they were already in Cuba.[17]

10

HONEYMOON

J ohn McCone, the sixty-year-old silver-gray bespectacled CIA chief who had been the first to alert President Kennedy about the presence of Soviet surface-to-air missiles in Cuba in August, was spending the first weeks of September on the French Riviera. He missed the all-important meeting with the president on September 4, when Kennedy and his advisers decided what should be done about the news that McCone's suspicions had materialized and the Soviets had indeed put their SAMs on Cuba. McCone had very good reason to be away from Washington: he had just married the fifty-year-old Theiline Pigott, the widow of Paul Pigott, the wealthy president of the Pacific Car and Foundry Corporation, and was now on his honeymoon.[1]

While the French Riviera honeymoon was the beginning of a happy marriage that would last almost thirty years, and the weather was perfect for swimming and sunbathing, for McCone it was at times a torturous experience, as he had little influence on decisions then being taken in Washington on matters that deeply concerned him. As he read the cables he was receiving daily from his subordinates in DC, McCone grew more and more convinced that the Soviets had put the SAMs on the island for a reason, and the reason was to protect the delivery of much more dangerous missiles that could carry nuclear warheads. The CIA chief shared his concerns with his second in command, General Marshall Carter, who was substituting for him in Washington. The deployment of SAMs in Cuba, cabled McCone on September 10 from his French getaway, had been undertaken "for purpose of ensuring secrecy of some offensive capability such as MRBMs [medium-range ballistic missiles] to be installed by Soviets after present phase completed and country secured from overflights."[2]

Carter, a balding fifty-three-year-old officer who had made his career as an aide to General George C. Marshall in his capacities as chief of staff of the US Army, secretary of state, and then secretary of defense, did not disagree with his chief but never shared his cables with the White House. He therefore had trouble convincing other members of the administration that the situation was indeed as dangerous as McCone suggested, and that it required constant monitoring by regular flights over Cuba.

The previous few days had been anything but a success for the CIA U-2 program. Since the fateful U-2 flight of August 29 that had discovered the Soviet SAMs, CIA spy planes had received a lot of bad press around the world. On the next day, August 30, the Soviets spotted a U-2 in their air space near Sakhalin Island in the Far East. The US government apologized for the incident, and Khrushchev even expressed satisfaction with the Kennedy administration's handling of it while meeting with Stewart Udall on September 7. But the U-2 continued to cloud US-Soviet relations, as the Chinese shot down a U-2 over their territory the following day, September 8. Two U-2 accidents resulting in international scandals and public embarrassment for the US government in less than ten days could not but affect espionage operations elsewhere, and overflights of Cuba became a matter of growing concern to the State Department, which had to do all the explaining in the international arena.[3]

Secretary of State Dean Rusk asked McGeorge Bundy, Kennedy's national security adviser, for a meeting with the CIA, and Bundy obliged, passing to the CIA Rusk's questions about U-2 flights along with his "hope" that there would be no further accidents that week. Rusk wanted to know how important the overflights were for intelligence gathering; whether it was possible to limit intelligence gathering to peripheral flights over international waters; and, finally, whether there was anyone among those planning U-2 missions who wanted to provoke an incident. The secretary of state did not trust his CIA counterparts![4]

Rusk was the first to speak at the meeting called by Bundy on September 10. "Pat, don't you ever let me up?" he addressed General Carter. "How do you expect me to negotiate on Berlin with all these incidents?" Before Carter could say anything, Robert Kennedy, who apparently favored the continuation of overflights, responded to Rusk's question with a joke: "What's the matter, Dean, no guts?" But he had nothing to say about Rusk's main argument: Berlin seemed to be a much bigger and more urgent problem than Cuba. Rusk wanted to stop overflights of the island but agreed to flights over international waters.[5]

Looking for a compromise, Bundy suggested that U-2 flights over the island could continue, but not along its entire length. Instead they should cross it to avoid being tracked and shot down by surface-to-air missiles. Besides, it was suggested that the flights would not take place if at least 25 percent of the island was covered with clouds; otherwise, the risk of overflights would not be justified by the received results of photo shooting. Carter was anything but pleased and considered that only a temporary solution. He told the gathering; "I want to put you people on notice that it remains our intention to fly right up over those SAMs to see what is there." He got no response and complained after adjournment: "There they all go again and no decisions."[6]

McCone, his French honeymoon paradise turning into a political cage, was more than upset. The possibility of Soviet deployment of ballistic missiles weighed on his mind. On September 16 he cabled Carter: "[W]e must carefully study the prospect of secret importation and placement of several Soviet MRBMs which could not be detected by us if Cuban defenses deny overflight." McCone's warning made no impact. The overflights were not resumed until October 14, owing to the prohibition and bad weather. The Soviets received a gift of five weeks to deploy nuclear-armed missiles in Cuba without being watched by American airplanes. Khrushchev's gamble seemed to be paying off.[7]

◊◊◊

WITH MCCONE STILL TRYING TO ENJOY HIS HONEYMOON IN France, and little real intelligence to go on, even his own people in the CIA remained complacent with regard to the Soviet buildup in Cuba. The Special National Intelligence Estimate issued on September 19 was anything but alarmist. "We believe," wrote the authors, "that the USSR values its position in Cuba primarily for the political advantages to be derived from it, and consequently that the main purpose of the present military buildup in Cuba is to strengthen the Communist regime there." The authors of the estimate considered the possibility of future placement of Soviet nuclear missiles on the island but thought it unlikely at the moment. "It would indicate a far greater willingness to increase the level of risk in US-Soviet relations than the USSR has displayed thus far, and this would have important policy implications in other areas."[8]

The CIA analysts estimated that Soviet military personnel on Cuba did not exceed four thousand. They counted seventy Soviet ships that had dropped anchor in Cuban ports since mid-July, bringing to Cuba about a dozen MiG-21 jet interceptors, six guided-missile patrol boats, and missiles and equipment for twelve SAM sites that had been spotted on the island. The CIA turned out to be good at counting ships, not particularly good at counting armaments and equipment, and astoundingly bad at counting people. More than forty thousand Soviet servicemen were transported to Cuba between mid-July and mid-October 1962, most of them by mid-September, when the CIA estimate was prepared. Hiding in tween decks for most of their sea voyage to Cuba, they remained invisible to American planes, as were most of their missiles and equipment.[9]

In Cuba extraordinary security measures were taken to conceal the movement of Soviet missiles and equipment to localities chosen by Soviet commanders and their Cuban advisers. The Cuban military and police guarded the ports where Soviet ships unloaded their cargoes, including the S-75 Desna missiles, which were taken to their preselected locations at night. The missiles and their crews belonged to two antiaircraft divisions. Their overall command was executed by Lieutenant General Stepan Grechko, commander of the air defenses of the Moscow region. Each of the divisions under Grechko's command had three regiments, each consisting of four squadrons. Each squadron had one launching site with six launchers. Thus, between the two divisions, there were twenty-four launching sites and 144 launchers. The plan was to supply each launcher with four S-75 Desna missiles, 576 missiles altogether. According to a later CIA estimate, during the first week of August the construction of SAM sites began in locations near Matanzas, Havana, Mariel, Bahía Honda, Santa Lucia, San Julián, and La Coloma.[10]

The launch sites photographed by a U-2 plane on August 29 belonged to the eleventh antiaircraft division, formed in the Ukrainian city of Dnipropetrovsk and commanded by Major General Mikhail Tokarenko. Captain E. N. Evdokimov, deputy commander of one of the regiments of the division, later recalled: "All squadrons of the regiment took up their positions in the course of August." They "formed a defensive zone covering the western part of Cuba from the north; the duty of that group in battle was to protect the launch sites of the two R-12 missile divisions and the airfield where the IL-28 carrying nuclear weapons were based (San Julian)."[11]

The forty-three-year-old Tokarenko was a former pilot who had completed 465 missions during World War II, taken part in fifty battle encounters with enemy planes, and downed twenty of them. He was awarded the gold star medal of the Hero of the Soviet Union, the highest Soviet military decoration, in April 1945. Having assumed command of the antiaircraft division in Dnipropetrovsk in 1961, Tokarenko was eager to prove himself worthy of the appointment. It turned out that he was too eager for his own good. He would not survive in his position for even a few weeks, his crime being a cavalier attitude toward the secrecy of the mission.

On July 24, while visiting the Pinar del Río region on the western tip of Cuba to look for good locations for one of his launch sites, Tokarenko decided to reassure the Cuban officers there that the Soviet Union would not abandon their country. "Guys, don't worry, the Soviet people won't abandon Cuba in this period, when its fate is being threatened," declared Tokarenko. "Right now, as we speak with you, ships are already crossing the ocean with our troops, who will help you defend your independence." The statement made a strong impression on the Cubans, who were pleased to hear the news and discussed it among themselves. It also made a strong but unfavorable impression on General Pliev. The next day Tokarenko was relieved of his duties as division commander for disclosing a state secret. That would be the end of his military career. The Cuban officers who had heard his words were detained to preclude further dissemination of information about the coming Soviet buildup on the island.[12]

The Soviet cargo ships with the R-12 MRBMs that John McCone had been so concerned about during his French vacation and General Tokarenko implied were on their way to save Cuba, began arriving in Cuban ports during the last weeks of August. The first was the cargo ship *Omsk*, which had left Sevastopol harbor on August 5 and arrived in Casilda, a seaside village near the city of Trinidad in central Cuba, on August 19. On board were six R-12 missiles accompanied by the officers and men of Colonel Ivan Sidorov's 637th missile regiment. As the docks of the Casilda sugar factory could handle only one ship at a time, and there was nowhere to put the missiles and equipment for storage, Sidorov, his men, and their cargo had to stay on board the *Omsk* as it lay at anchor in Casilda harbor. According to Statsenko's later report, the *Omsk* and those R-12 missiles were finally unloaded on September 9. That day the first MRBM landed on Cuban soil.[13]

General Igor Statsenko, the commander of the missile division, was the first to greet Sidorov and his men in Cuba. He had arrived by air in the third week of July, and by the time Sidorov reached the island, Statsenko had got a suntan, grown a mustache, and, to many, looked like a Cuban. One of the planners of the Anadyr operation, General Anatoly Gribkov, who had met Statsenko before his departure for Cuba and then saw him in action in October, was impressed by his stature: "Young, smart, and dressed, like all the servicemen and officers, in civilian clothes: dark gray pants, short-sleeved check shirt. His flawless military bearing was a delight to see." Sidorov took an immediate liking to his new commander. "He was a life-loving, energetic and strong-willed general with fine organizational skills and sufficient experience of service in the missile forces," recalled Sidorov.[14]

Statsenko's first task was to organize the unloading of the missiles, equipment, and accompanying personnel. Even more than with the SAMs, the key concern with the MRBMs was to ensure the secrecy of the operation. Statsenko later wrote: "The missiles were unloaded from the ships only at night, with the ships and ports fully darkened. While the missiles were being unloaded, the external approaches to the ports were guarded by a specially designated mountain rifle battalion of three hundred men transferred from the Sierra Maestra region." That was not all. "Within the defensive perimeter of the ports, there were the personnel of newly arrived subunits and groups of strategic operational officers assigned by the staff," continued Statsenko. "Navy ships and cutters protected the seaward approaches to the ships that were being unloaded, as did specially vetted and selected fishermen from among the local Cuban population. Every two hours, specially selected divers checked the submerged parts of ships and the harbor bottom near the piers."[15]

Once the missiles were unloaded, Statsenko's next task was to bring them to their places of deployment. He was in a hurry. The discovery of the SAMs by U-2 airplanes forced Khrushchev and the General Staff to revise the missile deployment schedules, cutting time needed for the transportation and installation of the missiles. According to the new timetable, regiments such as Sidorov's with R-12 launchers were supposed to be combat-ready by November 1, while the R-14 intermediate ballistic missile regiments were to prepare for combat between November 1, 1962, and January 1, 1963. The problem was that the missiles and accompanying equipment only began to reach Cuba on September 9. The arrival of all personnel, missiles, and equipment of Sidorov's regiment, the first to come to the island, was not completed until the first weeks of October. The situation with other regiments was even worse.[16]

Transporting the missiles to designated areas sometimes two hundred kilometers distant from the ports of disembarkation created numerous security problems. The columns moved only at night, between midnight and 5:00 a.m. To keep the itineraries and destinations secret, reported Statsenko, "when routes were closed, imitation car accidents were staged, with the removal of the 'wounded,' as well as the 'maneuvers' of the Cuban army." As if that were not enough, "an hour or an hour and a half before the missile column set out on its itinerary, a specially formed column of Cuban trailers or heavy trucks was dispatched along false itineraries." The Soviet columns included dozens of vehicles. First came "the motorcyclists with radio equipment; a Cuban vehicle with an operational officer, interpreter, and guards; two light vehicles with the commanders of the column; and a security vehicle," wrote Statsenko. Only then did the "missiles and tractors, a crane, and extra tractors" follow. The procession ended with a "security vehicle with Cuban guards and motorcyclists with radio equipment." The Soviet officers and soldiers were dressed in Cuban uniforms and prohibited to speak Russian. They would communicate with one another with the help of a couple of memorized Spanish words and phrases.[17]

The task of delivering the R-12 missiles to their assigned stations created numerous logistical problems. More than 22 meters long, the missiles were transported by even longer trailers. Statsenko, who personally supervised the movement of the first regiment of his division, gave Colonel Sidorov one week to prepare the route for his missiles from Casilda to an area near Calabazar de Sagua, approximately 100 kilometers as the crow flies but twice as far along narrow Cuban roads. In some places Sidorov and his men reinforced the bridges; elsewhere they built entirely new roads. Hardest of all was navigating the narrow streets of Cuban towns along the route. "In the town of Caunao," recalled Sidorov, "there was a sharp right turn with a 30-degree incline. To obtain the requisite turning radius, it looked as if we would have to demolish a statue in honor of the first cosmonaut, Yurii Gagarin, and the three-story municipal building. There was no other way." Eventually he found the solution: the column passed the city in one direction without making the tricky turn, got onto another road outside the town, reentered the town from a different direction, and passed through it again with no need to take the turn and demolish two of the city's landmarks.[18]

By the end of September Statsenko and Sidorov had delivered the missiles and the rest of the equipment to the regiment's designated stations. Now they had to build the launchpads from scratch, a task even more difficult than unloading and transporting the missiles. The Soviet soldiers, accustomed to the hardships of Russian and East European winters, were completely unprepared to work in tropical conditions exacerbated by the arrival of hurricane season. Statsenko later complained about the timing of missile deployment chosen in Moscow: September and October were months of tropical storms and hurricanes. General Gribkov, one of the planners of the operation, realized how bad the situation was when he came to Cuba in October. "Because of the heat (temperatures reaching 35–40° C and more) and high humidity, the regimental commander decided to change crews every hour," recalled Gribkov, describing his visit to one of Statsenko's regiments. "The ground was rocky, and in such conditions engineering equipment was not very efficient, so most of the work was done by hand."[19]

Despite the unbearable heat and humidity, endless rain, and disease besieging the Soviet combat, General Statsenko ordered Sidorov to get his regiment ready for military duty by October 22, one week ahead of the deadline established by Pliev. Sidorov did his best not to disappoint his commander. "In a brief period," recalled Sidorov, "in exhausting conditions, the personnel . . . carried out a huge task: concrete monoliths with anchoring bolts were poured to a meter's depth beneath the launch pads; storehouses for nuclear warheads were built from prefabricated parts; twelve kilometers of gravel roads were built on site; more than 1,500 blasts of rock formations were carried out; storehouses, mess halls, and housing tents were built and equipped with services."[20]

The first of Sidorov's R-12 launchers was combat-ready on October 8, the second on October 12. By October 18, four days before Statsenko's deadline, the whole regiment was combat-ready. They were prepared to fire their missiles at ten hours' notice—the time required to deliver nuclear warheads to the launch sites. The first warheads were delivered to Cuba on October 4, when the cargo ship *Indigirka* brought sixty nuclear charges for R-12 and R-14 missiles to Mariel, 40 kilometers west of Havana.[21]

◊◊◊

IN HIS HONEYMOON CAGE ON THE FRENCH RIVIERA, THE CIA chief John McCone was growing ever more furious with the lack of new intelligence on the Soviet buildup in Cuba. He was extremely unhappy with his deputy, General Carter, and considered firing him. McCone believed that Carter had mishandled the Cuban situation during his absence: he had not taken the initiative to share his cables with the White House—McCone had never instructed him to do so; he had not stood up to Rusk, whose opposition to U-2 overflights had led to their suspension; and, last but not least, he had approved the Special National Intelligence Estimate of September 19, which suggested that the Soviets would not deploy their missiles in Cuba.[22]

McCone returned to DC on September 26 to the news that a CIA source had spotted a Soviet R-12 ballistic missile (SS-4 Sandal in the American classification) being transported on Cuban roads on September 12. Now he had more reason for concern than ever before. His subordinates were picking up information from Cuban refugees about the extraordinary measures of precaution and secrecy taken by the Cuban police and military to conceal the arrival and deployment of the Soviet military units. The CIA officers were duly putting that information on their maps, but without the U-2 overflights along the entire length of the island there was no way to check the information and assess the scope and the nature of the Soviet buildup.

On October 9, McCone went to see John Kennedy. In attendance were Robert Kennedy, McGeorge Bundy, and other presidential advisers. Together with Deputy Secretary of Defense Roswell Gilpatric, McCone submitted a recommendation to resume the program of overflights of Cuba. Peripheral overflights of Cuba could neither confirm nor disprove the information coming from CIA sources on the ground. McCone needed the resumption of flights over the island itself and was particularly interested in the situation in western Cuba, where the first SAMs had been spotted and which peripheral flights could not reach with their cameras. The U-2 planes were to check the accuracy of reports on the sighting of R-12 MRBMs and assess the readiness of the SAM sites that previous overflights had shown to be under construction in late August and early September.[23]

It had been more than a month since the last U-2 overflight of Cuba on September 5, and the pressure on Kennedy to authorize a new U-2 mission was growing. He and his advisers knew that flying over the SAM sites was a dangerous undertaking. The chances of a U-2 being shot down were assessed at one in six. As no one believed that the administration could risk having a CIA pilot captured, Secretary of Defense Robert McNamara proposed that CIA pilots be replaced with Air Force pilots: in case a U-2 plane was shot down and the pilot captured, he would say that he had been on a peripheral flight over international waters (the operation conducted by the US Air Force) and simply lost his way.[24]

Kennedy made his decision on October 10. It took another three days to train an Air Force pilot to fly a CIA U-2C plane and then for the weather to clear and make possible the dangerous flight over known SAM sites. Mission 3101, as the overflight of the San Cristóbal area was designated by the CIA, was entrusted to Major Richard S. Heyser, a thirty-five-year-old veteran of the Korean War. Heyser, who served with the 4028th Strategic Reconnaissance Squadron of the 4080th Strategic Reconnaissance Wing, took off from Edwards Air Force Base in California at 11:30 p.m. on October 13. His ultimate destination was McCoy Air Force Base in central Florida, but he would get there only after overflying western Cuba. It was supposed to be a seven-hour flight, only seven minutes of which the pilot would spend over Cuba.

Major Heyser entered Cuban airspace at 7:30 a.m. October 14 at an altitude of 72,500 feet and switched on his camera, which was capable of capturing an area up to one hundred nautical miles wide beneath the plane. Everything went as planned. No missiles were fired from below, and the SAM sites, whether ready or not, remained silent. Heyser landed at McCoy Air Force Base at 9:20 a.m. ET on Sunday, October 14. His film was flown immediately to Andrews Air Force Base near Washington, DC. It then went for development at the Naval Photographic Intelligence Center. CIA experts at the National Photographic Interpretation Center in Maryland received the film on Monday, October 15. They would begin the week with a startling discovery: John McCone had been right all along—the Soviets had deployed MRBMs on the island.[25]

11

"WIPE THEM OUT"

Tuesday, October 16, began for John Kennedy like any other day, reading newspapers. He had a habit of doing that first thing in the morning, while still in bed. That morning he could not miss the lead article in the *New York Times* covering the reception he had given Ahmed Ben Bella, the prime minister of newly independent Algeria. The article was accompanied by the photo of Jackie Kennedy and the president's twenty-two-month-old son, John Jr., watching the ceremony and a twenty-one-gun salute from behind the bushes of the White House Rose Garden. Ben Bella, released from a French prison slightly more than three months earlier, had come to the White House to discuss bilateral relations and thank Kennedy for his support of his country's anticolonial struggle. He did so publicly, and the coverage was good for Kennedy.[1]

Also quite favorable was the coverage in the *Washington Post*, whose reporter wrote that "the president disabused Ben Bella of any ambitions that he might serve as a mediator between the United States and Cuba." In fact, knowing that Ben Bella's next stop after Washington would be Havana, Kennedy tried to use him to pass a message to Castro. He told the Algerian leader that he was prepared to make peace with the "national communist" regime in Cuba as long as Castro did not try to challenge the status quo in Latin America. When Ben Bella asked whether Kennedy had in mind a regime like those in Yugoslavia or Poland, Kennedy responded in the affirmative. He also told Ben Bella what was unacceptable to his administration: the transformation of Cuba into a Soviet military base armed with offensive weapons, and efforts to spread communist revolution in the rest of Latin America. Kennedy was offering Castro a deal without saying so openly.[2]

But anyone who looked at the front page of the New York Times that morning realized that Kennedy's room for maneuver on Cuba was limited. He was under growing pressure to act against the Castro regime. "Eisenhower Calls President Weak on Foreign Policy," went the headline of a report on Eisenhower's address at a Republican dinner in Kennedy's stronghold of Boston. The former president, who had hitherto kept his criticism of Kennedy and his administration to himself, broke the unwritten rule of not criticizing his successor and rejected Kennedy's earlier assertion that his administration had ignored Latin America for eight years. "In those eight years we lost no inch of ground to tyranny," wrote the Times, quoting Eisenhower. "We witnessed no abdication of international responsibility. We accepted no compromise of pledged word or withdrawal from principle. No walls were built, no threatening foreign bases were established."[3]

The reference to the wall was a dig at Kennedy's tacit acceptance of the Berlin Wall. The reference to military bases was a clear hint at Cuba. Anyone who followed media coverage of the growing Cuban controversy knew that Kenneth Keating, Republican senator from New York, was claiming day in and day out that there were in fact nuclear-armed missiles in Cuba and that the administration was doing nothing to deal with the threat. It did not look good for the president. The 1962 congressional elections were getting into high gear, and the Republicans had enlisted the most powerful weapon in their arsenal, the former president. He toured the country endorsing Republican candidates for Congress and attacking Democratic ones, including Jack Kennedy's youngest brother, Edward, who was running for the Senate. The dinner at which Eisenhower lashed out at Kennedy was attended by six thousand people, the speech was televised, and now the media was giving it extensive coverage.[4]

◊◊◊

McGEORGE BUNDY FOUND KENNEDY MORE THAN DISTRESSED by Eisenhower's statement when he showed up in his bedroom sometime after 8:00 a.m. The national security adviser had no comforting news to share. "Mr. President, there is now hard photographic evidence that the Russians have offensive missiles in Cuba," he told Kennedy. The U-2 overflight of Cuba authorized by Kennedy a few days earlier had revealed the installation in Cuba of surface-to-surface ballistic missiles capable of reaching most of the eastern United States. Bundy had received the news the previous night but decided not to disturb Kennedy, giving him the opportunity to get a good sleep after an exhausting day that included not only the reception of Ben Bella but also campaigning.[5]

Kennedy felt betrayed. "He can't do this to me," said the president to Bundy, meaning Khrushchev. The Soviet leader had broken his public word not to place offensive weapons on Cuba and his private assurances that he would do nothing to upset Soviet-American relations before the November congressional elections. Kennedy called Khrushchev a "fucking liar" and an "immoral gangster" when he met his brother later that day. In September the Soviet ambassador to the United States, Anatoly Dobrynin, had assured the White House on Khrushchev's orders that there would be no escalation over Berlin. On October 4 and 6— only a week before the unexpected news of the missiles reached John Kennedy—Robert Kennedy met with his Soviet contact, the military intelligence officer Georgii Bolshakov, who had visited Khrushchev in Pitsunda in mid-September. Bolshakov recited by heart Khrushchev's new message: no aggravation before the November elections.[6]

Kennedy asked Bundy to summon his key foreign policy advisers to the White House close to lunchtime, the first opening in his busy schedule for the day. As he began the succession of long-scheduled meetings and ceremonial functions, it seemed to him that it was the beginning of the end of his presidency. It looked as if Eisenhower and Republicans such as Senator Keating had been right all along. "You still think the fuss about Cuba is unimportant?" Kennedy asked his appointments secretary and confidant Kenneth O'Donnell during a break between his morning meetings. "Absolutely," responded O'Donnell. "The voters won't give a damn about Cuba." When Kennedy shared the news of the missiles, O'Donnell was incredulous. 'I don't believe it," he told the president. "You better believe it," Kennedy fired back. "Ken Keating will probably be the next president of the United States."[7]

The meeting of top foreign policy and security advisers called to assess the new intelligence information on Cuba and advise the president on a course of action began in the Cabinet Room of the West Wing at 11:50 a.m. Around the table, apart from the president himself, were Bobby Kennedy, McGeorge Bundy, Robert McNamara, Dean Rusk, and top figures from the State and Defense departments. John McCone, the CIA director, who had missed key meetings on Cuba in September, was absent again, and once again the cause of his absence had to do with his new family. His wife's son by her first marriage, and now his stepson, had died in a race-car crash, and McCone had to attend the funeral. He would be back in DC the next day, but for now the CIA was represented by McCone's deputy, General Marshall Carter.[8]

"There's a medium-range ballistic missile launch site," said Carter, who began his presentation by showing the president a U-2 photo. His words were saved for posterity by the secret recording system that Kennedy had installed in his Cabinet Room and had now activated. He had begun taping meetings with his advisers in the late summer of 1961. The top-secret project was probably launched with an eye to helping the president keep track of his decisions and advice given by others, as well as the possible preparation of another autobiographical book.

"How do you know this is a medium-range ballistic missile?" Kennedy asked those present at the meeting. "The length, Sir," answered Arthur Lundahl, the founding director of the National Photographic Interpretation Center, who was assisting Carter with the presentation. His photogrammetrist had measured the photos with special equipment the previous day and concluded that the missiles were approximately 65 feet long.[9]

Lundahl's other aide, Sidney Graybeal, showed the president pictures of Soviet ballistic missiles photographed at a military parade in Moscow. Graybeal, a former pilot who had flown thirty-two combat missions during World War II and joined the CIA after the war to become a guided-missiles intelligence analyst, knew more about the Soviet missiles than anyone else in the room. He explained to the president that medium-range Soviet missiles with a 630-mile range were 67 feet long, while intermediate-range missiles with a range of 1,100 miles were 73 feet long. Those spotted by the U-2 were approximately 67 feet long, indicating medium-range missiles. But if they had been photographed without their 4- or 5-foot nose cones, explained Graybeal, then they might well be intermediate-range missiles. Everyone in the room who bothered to do the calculation and look at the map had reason to worry. Intermediate-range missiles could reach not only Washington and New York but also Boston, Chicago, and Denver.

"Is this ready to be fired?" was Kennedy's next question, referring to the photos just shown to him. Graybeal told the president that the missiles under discussion were not yet combat-ready. Only one missile had been photographed at a launch site. He could not locate fenced areas near launch sites, which would be expected if the Soviets had already delivered nuclear warheads. Probed by those present at the meeting, Graybeal admitted that if everything were in place, it would take the Soviets "in the order of two to three hours before they could get that one missile up and ready to go." Kennedy wanted to know more about the missiles and their readiness. He authorized additional U-2 flights, but that was not enough. Neither he nor the others in the room thought that they could simply bide their time under the circumstances. They had to come up with a plan of action.[10]

Kennedy asked Dean Rusk, who had produced the first draft of the president's statement on the discovery of the SAM sites in early September, to share his thoughts. Rusk, who had been informed about the results of the U-2 flights the previous evening, even before the news was broken to the president, had clearly given the issue a lot of thought and was now ready to propose two possible scenarios. "I do think that we have to set in motion a chain of events that will eliminate this base," began Rusk. "The question then becomes whether we do that by a sudden, unannounced strike of some sort, or we build up the crisis to the point where the other side has to consider very seriously about giving in, or even Cubans themselves take some action on this." Rusk had set the agenda for the discussion for hours and days to come. There was an unspoken agreement in the room that the missiles had to go, no matter what. The question now was whether to give priority to diplomacy or military action.

Rusk believed that a strike was justified if the military situation did not allow time for diplomacy. The strike could be executed on its own or as part of an invasion of the island. But if time allowed, Rusk favored diplomacy, which would include informing if not consulting with US allies in Europe as well as Latin American clients and partners. He was also in favor of approaching Castro and pointing out to him that Khrushchev had victimized Cuba by putting ballistic missiles on the island and opening it to American intervention. He also wanted to let Khrushchev know that "there is an utterly serious crisis in the making here." He added: "Mr. Khrushchev may not himself really understand that or believe that at this point."[11]

As the discussion moved into the evaluation of pros and cons of the options proposed by Rusk, Kennedy wondered how much time he had to decide on a course of action before the information about the discovery of the missiles was leaked to the media or to his opponents in Congress. Secretary of Defense Robert McNamara gave the president one week: "[W]e should assume that this will become fairly widely known, if not in the newspapers, at least by political representatives of both parties." Rusk was in agreement: Senator Keating had already been talking about the construction of intermediate-missile launch sites on October 10. Presumably, he had obtained his information from Cuban refugees.[12] Shockingly, the time frame for the decision was decided not on the basis of how soon the Soviets would be able to make their missiles operational, but on the assumption of how long the news could be kept secret.

Whether the time frame was one week or two, Kennedy could not count on having much time before he had to act. But what action should he take? As the discussion progressed, Rusk's two options, strike and diplomacy, turned in Kennedy's mind into four: a surgical air strike against ballistic missiles; a general air strike against all types of missiles and the Soviet air force on the island; a general air strike accompanied by a naval blockade of the island; and, finally, diplomacy. Robert Kennedy immediately reminded his brother of a fifth option—the invasion of Cuba. Now there were five options altogether, and only one of them was diplomatic.

John Kennedy clearly did not think much of diplomacy. In the past, Richard Nixon had suggested that Kennedy was incapable of standing up to Khrushchev. After the Vienna summit, Kennedy assumed that Khrushchev himself was of the same opinion, considering him "stupid" and having "no guts." "If he thinks I'm inexperienced and have no guts, until we remove those ideas we won't get anywhere with him," Kennedy told a sympathetic reporter after the summit. The news about the Soviet MRBMs on Cuba suggested that Kennedy had to do something drastic about the perception that he was a weak president.[13]

Kennedy assumed that appealing to Khrushchev might prompt the Soviets to speed up preparations for a nuclear strike. NATO allies would be of little help but might raise objections against a US attack on Soviet missile installations in Cuba: the Europeans had lived under the threat of Soviet missiles for years and would probably think of such an attack as making them vulnerable to Soviet retaliation. "I expect they'll just object," Kennedy told the gathering about the British. "Just have to decide to do it. Probably ought to tell them, though, the night before."[14]

Closer to the end of the meeting, Kennedy summarized all available options once again, but his own list had been reduced to two—a surgical strike against the missiles and a general strike. "I don't think we've got much time on these missiles," Kennedy told his advisers. "We can't wait two weeks while we're getting ready to roll." That was the time required to prepare an all-out invasion of the island. Kennedy's preferred solution was a surgical strike. "Maybe we just have to take them out and continue our other preparations if we decide to do that," suggested the president. He later added, with more conviction: "We're certainly going to [do] number one." He had in mind a surgical strike. It was up to him to show resolve and respond to Khrushchev before the information was leaked to Congress. He certainly did not want Kenneth Keating to become the next president of the United States.[15]

Rushing to his next appointment, lunch with the crown prince of Libya, Hasan Al Rida Al Sansusi, Kennedy told his advisers to be back at 6:00 p.m. to continue the discussion. "I just hate to even waste these six hours," one can hear the president saying on the secretly made tape of the conversations just before the meeting broke up.[16]

◊◊◊

KENNEDY HAD LEFT THE LATE-MORNING MEETING ON CUBA convinced that he had to use military force. That conviction stayed with him for the rest of the day. At lunch with Al Rida Al Sansusi, Kennedy told Adlai Stevenson, his representative at the United Nations, "I suppose the alternatives are to go in by air and wipe them out or to take other steps to render the weapons inoperable." Stevenson urged the president to "explore the possibilities of the peaceful solution" before deciding on an air strike, but Kennedy was not responsive. Robert Kennedy, who could read his brother's mind better than anyone else, believed that he was leaning toward a military solution to the crisis and said as much to the CIA group that was running clandestine operations against Cuba; he met with them in the afternoon.[17]

Throughout the day, Kennedy kept struggling to understand why Khrushchev had decided to do what he did, but could not find an answer. "We certainly have been wrong about what he's trying to do in Cuba," he told his advisers when they began their evening meeting on the rapidly evolving crisis. General Maxwell D. Taylor, the sixty-year-old chairman of the Joint Chiefs of Staff, whom Kennedy had first asked to lead a group investigating the Bay of Pigs disaster and then appointed to the position held earlier by General Lyman Lemnitzer, stressed the psychological impact the Soviet missiles in Cuba would have on the Americans. His chiefs of staff argued that the Soviet missiles in Cuba would significantly change the strategic balance. But McNamara was skeptical. He personally believed that they would not change it at all. "I agree, what difference does it make?" said Kennedy in reaction to McNamara's suggestion. "They have got enough to blow us up anyway."[18]

Kennedy's mind kept returning to that question as the discussion moved on. A few minutes later he asked again: "If it doesn't increase very much their strategic strength, why is it—can any Russian expert tell us—why they?" Without finishing his question, Kennedy continued: "[I]t's just as if we suddenly began to put a major number of MRBMs in Turkey. Now that'd be goddam dangerous, I would think." Undersecretary of State Alexis Johnson interjected a sobering remark: "We did it." Kennedy was unimpressed: "Yeah, but it was five years ago." But Johnson would not give up. "That's when we were short on ICBMs," he told Kennedy. Unknowingly, he pointed at one of the key factors that motivated Khrushchev's actions in Cuba: his lack of long-range intercontinental missiles. But no one continued that line of argument. Kennedy in particular failed to draw the parallel between the Soviet Union and the United States a few years earlier. "But that was a different period then," he told his advisers.[19]

Whatever Khrushchev's motivations were, Kennedy was determined to show the country and the world that he was not a "weak" president, as Eisenhower had suggested, and eliminate the threat to the country. The military solution Kennedy preferred was a surprise surgical strike on the Soviet missiles in Cuba. Unexpectedly, that evening Kennedy's proposal to execute a surgical strike met with united opposition from the most unlikely allies: the State Department, the Department of Defense, and the Joint Chiefs of Staff. The competition between the departments of Defense and State that had characterized much of American history in the twentieth century was simply absent. McNamara and Rusk disliked the president's choice for different reasons. If Rusk, backed by Bundy, wanted to give diplomacy a chance, McNamara was concerned about the effectiveness of the strike, and the chiefs believed that a strike could put the Soviets on alert, complicating the invasion of the island.

McNamara presented his opposition to the president's plan at the very first meeting of the group. He was in favor of a strike only if the Soviet missiles were not yet operational. "Because, *if* they become operational *before* the air strike," argued McNamara during the late-morning session with Kennedy, "I do not believe we can state we can knock them out before they can be launched. And if they're launched there is almost certain to be chaos in part of the East Coast or the area in the radius of 600 to 1000 miles from Cuba." The military shared McNamara's concerns. "The Chiefs are strong in their recommendation against that kind of an attack, believing that it would leave too great a capability undestroyed," McNamara told the president during the evening session. General Taylor added that in the opinion of the chiefs "it would be a mistake to take this very narrow, selective target because it invited reprisal attacks and it may be detrimental." That afternoon, the Joint Chiefs of Staff agreed at their meeting to push for an invasion whether the Soviets had operational nuclear weapons on the island or not.[20]

McNamara disliked Kennedy's surgical strike option but was also critical of the diplomatic option proposed by Rusk, as it would give the Soviets time to build up their nuclear capabilities on the island and prepare for a possible invasion, which he believed could start a nuclear war. He proposed a new course instead: to impose a naval blockade on the island. Rusk's original plan, which he proposed that morning, envisioned a blockade as part of the general strike option, but now McNamara proposed to decouple them. He wanted to issue a statement with the following message: "[W]e would immediately impose a blockade against offensive weapons entering Cuba in the future and indicate that, with our open surveillance reconnaissance which we would plan to maintain indefinitely into the future, we would be immediately prepared to attack the Soviet Union in the event that Cuba made an offensive move against this country."[21]

McNamara's proposal caught many by surprise. It looked as if he were bringing the possibility of nuclear war closer instead of warding it off. "Attack who?" asked Bundy. "The Soviet Union," responded McNamara. He added that his third way "lies short of military action against Cuba." Kennedy was skeptical. On the one hand, he assumed that the proposed statement "would secure a good deal of political support" and "would put the burden on the Soviets." On the other hand, it would complicate the conduct of a military operation. "We would lose all the advantages of our strike," observed Kennedy. He was committed to the strike and had serious reservations about any warning to Khrushchev, public or private. Kennedy thought that he had already warned him once and saw no benefit in doing so again.[22]

The blockade option did not pass. Not only Robert Kennedy but also Bundy, who was usually supportive of McNamara, questioned how the blockade would be implemented and whether one would have to shoot to stop a Soviet ship if the captain refused to submit it to inspection. McNamara was for shooting. This looked like a delayed military action that would be aimed not only against missiles but also against Soviet ships in international waters. McNamara continued to argue his case. His solution was surveillance of the island and a naval blockade to prevent the arrival of any new offensive weapons, as well as the threat of an attack not on Cuba but on the Soviet Union itself if preparations were made to launch the missiles.

McNamara's attempt to gain supporters failed. "I do not think there is a military problem there," argued the secretary of defense. As Bundy expressed his agreement with that statement, McNamara continued: "This is a domestic political problem. In the announcement we did not say we'd go in and not [that] we'd kill them. We said we'd act." He was referring to the statement issued by Kennedy on September 4 and presented the introduction of the blockade as an action promised by the statement. General Carter of the CIA was among the skeptics: "Well, as far as the American people are concerned, action means military action, period." "Well, we have a blockade," responded McNamara. "Search and removal of offensive weapons entering Cuba." Carter was not impressed. "I think it's an alternative," he told McNamara, keeping the blockade apart from the military action but signaling his readiness to consider it. "I think it's a perfect solution by many means," replied the adamant McNamara.[23]

Kennedy held fast to his original idea of ordering a strike against the missile sites but still had some time to arrive at a final decision. A surgical strike was a military solution to his political problem. "[T]his is a political struggle as much as military," he told his advisers that evening. He agreed with McNamara that the missiles did not change the military balance, but politically he felt himself in a bind. "Last month I said we were not going 'to allow it.' Last month I should have said we don't care. But when we said we're *not* going to, and then they go ahead and do it, and then we do nothing, then I would think that our risks increase." He felt that he needed to act decisively.[24]

In the past, every time Kennedy was bullied, outmaneuvered, or defeated by Khrushchev in their personal meetings, as at Vienna in June 1960, he would strike back by asking Congress either to increase the defense budget or to call up reservists, or both. He was overcompensating at home for diplomatic defeats abroad, not only to warn Khrushchev but also to protect himself politically in his own country. He was strengthening the American military and sending threatening signals to his nemesis. But this time was different. Kennedy felt that he had to use force. His brother Robert Kennedy was even more radical. He proposed a staged attack on the American base at Guantánamo Bay or the sinking of an American ship to justify the invasion, urging the group to go for invasion even if that incurred the possibility of a general war. Robert urged the rest "just to get into it and get it over with and take our losses."[25]

◊◊◊

THE MEETING ENDED WITHOUT REACHING A DECISION. ROBert Kennedy counted eleven participants in the discussion favoring a blockade and seven advocating a strike. The latter group actually included nine people, if one counted the president and Robert Kennedy himself. Still, there was no consensus and no recommendation to the president. Rusk would go back to the State Department to resume meetings with his staff there. McNamara went to the Pentagon, where he would spend the first night of the crisis. John Kennedy went to a dinner in honor of his departing "Russia hand" Charles Bohlen, who was leaving for an ambassadorial appointment in Paris. Kennedy tried to convince Bohlen not to go, as he valued the latter's expertise, but Bohlen believed that a reversal of course would only raise unwanted questions and speculation. Both men were determined to keep the unfolding Soviet crisis secret from the media as long as possible.[26]

What neither Kennedy nor his advisers knew or could imagine at the time was that Soviet ballistic missiles were already combat-ready. Nuclear warheads for two of Colonel Sidorov's launch sites had been delivered ten days earlier. It was more than likely that a strike against the ballistic missiles sites in Cuba would have provoked the Soviet use of nuclear weapons. The General Staff in Moscow had a draft order ready to be signed allowing Soviet commanders in Cuba to use tactical nuclear weapons, which had arrived in Cuba as well, if they were attacked. The nuclear war that Kennedy was so desperate to avoid would have broken out almost immediately if his strike plan had been carried out. Luckily, he decided to take a pause.

12

QUARANTINE

On Saturday, October 20, it looked as if some unknown virus had hit the entire leadership of the United States. President Kennedy interrupted his three-day, five-state campaign trip in the Midwest, where he was speaking in support of Democratic candidates to Congress, because of a cold. He was returning to the capital. Vice President Lyndon Johnson cut short his stay in Honolulu and headed back to Washington, also citing a cold.

The White House press secretary, Pierre Salinger, broke the news to reporters about Kennedy's change of plans as they boarded a bus at the Sheraton-Blackstone Hotel in Chicago to follow the president to his next campaign stop in Milwaukee. He told the reporters that the president had developed a "slight upper respiratory infection" and was taking "normal medication for a cold, aspirins and antihistamines." His body temperature was allegedly one degree above normal. The reporters were incredulous: Kennedy looked normal. Pierre Salinger was equally suspicious and decided not to return on the press plane but to join the president on Air Force One. "Mr. President, you do not have a cold.

Something strange is happening," he said to Kennedy when they were alone. "The minute you get back in Washington, you are going to find out what it is," responded Kennedy. "And when you do, grab your balls."[1]

Robert Kennedy later recalled that he had phoned his brother before 10:00 a.m. to request his return to Washington. He believed that the discussions held by Kennedy aides with and without the president on October 16 had run their course, and the president had to make his final decision on which way to go with regard to Cuba. "It was now up to one single man," wrote Bobby. "No committee was going to make this decision." Upon receiving his brother's call, John Kennedy rushed back to Washington. Unbeknownst to him, he was flying right into the zone now covered by the Soviet missiles in Cuba. As his plane was in the air, the first Soviet R-12 medium-range missiles were being made fully operational near Sagua la Grande in western Cuba.[2]

Colonel Ivan Sidorov and his men of the 79th Missile Regiment celebrated their first victory with a small rally. "We will defend Cuba as our Motherland," read a slogan hanging over the makeshift podium made of a few sacks of soil brought from the Soviet Union. Next to the podium they placed a red-and-white-striped pole symbolizing a Soviet border post. The speeches were met with applause, gunfire, and slogans in Russian and Spanish: *Rodina ili smert'*—*Patria o muerte.* "Motherland or death." The Soviet rocket men had just found a new motherland. They were prepared to die for it and spread death in the process. Given the R-12's operational range of 2,080 kilometers, Sidorov's missiles would have fallen short of Chicago (2,233 kilometers away) but could easily have reached the DC area, only 1,812 kilometers away, where the president's plane would land in the early afternoon.[3]

◊◊◊

THE PRESIDENT HAD LEFT WASHINGTON ON THE MORNING OF Friday, October 19. He had spent the previous day in and out of sessions with his advisers, brainstorming the Cuban problem. They dealt with a new batch of disturbing news. Its bearer, as before, was the CIA imagery intelligence expert Arthur Lundahl, who had presented the U-2 photographs to Kennedy two days earlier.

Shortly after 11:00 a.m. on October 18, Lundahl told the president and his advisers that a U-2 camera had detected a launch complex approximately 20 miles southwest of Havana. Its presence suggested the deployment of intermediate-range ballistic missiles (IRBMs) whose range was roughly twice that of the previously spotted MRBMs. "We have never identified, irrevocably, the signature of the Soviet intermediate range ballistic missile, which is estimatedly a 2,000 mile missile," declared Lundahl. "But the elongation of the pads and location of the control bunkers, between each pair of pads, has been the thing that suggested to our hearts, if not our minds, the kind of thing that might accompany an IRBM." Whatever was preoccupying the minds of those present, Lundahl's information was grim enough to make their hearts sink. Lundahl told Kennedy: "[T]he orientation of the axis of the pads, 315 [degrees] . . . will bring you into the central massif of the United States."[4]

The news that the Soviets were bringing to Cuba intermediate-range missiles covering the better part of the United States strengthened John Kennedy's advocacy of an unannounced strike on the Soviet missile installations. He had taken that position during the first day of the crisis. "President seemed inclined to act promptly if at all, without warning, targeting on MRBM's and possible airfields," wrote McCone in his note on the meeting with Kennedy that day. "Stated Congressional resolutions gave him all authority he needed, and this was confirmed by Bundy, and therefore seemed inclined to act."[5]

Lundahl's report had a profound impact on those in the room. Dean Rusk, who had earlier opposed Kennedy's surgical strike option, was now ready to join the president: "I think this changes my thinking on the matter," said Rusk before declaring himself in favor of the strike. But he wanted it to be preceded by a warning. "We all of course remember *The Guns of August*, where certain events brought about a general situation which at the time none of the governments involved really wanted," remarked Rusk, referring to Barbara Tuchman's examination of Europe's sleepwalking into World War I. He knew about Kennedy's fascination with the book and clearly wanted to get the president on his side. "There is a possibility, only a possibility," continued Rusk, "that Mr. Khrushchev might realize that he's got to back down on this."[6]

The reference to Tuchman's book failed to sway Kennedy. He was as committed to the idea of an unannounced strike as he had been the previous day, when McCone visited him in the White House. He was also less than enthusiastic about approaching Khrushchev, whom he expected to respond to the warning with a warning of his own: "[I]f you take them out, we are going to take Berlin" or "We are going to do something else." Kennedy believed that striking first and negotiating second was a better alternative. But he could not stop thinking about Berlin and the impact that Khrushchev's actions there would have on America's European allies. "If he grabs Berlin," remarked Kennedy, "everybody would feel we lost Berlin, because of these missiles, which I say, do not bother them." "What do we do when he moves into Berlin?" asked Robert Kennedy. Bundy, who had had more than enough trouble with Berlin in the previous few months, suggested with a chuckle that it would be good to trade it off "and not have it our fault."

That was clearly an impossibility. "We have US troops there. What do they do?" remarked McNamara. "They fight," responded General Taylor. "And they get overrun," joined in John Kennedy. "It's then general war," said one of the participants, continuing that line of thinking. "You mean nuclear exchange?" inquired Kennedy. Rusk, for once, was not advocating diplomacy. "You would have to start at least with tactical nuclear weapons," he told the president. "The question really is to what [degree] action we take lessens the chances of a nuclear exchange, which obviously is the final failure. And at the same time, maintain some degree of solidarity with our allies," said Kennedy, drawing a line under that part of the discussion.[7]

◊◊◊

THE SITUATION LOOKED GRIM WHEN JOHN KENNEDY LEFT his advisers for lunch and returned to his prearranged schedule. It happened to include a meeting that might dramatically alter the course of the rapidly expanding Cuban missile crisis: the White House was about to be visited by no less a figure than the Soviet foreign minister, Andrei Gromyko.

Gromyko was visiting the United Nations and made a stopover in the American capital. Khrushchev and his colleagues in the Presidium wanted Gromyko to feel Kennedy out and try to predict his possible reaction to the impending Soviet announcement, to be made after the congressional elections, of the placement of missiles in Cuba. John McCone had a different agenda for Kennedy. In the memorandum he had submitted to the president the previous day, he warned him that "the United States should not act without warning and thus be forced to live with a 'Pearl Harbor indictment' for the indefinite future." He wanted Kennedy to "notify Gromyko and Castro that we know all about this" and "give them 24 hours to commence dismantling and removal of MRBMs, coastal defense missiles, surface to air missiles, IL 28s and all other aircraft which have a dual defensive-offensive capability, including MIG 21s."[8]

Kennedy met with Gromyko in the presence of Rusk, and they did not follow McCone's advice. Kennedy was still in favor of an attack without warning, while Rusk believed that it was premature to mention anything to Gromyko before the internal deliberations were over and the president had made up his mind. One way or another, Kennedy and Rusk remained silent about the missiles. Gromyko, for his part, acted as if the missiles did not exist. His main topic was Berlin, where he threatened escalation after the November elections. On Cuba, he attacked the United States for old-fashioned imperialism. He admitted that the Soviets had supplied weapons and trained Cubans in their use. Gromyko referred to the weapons delivered by the Soviets as "defensive," thereby contradicting Kennedy's description of them earlier in the conversation as "offensive" weapons. By this logic, if the Soviet ballistic missiles were to be used to defend Cuba, then they were not "offensive" weapons, as Kennedy had referred to them in his statement of September 11. With this diplomatic legerdemain, Gromyko was seeking to assert that the Kennedy administration could have no legitimate objection to the Soviet weapons deployed on the island.

"President Kennedy listened astonished, but also with some admiration for the boldness of Gromyko's position," wrote Robert Kennedy in his account of the crisis. Kennedy was silent on the missiles but said that he had been prepared to give assurances that there would be no invasion of Cuba. However, the Soviet shipments of arms to the island, beginning in July, had changed the situation. Kennedy called it "the most dangerous situation since the end of the war." Gromyko wrote in his memoirs that Kennedy kept talking about the "offensive weapons," and never asked him about the missiles. "Mr. President," he was supposed to tell Kennedy if confronted with the missile question, "the Soviet Union delivered to Cuba a limited number of missiles of the defensive character. They will never threaten anybody." But Kennedy never asked the feared question. "There was no need for me to say whether there were any or not," recalled Gromyko.[9]

Gromyko noticed the change in Kennedy's tone, finding him nervous and Rusk unusually tense, but failed to attribute the rising tension to the discovery of the missiles. Anatoly Dobrynin, the Soviet ambassador in Washington, remembered later that Gromyko was pleased with its outcome. "He was completely misled by Kennedy's conduct," wrote the ambassador in his memoirs. When he filed his report about the meeting with Kennedy, Gromyko wrote that public support for the invasion of Cuba was fading, while the media were paying more and more attention to Berlin. He did not see any signs of an imminent invasion. "Everything we know about the U.S. position on Cuba," wrote Gromyko, "permits the conclusion that the situation is in general wholly satisfactory."[10]

The meeting with Gromyko, which began at 5:00 p.m., ended after 7:15. Throughout the day, Kennedy heard reports from his Cuban advisory team on the meetings that they had conducted in smaller groups. At 9:15 p.m. he called them all into the White House to assess the situation. While Kennedy himself continued to favor a surgical strike, the momentum for that solution, which had developed in response to news about the Soviet IRBM launch sites in Cuba, had been lost. "During the course of the day, opinions had obviously switched from the advantages of a first strike on the missile sites and on Cuban aviation to a block-ade," dictated Kennedy into a microphone when the meeting was over. After recounting the positions taken by his advisers, he remarked: "The consensus was that we should go ahead with the blockade beginning on Sunday night."[11]

McNamara's old idea of a navy blockade was listed as one of the options in the memorandum that McCone had prepared for the presi-dent. It was reintroduced in the morning discussion with the president by Llewellyn Thompson, the former ambassador to Moscow, whom Kennedy had invited to participate in the deliberations. Thompson was critical of Rusk's idea of issuing a warning: as Kennedy had implied, that would give Khrushchev an opportunity to threaten American mis-siles in Turkey and Italy. But he also did not like the president's strike-without-warning option. "If you do this first strike, you would have killed a lot of Russians," remarked Thompson. "What is your prefer-ence, Tommy?" asked the bewildered Bundy, since the ambassador seemed to be offering nothing but criticism. "My preference is this blockade plan," responded Thompson.[12]

"What do we do with the weapons already there?" asked Kennedy, reacting to Thompson's suggestion. "Demand they're dismantled and say that we are going to maintain constant surveillance, and if they are armed, we would then take them out," responded the ambassador. Kennedy was not convinced. He saw the benefits of the blockade but was afraid that in response to the blockade of Cuba, Khrushchev would "grab Berlin." At the end of the day, with the tide turning against him, Kennedy was apparently wavering. According to the summary of the evening deliberations that he dictated into a secret tape recorder, he was considering "a limited blockade for a limited purpose." But he was not rushing to make a decision. "It was determined," dictated Kennedy into the microphone, "that I should go ahead with my speeches so that we don't take cover off this, and come back Sunday night."[13]

The speeches to which Kennedy referred were to be delivered in the course of a preplanned campaign trip to the Midwest. He was going to maintain the appearance that everything was normal, that there was no crisis of any sort, and that he was following a schedule determined long in advance.

◊◊◊

ON FRIDAY MORNING, OCTOBER 19, BEFORE FLYING OFF TO Illinois, John Kennedy met with the Joint Chiefs of Staff. Except for their chairman, General Taylor, they had been excluded from Kennedy's advisory group on the Cuban crisis and were holding meetings of their own. Ever since the Bay of Pigs disaster, they had been advocating the idea of going back to Cuba in full force. The discovery of the Soviet SAMs and, later, MRBMs, and now the launch sites of IRBMs, was a godsend to the chiefs: in their eyes, the placement of Soviet missiles in Cuba made an invasion absolutely necessary. But the signals they were getting from Taylor and McNamara, who had taken part in the deliberations with the president, were more than worrisome: invasion was not high on the president's agenda. The long-awaited meeting with the president presented the chiefs with an opportunity to get him on their side.

Kennedy began the meeting with a discussion of the difficult choice with which the Soviet action presented him. "If we do nothing, they have a missile base there," said Kennedy, knowing perfectly well that that option was not acceptable to the generals. "If we attack Cuba, the missiles, or Cuba in any way, then it gives them a clear line to take Berlin," continued Kennedy. A few minutes into his presentation, he commented on the loss of Berlin: "Which leaves me the only one alternative, which is to fire nuclear weapons—which is a hell of an alternative." He sounded more positive on the blockade but saw a problem there as well: the Soviets could start a blockade of Berlin, blaming him for creating a crisis and alienating American allies in Europe. "So I don't think we've got any satisfactory alternatives," concluded Kennedy. "When we balance off that our problem is not merely Cuba, but it is also Berlin."[14]

The chiefs knew that a blockade was emerging as the preferable course of action among the president's advisers and decided to change tactics, remaining silent on outright invasion and advocating instead an all-out air strike at the Soviet installations. They hoped it would lead to invasion one way or another. The charge was led by General Curtis LeMay, the Air Force chief of staff, a tough-speaking and hard-driving officer who had commanded the firebombing of Tokyo in March 1945, overseen the Berlin airlift in 1948–49, and masterminded the creation of the US Strategic Air Command's capability to deliver nuclear weapons. He argued against a blockade, as it would give the Soviets plenty of time to hide their missiles and protect them from an air attack. "Now as for the Berlin situation," continued LeMay, addressing the president's main concern and the source of his objection to the general strike option, "I do not share your view that if we knock off Cuba, they are going to knock off Berlin." LeMay went on: "If we do not do anything to Cuba, then they're going to push on Berlin and push *real hard* because they've got us on the run."

LeMay was barely hiding his disdain for the young, inexperienced, and, in his opinion, indecisive president. "This is almost as bad as the appeasement at Munich," said LeMay about the proposed blockade. This was more than disagreeing with the president: it was tantamount to a personal attack. The appeasement at Munich was closely linked in public perception with Joseph Kennedy's tenure as US ambassador in London on the eve of World War II. LeMay did not stop there. "You are in a pretty bad fix," he told the president. He argued that a blockade followed by negotiations would be perceived as showing weakness both at home and abroad. Kennedy had had enough. He interrupted the general: "What did you say?" LeMay repeated the phrase: "You are in a pretty bad fix." "You are in there with me," Kennedy shot back with a forced laugh. "Personally."[15]

The meeting did not go well. If anything, it reinforced Kennedy's distrust of the military. But their skepticism about a blockade was not lost on him, given his own doubts about it. Kennedy decided not to rush in making a final decision; he would stick to the original plan, and allow his advisers to continue their deliberations for another day or two. With most of them leaning toward a blockade, he asked Bundy to keep the strike alternative alive. He left Robert Kennedy in charge of the continuing discussions.[16]

When it came to Cuba, Robert Kennedy was nothing if not a hawk. Back in August he had been supportive of John McCone, who suggested that the Soviets might deploy nuclear missiles in Cuba. After the missiles were discovered on October 14, Robert pushed for an invasion when even General Taylor had his reservations about it. President Kennedy's tapes caught his brother calling for an invasion whether that might cause a nuclear war or not and proposing to sink an American ship or stage an attack on the Guantánamo base to justify an invasion. He was among the most consistent critics of the blockade option.[17]

But as negotiations on the Cuban crisis continued in Washington in the president's absence, Bobby positioned himself first and foremost as a spokesman for his elder brother. Endowed with a new sense of responsibility, he now argued in favor of a strike, preceded by a warning to Khrushchev. In this he reflected his brother's concern that a surprise attack like the one on Pearl Harbor would not sit well with the American public. As the deliberations continued through Friday and it became clear that the pro-blockade faction was winning the argument, Robert Kennedy's position evolved further, and he joined the majority, while still concerned that the administration was wasting its chance to get rid of Castro. On the morning of Saturday, October 20, Robert Kennedy reviewed a draft speech prepared by the president's adviser Ted Sorensen, which argued for a blockade. He decided that the time had come to call his brother back to Washington.[18]

◊◊◊

"GENTLEMEN, TODAY WE'RE GOING TO EARN OUR PAY," KENnedy told the members of his Cuba advisory committee when he joined them upon his return to Washington. "You should all hope that your plan isn't the one that will be accepted." The first to report was Ray

Cline, the CIA deputy director for intelligence. "We believe the evidence indicates," said Cline, "the possibility that 8 MRBM missiles can be fired from Cuba today." In the course of the previous week, they had learned about the medium-range ballistic missiles stationed in Cuba, then about preparations to place intermediate ones; now it was clear that some of the missiles in place were ready to be fired.[19]

After listening to Cline's report, John Kennedy opened the discussion. While most of the group favored a naval blockade, individual views about its purpose and hopes associated with it varied. Rusk believed that it would buy time and keep options open for further action, whatever it might be. McNamara hoped that it would present an opportunity to start discussions on exchanging the Soviet missiles in Cuba for the American ones in Italy and Turkey. Finally, McCone, Llewellyn Thompson, and Robert Kennedy wanted the blockade to serve as an ultimatum to Khrushchev to remove the missiles. It could be followed by a strike. Only General Taylor, with the backing of the unhappy chiefs of staff, and Bundy, who was there on the president's orders to keep the strike option open, remained in favor of a strike.[20]

As the meeting progressed, McNamara presented a case in favor of a blockade. For him the operational missiles constituted a red line that he was not prepared to cross with a military strike against Cuba. He favored a blockade, followed by a military action if necessary. But he favored negotiations and was prepared to make concessions on Turkey, Italy, and, if necessary, on the Guantánamo base in Cuba. Bundy presented his case for an unannounced strike. He submitted a draft presidential speech, which read: "My fellow Americans. With a heavy heart, and in necessary fulfillment of my oath of office, I have ordered—and the United States Air Force has now carried out—military operations, with conventional weapons only, to remove a major nuclear weapons build-up from the soil of Cuba." Robert Kennedy, ostensibly in the "blockade" camp, kept making comments suggesting that his heart was still with the "strikers." Like General Taylor, he believed that the time to strike was now or never. Bobby proposed to threaten Khrushchev with the transfer of nuclear weapons to the West Germans.[21]

John Kennedy had to make his choice. It appears that the key factor for the president had become the CIA report on the discovery of the eight operational missiles. The chances that the strike would produce a nuclear response and ultimately a nuclear war had increased dramatically. Reluctantly, Kennedy abandoned the strike camp he had been leading for the whole week and joined the majority. "The President said he was ready to go ahead with the blockade and to take actions necessary to put us in a position to undertake an air strike on the missiles and missile sites by Monday and Tuesday," reads the protocol of the meeting. The reference to the airstrike was a concession to those who still wanted a strike or even an invasion. There would be no negotiations, just a demand to Khrushchev to remove the missiles, backed by readiness to strike. It would be the limited strike that Kennedy had favored from the very beginning, not the extensive one covering airplanes and other installations advocated by the chiefs.[22]

On the morning of Monday, October 22, after having reviewed his options once again with his advisers, John Kennedy placed a call to his predecessor Dwight Eisenhower. The general was supportive of the blockade option but clearly looked at it as a prelude to the invasion. He dismissed Kennedy's concerns that Khrushchev could attack West Berlin or use nuclear weapons in response to the invasion of the island. "Something may make these people shoot them off," remarked Eisenhower with reference to the Soviet nuclear weapons. "I just don't believe this will." "Yeh, right," responded Kennedy with a chuckle. He was not convinced.[23]

At 7:00 p.m., after informing the leadership of the Senate and the House of Representatives on Monday afternoon about the burgeoning crisis and his plan to impose a blockade of Cuba, Kennedy went in front of television cameras to deliver his address to the nation. "Good evening, my fellow citizens," he began in a somber tone, projecting a sense of urgency but also resolve and self-confidence. "Within the past week unmistakable evidence has established the fact that a series of offensive missile sites is now in preparation on that imprisoned island. The purpose of these bases can be none other than to provide a nuclear strike capability against the Western hemisphere." He warned Khrushchev that a nuclear missile fired from Cuba would be met with "full retaliatory response upon the Soviet Union."

Kennedy announced seven steps he was taking to protect the United States from the imminent threat posed by the missiles. The first was the declaration of a "strict quarantine on all offensive military equipment" being shipped to Cuba. Concerned more than ever about the possibility of Soviet retaliatory action in Berlin, Kennedy pointed out the limited character of the blockade: "We are not at this time, however, denying the necessities of life as the Soviets attempted to do in their Berlin blockade of 1948." The seventh and last point contained a demand to Khrushchev. "I call upon Chairman Khrushchev," declared Kennedy, "to halt and eliminate this clandestine, reckless, and provocative threat to world peace and to stable relations between our two nations."

The die was cast. After a long vacillation that had allowed the Soviets to continue the construction of missile sites and the delivery of new missiles and nuclear warheads to the island, Kennedy had decided to act. He had no clue how his declaration would be met in the Kremlin. All that now remained was to wait.[24]

IV

MOMENT
of
TRUTH

13

MOSCOW NIGHT

The US media reports that arrived in Moscow on Monday, October 22, 1962, left no doubt that there was a major crisis in Washington, with all arrows pointing toward Cuba.

Kennedy managed to keep secret the meetings of his advisers in the course of the week, but over the weekend the media picked up clear signs that something was wrong: high officials kept coming to their offices and staying there until late hours, the lights in their windows sending an alarm far beyond the DC area. Kennedy asked the publishers of the *New York Times* and *Washington Post* not to publish anything on the subject. The newspapers did not publish anything that their reporters acquired from confidential sources in the government, but articles based on open or nonconfidential information continued to appear in the press. The reporters had already figured out that the crisis concerned Cuba, and that a major new policy move was about to be announced, possibly a blockade of the island.[1]

"Capital's Crisis Air Hints at Development on Cuba; Kennedy TV Talk Is Likely," read a huge headline on the front page of the *New York*

Times for October 22. An article titled "Top Aides Confer. U.S. Forces Maneuver off Puerto Rico—Link Is Denied," filed the previous day, began by stating, "There was an air of crisis in the capital tonight." According to the article, whose author was not identified, Kennedy's return to the White House allegedly for health reasons had spurred feverish activity in Washington. "But the speculation in Washington was that there had been a new development on Cuba that could not be disclosed at this point," continued the anonymous author. He or she expected Kennedy to make a radio and television address "in the next day or two." An announcement of the address came in a radio broadcast on the morning of October 22. It was scheduled for 7:00 that evening. For reporters and the public at large, there was nothing to do but wait.[2]

Today's news in Washington and New York became tomorrow's news in Moscow. On the morning of October 23 the country's leading newspaper, *Pravda*, appeared with a headline written the previous night: "The Ruling Circles of the USA Are Playing with Fire." The Soviet reporter recounted an article that had appeared the previous day in the *New York Herald Tribune*. It had all the hallmarks of similar reports in that day's American newspapers: Kennedy had interrupted his tour of the country; lights were on in Washington offices late into Sunday night; and naval exercises were underway in the Caribbean. *Pravda* also featured a United Press International piece whose author wrote that a conference of commanding officers of the naval exercises had been canceled, and that journalists were not allowed on ships heading toward Cuba.[3]

No nuclear missiles were mentioned in the American or Soviet reports, but those in the know at the Kremlin assumed that the crisis was about them. "They have probably discovered our missiles," a disturbed Nikita Khrushchev told his son Sergei when he received a report about Kennedy's forthcoming address. It was the evening of October 22 in Moscow, and Khrushchev was at home in his apartment in the Lenin (now Vorobiev) Hills. He immediately summoned the members of the party Presidium to the Kremlin. Anastas Mikoyan, the most vocal opponent of the deployment of nuclear weapons in Cuba, received the news at his country house near Moscow. He called Khrushchev's second in command, Central Committee Secretary Frol Kozlov, who told him the reason for the urgent meeting: it was expected that Kennedy would make a major foreign policy announcement.[4]

According to the protocol of the Kremlin meeting, Khrushchev wanted to discuss "positions toward further steps in regard to Cuba and Berlin." Ironically, the official agenda echoed the title of that day's article in the *New York Herald Tribune* by Warren Rogers, "Top-Secret Doings in the Capital; A Cuba-Berlin Strategy Step?" In fact, the only item to be discussed that night in the Kremlin was Cuba. According to the protocol of the meeting and the memoirs of Mikoyan, Berlin was not mentioned even once. Mikoyan recalled that once the members of the Soviet leadership got together, they realized what was on the agenda: "We understood this had something to do with Cuba."[5]

It was close to 10:00 p.m. on October 22. By that time, the Soviet leaders already knew that Kennedy's televised address was scheduled for 7:00 p.m. EST, which would be early morning on October 23 in Moscow. They had a few hours on their hands to discuss the situation before Kennedy made his announcement. "Not yet knowing the content of the speech, we exchanged views about expected issues from the US government's positions, what steps it would take and possible countermeasures on our end," recalled Mikoyan. "Anything at all could be expected from them," he wrote, describing the tense atmosphere in the room.[6]

◊◊◊

KHRUSHCHEV OPENED THE MEETING AND GAVE THE FLOOR TO the minister of defense, Marshal Rodion Malinovsky. Normally a hawk when it came to Khrushchev's policies on Cuba, he was trying to calm his boss and his colleagues. Malinovsky urged them to avoid any hasty action. "I do not think that the USA right now could embark on blitzkrieg operations. It is not such a country," began Malinovsky. Instead he expected threats and suggested that Kennedy's speech was a "preelection stunt." In the worst case, continued Malinovsky, "If an invasion of Cuba is declared, this will be after another 24 hours have passed in order to get ready. I think that we will not end up in a situation in which the missiles are placed on high alert."

Malinovsky was followed by General Ivanov, the secretary of the Defense Council, who reported on the state of the Soviet armed forces in Cuba: more than forty thousand officers and soldiers were already on the island; three of the four R-12 regiments, with their missiles and equipment, were taking their positions, as were those in charge of the Luna tactical nuclear weapons and the nuclear warheads. The R-14 regiments and their equipment were still en route.[7]

Khrushchev backed his minister of defense: for the moment there was no reason to put the strategic missiles on high alert. "The point is that we do not want to unleash a war," he told his colleagues. "We want to intimidate and restrain the USA vis-à-vis Cuba." Mikoyan and others had heard those assurances before, but now it was a very different situation—the Americans had probably discovered the missiles, and the initiative had been taken out of Khrushchev's hands. Khrushchev admitted that the American announcement had taken him by surprise. "The difficult thing is," continued the Soviet leader, "that we did not consolidate all that we wanted and did not publish the treaty with Cuba." And then he mentioned what was probably on everyone's mind—the danger of uncontrolled escalation of the conflict. "The tragic thing is," said Khrushchev, according to the brief protocol of the meeting, "that they can attack, and we will respond. This could escalate into a large-scale war."

Khrushchev was convinced that the American invasion of Cuba was in the making. "Conclusion (is being made): An attack is being organized against Cuba," reads one of the lines in the terse protocol of the meeting. The question was what Kennedy's next step would be. "They might declare a blockade, or they might take no action," speculated Khrushchev or one of his colleagues. No action required no response. But in case an attack should take place, they considered two scenarios. "One scenario: declare on the radio that there already is an agreement concerning Cuba," reads the protocol of the meeting. Such an announcement was supposed to serve as a warning to the Americans that escalation of the conflict would lead to a direct confrontation with the Soviet Union. Khrushchev's other option—the protocol referred to it as "another scenario"—proposed to declare the conflict a US-Cuban affair in which the USSR had no legal or military involvement. "In case of an attack, all the equipment is Cuban, and the Cubans declare that they will respond," reads a record of the meeting.[8]

According to Mikoyan's recollections, the author of that scenario was Marshal Malinovsky. "This idea appealed to Khrushchev," remembered Mikoyan. He explained the reasons: "Of course at that point Kennedy's appeal to the USSR [to remove the weapons] became senseless. . . . Negotiations should have been conducted with Cuba, but we were no longer [an] interested [party]. All the while the risk of a nuclear strike against the Soviet Union was supposedly lessened." Mikoyan considered that logic superficial. In his own words, he "took the floor and resolutely objected." In his mind the Americans had already accustomed themselves to the idea that the USSR had nuclear weapons, but nuclear weapons capable of striking the United States in Fidel Castro's hands were another matter altogether. He predicted that the Americans would "panic and immediately come down on Cuba with all of their might. There would be nothing left of the people, island, our troops. Our efforts would be nothing more than a cruel joke."[9]

Mikoyan managed to get Khrushchev and other members of the Presidium on his side. The idea of publishing the agreement on mutual military assistance between Cuba and the USSR would ultimately be rejected as well. What they agreed on was putting the Soviet troops in Cuba on full alert. "First and foremost, we decided to task Malinovsky with ordering the commander of our forces in Cuba, General Pavlov [Pliev], to prepare for defense of Cuba with military action in the event of an American invasion, and if that failed, to use the intermediate-range missiles," recalled Mikoyan. They were ready to use strategic nuclear weapons. Malinovsky prepared a draft telegram to Pliev saying exactly that: "[A]ll means at Pavlov's disposal should be in a state of readiness." It then suddenly dawned on Khrushchev that they were giving Pliev authorization to use the ballistic missiles. "If all means without reservations, that means missiles too, that is, the outbreak of thermonuclear war," said Khrushchev. "How can that be possible?" It was a faux pas on the part of Malinovsky, and Mikoyan did not fail to record it in his recollections as a case of "extreme recklessness." The instruction was corrected in line with Khrushchev's objection.[10]

Both the Mikoyan memoirs and the protocol of the meeting suggest that not all nuclear weapons were ruled out. "Make all the effort initially not to use atomic [weaponry]. If there is a landing assault—the tactical atomic weaponry, but the strategic [not] until orders are given [from Moscow]," reads the protocol of the meeting. What Khrushchev and others had in mind when they talked about tactical weapons were the Luna nuclear-tipped missiles, which had already been delivered to the island. As for strategic forces, they explicitly excluded from their order the "means in the custody of Statsenko." The reference was to the R-12 missile regiments already deployed in Cuba under the command of General Igor Statsenko. Malinovsky proposed not to rush with an order before Kennedy's announcement: "[W]ait until 1:00 a.m., or else they will be given grounds for using atomic weaponry."[11]

Khrushchev and his colleagues were now waiting for Kennedy's speech. They were ready for the worst, and, while maintaining control over strategic nuclear weapons, were prepared to allow Soviet commanders in Cuba to use tactical ones. The mood in the Kremlin was close to panic. "That's it. Lenin's work has been destroyed," was Khrushchev's first reaction to the American discovery of the Cuban missiles, as recalled by his KGB chief, Vladimir Semichastny.[12]

◊◊◊

THE SOVIET AMBASSADOR TO WASHINGTON, ANATOLY Dobrynin, received a message from Dean Rusk to come to his office in the State Department at 6:00 p.m. that day. It was the afternoon of October 22, and Dobrynin was in New York, seeing off the departing Soviet foreign minister, Andrei Gromyko, who was returning to Moscow with the upbeat message that there were no developments concerning Cuba. Dobrynin tried to move the meeting to the next day, but Rusk's messenger insisted on seeing the Soviet ambassador that evening. Dobrynin suspected that something important had happened, but he did not know what.

At 6:00 p.m., one hour before the start of the president's television address, Dobrynin showed up in Rusk's office. "Rusk looked unusually serious," remembered the ambassador later. He handed him the text of the forthcoming presidential speech. It was accompanied by a personal letter to Khrushchev in which Kennedy stated that his desire was to avoid misunderstanding between the two governments. He also issued a warning to Khrushchev: "I must tell you that the United States is determined that this threat to the security of this hemisphere be removed." The letter ended with a call for a dialogue: "I hope that your Government will refrain from any action which would widen or deepen this already grave crisis and that we can agree to resume the path of peaceful negotiation."[13]

Rusk warned Dobrynin not to underestimate American will and determination—a key point of Kennedy's letter. Dobrynin knew nothing about the deployment of the missiles in Cuba, and for him the text of the president's statement came as a complete surprise. According to Rusk, Dobrynin's face went pale. "I saw him age ten years right in front of my eyes," recalled Rusk. Whatever he told Rusk in return, Dobrynin sent an encouraging report to Moscow. Rusk, wrote Dobrynin, "was clearly in a nervous and agitated mood, even though he tried to conceal it." Never having been informed by his government about the missiles, Dobrynin continued to deny their presence in Cuba. "Rusk," he wrote to Moscow, "was told that the actions of the USA government cannot be justified by the absolutely unconvincing motives which are not grounded in the factual situation . . . and that all responsibility for possible grave consequences of the aforementioned actions of the United States will be entirely on the American administration."[14]

In the Kremlin, Khrushchev and his colleagues received the text of Kennedy's speech not from Dobrynin but from the Ministry of Foreign

Affairs, to which it had been delivered by an American diplomat one hour before the start of Kennedy's address, the same time Rusk handed a copy of the speech to Dobrynin. The news that Kennedy was about to declare a naval blockade instead of the feared invasion of Cuba was met with a sigh of relief, if not jubilation. "This is not a war against Cuba but some kind of ultimatum," declared Khrushchev. "We've saved Cuba!" He could live with a blockade. "Even earlier, when making a decision on sending missiles to Cuba, we had anticipated the possibility not of military action against Cuba on the part of the United States, but of a blockade of Cuba," recalled Mikoyan. "Proceeding from that, we anticipated that in case of such a turn of events we could obtain a resolution of the matter through the United Nations instead of resorting to military action."[15]

The question was what to do next. According to Mikoyan, Khrushchev immediately dictated the main points of the Soviet statement on the blockade. "The USSR gov't is appealing to the peoples of the USSR—and is informing them," reads the protocol of the meeting. "[Keep] working. [We are taking] measures so that we are not caught unawares." When Khrushchev finished dictating, it was long past 1:00 a.m. on October 23. They decided to take a break, get some sleep, and reconvene in the morning to discuss further steps. Sleep meant snoozing on the couches in their offices. Khrushchev did not undress. He wanted to be fully ready in case unexpected news reached the Kremlin. "I was ready for alarming news to come at any moment, and I wanted to be ready to react immediately," he recalled later. Khrushchev did not want to be caught with his pants down in the middle of a major crisis, as he believed had happened to the French foreign minister during the Suez Crisis.[16]

According to Mikoyan, they planned to reassemble at 8:00 a.m. on October 23, but the meeting was moved to 10:00 a.m. They focused on the discussion of the statements, letters, and communications they had to issue. The idea of giving General Pliev authority to use tactical nuclear weapons was now abandoned. The order that Marshal Malinovsky had sent to Cuba at 11:30 p.m. the previous evening remained in force. It read: "In connection with the possible landing of Americans participating in the maneuvers in the Caribbean Sea on Cuba, undertake urgent measures to increase combat readiness, and to repel the enemy by joint efforts of the Cuban army and all units of the Soviet troops, excluding the weapons of Statsenko's and of all Beloborodov's cargo."[17]

"Beloborodov's cargo" meant the nuclear warheads for both strategic and tactical missiles, which had been delivered to Cuba on the same ship, *Indigirka*, and remained in the custody of Colonel Nikolai Beloborodov. The directive prevented Pliev from using any nuclear weapons whatever. The alternative one, which gave him that right, and which Malinovsky recommended to delay until the delivery of Kennedy's speech, was never forwarded to Cuba. Instead, Malinovsky, who was clearly worried about the possibility of losing control over the situation on the ground, ordered Pliev to establish a reliable radio connection with Moscow.

A key decision made that morning concerned the Soviet ships heading toward Cuba, and potentially right into the hands of the American navy. "We decided to turn all vessels proceeding to Cuba with weapons back to Soviet ports, while leaving civilian vessels with technical equipment on course until the situation and the details of the quarantine became clear. But not to declare this to the USA immediately," wrote Mikoyan, recalling the morning's discussion. The protocol of the meeting suggests that the decision was approved unanimously, but not all the ships were ordered back. The dry cargo ship *Aleksandrovsk*, with the second load of nuclear warheads, then approaching Cuba, was ordered to remain on course. So were the four Soviet submarines armed with nuclear missiles.[18]

The protocol of the Presidium meeting registers different stages in the process of decision-making on the return of the Soviet ships. First it was agreed to stop new shipments of weapons and order ships that were in the Mediterranean but had not passed Gibraltar to return to the Black Sea. Then they decided to turn back ships that were in the Atlantic but had no chance of reaching Cuba before the imposition of the blockade, with the special exception of the *Aleksandrovsk*. Equally complex was the decision on the nuclear submarines. First they agreed to halt their movement to Cuba and keep them on the "approaches" to the island but later reversed that decision and ordered them to remain on course to Cuba. Mikoyan explained that the idea to keep the submarines away from Cuba was his. He was concerned that their discovery would produce the same kind of reaction in the United States as that caused by the discovery of the missiles.[19]

Khrushchev agreed, and Mikoyan's position was recorded in the protocol. But then Malinovsky was given the floor, and he insisted that the submarines remain on course. He was supported by two or three members of the Presidium, and despite Khrushchev's original backing of Mikoyan's idea, they decided to do as Malinovsky advised. Mikoyan lost the battle once again. First he had been overruled on the issue of missiles, and now on the movement of submarines. He retreated but did not surrender and would keep fighting in the days to come.[20]

They then discussed the content of Khrushchev's letters to Kennedy and Castro. In the draft of Khrushchev's letter to Castro, the Soviet leader no longer claimed victory. "It was halfway successful, and half not," went the line of argument. "It is positive that the whole world is focused on Cuba. . . . Time will pass, and if needed, it [weaponry] will again be sent." The Presidium instructed Khrushchev to ignore Kennedy's demand to remove nuclear weapons from Cuba. The protocol read as follows in that regard: "Regardless of the class of weaponry, it has been delivered. It has been delivered with the aim of defending Cuba against aggression." If Kennedy wanted Khrushchev to remove nuclear weapons from Cuba, Khrushchev wanted Kennedy to lift or, rather, not introduce, the blockade. "I hope," went Khrushchev's letter to Kennedy, "that Government of United States will show prudence and renounce actions pursued by you, which could lead to catastrophic consequences for peace throughout world."[21]

By midday on October 23, the marathon meeting of more than twelve hours, with a short break for sleep, was finally over. Khrushchev and the members of the Presidium went to lunch. The situation seemed to be back under control. The previous night Khrushchev, like Kennedy during the first day of the crisis, had opted for military action. If Kennedy argued in favor of a strike, Khrushchev would be prepared to use tactical nuclear weapons, followed by strategic ones if the situation required them. But with Kennedy taking a moderate line and choosing a blockade instead of a strike or invasion, Khrushchev, to his relief, did not get a chance to approve the use of tactical nuclear weapons. For all the differences between the two men, and the misjudgments and misunderstandings that accompanied their search for the right decision, they had something in common. They dreaded a nuclear war.

14

BLINKING IN THE DARK

R obert Kennedy did not hide his frustration with Anatoly Dobrynin when he visited the Soviet ambassador late in the evening of October 23. "What would have been the point of us contacting you via the confidential channel, if, as it appears, even the Ambassador, who has, as far as we know, the full trust of his government, does not know that long-range missiles which can strike the USA, rather than defensive missiles which are capable of defending Cuba from any sort of attack on the approaches to it, have already been provided to Cuba," Robert told Dobrynin. As it appears from his report on the meeting, he acted on the instructions of the president but told Dobrynin that he had come on his own.

Robert Kennedy "was in an obviously excited condition and his speech was rich in repetitions and digressions," reported Dobrynin to Moscow. Kennedy listed the assurances given publicly and privately by Khrushchev and Dobrynin himself that the weapons delivered to Cuba were defensive. Kennedy went on to mention the promise that nothing would be done to aggravate Soviet-American relations before the November elections. "The President felt himself deceived, and deceived intentionally," he said to Dobrynin. "He is convinced of that even now. It was for him a great disappointment, or, speaking directly, a heavy blow to everything in which he had believed and which he had strived to preserve in personal relations with the head of the Soviet government: mutual trust in each other's personal assurances."

To Kennedy, Dobrynin looked "extremely concerned." He stood by his earlier statement: as far as he knew, there were no missiles in Cuba. He also improvised, assuring Robert Kennedy that Khrushchev valued personal relations with his brother. All he had to go on were Khrushchev's recent official statements. Whatever trust the Kennedy brothers had had in their Soviet counterparts—John in Khrushchev and Robert in Dobrynin—was now gone. But they still had nothing to guide them in predicting Soviet behavior except the words of the Soviet ambassador in Washington, who they correctly guessed was being kept in the dark by his own government.

As he was bidding farewell, Kennedy asked Dobrynin the question that had brought him to the Soviet Embassy: "What sorts of orders did the captains of the Soviet ships bound for Cuba have, in light of President Kennedy's speech yesterday and the declaration which he had just signed about the inadmissibility of bringing offensive weapons to Cuba?" Dobrynin, who knew nothing about the instructions sent to the ships from Moscow the previous night, as he had known nothing about the missiles, told Kennedy that as far as he knew, the captains were following their usual instructions, "not to obey any unlawful demands to stop or be searched on the open sea, as a violation of international norms of freedom of navigation." "I don't know how all this will end, for we intend to stop your ships," said Robert Kennedy before leaving the Soviet embassy. "But that would be an act of war," responded Dobrynin. As he remembered later, Robert "shook his head and left."[1]

The lines of communication between the two sides were broken, signals received were unclear, and those they sent themselves were often misunderstood by the other side. They were moving in the dark, hoping not to stumble into each other, but unconsciously speeding on a collision course.

◊◊◊

THE QUESTION OF HOW TO IMPLEMENT THE NAVAL BLOCKADE of Cuba without causing a Soviet-American war moved to the top of President Kennedy's agenda on October 23, the day after his television address. That morning he transformed his informal group of advisers on the Cuban missile crisis into the Executive Committee of the National Security Council, or ExCom.

The first meeting of ExCom began at 10:00 a.m. on Tuesday, October 23. "There was a certain spirit of lightness—not gaiety certainly, but a feeling of relaxation, perhaps," wrote Robert Kennedy, recalling the atmosphere in the White House Cabinet Room. "We had taken the first step, it wasn't so bad, and we were still alive." The official Soviet statement transmitted by TASS that morning announced that the Soviet Army command had canceled the planned demobilization of conscripts, but there was no news of planned military actions. McGeorge Bundy called the Soviet statement a "rehash of stuff we've heard before." Dean Rusk was relieved: "We've passed the one contingency: an immediate, sudden, irrational strike." The Soviets seemed to be on the defensive. Washington knew nothing about the nuclear submarines approaching the island.[2]

The first to report that morning was the CIA director, John McCone. On the new batch of photos taken by U-2 pilots, his photography experts could not locate the Soviet missiles they had seen there earlier. Regrettably, this was not an indication that Khrushchev had listened to Kennedy and was removing the missiles from the island. McCone pointed to evidence of "extensive camouflage." The Soviets were not removing but hiding their missiles from view. "It was never clear why they waited until that late date to do so," recalled Robert Kennedy, describing the thoughts of those in the room. "We caught them without their contingency [plan]," said Deputy Undersecretary of State for Political Affairs Alexis Johnson, not without satisfaction.[3]

According to Robert Kennedy, "the relaxed lighter mood had completely disappeared" in the room when the ExCom began discussing American contingency plans in case of a Soviet military response either in Cuba, or, as John Kennedy feared, in West Berlin. As McNamara reported on the possible response to a potential shooting down of a U-2 plane by a Soviet missile., they agreed that the response would have to be limited to that particular site, not broadened to an attack on all Soviet installations in Cuba. Turning to Germany, they decided against suspending the usual traffic between Western Germany and Berlin. After the end of the session, President Kennedy called General Lucius Clay, a veteran troubleshooter but also a troublemaker in West Berlin. The general sounded ready to serve his country in what had arguably again become the most dangerous place on earth. He told the president: "I am available anytime for anything."[4]

The most urgent matter on the ExCom agenda that day was the implementation of the naval blockade. By 6:00 p.m., when the ExCom met for its evening session, there was good news from the Organization of American States (OAS), which had approved the blockade unanimously. It was an unexpected result, as there had been concern that even two-thirds would not be easy to get. They could now move ahead with the formal declaration of the blockade, but first they had to decide what to do with Soviet ships in the Atlantic. ExCom agreed that those on the way to Cuba should be stopped, but what were they to do with those that turned back? Let them go undisturbed, or intercept them? John Kennedy believed that the ships should not be stopped, but he found it difficult to convince his brother of his approach.

Robert Kennedy was a late arrival to the blockade camp and saw it as a prelude to a military strike against Cuba. Now he saw the blockade as an opportunity to stop and search any Soviet ship in hopes of uncovering evidence that it was delivering offensive weapons to Cuba. "It would be a hell of an advantage to be able to come in and have pictures of the missiles," he told the gathering. "And also, I would raise the point that there possibly would be an intelligence advantage to be able to examine some materials." He wanted to establish a zone within which all ships would be stopped and searched, no matter which way they were going. He had a cover story ready for such action: "Say you don't know, when they turn around, whether they're going to try to come into Cuba in a different fashion."[5]

John Kennedy was not impressed. He believed that the Soviets would turn back ships transporting weapons, so that the search would produce nothing but an international scandal. He was also unsure at what distance they should begin interception: one ship had been spotted 1,800 miles from Cuba. The president clearly had doubts whether it constituted a legitimate target, but his brother had none: "I don't think that's too far. If it keeps coming . . ." McNamara was opposed to interception at such a distance and played for time: "I recommend that we not, tonight, decide the issue on that particular ship that's 1,800 miles out." He suggested following the ships' movements for the time being. Robert Kennedy was clearly disappointed. "As I say, I don't see any problem," he began, before continuing: "I think it would be damn helpful to come in with that kind of evidence."[6]

Dean Rusk joined the debate on the side of the president. "If they seem to turn around, give them the chance to turn around and get on their way," he told the gathering. Robert Kennedy jumped back into the discussion, pushing his argument on how to deal with the "hullabaloo" that could be created by the intercept: seizing weapons and taking pictures of them would make Soviet complaints groundless. "Well, I think I can see that, Bob," responded the clearly worried Rusk. "The problem here is that, from the Soviet point of view, they're going to be as sensitive as a boil." He reminded Robert and others of the purpose of the blockade as he saw it: to keep the Soviets out of Cuba. John Kennedy entered the discussion as a peacemaker. He proposed to postpone the decision until the next day.

The president's proposal was accepted. For the moment, Rusk probably wanted nothing more. The delay allowed him to give diplomacy a chance. With Llewellyn Thompson, he produced a draft letter from Kennedy to Khrushchev urging Soviet ships to stay away from the quarantine line. "The idea was," said Thompson, explaining the purpose of the letter: "they [Khrushchev and the Soviet leadership] will tonight all be deciding on what instructions are going to the ships." The draft letter read: "I hope that you will issue immediately the necessary instructions to your ships to observe the terms of the quarantine. . . . We have no desire to seize or fire upon your vessels." Kennedy agreed to send the letter but insisted on dropping the last sentence.[7]

What helped Rusk and his peace initiative was the president's growing concern about the practical implementation of the blockade, especially the seizure of Soviet ships. "That's what could happen," said Kennedy, outlining possible difficulties following the announcement of a blockade. "They are going to keep going. And we are going to try to shoot the rudder off, or the boiler. And we're going to try to board it. And they're going to fire a gun, then machine guns. And we're going to have one hell of a time trying to get aboard that thing and getting control of it, because they're pretty tough, and I suppose there may be armed soldiers or marines aboard their ships." "Or they might give orders to blow it up or something," responded Robert Kennedy, continuing that line of thought. He was no longer insisting on the interception of Soviet ships. Ultimately, he was there to support his brother. In his memoirs he said nothing about his hawkish stand but praised his brother's prudence and caution.[8]

After 7:00 p.m., when everyone had left, and John and Robert were alone, they reflected on the situation created by Khrushchev's deception and the declaration of the blockade. "It looks like hell—looks real mean. Doesn't it?" said the president to his brother. He then added: "But on the other hand, there is no other choice. If they get this mean on this one, it's just a question of where they go about it next. No choice. I do not think there was a choice." John Kennedy had Khrushchev's policies in mind, but Robert was also thinking of the domestic situation. "Well, there isn't any choice. I mean, you would have been, you would have been impeached." The president did not disagree. "That's what I think," he told Robert. "I would have been impeached."

Robert Kennedy wondered whether he could do a better job by helping his brother to establish a back channel to the Soviets. John Kennedy was still hurt by what he called Khrushchev's "horseshit about the election," delivered by Robert's main confidential contact, the Soviet intelligence officer Georgii Bolshakov. John Kennedy brought up his name: what did he have to say about the instructions given to the Soviet captains? "He said they are going to go through." Robert Kennedy no longer sounded like a reckless teenager looking for any opportunity to get into a fight. Instead, he suggested that it might be a good idea to have Soviet ships inspected by boarding parties consisting not only of Americans but also of OAS representatives. Should conflicts arise over the boarding of ships, he preferred that they be international rather than exclusively American. The latter might lead directly to war.[9]

After the ExCom meeting, when the brothers left the Cabinet Room with its tape recorder, they moved to the Oval Office, where John Kennedy shared with Robert, Ted Sorensen, and his appointments secretary, Kenneth O'Donnell, his concerns about the danger of "miscalculation—a mistake in judgment." According to the account presented in Robert's memoirs, John once again brought up Barbara Tuchman's *Guns of August*. "They somehow seemed to tumble into war," he remarked, "through stupidity, individual idiosyncrasies, misunderstandings, and personal complexes of inferiority and grandeur." In an earlier draft of Robert Kennedy's summary of the discussion, there was no mention of *The Guns of August*. Instead there was a passage on World War I: the president considered the guarantees given by Britain to Poland in 1939 to have been a mistake. Like his father in 1939, John Kennedy believed that Britain should not have gone to war. In the current crisis he did not want the United States involved in any international agreement or arrangement of its own making that would automatically lead it into war.[10]

After the meeting was over, Robert Kennedy went to see Dobrynin in order to ensure that there would be no misunderstandings.

◊◊◊

IN MOSCOW, NIKITA KHRUSHCHEV WAS STRUGGLING WITH his own dilemma: he could not allow the Americans to search his ships in international or Cuban waters without looking weak, but neither could he afford a military confrontation in the Caribbean, being well aware that in case of an American invasion of Cuba, it would be difficult if not impossible to prevent the use of nuclear weapons. His solution was quite simple: to accelerate the passage of those ships that could reach Cuba before the start of the blockade and turn back those that could not.

The orders, issued in the morning of October 23, Moscow time, were received by ships in the Mediterranean about the same local time. The captain of the dry cargo ship *Mednogorsk* received his orders to turn back at 10:15 a.m. on October 23. The order came in the form of a coded telegram from the minister of the Soviet merchant fleet, Viktor Bakaev. The *Mednogorsk* was then in the Mediterranean off the shore of Algeria. The ship was carrying 2,400 tons of military equipment, with 274 officers and soldiers on board. Ignoring the protests of crew members who were eager to complete the journey, the captain did as ordered—the *Mednogorsk* turned back and, after clearing the Dardanelles, entered the Black Sea and headed for its home port of Mykolaiv.[11]

The ships closer to the Cuban shores were ordered to proceed to the island—five ships altogether. One, the cargo ship *Divnogorsk*, was spotted by American airplanes on the approaches to Cuba on the night of October 22. As reported later by a KGB officer on board the ship, a US airplane with its searchlights on overflew the *Divnogorsk* not once or twice but seven times. But apart from those acts of surveillance, bordering on harassment, the ship was left alone: no signals or orders were issued to stop it. The *Divnogorsk* reached the port of Mariel safely at 2:00 a.m. on October 23. Only then was the captain informed that the United States had introduced a blockade of the island, and "American naval vessels and airplanes were scouring the Caribbean Sea, the straits and Cuban ports in order to seize our transports." They all heaved a sigh of relief.[12]

Among the vessels specifically ordered to remain on course was the dry cargo ship *Aleksandrovsk*. It was bringing the most dangerous cargo of all, twenty-four nuclear warheads for the IRBM R-14 missiles still en route, and forty-four warheads for the cruise missiles already on the island. Khrushchev and his advisers decided that the *Aleksandrovsk* should head for the nearest Cuban port as quickly as possible. It was supposed to dock at Mariel, but the Soviets intercepted American communications indicating that they were looking for a ship adapted for carrying nuclear warheads, and two American planes overflew the port of Mariel on the afternoon of October 23. The *Aleksandrovsk*, running behind schedule, was ordered to change course and head for the port of La Isabela. Moscow waited eagerly to hear whether it had managed to beat the blockade. The letter from President Kennedy received in Moscow early in the morning of October 24 gave the exact time when the blockade was to be implemented: "14:00 hours Greenwich time October twenty-four."[13]

◊◊◊

IN WASHINGTON, THE OCTOBER 24 MEETING OF EXCOM started exactly at the minute and hour of the official implementation of the blockade. It was 10:00 a.m. Eastern Standard Time on the US East Coast and 14:00 Greenwich Mean Time. The meeting began, as usual, with the report of the CIA director, John McCone, who informed his colleagues that there were twenty-two Soviet ships en route to Cuba. Seven of them had received urgent messages at 1:00 a.m. Moscow time on October 23. All twenty-two received additional messages at 2:30 a.m. EST on October 24. McCone did not know the content of the coded messages, but control over the ships had passed from the headquarters of the Black Sea cargo fleet in Odesa to the headquarters of the Soviet merchant fleet in Moscow.

ExCom was ready to discuss the interception of the ships that did not change their course. Late the previous night John Kennedy had decided after a conversation with his old friend, the ambassador of the United Kingdom, David Ormsby-Gore, that the quarantine line should be established 500 nautical miles off the shores of Cuba. He contacted McNamara immediately, and now they were all working from the same script: the quarantine zone would begin 500 miles away from the island. Dean Rusk's suggestion of the previous day to begin by intercepting a Soviet ship not carrying weapons did not get much support: the administration might be embarrassed if its navy were found stopping ships with baby food. They were looking for ships with weapons on board.

McNamara singled out the *Gagarin* and another Soviet dry cargo ship, the *Kimovsk,* as primary targets. They had discussed the *Kimovsk* the previous day, when it was approximately 1,800 miles from Cuba, and decided to wait an extra day to see where it was heading. They did not know where the *Kimovsk* and the *Gagarin* were at that point but assumed that the vessels were approaching the quarantine line. It was also assumed that they were being escorted by Soviet submarines, making them prime suspects of carrying missiles. McNamara reported that the *Gagarin* had declared its cargo as technical equipment and its port of destination as Conakry—in his opinion, "a typical declaration of an offensive weapons-carrying ship from the Soviet Union." He continued: "We have checked back the records, and this appears to be a typical way by which they propose to deceive."[14]

McNamara got it right: the *Gagarin* was indeed carrying missiles. The ship left Mykolaiv late in the evening of October 10 with equipment for the two detachments of the R-14 missile regiment stationed in the Ukrainian city of Okhtyrka. When crossing the Bosporus, the ship had given its destination as Conakry, but a Turkish navigator at the straits had suggested that in fact it was headed for Cuba, so the true destination seemed to be an open secret. Early in the morning of October 22, the day Kennedy gave his television address, the *Gagarin* was approaching the Bahamas, where it encountered a US Navy ship that ordered it to stop. The captain ignored the order. After numerous further attempts to signal the *Gagarin*, the American vessel left: the whole episode had lasted less than fifty minutes.[15]

The *Kimovsk* was also guilty as charged. In August that Finnish-built cargo ship, whose home port was Leningrad, delivered to Cuba thirty-one Soviet tanks and 150 officers and soldiers from the 6th Tank Army of the Kyiv military district. On September 22 it returned to Cuba, delivering a 2,200-ton load, including eight medium-range R-12 missiles and officers and soldiers of the 79th Missile Regiment of Colonel Ivan Sidorov. His missiles would be combat-ready on October 10. Now the *Kimovsk* was back, carrying intermediate R-14 or SS-5 Skean missiles and the units that serviced and operated them.[16]

"Both of these ships," McNamara told the ExCom, "are good targets for our first intercept." He then added: "Admiral Anderson's plan is to try to intercept one or both of them today." The reference was to the chief of naval operations, Admiral George Whelan Anderson Jr. John Kennedy was concerned about the details of the operation. "Which one are they going to try to get?" the president asked his secretary of defense. "Both of them?" McNamara's response was in the affirmative, although he considered the *Kimovsk* the primary target. "What kind of ship is going to try to intercept?" continued Kennedy. "A destroyer?" He was informed that the aircraft carrier *Essex*, with antisubmarine helicopters on board, was getting ready to help intercept the Soviet ships by diverting the Soviet submarines that were presumably escorting them from the point of interception.

Suddenly, McCone interrupted what seemed to be a Kennedy-McNamara discussion: "Mr. President, I have a note just handed to me. . . . All six Soviet ships currently identified in Cuban waters—and I don't know what that means—have either stopped or reversed course." If anyone questioned the propriety of the CIA chief interrupting of the secretary of state's presentation, their concerns vanished as soon as he broke the news. Rusk asked what "Cuban waters" meant. McNamara suggested that the reference was to ships leaving Cuba, but Kennedy asked for clarification: "Why do not we find out whether they are talk-

ing about the ships leaving Cuba or the ones coming in?" Rusk provoked laughter when he added: "Makes some difference."[17]

McCone immediately left the room to investigate the report. Kennedy and his advisers continued discussing how the submarines
accompanying the *Kimovsk* and the *Gagarin* could be made to surface.
McNamara suggested practice depth charges. "Warning depth charges
will be used if sonar signal does not get through," were McNamara's
words as recorded by Robert Kennedy in his notes on the meeting. He
continued with the president's reaction: "I assume if we sink [a] Russian ship that they will close down Berlin." John Kennedy was growing
steadily more tense. The ghost of nuclear war was rising in his imagination from beneath the waves hundreds of miles away.

"We don't want the first thing we attack as a Soviet submarine,"
John Kennedy told his aides. "I would rather have a merchant ship."
But McNamara would not back down. He was adamant that the Soviet
submarines should be forced to surface before anything was done with
the *Kimovsk* or the *Gagarin*. "I think it would be extremely dangerous,
Mr. President, to try to defer attack on this submarine in the situation
we are in," he told Kennedy. "We could easily lose an American ship
by that means." The president gave up. "OK. Let's proceed," he was
caught saying by the secret microphone in the Cabinet Room. "President Kennedy had initiated the course of events, but he no longer had
control over them," wrote Robert Kennedy later. It was a key moment in
the deliberations: the president had signed off on the order to intercept
Soviet ships.[18]

Across the table, Robert Kennedy saw the signs of his brother's
disturbance. "His hand went up to his face and covered his mouth," he
wrote later. "He opened and closed his fist. His face seemed drawn, his
eyes pained." Their eyes met. "For a few fleeting seconds, it was almost
as though no one else was there and he was no longer the President,"
recalled Robert. He was thinking of the supreme trials that his brother
had endured in the course of his life: the illness that almost killed him;
the shock on learning of the death of his older brother, Joseph; the loss

of his infant son, Patrick. "I think these few minutes were the time of gravest concern to the President," wrote Robert later.[19]

Kennedy was bracing himself for the worst—a likely sinking of a Soviet ship, the Soviet imposition of a Berlin blockade, an American airlift to save the city, and the Soviet shooting down of American planes. "What do we do then?" he asked the gathering. McNamara's deputy, Paul Nitze, began to enumerate possible responses: "We've got our fighters up in the corridor and we try to shoot down their planes." Nitze was still continuing his exposition when McCone reentered the Cabinet Room. "What have you got, John?" "These ships are all westbound, all inbound for Cuba," responded McCone. He did not know where the ships were at the moment but knew that "they either stopped them or reversed the direction." And so the ships were moving away from Cuba. Among the six listed by McCone were the *Kimovsk* and the *Gagarin*.

"We are eyeball to eyeball, and I think the other fellow just blinked," whispered Dean Rusk to McGeorge Bundy when he heard that the Soviets ships had turned away from Cuba. "Well, let's just say that, if this report is accurate, then we're not going to do anything about these ships close to Cuba," suggested Kennedy. "We're not planning to grab any ship that is not proceeding toward Cuba," said McNamara, echoing the president. Robert Kennedy had abandoned his previous position that the ships had to be stopped that day no matter where they were heading. "Well, will that information get to the Navy?" he asked, reacting to McNamara's statement. For once he and Rusk were in agreement. "Yeah, we better be sure the Navy knows that they're not supposed to pursue these ships," said Rusk, supporting the younger Kennedy. "The meeting droned on," remembered Robert Kennedy. "But everyone looked like a different person. For a moment the world had stood still, and now it was going around again." The order to attack the ships was recalled.[20]

◊◊◊

THE "EYEBALL TO EYEBALL" METAPHOR BECAME THE FOUND-ing myth of the historiography of the Cuban missile crisis. The dramatic moment in which Kennedy, speaking at the morning meeting of ExCom on October 24, gave the order to go after the Soviet vessels, which Robert Kennedy so amply described in his memoir, was indeed every bit as dramatic and potentially dangerous as it emerges from the book. It was also the moment that encapsulated everything Kennedy was afraid of as he kept coming back to Barbara Tuchman's book and thinking about the danger of misinformation and misunderstanding. Being misled by outdated and incomplete intelligence, he gave the order to attack ships that unbeknownst to him had already changed course and turned back from Cuba more than twenty-four hours earlier.

Neither Kennedy nor the members of the ExCom had access to the latest information supplied by Navy surveillance planes. It took hours for that information to get to the White House, forcing the president and his aides to make their decisions in virtual darkness. When McNamara first mentioned the dry cargo ship *Kimovsk* in the ExCom discussion on October 23, it was already on its way back to the Soviet Union. At 3:00 a.m. on October 23 the *Kimovsk* was spotted 300 miles east of the future quarantine line drawn 500 nautical miles from the eastern tip of Cuba. By 10:00 a.m. on October 24 the ship had traveled hundreds of miles farther east. The location of the *Kimovsk*, coupled with intercepted communication to the effect that it was heading toward the Baltic Sea, suggested that it was on its way home, not executing a maneuver to deceive the Americans and return to Cuba from a different direction.[21]

The *Gagarin* was going back as well, heading not for Odesa or the Black Sea but for Baltiisk on the Baltic Sea. Its thirty-seven-year-old captain, Kim Holubenko, had been ordered to turn back at 8:30 a.m. on October 23. Holubenko complied immediately. The *Gagarin* was already headed back east when, soon after 6:00 p.m. on October 23, a four-engine American plane dropped two explosives in front of the ship after flying over it three times with the plane's searchlights turned on. Shortly afterward, at 7:01 p.m., another American plane showed up. With searchlights on, it overflew the *Gagarin* six times. At 7:40 p.m., a third plane flew over the ship a mere 70 meters above its mast.

Between 8:43 and 9:10 p.m. the ship was overflown by a fourth plane. A fifth did the same, with searchlights on and off, at 11:34 p.m. The US Navy airplanes did not leave the ship to its own devices until 1:40 a.m. on October 24.[22]

Holubenko would later report on his trip to Cuba directly to Nikita Khrushchev and receive from his hands the highest Soviet award, the golden star of Hero of Socialist Labor. He would also meet and take a photo with the man after whom his ship was named, the astronaut Yurii Gagarin. Holubenko would be remembered for stories in which he allegedly forced an American ship to leave the *Gagarin* alone by ordering water to be shot into the air from a fire hose. According to Holubenko, the Americans assumed that his ship had some kind of secret weapon on board. The Soviets were in the process of developing their own myths of the "eyeball to eyeball" confrontation on the Atlantic.[23]

The two adversaries had indeed met eyeball to eyeball in the Caribbean, and one of them had blinked first. The problem was that they could hardly see each other's eyes, to say nothing of eyeballs. A dark room of deception and mutual suspicion was made even darker by lack of reliable and timely information, and when one side blinked, it took the other side more than a day to realize what had happened. The nuclear age preceded the arrival of the information age by at least a few decades. In October 1962, that gap might very well have led to the return of the Stone Age.

15

WOODEN KNIFE

The Romanian communist leader Gheorghe Gheorghiu-Dej, who made a stopover in Moscow on October 23 on his way back from a state visit to Indonesia, found Khrushchev in a highly agitated if not panicky state. Khrushchev was extremely upset when his minister of defense, Marshal Malinovsky, reported that the US Navy was on high alert and that preparations for a blockade of Cuba were underway. According to the recollections of Gheorghiu-Dej, who was present when Malinovsky reported the news, and whose words were relayed later by one of the Romanian intelligence chiefs, Ion Mihai Pacepa, "Khrushchev flew into a rage, yelling, cursing and issuing an avalanche of contradictory orders."

The Romanians suspected that Khrushchev had been drinking that morning, but they were wrong. The Soviet leader was exhausted for lack of sleep: Gheorghiu-Dej arrived right after the marathon all-night session that saw Khrushchev first brace himself for nuclear war in the event of an American invasion of Cuba and then decide how to react to the announcement of the blockade. He was furious. At the Kremlin reception in honor of the Romanian leadership, "Khrushchev swore at Washington, threatened to 'nuke' the White House, and cursed loudly every time anyone pronounced the words America or American," wrote Pacepa. Khrushchev then surprised Gheorghiu-Dej with an invitation to join him and the rest of the Soviet leadership for a visit to the Bolshoi Theater.[1]

Khrushchev recalled designing the visit as a public relations move. He said to his aides: "Comrades, let's go to the Bolshoi Theater. The atmosphere in the world is tense now, but we'll make an appearance in the theater. Our people and foreigners will see it, and that will begin to have a calming effect. If Khrushchev and other leaders are sitting in the theater at such a time, then everyone can sleep soundly." He then added: "But we ourselves were very anxious at the time." Foreign Minister Andrei Gromyko, who was among those invited to the performance, later recalled: "I don't remember what was playing in the theater. And probably none of the Politburo members in attendance were interested in what was happening on stage. Opera, ballet or drama—it was all the same to them all. Everyone was thinking of what was going on there, in the Western hemisphere. But they all sat properly and calmly in their seats, applauding as avid theatergoers should."[2]

On stage was the classic Russian opera *Boris Godunov* by Modest Mussorgsky, with the Metropolitan Opera star Jerome Hines in the leading role. *Pravda* reported next day on Hines's very successful performance: he received a standing ovation and six curtain calls. Khrushchev, according to the Romanian leader's recollections, "went out of his way to present personal congratulations" to Hines. In the company of Gheorghiu-Dej and the Soviet leaders he went backstage, where he complimented Hines on his good Russian and raised a toast to "peace and friendship between our countries."[3]

The Romanians, who had earlier seen Khrushchev cursing after hearing the word "America," were not sure what to think. Khrushchev was clearly off balance. He had been caught red-handed delivering missiles to Cuba and now did not know what to do. He tried his usual bullying tactics, menacing Kennedy with veiled threats of nuclear war and talking tough in front of his communist comrades. It was especially important to do so before the Romanians, who had begun to distance themselves from Moscow after Khrushchev's withdrawal of Soviet Army units from their country in 1958 began and had refused to side with the Soviet leader in his conflict with Mao Zedong.[4]

But the bullying tactics no longer worked. Kennedy was proceeding to implement the blockade, and Khrushchev was at a loss to respond effectively. The boomerang of nuclear war with which Khrushchev threatened Kennedy was coming back to haunt him. Vasilii Kuznetsov, the Soviet deputy foreign minister in charge of Soviet-American relations, told a trusted colleague that in the first days after Kennedy's television address, the Moscow leadership was paralyzed by "the confusion that reigned there, which was only covered up by Khrushchev's blustering public statements." In reality, continued Kuznetsov, "from the very beginning of the crisis, fear of the possible course of further developments arose within the Soviet leadership and increased with every passing hour."[5]

◊◊◊

THE ROMANIANS LEFT MOSCOW ON OCTOBER 24, THE DAY after their arrival, but not before Gheorghiu-Dej witnessed another of Khrushchev's outbursts. The Soviet leader was having breakfast with his Romanian guests when he received a report from the head of the KGB, Vladimir Semichastny. According to a decoded cable, Kennedy had canceled his planned visit to Brazil and was ordering the imposition of a naval blockade of Cuba. Khrushchev's face grew red as he read the cable. He started cursing "like a bargeman," threw the paper on the floor, and stamped on it with his heel. "That's how I'm going to crush that viper," he shouted, also calling Kennedy a "millionaire's whore." "If Kennedy had been there, the lunatic would have strangled him dead on the spot," Gheorghiu-Dej told his assistants upon his return to Bucharest.[6]

Gheorghiu-Dej was not the only foreign visitor whom Khrushchev met on October 24. Another was the president of the Westinghouse Electric International Company, William E. Knox. A prominent businessman who had managed his company's relations with the Soviet foreign trade agency, Amtorg, during the war, Knox was on a business trip to the USSR when he was summoned to see Khrushchev at an hour's notice. *Pravda* reported that the meeting took place at Knox's request. It lasted three hours. The Soviet leader went on the offensive, stating that Kennedy's announcement of October 22 was the result of his inexperience, electoral pressures, and outright hysteria. Kennedy was a young man, said Khrushchev, younger than Khrushchev's own son, and he could not imagine Eisenhower acting in such a manner.[7]

Khrushchev rejected Knox's suggestion that he had deceived Kennedy, but then made the most striking statement of the entire meeting, admitting that he had deployed not just ballistic missiles but also nuclear warheads in Cuba. "The Soviet Union had antiaircraft missiles in Cuba, as well as ballistic missiles with both conventional and nuclear warheads," reads the State Department summary of Knox's conversation with Khrushchev. The missiles were 100 percent under Soviet control and could be fired only in defense of Cuba and only on his personal orders, continued Khrushchev. If the Americans did not believe him, they could try to attack Cuba, and Guantánamo would be wiped out the first day of the conflict. According to another account, Khrushchev told Knox that he did not want war, but if the United States decided to start one, he was ready. "We'll all meet in hell," he told the surprised businessman.

But it was not all attacks and threats. Khrushchev wanted Knox to know that he was prepared to meet with Kennedy in the United States, the Soviet Union, at sea, or anywhere else. He remarked that the conflict was untimely, since Gromyko and Rusk had reached an understanding on a nuclear test ban and European frontiers. He then told Knox a joke about a man who did not like the smell of his goat but eventually learned to live with it. The Soviet Union had its goats in Italy and Greece and had learned to live with them. The United States was getting its goat in Cuba. The message to Kennedy was clear: I did indeed place nuclear missiles in Cuba, as you did on my borders. Get used to it.[8]

On the same day Khrushchev responded to Kennedy's letter of the previous day requesting him to turn Soviet ships back from the quarantine line. Early that morning, he had received the good news that the *Aleksandrovsk,* with nuclear warheads on board, had successfully reached Cuba, and he felt confident enough to go on the attack. He accused Kennedy of having declared the blockade "out of hatred for the Cuban people and its government, but also because of considerations of the election campaign in the United States." He also declared the blockade unlawful. "The Soviet Government," read the letter, "considers that the violation of the freedom to use international waters and international air space is an act of aggression which pushes mankind toward the abyss of a world nuclear-missile war." Refusing to order his captains to turn back, Khrushchev threatened resistance and retaliation: "We will . . . be forced on our part to take the measures we consider necessary and adequate in order to protect our rights. We have everything necessary to do so."[9]

The letter was approved by the Presidium of the Central Committee, which met that day to discuss the evolving Cuban situation. But Khrushchev clearly did not consider the official response to Kennedy strong enough. He decided to send the president a personal letter as well. His courier was supposed to be Georgii Bolshakov, through whom in September he had passed a verbal message to Kennedy: "We repeat again that the Soviet Union is delivering only defensive weapons to Cuba." He promised to do nothing to complicate Kennedy's situation in the run-up to the congressional elections in November. It was the violation of the promise delivered by Bolshakov that upset Kennedy so much. Now Khrushchev wanted Bolshakov to deliver another message to Kennedy. Since it was extremely long, it could not be memorized and took the form of a letter.[10]

Khrushchev was clearly in a bellicose mood when he dictated his response to Kennedy's demand to stop the ships. "You cannot fail to remember that both Hitler and Napoleon used such language in their day when speaking with small countries," asserted Khrushchev. "Do you really think even now that the USA is made of one dough and countries that you threaten another?" asked Khrushchev rhetorically, continuing his attack. In order to muddy the waters, Khrushchev took full advantage of Kennedy's references to offensive weapons rather than nuclear ones in his letters and pronouncements. On the one hand the Soviet leader denied the presence of Soviet nuclear weapons in Cuba on the grounds that they were not offensive, while on the other he implied that such weapons were there and asserted that they were under Soviet control.

Khrushchev suggested that the weapons that he, like Kennedy, never called "nuclear" could be removed, but only as part of a comprehensive agreement on nuclear disarmament. "Under such conditions," continued Khrushchev, "I think that we would not remove all weapons from Cuba but simply drown them in the vicinity if you were to do the same with your weapons." Turning the Caribbean into the world's nuclear dumping ground struck Khrushchev as a mutually beneficial solution. The letter ended with a threat of nuclear war: "But if any aggressor should attack Cuba, in that case the weapons themselves will start firing in retaliation."[11]

Khrushchev apparently dictated his personal letter late in the day, after the meeting of the Presidium. He had admitted the presence of nuclear weapons to Knox and now implied the same in writing: there were nuclear arms on the island; they were operational and under Soviet control; and they were rigged to go off in the event of an attack on Cuba, leading to Soviet-American conflict and the start of a nuclear war. Khrushchev postponed its dispatch, planning to get approval from the Presidium the following day. He went to bed on October 24 fully resolved to blackmail Kennedy with the use of nuclear weapons in the event of an American invasion of Cuba.

◊◊◊

ON OCTOBER 25, SOVIET NEWSPAPER HEADLINES VERY MUCH reflected Khrushchev's mood of the previous day. *Izvestiia*, edited by

Khrushchev's son-in-law, Aleksei Adzhubei, published a front-page poem by one of the leading Soviet poets, Nikolai Dorizo, attacking the naval blockade of Cuba and expressing the conviction that it would be broken. "The waves will break the blockade, Cuba / The sun will break the blockade, Cuba / And victory will be yours, Cuba," read the poem.[12]

Despite the upbeat tone of the Soviet media, for Khrushchev the morning began with bad news. To his official letter protesting the imposition of the blockade, Kennedy responded with a terse telegram that consisted of only two full paragraphs but left no doubt that Khrushchev's bullying tactics were not working. War or no war, Kennedy was moving ahead with the blockade. "I ask you to recognize clearly, Mr. Chairman, that it was not I who issued the first challenge in this case, and that in the light of this record these activities in Cuba required the responses I have announced," wrote Kennedy. "I repeat my regret that these events should cause a deterioration in our relations. I hope that your Government will take the necessary action to permit a restoration of the earlier situation."[13]

Kennedy's terse response pointed, in Khrushchev's mind, in one direction, and one direction only: the Americans were preparing for military action. It was to target not only Cuba but also the Soviet Union. Global nuclear war was imminent—a matter of hours, not days. On the morning of October 24, Soviet military intelligence officers stationed at the Soviet embassy in Washington intercepted an order to Strategic Air Command (SAC) units to raise their Defense Readiness Condition (DEFCON) to level 2, just short of level 1, which was reserved for conditions of open warfare. Never before had US strategic forces been put on that level of alert. The fleet of 1,479 bombers and 182 ballistic missiles, with 2,962 nuclear warheads at their disposal, was getting ready to strike targets in the Soviet Union.[14]

The DEFCON order was implemented at 10:00 a.m. EST on October 24, the same day and time as the naval blockade of Cuba. A few minutes later General Thomas S. Power, the tough-talking commander in chief of SAC, went to a microphone and spoke over unprotected communication lines to his staff, scattered across dozens of military bases and bunkers throughout the world. "This is General Power speaking," he began. "I am addressing you for the purpose of reemphasizing the seriousness of the situation the nation faces. We are in an advanced state of readiness to meet any emergencies, and I feel that we are well prepared." Power had the president's authorization to raise the level of alert, over unprotected communication lines, but he had no authority to address his troops in the same manner. Apparently, that did not matter to him, but Kennedy was losing his monopoly on communicating with Khrushchev. The military was opening its own hotline with the Soviet Union.[15]

Whether the text of Power's address was intercepted and delivered to Khrushchev or not, Soviet military intelligence intercepted the Joint Chiefs of Staff order of October 24 to SAC to raise its DEFCON to level 2. Soviet radar followed the American nuclear armed bombers as they approached the borders of the Soviet bloc before making an abrupt turn over the Adriatic Sea. They repeated that maneuver again and again. It is not exactly clear when the news was delivered to Khrushchev (it was either October 25 or 26) but there is no doubt that he got the message. The Soviet deputy foreign minister, Vasilii Kuznetsov, confided a few weeks later to one of his junior colleagues that after receiving the information about SAC going to the highest prewar level of DEFCON, Nikita Khrushchev "shat his pants."[16]

While some of Kennedy's advisers believed that raising the DEFCON level was useful, as it might deter the Soviets from taking action against US targets in Europe, the news helped convince Khrushchev that the Americans were getting ready not just to attack Cuba but also to hit Moscow. He concluded that the letter he had wanted to send via Bolshakov the previous day would make things even worse. Leonid Brezhnev remembered how in a panic, Khrushchev recalled the telegram he had already ordered to be sent to Kennedy. Instead, he called a Presidium meeting to present his colleagues with a very different agenda. Khrushchev was sounding a retreat.[17]

◊◊◊

"The Americans say that the Soviet installations in Cuba must be dismantled," he told the gathering. If they were expecting an emotional outburst full of expletives, they were in for a surprise. "Perhaps that should be done: it's not capitulation on our part because, if we shoot, they'll shoot back," said Khrushchev, surprising his colleagues. "The Americans have taken fright—no doubt about that, evidently," he declared, projecting his own state of panic onto his American counterpart. He continued: "Kennedy slept with a wooden knife." When the bewildered Mikoyan asked what that might mean, Khrushchev explained that according to a popular saying, those who go to hunt bear for the first time take along a wooden knife to clean their trousers.

He then presented his policy toward Cuba as a victory rather than a defeat. "We have now made Cuba a focus of world attention; we have knocked two systems together head to head," he continued, claiming that his gamble had paid off. He then explained the deal that he was going to offer the Americans: "Kennedy says to us: take your missiles out of Cuba. We answer: give firm guarantees and promises that the Americans will not attack Cuba. That's not bad. We could take out our R-12s and leave other missiles there." By "other missiles" he probably meant tactical nuclear weapons.

"This is not cowardice," said Khrushchev, returning to the subject of capitulation, "it's a reserve position." If so, then it was the first that Khrushchev's colleagues had heard of it. He reassured them that the removal of the missiles would not hurt Soviet prospects of staying on par with the United States. "Besides, there's no need to bring the situation to a boiling point; we can destroy the USA from the territory of the USSR just as well," he argued. "We should play our part, but without trying to wiggle out, without losing our heads. The initiative is in our hands; there is nothing to fear." He then turned the whole issue of fear inside out. "Began and chickened out," Khrushchev told his aides: the note in the protocol is too laconic to make it clear whether he meant the Americans or himself. He then continued. "Fighting is not to our advantage: the future does not depend on Cuba but on our country—that's for sure."

The members of the Presidium, some of whom, like Mikoyan, were clearly relieved, supported their boss. "A correct and reasonable tactic," wrote the notetaker, summarizing their views. "Now Cuba is not the same as it was before the events. Do not aggravate the situation. In this manner we will strengthen Cuba." This resonated with Khrushchev's own argument. He said to the gathering: "Cuba will be different from what it was earlier. They [the Americans] are threatening an economic blockade, but the USA will not attack Cuba. We should not aggravate the situation but conduct a rational policy. That way we will strengthen Cuba and save it for two-three years, and in a few years it will be even harder to get the better of it."

With the decision reached and consensus attained, the meeting moved on to discuss how to break the news of the Soviet withdrawal of nuclear weapons to Castro. "Some things worked out well, others did not," said Khrushchev, trying to strike a philosophical tone. "What we have right now is a positive moment. What is the positive side of this? The fact that the entire world is focused on Cuba. The missiles played their positive role." Khrushchev apparently wanted to soften the blow to Castro by saying that the withdrawal of the missiles might be temporary. Gromyko, along with two party officials, was entrusted with the task of putting those thoughts on paper.[18]

But even before getting into negotiations with Kennedy or informing Castro about the withdrawal of the missiles, the worried Khrushchev decided to start the de-escalation process right away. What only yesterday had been welcomed with great relief—the delivery of nuclear warheads for the R-14 intermediate-range missiles to Cuba on the cargo ship *Aleksandrovsk*—was now perceived as a potential problem to deal with. On Khrushchev's orders, Defense Minister Rodion Malinovsky cabled General Issa Pliev, the commander of the Soviet forces in Cuba, to ship the warheads back. "In connection with the fact that US Navy is blockading approaches to Cuba, we made a decision not to send 665 and 668 RP [missile regiments] to you. You should not unload warheads for R-14 from transport ship *Aleksandrovsk*," read the cable. "If they are already unloaded, organize secret loading back onto *Aleksandrovsk*," continued Malinovsky. "Transport ship *Aleksandrovsk* with the warheads for R-14 should be prepared for transportation back to the Soviet Union." In case of emergency, the captain was to sink the ship with the nuclear warheads.[19]

◊◊◊

ON OCTOBER 25, THE DAY KHRUSHCHEV DECIDED TO REMOVE his ballistic missiles from Cuba in exchange for Kennedy's promise not to invade the island, the Soviets suffered a major public relations defeat at a meeting of the UN Security Council, where they tried to deny the existence of such missiles in Cuba.

The key figures in the televised drama were the American representative to the UN, Adlai Stevenson, and his Soviet counterpart, Valerian Zorin. The Soviet representative left himself open to an attack by Stevenson when he claimed that the Americans had nothing but "false evidence" to prove the presence of Soviet missiles in Cuba. Why, he asked, did Kennedy not mention the missiles when he met with Gromyko on October 18? "Because no such facts exist," asserted Zorin, answering his own question. "The Government of the United States has no such fact in its hands except this falsified information of the United States Intelligence Agency, which are being displayed for review in the corridors and vestibules of the UN and which are sent to the press. Falsity is what the United States has in its hands, false evidence."[20]

Stevenson decided to fight back. "I want to say to you, Mr. Zorin, that I do not have your talent for obfuscation, for distortion, for confusing language, and for doubletalk," he began. "And I must confess to you that I am glad that I do not!" After suggesting that Zorin was flip-flopping on the issue of whether there were any Soviet weapons in Cuba and whether they were offensive or defensive, he continued: "All right, sir, let me ask you one simple question: Do you, Ambassador Zorin, deny that the U.S.S.R. has placed and is placing medium- and intermediate-range missiles and sites in Cuba? Yes or no—don't wait for the translation—yes or no?" Zorin responded, after waiting for the translation: "I am not in an American court of law, and therefore do not answer a question put to me in the manner of a prosecuting counsel . . . you will have your answer in due course."

Stevenson pressed on: "You can answer yes or no. You have denied they exist. I want to know if I understood you correctly. I am prepared to wait for my answer until hell freezes over, if that's your decision. And I am also prepared to present the evidence in this room." Stevenson's aides brought enlarged photographs of Soviet missile sites under construction taken by U-2 pilots in the vicinity of San Cristóbal. There were photographs taken in August, when no construction could be observed, and ones taken a week and a few days prior to the presentation, demonstrating the dramatic change in the landscape and the appearance of tents and missile installations where there had been none before. Stevenson's performance impressed President Kennedy, who remarked, watching the exchange on television, "Terrific. I never knew Adlai had it in him."[21]

The next day the *New York Times* came out with a huge front-page photo of Stevenson presenting his evidence, making the showdown at the United Nations the day's top story. It would appear that Khrushchev was never informed about the public relations fiasco at the UN. Zorin tried to put a brave face on his performance both in public and in his reports to the Kremlin, in which he wrote: "We ridiculed the maneuver that Stevenson had made at the session in showing the photographs which had been fabricated by American intelligence and assigned the role of 'irrefutable' evidence of the presence in Cuba of nuclear-missile arms." Like Dobrynin in Washington, Zorin in New York was kept in the dark by his government regarding the deployment of missiles in Cuba. Otherwise he would probably have behaved differently on the day when his boss in the Kremlin decided to give up the Soviet missiles in Cuba—missiles that, according to Zorin, had never been delivered to the island.[22]

16

THE AMERICANS ARE COMING!

Every major piece of intelligence that Nikita Khrushchev received on Friday, October 26, suggested that the Americans were getting ready for a major military action that would start with an invasion of Cuba. That day, military intelligence reports conveying information on the preparation of US hospitals for possible casualties were supplemented by information from KGB officers and diplomats stationed in Washington. Some of it was supplied by the ambassador himself.

The previous day, Anatoly Dobrynin had sent an urgent cable to Moscow: "This night (around 3 o'clock in the morning Washington time) our journalist [. . .] was at the bar of the press club of Washington where usually many correspondents gather. Barman approached him [. . .] and whispered that he had overheard a conversation of two prominent American journalists (Donovan and Rogers) that the President had supposedly taken a decision to invade Cuba today or tomorrow night. Our correspondent also had an opportunity to talk to Rogers, a correspondent of the *New York Herald Tribune*, permanently accredited to the Pentagon. He confirmed that report."[1]

The Soviet journalist to whom Dobrynin referred in his cable was in fact a KGB officer who had reported news that he picked up in a Washington bar to his superior, the head of the KGB Washington station, Aleksandr Feklisov. Feklisov in turn shared the information not only with his superiors in Moscow but also with the ambassador. Dobrynin, who had established a line of communication through Robert Kennedy to the president himself, was eager to maintain it as the only channel for confidential contacts with the two American leaders. He routinely downplayed the importance of his competitors, the KGB and military intelligence officers such as Feklisov and Georgii Bolshakov, in both Washington and Moscow. But this case was different. With the KGB reporting that Kennedy was going to invade Cuba within the next twenty-four hours, Dobrynin no longer sought to undermine his competitors but jumped on the intelligence services bandwagon, eager to deliver the information to Moscow as soon as possible.[2]

There was little doubt in Khrushchev's mind that he had to act quickly. Luckily, he had a solution ready in the form of the offer to Kennedy approved by the Presidium the previous day: he would remove the missiles from Cuba in exchange for a pledge not to invade the island. What remained was to call in the stenographer to take down Khrushchev's draft letter, which his aides would turn into a coherent text. By the afternoon of October 26, the letter was ready, and a courier delivered it to the US embassy in Moscow at 4:43 p.m. Moscow time. As always, it was a long and rambling missive, with a count of 2,748 words in English translation. It took hours to transmit the text to Washington, and the White House did not receive it until 9:15 p.m. that evening.[3]

Khrushchev began on a conciliatory note. "Dear Mr. President," read the text delivered to the embassy, "I have received your letter of October 25. From your letter, I got the feeling that you have some understanding of the situation which has developed and (some) sense of responsibility. I value this." He was referring to the terse letter in which Kennedy had declared his intention to go ahead with the blockade despite Soviet protests, but Khrushchev preferred not to mention that. He was pulling his punches because he wanted Kennedy to accept his proposal, which read as follows: "We, for our part, will declare that our ships, bound for Cuba, will not carry any kind of armaments. You would declare that the United States will not invade Cuba with its forces and will not support any sort of forces which might intend to carry out an invasion of Cuba. Then the necessity for the presence of our military specialists in Cuba would disappear."

What Khrushchev was prepared to offer Kennedy was far short of the mandate given him by the Presidium. He never explicitly admitted the presence of nuclear missiles on the island and never proposed to remove them. Instead, he gave a vague promise to remove "military specialists." Khrushchev was initiating a bargaining process, his immediate goal being to stop the escalation of the conflict. "Mr. President," he wrote, "we and you ought not now to pull on the ends of the rope in which you have tied the knot of war, because the more the two of us pull, the tighter that knot will be tied. And a moment may come when that knot will be tied so tight that even he who tied it will not have the strength to untie it, and then it will be necessary to cut that knot, and what that would mean is not for me to explain to you, because you yourself understand perfectly of what terrible forces our countries dispose."[4]

With the letter signed and delivered to the American embassy, all that remained for Khrushchev to do was wait. He did not know which would come first, a response or an invasion.

◊◊◊

ON OCTOBER 26 KHRUSHCHEV WAS NOT THE ONLY POLITICAL leader deeply concerned about an impending invasion of Cuba. Even more convinced of its inevitability and concerned about its outcome was Khrushchev's Cuban ally, Fidel Castro.

Ever since Kennedy's televised address of October 22, Castro had been trying to reassure his people and rally them around the goal of defending their now socialist *patria*. He had put the Cuban military forces on high alert a few hours before Kennedy's speech, anticipating that the address would deal with Cuba. On October 23 Castro gave a lengthy televised interview, responding to Kennedy by repeating lines from his speech and ridiculing his professed concern about the freedom and well-being of Cubans. Castro declared himself open to dialogue but stressed: "Anyone who tries to come and inspect Cuba must know that he will have to come equipped for war. That is our final answer to illusions and proposals for carrying out inspections on our territory." He did not confirm or deny the presence of nuclear weapons on Cuban soil but asserted that all weapons were defensive.[5]

Castro's firm stand helped to calm his supporters. The panic that had swept the corridors of power in Havana after Kennedy's address gave way to relative calm in the next few days. But with heightened activity at the UN on October 24–25, resulting in the Stevenson-Zorin interchange, a new wave of panic hit Havana. Castro's agents in New York, working under cover of the state news agency Prensa Latina, had intercepted an American telegram suggesting that Kennedy was preparing an ultimatum to the acting UN secretary general, U Thant, demanding the removal of offensive weapons from Cuba. Castro was worried. If Kennedy delivered such an ultimatum, it could mean the diplomatic preparations for an invasion. Castro was convinced of the reliability of his intelligence by the increasing American overflights of the island.[6]

On Friday, October 26, diplomats accredited to the Cuban government in Havana began to pick up signs of tension. "The Cubans have further expanded their battle preparedness and are now at maximum readiness," reported the Czechoslovak ambassador in Havana, Vladimir Pavlíček. The Yugoslav ambassador, Boško Vidaković, who visited the Cuban president, Osvaldo Dorticós, that afternoon, found him in a state of utmost concern. The Brazilian ambassador in Cuba, Bastian Pinto, reported to his capital on the basis of his conversation with Vidaković that "Dorticós, extremely perturbed, told him that American planes are making low-level flights over Cuba and, according to information obtained in recent hours, the American attack is imminent;

it would even be a 'miracle' if the attack does not come this evening, repeat: this evening."[7]

While Dorticós met with friendly ambassadors, hoping to mobilize the international community against the invasion that he expected at any moment, Castro rallied his troops and readied his defenses. He ordered his military commanders to put the army on highest alert. He also issued a warning to the Americans in a communiqué addressed to U Thant: "Cuba does not accept the vandalistic and piratical privilege of every warplane to violate our airspace. Therefore any warplane that invades Cuban airspace does so at the risk of meeting our defensive fire." Castro meant what he said. He ordered fifty aircraft batteries to take positions across the country and start shooting down American airplanes beginning the next morning.[8]

Later in the day, Castro visited Soviet military headquarters to inform General Pliev of his order. Their meeting lasted the whole afternoon. Castro maintained that overflights could no longer be tolerated because they would make the Cuban and Soviet positions vulnerable when the invasion came. He asked Pliev to disperse his missiles. He and Dorticós then visited the Soviet ambassador, Aleksandr Alekseev. Castro wanted the Soviets to use the American violation of Cuban airspace as a pretext to declare that the weapons Kennedy was talking about were indeed in Cuba but under Soviet control. This was similar to the line considered by Khrushchev in his draft letter to Kennedy of October 24, which was supposed to be delivered by Georgii Bolshakov but was never dispatched because of Khrushchev's change of mind.[9]

As day turned into evening and evening into night, Castro decided that his oral intervention with Pliev and Alekseev had been insufficient. He was getting more intelligence supporting his earlier belief that the Americans were coming. President João Goulart of Brazil informed him that he had forty-eight hours to dismantle the missiles or be attacked. Castro wanted Khrushchev to know what was going on. In the early hours of October 27, he went back to see Alekseev. The two drank beer and ate sausages as they discussed the content of the letter to be sent to Moscow. But the ambassador considered Castro's information so urgent that he hastened to send word to Moscow even before the draft was completed. He telegraphed: "Castro is with us at the embassy and is preparing a personal letter for N. S. Khrushchev that will immediately be sent to him." He then added: "In Castro's opinion, the intervention is almost inevitable and will occur in approximately 24–72 hours."[10]

It took Castro, with Alekseev's help, close to three hours to complete the letter: he did not leave the Soviet embassy until 5:00 a.m. Castro expected an American attack in the form of an air strike or a land invasion in the next one to three days, as Alekseev had reported earlier. Castro promised that the Cubans would "offer strong and decisive resistance to whatever form this aggression may take" but warned the Soviet leader that "the imperialists might initiate a nuclear strike against the USSR as well." "In those circumstances," continued Castro, "the moment would be right for considering the elimination of such a danger, claiming the lawful right to self-defense." In fact, he proposed that Khrushchev use nuclear weapons first. "However difficult and horrifying this decision may be, there is, I believe, no other recourse," wrote the Cuban leader.[11]

Alekseev, who took part in composing Castro's letter and subsequently found himself in trouble for having participated in such a warmongering exercise, denied that Castro wanted Khrushchev to attack the United States with nuclear weapons. "I think," said Alekseev later, in one of his interviews, "that he was just warning that we had to be on guard that anything could happen, including, as he thought, that the Americans could use nuclear weapons." That is not how Khrushchev read Castro's letter when he received it. His reaction to the Cuban's proposal would become steadily more negative over time. His original determination to use nuclear weapons against an American invasion force had long disappeared, yielding to a desire to avoid military conflict and thus nuclear war at almost any price.[12]

◊◊◊

The apprentice: happy, idealistic, inexperienced. JFK on his Inauguration Day, January 20, 1961. (JFK LIBRARY)

Fidel Castro and his comrades enter Havana on January 8, 1959. In Washington, the Cuban revolution heightened fears of communist takeovers in the Western Hemisphere. In Moscow, it inspired Soviet hopes for the approaching collapse of global capitalism. (EVERETT COLLECTION HISTORICAL/ALAMY STOCK PHOTO)

Stepping into a trap. Trying to improve his standing at home and abroad after the disastrous attempt to invade Cuba at the Bay of Pigs, Kennedy rushed into a meeting with Khrushchev, only to get another beating and receive an ultimatum to leave West Berlin. Vienna, June 4, 1961. (KEYSTONE PRESS / ALAMY STOCK PHOTO)

In May 1962, concerned about the possibility of losing Cuba either to another US-backed invasion or to a Maoist coup in Havana, Khrushchev decided to install Soviet missiles on the island. He is shown here in the company of his key foreign policy advisers. Seated next to the Soviet leader is his minister of defense, Marshal Rodion Malinovsky, who supported Khrushchev's Cuban adventure. First Deputy Prime Minister Anastas Mikoyan, who opposed it, is third from left. (KEYSTONE PRESS / ALAMY STOCK PHOTO)

Cavalryman. General Issa Pliev, a hero of World War II, brutally suppressed a popular uprising in the southern Russian town of Novocherkassk in June 1962. He was handpicked by Khrushchev and Malinovsky to lead the Soviet task force in Cuba. (MIL.RU)

Rocket man. In the summer of 1962 the forty-four-year-old General Igor Statsenko, stationed in Ukraine, was dispatched by Khrushchev to Cuba along with his men and missiles. Despite the unforgiving terrain and punishing climate, Statsenko managed to make his missiles battle-ready before President's Kennedy televised address on October 22, 1962. (MIL.RU)

Submariner. Captain Vasilii Arkhipov, the commander of the Soviet nuclear-armed submarines in the Atlantic and the man credited with saving the world from the nuclear exchange in the Sargasso Sea. (COURTESY OF THE ARKHIPOV FAMILY)

Throughout the crisis, JFK managed to keep the military under control with the help of the new chairman of the Joint Chiefs of Staff, General Maxwell D. Taylor, shown here at his swearing-in ceremony on October 1, 1962. On the right is Attorney General Robert Kennedy, his brother's loyal lieutenant and a key hawkish figure in the crisis. (JFK LIBRARY)

The Soviet medium-range R-12 missile installations in Cuba were first detected by a U-2 spy plane on October 14, 1962, setting off the crisis. This photo of the installations was presented to the United Nations on October 25, 1962. (PICTORIAL PRESS LTD / ALAMY STOCK PHOTO)

MEDIUM RANGE BALLISTIC MISSILE BASE IN CUBA

SAN CRISTOBAL

LAUNCH POSITION

MISSILE-READY TENTS

MISSILE ERECTORS

LATE OCTOBER

The Executive Committee of the National Security Council, a group of advisers to the president, began deliberations about the crisis on October 16, 1962. Its members are shown here at a session on October 29. Their discussions were secretly recorded by JFK—a breach of trust but a boon to historians. (JFK LIBRARY)

Face to face with the adversary. Soviet foreign minister Andrei Gromyko (second from right) and Soviet ambassador to the United States Anatoly Dobrynin (third from right) meet with the president on October 18. Kennedy did not mention the missiles at this meeting, leading Gromyko to conclude that the Americans were in the dark. He was mistaken: not only did JFK know about the missiles, but he wanted them destroyed with an airstrike. (JFK LIBRARY)

The blockade went into effect on October 23, 1962, raising fears of US-Soviet armed conflict over passage rights. Here an American Lockheed P-2 Neptune airplane is captured by a KGB camera as it flies over one of the Soviet ships. (ARCHIVE OF THE STATE SECURITY SERVICE OF UKRAINE)

Unsung heroes. U-2 pilots waiting for an audience with Kennedy a few days after a Soviet missile downed a U-2 plane piloted by Major Rudolf Anderson. The pilots would be introduced to the president by his longtime nemesis, General Curtis LeMay, chief of staff of the United States Air Force (far right). LeMay led the opposition to JFK in the Joint Chiefs of Staff caucus and demanded an all-out attack on Cuba. (JFK LIBRARY)

As Kennedy and Khrushchev reached a deal to resolve the crisis on October 28, Castro rebelled against his Soviet ally and refused to allow US or UN inspection of the missile sites in Cuba. Khrushchev tried in vain to bully his unruly client into submission. The two are shown here during Castro's 1963 visit to the USSR, Khrushchev's attempt to restore relations. To Castro's left is the Soviet ambassador to Cuba, Aleksandr Alekseev, a former KGB resident there. (ZUMA PRESS, INC. / ALAMY STOCK PHOTO)

The Soviets agreed to what some called a "strip search," the American inspection of their ships carrying missiles back to the USSR. Here the USS *Blandy* approaches the Soviet cargo ship *Divnogorsk*. The captain of the *Divnogorsk* showed its R-12 medium-range missiles to the crew of the *Blandy* over the protests of the humiliated military commanders. The photo was taken by a KGB officer on November 9, 1962. (ARCHIVE OF THE STATE SECURITY SERVICE OF UKRAINE)

The winner. At his press conference on November 20, 1962, a jubilant JFK announces the withdrawal of Soviet missiles and bombers from Cuba.
(JFK LIBRARY)

The loser. Khrushchev never managed to recover his standing with his military chiefs, who backed a palace coup against the Soviet leader in October 1964. Marshal Rodion Malinovsky, standing next to Khrushchev in this 1964 photo, told his commanders after Khrushchev's ouster that neither the Russian nor the Soviet army had ever been subjected to such humiliation as during its withdrawal from Cuba.
(ITAR-TASS NEWS AGENCY / ALAMY STOCK PHOTO)

THE FIRST MAJOR PIECE OF INFORMATION ON CUBA THAT Khrushchev saw on Saturday, October 27, was not Castro's alarmist letter but a calmer if still very disturbing report from the commander of the Soviet forces in Cuba, General Issa Pliev.

The general had clearly been affected by Castro's high anxiety. He also knew about the new DEFCON level and was disturbed by the increased American overflights. He reported that the Cubans were expecting an air strike either during the night of October 26 or on the morning of October 27. "The decision to shoot down American military airplanes with antiaircraft artillery has been made by Fidel Castro in case of their invasion of Cuba," wrote Pliev. He was going to do the same. "In case of a strike against our installations on the part of American aviation, the decision has been made to employ all available antiaircraft resources," reported Pliev. He believed that the American intelligence services had identified "some areas in which Comrade Statsenko's installations were located." Pliev had no right to use nuclear weapons without authorization from Moscow but could launch his SAM missiles and was prepared to do so.[13]

Pliev's report was presented by Marshal Rodion Malinovsky to Khrushchev and the members of the Central Committee's Presidium as they met at the Kremlin that day for their now regular session to discuss the Cuban situation. The Presidium approved General Pliev's actions but instructed him not to escalate the possible conventional conflict into a nuclear one. He was once again prohibited from using nuclear weapons, including tactical ones, as well as aircraft without explicit instructions from Moscow. And the supervision did not end there: three separate telegrams were sent to Pliev. "Stop all work on deployment of R-12 and R-14—you are aggravating the United Nations," read one of the orders sent to Cuba by Malinovsky. "Camouflage everything carefully, work only at night." Pliev was also reminded that he had to send the *Aleksandrovsk*, which had brought the nuclear warheads for intermediate-range missiles to Cuba, back to the Soviet Union.[14]

Khrushchev was uncharacteristically calm that day. He wanted to keep Pliev from complicating the diplomatic game he was now playing with Kennedy and at the United Nations. He also saw a sign of hope and new opportunity in the reports coming from Cuba, no matter how alarmist they had been. It was afternoon in Moscow when the Presidium discussed the report. The night of October 26 and the morning of October 27 had come and gone with no news of an American attack on the island. "We must take into account that the US did not attack Cuba," Khrushchev told his colleagues. "Could they attack us right now?" he asked at another point in the discussion and immediately gave his own response: "I think they will not bring themselves to do it."

Unlike Castro and Pliev, Khrushchev no longer believed that an invasion was imminent. That view gave him some breathing space and additional room for maneuver. He was still committed to the idea of trading the missiles for concessions from the United States. To get those concessions, he was prepared to go further than he had done the previous day in his letter to Kennedy; in particular, to admit openly what he had only implied up to that point—the deployment of ballistic missiles in Cuba. "We will not eliminate the conflict if we do not give satisfaction to the Americans and do not tell them that our R-12 missiles are there," he told his colleagues. "I think that we should not be obstinate."[15]

But Khrushchev was prepared to make such an admission only for a price. He considered the fact that Kennedy had not so far attacked Cuba a sign of weakness to be exploited. "Did we commit a mistake or not?" he asked the members of the Presidium. "This can be assessed later on," continued Khrushchev before making his brazen new proposal: "And if we receive in return the elimination of the [US] bases in Turkey and Pakistan, then we will end up victorious." For Khrushchev's colleagues, his idea of throwing the missiles in Turkey into the equation came as a surprise. "Speaking frankly, we were not thinking about bases in Turkey at all," Khrushchev's well-informed ally Anastas Mikoyan would tell the Cuban leaders in early November 1962.[16]

The American missiles in Turkey had been very much on Khrushchev's mind since the inception of the Cuban affair. It was no accident that the idea of dispatching nuclear weapons to Cuba had come to him in May 1962 in the Black Sea port of Varna as he publicly denounced the Americans for turning the Turkish coast into a military base. But this was Khrushchev's first mention of Turkey not in order to argue that the Soviets had the right to place their missiles in Cuba but to suggest a potential bargain. He threw in Pakistan as well, which indicated that the idea was not yet fully formed in his mind. Since Pakistan had no nuclear weapons but served as a base for U-2 overflights of the USSR, Khrushchev was simply looking to increase the number of American strategic assets to which he could object. But as he and his aides began to work on the letter to Kennedy proposing the new deal, Turkey not only took priority over Pakistan but completely replaced it.

If one trusts Mikoyan, the idea of using the American missiles in Turkey as a bargaining chip came to Khrushchev from the US media. "During discussion of the dangerous situation we received information from the United States of America, including an article by [columnist Walter] Lippmann [in the *Washington Post* on October 25], where it was said that the Russians could raise the question of liquidating the USA bases in Turkey," recalled Mikoyan a few weeks later. "They were speaking about the possibility of such a demand inside American circles. This question was discussed in the USA. Turkish bases do not have great importance for us. They will be eliminated in case of war. True, they have certain political significance, but we don't pay them special importance, though we will seek their liquidation."[17]

Khrushchev began to dictate his letter to Kennedy there at the meeting of the Presidium. Seven members of that body, including Mikoyan, his nemesis Malinovsky, the cautious Gromyko, and the often-silent Brezhnev took part in the discussion and eventually approved the final text. As no reply had yet been received from Kennedy to Khrushchev's letter of the previous day, the new letter was styled as a response to Kennedy's reaction to U Thant's proposal to lift the blockade in exchange for Khrushchev's promise not to send weapons to Cuba. Khrushchev had agreed to U Thant's proposal, while Kennedy had not, but one could not tell that from Khrushchev's new letter to the president.

Unusually for the recent correspondence between the two leaders, Khrushchev's new missive began on a positive note. "Dear Mr. President," wrote Khrushchev, "I have studied with great satisfaction your reply to Mr. Thant concerning measures that should be taken to avoid contact between our vessels and thereby avoid irreparable and fatal consequences. This reasonable step on your part strengthens my belief that you are showing concern for the preservation of peace, which I note with satisfaction." Despite the argument he had made at the Presidium meeting, Khrushchev did not explicitly admit the presence of ballistic missiles and nuclear warheads on the island, calling them only "means that you regard as offensive." But he made it clear that they were under sole Soviet control, and his comparison of them with the American missiles in Turkey left no doubt what they were.

"You are disturbed over Cuba," continued Khrushchev, coming to his main point. "You say that this disturbs you because it is 90 miles by sea from the coast of the United States of America. But Turkey adjoins us; our sentries patrol back and forth and see each other. Do you consider, then, that you have the right to demand security for your own country and the removal of the weapons you call offensive, but do not accord the same right to us? You have placed destructive missile weapons, which you call offensive, in Turkey, literally next to us. How then can recognition of our equal military capacities be reconciled with such unequal relations between our great states? This is irreconcilable."

Khrushchev's offer read as follows: "We are willing to remove from Cuba the means that you regard as offensive. We are willing to carry this out and to make this pledge in the United Nations. Your representatives will make a declaration to the effect that the United States, for its part, considering the uneasiness and anxiety of the Soviet State, will remove its analogous means from Turkey." Khrushchev further proposed that the Soviet Union give a pledge at the UN Security Council to respect the independence and territorial integrity of Turkey, and that the United States give a similar pledge with regard to Cuba. He promised a bright future in Soviet-American relations if only the deal on Cuba and Turkey could be reached. That future included the signing of the nuclear test-ban treaty that was so dear to Kennedy's heart. The two deals could be negotiated and approved simultaneously, which could mean only one thing: Khrushchev was prepared to throw in concessions on the test-ban agreement in order to push through the Cuba-Turkey missile swap.[18]

Khrushchev gambled on Kennedy's reluctance to attack Cuba, but he had no guarantee that such an attack might not come soon. Accordingly, it was imperative to deliver the letter to the White House at top speed, ideally not only before a possible attack on the island but also before Kennedy responded to Khrushchev's offer of the previous day, which made no mention of Turkey and proposed only to remove Soviet "specialists" in exchange for an American pledge not to invade Cuba. He knew that it would take hours, perhaps a whole day for the letter to be delivered, translated, and then telegraphed in sections to Washington from the US embassy in Moscow. The new letter was significantly shorter than his previous one but still amounted to 1,575 words in English. The Presidium decided to broadcast the letter on Soviet radio as soon as possible.[19]

They rushed the letter to the Moscow radio center. It was aired at 5:00 p.m. Moscow time and picked up by international wire services in North America in the late morning of October 27. In Washington, Kennedy and his advisers were in for a major surprise: Khrushchev had sent two letters in as many days, and they conveyed two different messages.

V

BLACK
SATURDAY

17

TURKISH QUAGMIRE

John Kennedy was discussing the U-2 overflights of Cuba with the members of ExCom when Ted Sorensen, his legal counsel and speechwriter, silently handed him a news ticker tape. "Premier Khrushchev told President Kennedy yesterday," read JFK aloud for the benefit of those present, "he would withdraw offensive weapons from Cuba if the United States withdrew its rockets from Turkey." It was soon after 10:00 a.m. on Saturday, October 27.

The first to react to the news was McGeorge Bundy. "Hmm. He did not," said the national security adviser. Sorensen defended himself, if not the accuracy of the news he had delivered: "That's how it is read by both the associations that have put it out so far. Reuters has the same thing." Bundy repeated his denial: "He did not!" Sorensen now expressed his own doubt: "He did not really say that, did he?" "No, no," repeated Bundy. The news agencies referred to Khrushchev's letter of "yesterday," and Bundy remembered quite well that there had been no mention of Turkey in Khrushchev's letter of the previous day. President

Kennedy was the first to grasp what might be going on. "He may be putting out another letter," he told his advisers, referring to Khrushchev.[1]

Kennedy was right. The newswires were transmitting Nikita Khrushchev's new letter just released by Radio Moscow. There was a good reason why Kennedy was the first to grasp what was going on. If for Khrushchev throwing Turkey into the equation was a spontaneous last-minute decision, for Kennedy it was anything but an unexpected move on the part of Moscow. Turkey had been on his mind from the very start of the crisis, not as a propaganda tool but as a way of overcoming it. Kennedy, who believed that the nuclear-armed Jupiter missiles placed in Turkey by his predecessor, General Eisenhower, were outdated and useless, had been thinking of trading them off for the Soviet missiles in Cuba long before the arrival of Khrushchev's offer. He discussed that possibility as his preferred diplomatic scenario with his friend the UK ambassador to Washington, David Ormsby-Gore, on the afternoon of October 21, the day before he first addressed the nation. He was not sure back then whether he would be able to pull it off politically, but now it seemed the opportunity had finally presented itself.[2]

"Where are we with our conversations with the Turks?" Kennedy asked his advisers. "Hare says that is absolutely anathema as a matter of prestige and politics," responded Undersecretary of Defense Paul Nitze, referring to the reports from the American ambassador to Turkey, Raymond A. Hare. Nitze was clearly on Hare's side: the move could raise the question of whether the United States was going to denuclearize NATO. Kennedy knew that the unity of NATO would be in jeopardy if the Europeans assumed that the Americans were removing their nuclear shield and abandoning them to the Soviets. Nitze offered Kennedy a possible solution to his problem: if he told Khrushchev that he was prepared to discuss Turkey once the Cuban crisis was solved. Kennedy was skeptical. "No, I do not think we can," he told Nitze with regard to his proposal.

McGeorge Bundy suggested to ignore Khrushchev's proposal about Turkey and focus on his earlier letter, which did not mention it. "There's nothing wrong with our posture in sticking to that line," declared Bundy. Kennedy disagreed. He did not believe that Khrushchev would remove missiles from Cuba on any basis other than the removal of American missiles from Turkey. That and only that, in Kennedy's mind, would give diplomacy a chance. Thus he hoped that the initial wire reports were correct, and that Khrushchev had indeed offered a swap. "Let's wait and let's assume that this is an accurate report of what he is now proposing this morning," he told his aides.[3]

◊◊◊

JOHN KENNEDY AND HIS ADVISERS FIRST BROACHED THE question of the American missiles in Turkey at the very first session of his Cuban crisis group. On October 16, the first day of the crisis, Dean Rusk mentioned Turkey as he recounted for Kennedy John McCone's hypothesis explaining why Khrushchev might have decided to put his missiles in Cuba. Khrushchev, argued Rusk, knew that the United States had nuclear superiority over the USSR. "Also, we have nuclear weapons nearby, in Turkey and places like that," added Rusk.[4]

The Jupiters—the first nuclear-tipped medium-range ballistic missiles (MRBMs), designed by Hitler's main rocket man and one of the founders of the American missile program, Wernher von Braun—were capable of delivering a 2,000-pound nuclear bomb at a distance of up to 1,700 miles. They were built first and foremost for Europe, but the French refused to take them—President Charles de Gaulle was developing his own nuclear and missile programs. But the Italians and the Turks, who had no plans to go nuclear themselves, accepted the Jupiters in deals signed in 1959. The decisions were made by Eisenhower, but deployment of the missiles in both Italy and Turkey began under the Kennedy administration, in the summer of 1961.

There were political concerns about the deployment. Some Democratic senators, such as Albert Gore Sr., the father of future vice president Al Gore, questioned the wisdom of the move, considering the missiles nothing short of a provocation. He asked Dean Rusk what the American attitude would be if Khrushchev put missiles in Cuba.

Gore's comments, made at a closed session of the Senate in February 1961, were generally ignored at the time, and deployment proceeded as planned. By the end of 1961, Turkey had fifteen Jupiters that could be launched only by coordinated action of the Turkish and American military—the former operated the missiles, while the latter had control over the nuclear warheads.[5]

John Kennedy never considered the deployment of American missiles in Europe an asset to either American or European security—the Jupiters were perfect targets for the Soviets in case of military confrontation, and it seemed that on October 16 the very fact of their presence had slipped his mind. Shocked by what he considered Khrushchev's reckless deployment of Soviet missiles in Cuba, Kennedy seemed oblivious to any parallel between the Soviet and American missiles. McGeorge Bundy and Deputy Secretary of State Alexis Johnson reminded the president that the US had deployed the nuclear-armed missiles in Turkey. Kennedy still refused to see the parallel between what Khrushchev was doing in Cuba and what the Americans had done in Europe in 1959. "But that was during a different period then," he told his aides. That was exactly the point Johnson was apparently trying to make: Khrushchev, lacking ICBMs of his own, was now in the same position as Eisenhower five years earlier. What for Kennedy was a bygone period of a lack of long-range missiles was present-day reality for Khrushchev.[6]

It was the first day of the crisis, and Kennedy was in a bellicose mood, denying Khrushchev and his actions even a hint of legitimacy. Only on the third day of the crisis, October 18, did Kennedy finally admit the parallel between the Turkish and Cuban situations. In order to predict Khrushchev's next move, he was prepared to put himself in Khrushchev's shoes and suggested to the members of ExCom: "Let's say the situation was reversed, and he had made the statement about these missiles similar to the ones I made about [Cuba]. Similar to the ones about putting our missiles in Turkey. And he had made the statement saying that serious action could result if we put them in, and then we went ahead and put them in. Then he took them out some day." At that point Kennedy was thinking about "taking out" as attacking the missiles rather than removing them. But his thinking on the missiles in Turkey would evolve.[7]

On October 22, the day of his speech on the naval blockade of Cuba, Kennedy had first entertained the idea of trading Soviet missiles in Cuba for American missiles in Italy and Turkey. It was a reaction to Dean Rusk's proposal to force Khrushchev to cede control over his missiles in Cuba to the United Nations in exchange for a similar move by the United States with regard to its Jupiter missiles in Italy and Turkey. "There are only three places where nuclear missiles are present outside the territory of a nuclear power: Cuba, Turkey and Italy," argued Rusk. "This would be: Take them out of any country that is not a nuclear power," said Kennedy, reacting to Rusk's proposal. "Well, not 'take them out' at this phase. Just sit on them," responded Rusk, who simply wanted to make the Soviet missiles in Cuba nonoperational.

But Kennedy had hit on a bigger idea, that of trading Soviet missiles in Cuba for American ones in Italy and Turkey. "Why don't we go the whole way?" the president asked his reluctant secretary of state. Rusk was against referring to Italy and Turkey in the statement he was preparing for the United Nations. But Kennedy did not care about the statement: he was fascinated with his new idea. "This gives us an excuse to get them out of Turkey and Italy. As long as they are not connected with it [the American proposal to the UN], let's get them out of both places. We tried to get them out of that other place anyway."[8]

Later that day Kennedy asked Assistant Secretary of Defense Paul Nitze to look into the possibility of removing the missiles from both Italy and Turkey. He considered them worthless. The military knew that: with fifteen to twenty minutes required to prepare the missiles for launch, they were sitting ducks for a Soviet first strike—in fact, inviting it. Instead of deterring attack, they might well provoke it. But Nitze had political rather than military objections to the president's idea: the Europeans might perceive it as an American policy of removing the whole US nuclear arsenal from Europe. Kennedy assured the worried Nitze that removal of the missiles was his plan B. His plan A was to demand unilateral withdrawal of the Soviet missiles from Cuba.[9]

The Cuba-Turkey missile swap disappeared from the ExCom discussions. The State Department was opposed to it, and in the Department of Defense only the officers dealing with disarmament were in favor of it. But the swap became a subject of internal memos and, by October 25, it had spilled into the media. No less a figure than Walter Lippmann, who had coined the term "Cold War" back in 1947, proposed such a swap in his column "Today and Tomorrow" in the *Washington Post*. On the same day Rusk attacked the proposal at a meeting with reporters. He also sent a cable to Turkey reassuring its government of the continuing American commitment to their country's security. But the damage had already been done. Anatoly Dobrynin included Rusk's rebuff of Lippmann in his report to Moscow, and, according to Anastas Mikoyan, Lippmann's proposal became common knowledge in Khrushchev's circle.[10]

◇◇◇

ON THE MORNING OF OCTOBER 27, THE IDEA OF A TURKISH-Cuban swap was suddenly revived with the incoming news about Khrushchev's new public proposal. For Kennedy it emerged as the only hope for a peaceful resolution of the crisis. The blockade only sent a signal that the Kennedy administration was serious and could prevent the delivery of new missiles but did next to nothing about the existing ones. A trade could remove the missiles that Khrushchev had managed to deliver before the blockade began.

Kennedy was prepared to treat Khrushchev's new letter, whose content had not yet been independently confirmed, as an indication of Khrushchev's new and thus real negotiating position. Kennedy also saw no reason to refuse the swap, or even a possibility of doing so. As he insisted on discussing Khrushchev's new proposal even before a full summary of it had been delivered to the Cabinet Room, he told his skeptical aides: "We're going to be in an insupportable position on this matter if this becomes his proposal. In the first place, we last year tried to get the missiles out of there because they're not militarily useful, number one. Number two, it's going to—to any man at the United Nations or any other rational man, it will look like a very fair trade."[11]

Kennedy's aides stuck to their guns, opposing the very idea of engaging in a discussion with Khrushchev over Turkey. But Kennedy's weak position suddenly became stronger as more details about Khrushchev's proposal were released by the media. It was becoming clear that earlier media reports had not misrepresented its content. Kennedy felt vindicated. "It's going to be hung up there now," he told the aides. "This is their proposal." He did not want to hear any objections. "How much negotiations have we had with the Turks this week?" asked Kennedy, cutting short an aide's remarks. "Who's done it?" continued the president. "We haven't talked with the Turks," responded Rusk, adding: "The Turks have talked with us." "Where have they talked with us?" Kennedy kept pushing. "In NATO," responded Rusk. Kennedy was no longer hiding his frustration. "Yeah, but have we gone to the Turkish government before this came out this week? I've talked about it now for a week. Have we had any conversations in Turkey, with Turks?"

Rusk tried to defend himself, pointing out that the State Department had asked for the opinions of American ambassadors in Rome and Ankara. Undersecretary of State George Ball explained the rationale: "If we talked to the Turks, I mean that would be extremely unsettling business." Kennedy wanted none of that. "Well, this is unsettling now, George," he shot back. He then added, referring to Khrushchev: "[H]e's got us in a pretty good spot here." Kennedy had in mind the public relations consequences of Khrushchev's letter: "Most people would regard this as not an unreasonable proposal." But the antiswap party would not give up. "But what 'most people,' Mr. President?" asked Bundy, jumping back into the discussion. Kennedy ignored the question but explained his thought in more detail:

"I think you're going to have it very difficult to explain why we are going to take hostile military action in Cuba, against these sites . . . when he is saying: 'If you'll get yours out of Turkey, we'll get ours out of Cuba.' "[12]

Bundy's solution was akin to the one proposed earlier in the discussion by Nitze: ignore Khrushchev's Turkey proposal. "I do not see why we pick that track when he's offered us the other track within the last 24 hours," said Bundy. "But that offer is a new one," responded Kennedy. Once again, his argument fell on deaf ears. The ranks of the opposition to the president's proposal were growing by the minute. "And you think the public one is serious, when we have the private one?' asked Llewellyn Thompson, the former ambassador to Moscow, probing the president's defenses. Even Ted Sorensen had joined the anti-Kennedy camp. "I think it is clear that practically everyone here would favor the private proposal," he told Kennedy, referring to Khrushchev's first letter.[13]

Kennedy was outgunned and outvoted in his own ExCom. The key argument marshaled by his opponents was that making a deal with Khrushchev on Turkey would undermine American credibility with the NATO allies. "If we talked to the Turks, it would already be clear that we were trying to sell out our allies for our interests. That would be the view in all of NATO," argued Bundy. Kennedy demanded answers on what had been done to approach the Turks. He asked his aides to formulate a position on the second proposal, "because this is the one that's before us and before the world." Nothing helped. The president decided to sound a temporary retreat and play for time. "We first ought to get clarification from the Soviet Union of what they're talking about," proposed Kennedy. On that suggestion, everyone finally agreed.[14]

◊◊◊

KENNEDY LEFT THE EXCOM SESSION AROUND NOON TO ATTEND a meeting with American governors summoned to Washington to be asked to make civil defense preparations for a possible nuclear war. With the ExCom opposing a Cuba-Turkey deal, that prospect was becoming ever more real. The Chiefs of Staff were in the final stages of preparing their recommendation to Kennedy to execute a massive airstrike on Cuba as early as the next day, Sunday, October 28, or Monday, October 29. The strike would be followed by an invasion, the option favored by Robert Kennedy. A peaceful solution was clearly available, but Kennedy had difficulty taking the deal offered to him by Khrushchev.[15]

The official White House statement, released later that day, reflected Kennedy's defeat and his advisers' victory. It referred to "several inconsistent and conflicting proposals" made by Moscow in the previous twenty-four hours, stating that the crisis was about the threat posed by the Soviets to countries of the Western Hemisphere and that negotiations could start only after construction of the missile bases in Cuba stopped. That would make it possible to begin "seeking properly inspected arms limitations" for nations outside the Western Hemisphere. There was no mention of Turkey, Italy, or Britain by name. The statement was a setback not only for Kennedy but also for Khrushchev, who had no idea either of the president's real position on the issue or of the difficulties he had created for Kennedy by making his statement public.[16]

For the first time since the start of the crisis, Kennedy found himself closer to Khrushchev than to his own aides. Khrushchev had offered a deal that Kennedy was ready to accept. The question was whether he could do so politically. He was the only member of ExCom prepared to make the deal: everyone else was opposed. However, it was not only a question of the revolt of Kennedy's aides but also of the publicity accompanying Khrushchev's offer. Kennedy could not accept a public deal that would make him look weak, accommodating Khrushchev's whims and backing off from his original position. It was no less important to assure the NATO allies that he was not betraying them so as to shield himself and his country from the Soviet nuclear threat, with which the Europeans had lived for years.

It was a trap. Kennedy could not accept the Turkish "gift" that Khrushchev was offering him because it would require "ungifting" the missiles his predecessor had given to Turkey—a political impossibility. The two leaders were prepared and even eager to make a deal, but one of them had presented it in such a way that the other could not take it.

18

LOSING CONTROL

The Strategic Air Command had been at DEFCON 2 readiness since the morning of October 24. At any moment there were as many as seventy-two nuclear-armed B-52 planes in the air on the "Chrome Dome" mission: in case of a nuclear attack on the United States, they would strike Soviet targets in retaliation. The pilots and planes were assigned twenty-four-hour shifts. Joining the B-52s in the skies were KC-135 Stratotankers, ready to refuel them in flight. B-47 Stratojet bombers of an older design were dispersed at airfields throughout the United States to preclude the possibility that most or all of them might be incapacitated by a Soviet first strike.[1]

SAC was prepared to fight a nuclear war, while its creator and now United States Air Force Chief of Staff General Curtis LeMay was ready to invade Cuba. On the morning of October 27, at a meeting of the Joint Chiefs of Staff in the Pentagon conference room, known since World War II as the "tank," LeMay seized the initiative by proposing to draft a formal proposal to the president suggesting the speedy invasion of the island. It was after 10:00 a.m. that LeMay told the gathering: "We should write a simple paper, taking the latest intelligence into account, and again recommending the execution of a full-scale OPLAN 312 followed by OPLAN 316."

The first of these, codenamed "OPLAN 312–62," envisioned an air strike on the island targeting first missile, aircraft, and antiaircraft installations, then transportation and communication networks, and finally troop concentrations. Fifty-two aircraft would begin the operation, their number to be increased after the first six hours to 384, and after twelve hours to 470. OPLAN 316–61 envisioned the invasion of the island with two airborne divisions and one infantry division, joined by a Marine division and a brigade, accompanied by an armored combat command. The amphibious assault was planned to take place three days after the receipt of the order by the troops, and the airborne assault five days after that.[2]

When Robert McNamara joined the meeting around 1:30 p.m., soon after President Kennedy adjourned the morning meeting of the ExCom, the paper was ready and presented to him by the chiefs. It proposed the "early and timely execution" of OPLAN 312. McNamara asked what that actually meant, and LeMay answered: "Attacking Sunday or Monday." That meant the next day or the day after—October 28 or 29. McNamara was in favor of the strike but needed more time, as he had to wait until the issue of American missiles in Turkey was resolved. General Maxwell Taylor, the chairman of the Chiefs of Staff, proposed a compromise: "If there is no stoppage in missile work [in Cuba], chiefs recommend a strike after a reasonable period of time." McNamara agreed, with the proviso that "I would not accept a recommendation to strike 'now.'"

Before McNamara was ready to leave the meeting, the chief of the Joint Reconnaissance Group, Colonel Ralph Steakley, who had briefed Kennedy on the discovery of Soviet missile sites in Cuba on October 16, walked in. He informed those present that a U-2 airplane on a routine mission over the North Pole to collect air samples—a procedure required for monitoring possible Soviet nuclear tests—had lost its way and strayed into Soviet territory for reasons unknown. McNamara alleg-edly yelled: "This means war with the Soviet Union." It was 2:03 p.m. EST. By that time the U-2 was thirty to forty minutes late in returning to its base. McNamara excused himself and left the room to call Rusk. Through him, the news eventually reached Kennedy.[3]

Roger Hilsman, the Department of State chief of intelligence, found the president in the White House soon after he had taken his usual afternoon swim to ease his back pain. He told Kennedy that the Air Force had a U-2 reconnaissance plane over the Soviet Union being pursued by Soviet fighters. American fighters were now in the air try-ing to protect it. "The implications were as obvious as they were horren-dous," wrote Hilsman, recalling his own assessment of the situation. "The Soviets might well regard the U-2 as a last-minute intelligence reconnaissance in preparation for nuclear war."

John Kennedy took the news rather stoically, if not philosophically: "There is always some sonofabitch who doesn't get the word." Having served in the Navy during World War II, he had little trust in the mili-tary carrying out orders as received. Kennedy understood what was at stake. He could not but remember the crisis caused by the downing of a U-2 plane over the Soviet Union in 1960, which had derailed the planned summit between Eisenhower and Khrushchev. Now, in the middle of a much more serious crisis, a U-2 lost over Soviet territory might very well lead to war.[4]

◊◊◊

UNLIKE CAPTAIN GARY POWERS'S ILL-FATED FLIGHT OVER the Soviet Union on May 1, 1960, Captain Charles (Chuck) Maultsby's incursion into Soviet airspace on October 27, 1962, was not premedi-tated. Like Powers, Maultsby was collecting evidence needed to assess Soviet activity, but he had no intention of venturing into the skies over the USSR. Maultsby, who had been shot down over Korea during the Korean War and spent twenty-two months in Chinese imprisonment, had no desire to conduct a comparative study of communist prisons and labor camps. He was supposed to collect air samples outside Soviet borders but simply lost his way.

As a participant in "Project Star Dust," Maultsby had orders to fly his Lockheed U-2 spy plane to the North Pole, take samples of air that might or might not contain traces of Soviet or hydrogen atomic bomb tests, and return, all within approximately seven hours. There was one inherent hazard in this otherwise routine flight: because the magnetic North Pole is not coterminous with the geographic one, magnetic compasses cannot be used for orientation, forcing pilots to navigate by the stars. The only things the pilots could have with him were a sextant and star charts. They were also instructed to maintain radio silence. The U-2, a product of the latest twentieth-century technology, had to be navigated with the help of an eighteenth-century instrument on these flights.

Maultsby took off for the North Pole from Eielson Air Force Base near Fairbanks, Alaska, around midnight local time on Friday, October 26, with almost all the flight taking place in the early hours of October 27. The pilot's last electronic contact with earth occurred approximately an hour after takeoff, when he picked up a signal from the radio beacon on Barter Island off the northern coast of Alaska. That was also the point at which the pilots of the search and rescue planes that had accompanied him bade him farewell.

At first the unaccompanied flight went without a hitch. Maultsby checked his location and his route with the help of charts and sextant, but as he got closer to the North Pole, he had trouble orienting the sextant toward major stars indicated on the charts because his vision was blurred by flashes of colored lights in the sky. He was looking at the aurora borealis, or northern lights, a light phenomenon caused by the knotting together of a number of the sun's electromagnetic fields. Maultsby could not get his bearings by using the charts and sextant. He decided to fly toward what he believed to be the North Pole, collect the air samples in the filter-paper device and bottles designed for the purpose, and then turn back to fly home. But because the North Pole did not lie where Maultsby believed it to be, he got lost and could not find his way back.

The realization that he was lost came to Maultsby only after he had been flying for eight hours and his fuel supply was almost exhausted. He expected to pick up a radio signal from the Alaskan island he had passed on his way to the North Pole, but there was none. Instead, he heard the voice of a rescue pilot asking him to identify his location by the stars. Maultsby saw Orion 15 degrees to the left of his plane's nose. The rescue pilot who was supposed to meet him over Barter Island but could not do so suggested that Maultsby turn 10 degrees left, but then another voice suggested doing the opposite—turn 30 degrees right.

Unbeknownst to Maultsby, the second voice belonged to a Soviet controller who had spotted the U-2 flying over the Chukotka Peninsula, a thousand miles west of his route and Barter Island, with its radio beacon. The fact that Maultsby had been spotted by Soviet radar over the sovereign airspace of the USSR put him in danger, but Strategic Air Command intelligence officers at Offutt Air Force Base in Nebraska, who were spying on Soviet radar signals, had intercepted the Soviet controller's message and also learned Maultsby's position. Yet this did not mean that Maultsby would be rescued from his predicament, because SAC was not about to reveal its successful monitoring of Soviet radar signals.

Maultsby was unaware that ever since he crossed into Soviet airspace and heard the unfamiliar voice on his sideband radio, he had been hunted by Soviet jet fighters, which took off from their air bases in Pevek and, ironically, Anadyr, the town that shared its name with the Soviet Cuban operation. The SAC intelligence officers in Nebraska were tracking Maultsby's route and the Soviet jets speeding toward his plane but could do nothing without revealing their monitoring to the Soviets.[5]

In fact, they did not have to do anything. Soviet MIG fighters could not reach the high altitude at which the light U-2 plane was flying. The two MiG-17P all-weather fighter jets from the 25th Fighter Division of

Air Defense Forces that were sent in pursuit of Maultsby's plane could fly at a speed of more than 1,000 kilometers per hour and reach an altitude of 15,600 meters in fifteen minutes, but that did not count for much against a U-2 plane flying at an altitude of more than 21,000 meters. The MiGs had no chance of catching the U-2 but, just in case, the Alaska Air Command dispatched two Convair F-102 Delta Dagger interceptors to protect their spy plane and, if necessary, confront the MiGs once Maultsby crossed into American airspace.[6]

The F-102s could rise as high as 16,300 meters or 53,400 feet, not enough to reach U-2 altitude but perfect for intercepting the Soviet fighters. The MiGs were armed with two 23 mm autocannons with eighty rounds of ammunition per gun and one 37 mm autocannon with forty rounds of ammunition. The F-102s had no guns but were armed with twenty-four unguided rockets and nine Falcon air-to-air missiles. Under normal circumstances that would suffice to deal with MiG firepower and engage the Soviet jets in a firefight. But circumstances were not normal. The US Air Force was on DEFCON 2 alert, which meant that the Falcon missiles carried by the two F-102s were armed with nuclear warheads. If attacked, the F-102 pilots had no means of defending themselves but with the nuclear-tipped Falcon missiles.[7]

The MiGs unexpectedly turned back, never reaching American airspace because they were short of fuel. But so was Maultsby's U-2. He had enough fuel for roughly nine and a half hours and had already been flying more than nine hours. To save fuel he shut off the engine, making use of the U-2's huge wingspread to glide. The instructions he could barely hear from his navigator at home base directed him eastward, back to American territory. With no engine working and lights off, his cabin depressurized while his flight suit inflated. As the plane glided, it steadily lost altitude, and the prospect for Maultsby began to look like a cold death either in the air, on the snowfields of Chukotka, or amid the glaciers of Alaska.

It was then, when almost all hope was gone, that Maultsby spotted the two F-102 jets flying beside him. He was now under nuclear protection but without much fuel to spare or battery power remaining to communicate with the F-102 pilots. Yet he managed to hear their greeting: "Welcome home." They led him to an icy air strip at the radar station on Kotzebue Sound, an arm of the Chukchi Sea, where Maultsby managed to land his fuelless plane. It was a double miracle: not only did Maultsby not perish, but the scrambled American and Soviet jets did not engage in a fight over his plane.[8]

This did not yet mean a happy ending. The Soviets might very well assume that Maultsby's flight had been made in preparation for an all-out nuclear attack on the USSR. The question for Kennedy and his advisers was what to do with the pilot and his flight. Their main concern was not his well-being or the safety of his plane, which had not returned to the base yet, but the reaction it might produce on the part of Khrushchev.

◊◊◊

"THEY WILL PROBABLY BE MAKING A BIG BLAST OUT OF THAT in the next day or two," said Dean Rusk to the president and his aides during the afternoon session of ExCom, which began at 4:00 p.m. that day. No longer concerned about the possible outbreak of hostilities and nuclear war—the reaction that the news had provoked from McNamara as soon as he heard it—Rusk proposed issuing a public statement suggesting that the plane was on a routine mission and had got lost because of instrument failure. Kennedy was against any announcement whatever. "I think we are better off not to do it if we can get away with not having some leak," said the president. "Because I think our problem is to maintain our credibility with Khrushchev."

Kennedy was thinking about future negotiations with Khrushchev over the missile swap. He was prepared to negotiate the deal, but on one condition: Khrushchev had to stop the deployment of missiles already on Cuban soil. "I think we ought to be able to say that the matter of Turkey and so on, in fact all these matters, can be discussed if he'll cease work," said Kennedy to his advisers. "Otherwise, he's going to announce that we've rejected his proposal. And then, where are we?" He still was in the minority but kept pushing, and when he left the

room for a moment, Robert Kennedy, who sensed the new determination in his brother's attitude, told the gathering: "I think that he almost
said that he would be willing to discuss Turkish bases or anything that
they want to discuss." By "they" Robert meant the Soviets in general
and Khrushchev in particular.

Most of the ExCom members continued to oppose the removal of
the missiles from Turkey, suggesting that Kennedy propose to Khrushchev that they negotiate that issue once the Cuban crisis was resolved.
"Well, isn't that really rejecting their proposal of this morning?" asked
Kennedy. He wanted ExCom to discuss political and diplomatic means
of removing the missiles from Turkey, not debate the idea itself. "We
have the question of a choice between the bilateral arrangements with
Turkey—in which we more or less do it. Or whether we go through
NATO and let NATO put the pressure on, and also explain to the Turks
what's going to happen to them if it doesn't—if they end up slowing
things down." The opposition, represented by Bundy and Dillon, had
shifted gears, questioning whether approval to remove the missiles
could be obtained from either NATO or Turkey before Monday.[9]

John Kennedy kept pushing. "To be reasonable, we're not going to
get these weapons out of Cuba, probably anyway—but I mean, by negotiation. We're going to have to take our weapons out of Turkey. I don't
think he's not going to [remove missiles from Cuba]—now that he made
that public," said Kennedy, turning to Llewellyn Thompson. "I don't
agree, Mr. President," came the answer. As the discussion dragged on,
Robert Kennedy saved the situation by telling his brother, "Why do we
bother you with it, Mr. President? Why don't you let us work this out?"
The president responded that indeed they had to move on to other top-
ics, but they also had to decide on his response to Khrushchev. "Why
don't we try to work it out for you without you being there to pick it
apart?" responded Robert. Everyone laughed. The matter was relegated
to a drafting committee without being decided in principle.[10]

It was the first time during the crisis that Kennedy had faced such
strong opposition from his own aides. Unlike the members of Khrushchev's Presidium, who were formally equals of the Soviet leader and

had the same voting rights, the members of ExCom were there to advise the president and serve at his pleasure. But they exercised much more freedom in defending their positions than Khrushchev's colleagues could ever have dreamed of. Aides, however, were only part of Kennedy's problem. The Joint Chiefs of Staff were also in opposition to him, and with the Cubans now starting to shoot at American planes, Kennedy was at the mercy of his military commanders and developments on the ground that were beyond his control.

◊◊◊

THE INFORMATION THAT KENNEDY AND HIS AIDES RECEIVED during the afternoon session of ExCom from the Pentagon was alarming: antiaircraft batteries in Cuba were now shooting at low-flying American reconnaissance planes, forcing some of them to turn back. McNamara believed that if fire continued the next day, the US Air Force "must attack back, either the SAMs and/or MIG aircraft that would come against them or the ground fire that comes up." His other option was to respond on the next day with a general strike against all military targets in Cuba.

When the news of antiaircraft fire first arrived, Bundy reminded everyone that the Cubans had issued a warning about starting to shoot at American airplanes. But what McNamara now proposed was not a strike against Cuban antiaircraft batteries but against Soviet-operated SAM missiles and, potentially, against their other installations, including nuclear-armed ballistic missiles. "I'm rather inclined to take the more general response," Kennedy told his aides. He no longer believed that a strike against a selected antiaircraft battery or missile site would be effective. But he asked for more time to make a final decision. "Do the reconnaissance tomorrow," he told his aides. "If we get fired on, then we meet here and we decide whether to do a much more general [strike]." Kennedy was playing for time, which he needed if he were to attempt a diplomatic solution.[11]

It soon became apparent that he had no time at all. "The U-2 was shot down," said McNamara, interrupting the discussion in the Cabinet Room. Kennedy had just impressed on his aides the need to organize NATO support for the Cuba-Turkey swap as soon as possible. This news was not about Maultsby's plane but about another U-2 overflying Cuba about which they had been informed earlier in the day. "A U-2 was shot down?" asked John Kennedy in disbelief. "Was the pilot killed?" Robert Kennedy asked in turn. "The pilot's body is in the plane," came the answer from General Taylor. He added that the plane had been struck by a surface-to-air missile, which suggested that it had been fired not by the Cubans but by the Soviets.[12]

The U-2 plane on which McNamara reported had been piloted by a thirty-five-year-old veteran of the Korean War, Major Rudolf Anderson. It belonged to the 4028th Strategic Reconnaissance Weather Squadron of the 4080th Strategic Reconnaissance Wing, permanently stationed at Laughlin Air Force Base in Texas. But with the Cuban missile crisis in full swing and the CIA increasing its surveillance overflights, Anderson had been transferred to the East Coast. On the morning of October 27 he took off from McCoy Air Force Base in Orlando, Florida, heading for Cuba. He sent a coded message once he left American airspace and entered Cuban airspace at 10:12 a.m. EST.[13]

The news about Anderson's U-2 being overdue at the base reached the Joint Chiefs of Staff at 2:03 p.m. Forty-four minutes later, at 2:47 p.m., the Chief of Naval Operations Office Log recorded news of an announcement by the Cuban minister of defense that his forces "had fired at a hostile aircraft." By that time Anderson's U-2 was an hour overdue at his base, but there was no indication that the plane had been shot down. At 4:50 p.m. Admiral Charles Griffin, the deputy chief of naval operations, received a report about the downing of the plane. Immediately he ordered a revision of Plan 312 (Shoe Black), which contained instructions for "discriminatory retaliation in the event of shooting at reconnaissance aircraft." McNamara was notified soon afterward.

"Well, now this is much [more] of an escalation by them, isn't it?" were the first words uttered by President Kennedy on hearing the news. "Yes, exactly," responded McNamara. Kennedy was trying to make sense of what had just happened in the context of the two letters that Khrushchev had sent him in the last twenty-four hours. "How do we explain the effect of this Khrushchev message of last night and their decision [to shoot down an American plane]?" asked the president. "How do we interpret this?" responded McNamara. "I do not know how to interpret it."[14]

The dark room in which they were all operating as they tried to discern the rationale behind Khrushchev's contradictory letters had suddenly been darkened even more by the shocking news. The members of ExCom could not imagine that they were not the only ones losing control of their people on the ground and in the sky. Khrushchev was facing the same situation, and the consequences in his case were even more dangerous.

19

"TARGET DESTROYED!"

By the morning of October 27, few people in the Cuban leadership or among the Soviet commanders in Cuba doubted that an invasion was imminent. There was no need for spies or secret information from UN headquarters in New York or the KGB station in Washington to reach that conclusion. The evidence was right there in the sky above Cuba. It came with the noise of US Navy Vought F-8 Crusader airplanes, supersonic fighters that could also be used as bombers and surveillance planes. Since October 23 they had been crisscrossing Cuba on a regular basis, focusing on Soviet ballistic missile sites and military installations.

Operation "Blue Moon," initiated on October 17 and implemented on October 23, involved pilots and planes from two photographic squadrons reinforced by pilots from the US Marine Corps. They flew RF-8A Crusader planes with three CAX-12 trimetrogon cameras and two K-17 vertical cameras, all manufactured by Chicago Aerial Industries. Flying 1,000 feet over their targets (as compared to the 70,000-foot altitude of the U-2s), the pilots could get close-up photos of the sites, taking approximately four frames per second, or one shot every 70 yards. The planes flew in pairs, both aircraft equipped with cameras. They would take off from Boca Chica Naval Air Station at Key West, Florida, twice a day and, after flying over their targets, often multiple times (it took them approximately four minutes to go over Cuba), return to Florida, landing at the Naval Air Station in Jacksonville. Film collected there would be sent to Andrews Air Force Base for development and then to the CIA National Interpretation Center.[1]

The Crusaders flew unobstructed until October 27, when Castro gave the order to start shooting at the low-flying planes. It was Crusader photographs that Adlai Stevenson used at the United Nations on October 25. Commander William Ecker, the commanding officer of VFP-62, one of the light photographic squadrons, reminisced many years later about flying over Cuba in the midst of antiaircraft fire: "You could see the popcorn in your mirrors." "Popcorn" meant the white puffs of antiaircraft shells bursting in the wake of the fast-moving Crusader. "But we never got hit," noted Ecker.

Lev Evseev, a young officer with a Soviet Air Force unit in Cuba, remembered that both automatic rifles and antiaircraft guns were used to fire at the Crusaders. After someone fired an automatic rifle at a pair of the planes flying over his airfield, recalled Evseev, "Cuban anti-aircraft units, taking that as a signal, opened fire." Evseev found an ideal vantage point to witness the event. "I quickly climbed onto a wing of my plane (it was covered) and saw shells bursting ahead, above, and below the Americans flying overhead, but again and again they failed to make a hit," he recalled. "The Americans made three overflights, and high-caliber machine guns were fired three times. Shrapnel from anti-aircraft shells kept falling among us. But the Americans, having carried out their mission, flew away safe and sound."[2]

The unceasing Crusader overflights racked the nerves of Soviet commanders on the island and lent credibility to Castro's panicky claims that the Americans were coming. "Every hour there were dozens of planes overhead. The roar of motors shook the air. The atmosphere was that of a mass air strike with bombs dropping. The Americans were conducting a psychic attack," recalled General Leonid Garbuz, General Pliev's deputy in charge of combat readiness. Psychological warfare was not part of the American strategy, but the American commanders hoped that the Soviets would become so used to American planes in the air that when the time came for an air strike they would be caught off guard, unable to distinguish bombers from reconnaissance aircraft.[3]

On the evening of October 26 Garbuz was summoned to General Pliev's office after Pliev had spent a good half of the day in the company of Fidel Castro and other Cuban and Soviet commanders. Also in attendance was Pliev's deputy in charge of air defenses, General Stepan Grechko, and the chief of staff of the Group of Soviet Forces in Cuba, General Pavel Akindinov. The discussion, remembered Garbuz, focused on "what they [the Americans] had uncovered and what they hadn't . . . because tomorrow they could be fired upon and we'd have to decide what to remove and what to replace." The generals concluded that many of the ballistic missile sites under the command of General Igor Statsenko had been discovered by the Americans. "And we reported to Moscow—I wrote it in my own hand rather quickly—that our opponent had managed to uncover some strategic areas," recalled Garbuz.[4]

Pliev sent a telegram drafted by Garbuz to Moscow reporting that "[a] decision has been made to use all available antiaircraft resources in case of a strike against our sites by American aviation." Khrushchev and Malinovsky would approve the decision later that day, but it had gone into effect immediately. "We received a secret coded telegram: be prepared for military action; an American intervention is expected," recalled Captain Nikolai Antonets, chief of staff of the missile battalion of the 507th regiment, 27th Air Defense Division, in the vicinity of Banes in eastern Cuba. "We were allowed to go on air and turn on radio communications. Everyone felt that war was possible." Major Nikolai Serovoi, who was on duty that night at the headquarters of the 27th Division, remembered an even more specific instruction concerning the time of the invasion. "A coded telegram has been received: war at dawn tomorrow. Make the elements of the division combat-ready, but secretly," Serovoi was informed in a phone call from the division commander, Colonel Georgii Voronkov.[5]

The new order from Pliev was in line with instructions earlier received from Moscow. In the tense evening hours of October 22, when the agitated Soviet leaders gathered in the Kremlin in anticipation of Kennedy's announced speech on Cuba, Minister of Defense Rodion Malinovsky ordered Pliev to "undertake urgent measures to increase combat readiness and to repel the enemy by joint efforts of the Cuban army and all units of Soviet troops, excluding the weapons of Statsenko and all of Beloborodov's cargo." This meant that Pliev was authorized to use all non-nuclear-tipped weapons, including the surface-to-air missiles of the air defense units. The caveat was that he could do so only to "repel the enemy."[6]

For the moment, all they could do was wait for an American attack. But with American planes in the air, Cubans firing, and rumors of imminent invasion spreading like wildfire, Soviet commanders found the line between impending and actual attack becoming blurred.

◊◊◊

As Khrushchev sent Kennedy one letter and then another, looking for a way out of the Cuban nightmare, and Kennedy argued with his aides over the proposed missile swap in order to make an invasion of Cuba unnecessary, Soviet officers and soldiers on the island were living in a world of their own, unaware of the diplomatic moves at the highest levels. They were preparing to resist an invasion, and their main concern was to meet deadlines for deployment of the missiles on the island.

The commander of the 51st Missile Division, General Igor Statsenko, some of whose installations had been discovered and photographed by US overflights, as Pliev had reported to Moscow, had every reason to be proud of what he had accomplished. On September 8, the General Staff had ordered Statsenko to prepare the two regiments with medium-range R-12 missiles for combat by November 1. The regiments armed with intermediate-range R-14s were to be made battle-ready in November and December. Most of the missiles, men, and equipment of the intermediate-missile regiments were still en route to Cuba at the time of Kennedy's announcement and had to be turned back. But three medium-range missile regiments and a good part of the fourth regiment were already on the island, and Statsenko did all he could to get them ready before the November 1 deadline.[7]

The Soviet officers and soldiers who were rushing to make the missiles operational found themselves on difficult terrain and in unusual climatic conditions for which they were ill-prepared. Colonel Dmitrii Yazov, a future Soviet minister of defense, recalled that "[t]here were no awnings in the area where the regiment was stationed. Everything was stored in the open air. There were only tents for the personnel. Given the tropical heat and high humidity, conditions were ideal for the spread of bacteria in those tents. In just a few days cans of food began to swell and explode like bombs." And Yazov's men soon discovered another problem: the trees in the grove where they sought shelter from the burning sun turned out to be poisonous. "It was not a pleasant sight," wrote Yazov, recalling his visit to the makeshift regimental hospital. "Swellings, blisters under the eyes, and festering wounds. The patients tried to drive away clouds of mosquitoes hanging over the bunks. The air was heavy with the poisonous odor of guavas; a huge, ominous black cloud was creeping up on the camp." General Pliev, who visited Yazov's regiment, ordered its relocation to a safer place.[8]

Aleksandr Voropaev, a young sergeant at the time, remembered that in his infantry regiment, stationed in the town of Torrens near Havana, spoiled food almost led to a mutiny. Because of high temperatures and even higher humidity, food went bad very quickly. "Worms began to show up in pasta and porridge, more and more of them as time went on," he recalled. The worms in the food reminded many soldiers of the mutiny on the battleship *Potemkin*, the subject of a classic Soviet film directed by Sergei Eisenstein. There the revolt began with the discovery of worms in pieces of meat in the borscht served to the sailors.

The situation was serious enough for the commander of the regiment, Lieutenant Colonel Karpov, to summon his subordinates for a talk.

"What, do you think that the officers are eating different food?" wrote Voropaev, recalling his commander's words. "It's a different mess, but the food is the same. And the worms on the plates are the same. Yesterday they brought Lieutenant Colonel Krivoy and me . . . canned meat with pasta for lunch. And there were worms in his pasta and mine. We looked at each other, threw out the worms, and started eating what was available." Karpov promised that the situation would improve as soon as a ship with new food supplies reached a nearby port. The soldiers did not revolt, but their stomachs did. Voropaev wrote later: "I don't know whether it was from the worms or from the water that we drank directly from tubes lying on the ground, but dysentery appeared in the regiment and soon reached epidemic proportions. Out of the total personnel of about 1,300 men, more than 800 found themselves in the 'machine-gun companies'—an expression that became almost official."[9]

Kennedy spoke on the evening of October 22. The next morning at 8:00 a.m. Cuba time, General Statsenko put his entire division on high alert. By then he had under his command almost eight thousand Soviet officers and soldiers, thirty-six R-12 missiles, and the same number of warheads for them. Colonel Ivan Sidorov's first launching battery of intermediate ballistic missiles was ready on October 8, the second on October 12. By October 18, he recalled, his entire regiment was combat-ready (General Statsenko gave the date of October 20 in his report). By that date Sidorov's regiment was prepared to launch nuclear missiles against targets in the United States on two and a half hours' notice. There was one caveat: in order to fire, they needed nuclear warheads to be delivered to the site. That was just a matter of time, as the warheads were already in Cuba. And the Soviets had all the time they needed: Sidorov's missiles were ready to go two days before Kennedy's television address.

On October 24, Statsenko ordered the commanders of two other regiments, Colonels Sidorov and Bandilovsky, to "share" some of their fuel and other equipment with the missile regiment under the command of Colonel Soloviev, whose equipment never reached Cuba because of the blockade. They did as ordered. By October 25, Bandilovsky's entire regiment and one missile squadron of Soloviev's regiment were also on high alert. On the night of October 26, nuclear warheads were delivered from central storage to Sidorov's positions. By October 27 he was not just on high alert and ready to fire his missiles but also fully equipped to attack the United States with nuclear weapons. Kennedy's worst nightmare had suddenly become a reality.[10]

◊◊◊

GENERAL STATSENKO AND THE REST OF THE SOVIET OFFICERS and men spent the whole night of October 26 getting ready for the attack that they expected to begin at any minute. It did not come. "The day dawned, but it was quiet, and the radar found no targets in the sky. But everyone's nerves were strained to the breaking point, and people were weary after a sleepless night," recalled Major Nikolai Serovoi, an officer on duty at the headquarters of the 27th Antiaircraft Division in Camagüey in central Cuba.

Around 8:00 a.m. on October 27, with tropical rain picking up and the worsening weather making an attack less likely, Pliev beat a retreat, issuing a new order to his troops. "We were ordered to go on duty in smaller units and fire only in case of direct enemy attack," recalled Major Serovoi. Exhausted by the sleepless and nerve-racking night, the commander of Serovoi's division, Colonel Georgii Voronkov, and many of the officers left the command post to have a bite to eat and get some sleep. Serovoi, for whom it was the start of a second consecutive twenty-four-hour shift, remained at his post. He was exhausted. "We got no sleep the whole night," he recalled.[11]

It was around 9:00 a.m. that radar in Camagüey located a target—an airplane flying toward the eastern tip of the island at an altitude of more than 20 kilometers, or over 65,000 feet. The plane was being

piloted by Major Rudolf Anderson of the United States Air Force 4080th
Strategic Reconnaissance Wing. He had taken off in his Lockheed U-2F
from McCoy Air Force Base in Orlando, Florida, and was picked up by
Soviet radar at 9:12 a.m. Havana time entering Cuban air space over
Cayo Coco Island in central Cuba. At 9:20 Anderson was already flying over the headquarters of Colonel Voronkov's air defense division in
Camagüey. He then flew south to the town of Manzanillo, turning east
toward Santiago de Cuba and passing over Guantánamo Naval Base
before making a sharp eastward turn and heading over the northern
shore toward Banes, a town in Holguín province.[12]

Major Anderson spent more than an hour in Cuban airspace, maintaining radio silence and not responding to Soviet radio signals that
asked him to identify himself. His cameras were clicking the whole
time, taking new pictures of Soviet missile sites. The Soviet officers
knew exactly what was going on: the positions they had built with such
effort were being exposed. At the command post of the 27th Antiaircraft Division in Camagüey Major Serovoi was besieged with demands
from regimental commanders to allow them to shoot down the intruder.
Eager to see action at last, they had their Desna S-75 surface-to-air missiles, like the one that had shot down Gary Powers in 1960, ready to fire.

"The commanders of anti-aircraft missile regiments began asking
me insistently to allow them to open fire, maintaining that this was
indeed a direct attack," recalled Serovoi. "Others considered that the
scout could not be allowed to get away scot-free with his reconnaissance
data about our positions: after him, there would be a crushing bomb
strike against the positions. I repeat that at that moment we were intent
on repelling an attack; we had not yet 'cooled down.'"[13]

Major Serovoi called Pliev's headquarters, located in an underground bunker at the El Chico estate near Havana, where the duty officer was General Stepan Grechko, the fifty-two-year-old chief of staff of
the Moscow air defense region, who had been dispatched to Cuba to
serve as Pliev's deputy in charge of air defense. He had two divisions
armed with Desna S-75 surface-to-air missiles under his command.
They had been brought to Cuba ahead of Statsenko's missile regiments

to protect them from discovery by American U-2 spy planes. But now the Americans were flying unobstructed over Statsenko's installations, making Grechko's whole mission pointless. With a strike or invasion around the corner, the nuclear missile sites Grechko was supposed to protect were turning into sitting ducks for American bombers.

Serovoi told Grechko that "the unit commanders are insisting that the reconnaissance plane be destroyed." Grechko did not know what to do, and Pliev was not around. After a sleepless night the sickly commander, struggling with kidney disease, had gone to get some rest. General Garbuz, who reached the command post around 10:00 a.m. that morning, remembered Grechko telling him that he could not reach Pliev because he was sick. Serovoi recalled that the debate between Grechko's headquarters and the regimental commanders on whether to shoot down the American plane went on for at least half an hour. "General Grechko advised not to hurry, to wait, as he said 'I can't reach the commander,'" recalled Serovoi.[14]

When General Garbuz arrived at the headquarters, Grechko informed him that "[a] 'guest' has been circling around us for more than an hour. I think the order has to be given to shoot down the American plane because it can discover our positions to their fullest extent, and the reconnaissance data will be known to Washington in a few hours." Both generals knew that Pliev issued a prohibition against shooting at the American planes without his direct orders, but he was not around and out of reach. Grechko consulted with his other deputies. Most of them were missile officers who considered Pliev, as a former cavalry-man, a poor fit for the job, since he knew nothing about missiles. They all were in favor of shooting down the plane. Garbuz told Grechko: "[A]ll the missile starts have now been 'lit up,' and the secret information cannot be allowed to make its way to the Pentagon."

Grechko probably felt that the decision was now up to him, since air defense was his responsibility. A veteran of World War II who had seen a great deal of fighting on the German front, Grechko knew that reconnaissance flights of enemy airplanes would be followed by bombing. He had been wounded in 1943 in the course of a German attack on the headquarters of the army group to which he had been assigned. Grechko belonged to an elite group of Soviet commanders closely associated personally with Nikita Khrushchev. These included the former commander of strategic missile forces, Marshal Kirill Moskalenko, and Grechko's direct superior in the Moscow air defense district, General Pavel Batitsky, who had personally shot Khrushchev's archrival, Lavrentii Beria, in December 1953. Dispatched to Cuba directly from Moscow, while the others had come from the Soviet provinces, Grechko had more clout than other deputies of Pliev.[15]

After "the radar man said he would go back to Guantánamo in five minutes," recalled Garbuz, "Grechko said, 'I have made a decision to shoot him down.'" He added to Garbuz: "I guess we'll both answer for it." Garbuz agreed. "We both were responsible," he admitted decades later. In Camagüey Major Serovoi received the order to open fire from the commander of his division, Colonel Voronkov, who never told Serovoi who had given the order; Serovoi believed that Voronkov had issued it on his own. He passed on the order to the units of the division and immediately informed Pliev's headquarters, where General Grechko neither confirmed nor aborted the order. Whether the actual order originated with Garbuz, as he claimed, or with Voronkov, as suggested by Serovoi, Grechko as the senior officer in charge was now responsible for an order that was in clear violation of Pliev's instructions.[16]

It looked for some time, however, as if the order would have no effect, since precious time had been lost. While Grechko was hesitating about whether or not to shoot down the U-2, it disappeared from the radar screens. But the order remained in force, and a few minutes later, when the U-2 reappeared on radar after making a turn over the eastern tip of the island and proceeding westward, in the direction of Havana, Voronkov's men were ready. At the SAM launch site near the town of Banes, the commander of the SAM battalion, Major Ivan Gerchenov, his chief of staff, Captain Nikolai Antonets, and Lieutenant Aleksei Riapenko crammed into the cabin of the R-12 launcher and followed the target on the radar screen. Antonets, who was maintaining communications with regimental headquarters, asked Gerchenov: "What are we going to do? Shoot?" Antonets asked once for confirmation of the order, then a second time. "Wait, the order will follow any minute," came the answer.[17]

"Destroy the target with a salvo of three!" Lieutenant Riapenko, the launcher's target officer, heard those words in the voice of Major Gerchenov, who had finally got the order confirmed. "I switched all three firing channels to BR mode and pressed the 'Fire' button of the first channel," recalled Riapenko. "The missile took off from the launch pad. Then I reported: 'Target locked in!' The first missile had already been in flight for nine or ten seconds when the commander ordered: 'Fire two!' I pressed the 'Fire' button of the second channel. When the first missile exploded, a cloud appeared on the screens. I reported: 'One, explosion. Target connected. Target damaged!' After the explosion of the second missile the target abruptly began to lose altitude, and I reported: 'Two, explosion. Target destroyed!'"

◊◊◊

IT WAS 10:19 A.M. HAVANA TIME, 11:19 A.M. IN WASHINGTON, and 8:19 p.m. in Moscow. In the commotion that followed the order, one missile was shot after another instead of in an automatic burst. But that no longer mattered. The target was destroyed. Gerchenov commended Riapenko for acting calmly under enormous stress. When Riapenko emerged from the launch cabin, he was welcomed with much more exuberant expressions of appreciation. "They picked me up and began tossing me into the air—that was easy, as I weighed only 56 kilograms," recalled Riapenko. The man who had almost started a nuclear war was twenty-two years old and weighed 123 pounds. Jubilation was short-lived. Riapenko recalled that they considered what had just happened to be the beginning of a military conflict and expected retaliation.[18]

Major Serovoi reported the downing of Target 33 to General Grechko's headquarters. Once again Grechko was silent, neither congratulating Serovoi on the news nor reprimanding him for violating Pliev's order. A few hours later a group of Soviet officers visited the area where the U-2 had crashed. They apparently found Major Anderson's documents and personal belongings in the cockpit. It is not clear whether they saw his body. The regimental cipher clerk, Gennadii Tolshin, later recalled the text of the telegram that he sent to General Pliev on behalf of Colonel Voronkov: "To Pavlov. On October 27, 1962, at 10 hours 21 minutes, TARGET no. 33, a violating U-2 reconnaissance aircraft of the United States Air Force, was destroyed. It was piloted by Captain R. Anderson, United States Air Force, born in New York City, leaving his wife and three daughters. Voronkov."[19]

Radio Havana was the first to break the news about the downing of the American plane. Not only was it a major boost to Cuban morale, but also, whether Castro realized it or not, the destruction of Target 33 marked the success of his strategy. His panic over the coming attack affected Pliev, who eventually lost control of his troops, physically and psychologically exhausted by the prolonged suspense. When news of the downing of the plane finally reached Pliev, he was as ambiguous about it as Grechko had been. "The commander in chief did not criticize us," recalled Garbuz. At least for the present, he did not try to blame the violation of his and Moscow's order on his deputies. Whether intentionally or not, he had lost control over his subordinates. Like Riapenko and his fellow officers, Pliev and his commanders now awaited what would come next. As far as they were concerned, the Americans were about to retaliate.[20]

20

SECRET RENDEZVOUS

The shooting down of the U-2 airplane piloted by Major Anderson became a turning point in the deliberations that President Kennedy and his advisers conducted that day. Robert Kennedy later suggested that the news changed the atmosphere in the Cabinet Room of the White House. "There was sympathy for Major Anderson and his family," wrote Robert. "There was the knowledge that we had to take military action to protect our pilots. There was the realization that the Soviet Union and Cuba apparently were preparing to do battle. And there was the feeling that the noose was tightening on all of us, on Americans, on mankind, and that the bridges to escape were crumbling."[1]

What, then, was to be done in that situation? "They have fired the first shot," said Paul Nitze. General Taylor proposed to retaliate by destroying the missile site that had shot down the plane and following up with a general strike if shooting at other planes continued. "It's what we agreed to do two days ago," said the general. "It looked good then, and it still looks good to me," said a member of ExCom whose voice on the tape remains unidentified. He seemed to express the opinion of the majority.

Earlier in the meeting Kennedy had voiced his support for Taylor's advocacy of all-out retaliation for any shooting down of a US aircraft. But immediate retaliation against a missile site was impossible—it was getting dark in Cuba. "It's too late. This is why it gets into tomorrow," explained McNamara. Neither the president nor his advisers could make sense of what had just happened. They appeared to be certain of only one thing: the shooting down of the plane was a deliberate act in the dangerous game being played by the Kremlin and its master, Nikita Khrushchev.[2]

The problem of American missiles in Turkey, addressed in the morning and afternoon sessions of ExCom, remained on the agenda and took on new urgency in light of the loss of the U-2 over Cuba. Kennedy's idea of getting rid of the missiles had only one strong supporter—Robert McNamara. But his reasoning had nothing to do with Kennedy's. If the president wanted to remove the missiles in order to prevent invasion and possible war, his secretary of defense wanted them out because by now he was leaning toward invasion, as advocated by the chiefs. There was a chance that the Soviets might respond to an invasion with a military strike somewhere else, and the missiles seemed to be a likely target—"sitting ducks" waiting to be "taken out." "I would suggest that to minimize the Soviet response against NATO following a US attack on Cuba, we get those Jupiters out of Turkey before the Cuban attack," McNamara told the ExCom. The majority was not convinced.[3]

When Kennedy left the cabinet room around 5:00 p.m. to attend his scheduled appointments, there was still no consensus on a response to Khrushchev's proposal to swap missiles. With Kennedy away, his aides continued the discussion and drafted alternative versions of a letter from the president to Khrushchev. Robert Kennedy and Sorensen were putting the finishing touches on the draft, which made no mention of the missiles in Turkey. McNamara was arguing for unilateral withdrawal of the missiles from Turkey and an exchange of the land-based Jupiters for sea-based Polaris missiles, while McCone of the CIA, backed by George Ball, was preparing a message to Khrushchev that combined an ultimatum to stop shooting at American planes with what amounted to acceptance of his proposed swap.

Everyone was going in a separate direction. People were exhausted, irritable, and generally at a loss. To complicate matters, Curtis LeMay and the Chiefs of Staff rejected the idea of a retaliatory strike against the SAM missiles, as they believed—correctly, as it turned out—that some nuclear missiles were already operational in Cuba. A strike against a SAM might therefore provoke a nuclear response from the Soviets. Accordingly, the chiefs wanted not a discriminatory strike but an all-out attack on Cuba as soon as possible. The window of opportunity for Kennedy and Khrushchev to make a deal was closing rapidly, and on the afternoon of October 27 it was anything but clear whether they could make the deadline.[4]

◊◊◊

TWO HOURS LATER, ROBERT KENNEDY BRIEFED HIS BROTHER privately on the continuing debates in ExCom. "He talked about Major Anderson and how it is always the brave and the best who die," wrote Robert Kennedy, recalling a meeting with his brother on the evening of October 27. Describing the trend of his brother's thoughts, he went on: "The politicians and officials sit home pontificating about great principles and issues, make the decisions, and dine with their wives and families, while the brave and the young die." John Kennedy then switched to his favorite topic, the danger of miscalculation, but according to Robert the gist of the conversation was to make sure that "every opportunity was . . . given to the Russians to find a peaceful settlement which would not diminish their national security or be a public humiliation."[5]

Whether Robert Kennedy's recollection of the words spoken by his brother that evening is accurate or not, there is no doubt that the downing of the U-2 and the death of the pilot strengthened Kennedy's determination to prevent war in any way possible, which meant accommodating the Soviets. All day he had fought to convince his aides that the only way to get rid of the missiles in Cuba was to swap them for those in Turkey. General Taylor told the Chiefs of Staff in his report on the ExCom meeting that afternoon that the president "has been seized with the idea of trading Turkish for Cuban missiles."[6]

There is no indication that his commitment to that solution weakened in the course of the day. But in the discussion with Robert, the president approved a letter to Khrushchev drafted by him and Ted Sorensen that made no reference whatever to Turkey. An earlier draft had included the phrase, "You should just understand that the bases in Turkey are under NATO jurisdiction." But the final version ignored Khrushchev's swap offer altogether. The letter promised negotiations if Khrushchev halted the construction of missile sites in Cuba. The basis for negotiations was removal of the Soviet missiles under United Nations supervision. Based on that, the blockade would be lifted and assurances against invasion given by the United States and its Latin American allies.[7]

John Kennedy accepted Robert's draft of the letter because he already had another plan: to send his brother to the Soviet ambassador, Anatoly Dobrynin, to negotiate the swap in secret. After his meeting with Robert, John Kennedy returned to the room where the ExCom was still in session and, after a brief discussion, asked selected members of ExCom to join him in the Oval Office. He did not want Lyndon Johnson around but invited McGeorge Bundy, who left us the only detailed recollection of what happened there. The main item on the agenda was the oral message that Robert Kennedy was to deliver to Dobrynin, along with the letter drafted by Robert and Ted Sorensen.

The American missiles in Turkey were the elephant in the room. Everyone knew that Kennedy wanted to trade them, but they were not mentioned in the letter to be delivered to Dobrynin. It was clear that Kennedy wanted his brother to discuss them with the Soviet ambassador, but how? Dean Rusk offered a solution: Robert would tell Dobrynin that while there could not be a publicly announced quid pro quo on the missiles in Cuba and Turkey, once the crisis was resolved on the basis of Kennedy's letter the president would remove the American missiles from Turkey.[8]

The solution was as old as diplomacy itself—a secret deal. Rusk's formula was based on an idea proposed by Raymond Hare, the American ambassador to Turkey, in a cable received in Washington earlier that day. One of Hare's suggestions was "dismantling the Jupiters" either in "a more obvious relation to the Cuban crisis" or, alternatively, "on a strictly secret basis with the Soviets." He added that "stipulation of secrecy might not be too convincing since would involve good faith of Soviets who would always have option to reveal to detriment of US Turkish relations." No one knew better than Kennedy that Khrushchev, who had lied about the missiles only a few weeks earlier, was not to be trusted, but he had no choice but to put his trust in that man again.[9]

"The moment Dean Rusk made his suggestion it became apparent to all of us that we should agree," remembered Bundy. But the secrecy provision of the deal required silence not only from Khrushchev but also from those making the decision on the American side. "Concerned as we all were by the cost of a public bargain struck under pressure at the apparent expense of the Turks, and aware as we were from the day's discussions that for some, even in our closest councils, even this unilateral private assurance might appear to betray an ally, we agreed without hesitation that none not in the room was to be informed of this additional message," recalled Bundy.[10]

The "additional message" mentioned by Bundy was in fact the main message that Robert Kennedy had to deliver and, shockingly, it would be kept secret from the rest of ExCom, including Vice President Johnson and the chairman of the Joint Chiefs of Staff, General Taylor, as well as the head of the CIA, John McCone. Rusk, the alleged author of the formula accepted by the others, later underplayed his role in the conspiracy and stressed that he had been adamant in making sure that the removal of the missiles from Turkey was not included in the Cuban deal.

"I suggested that since the Jupiters in Turkey were coming out in any event, we should inform the Russians of this so that this irrelevant question would not complicate the solution of the missile sites in Cuba," wrote Rusk later. "We agreed that Bobby should inform Ambassador Dobrynin orally. Shortly after we returned to our offices, I telephoned Bobby to underline that he should pass this along to Dobrynin only as information, not a public pledge. Bobby told me that he was then sitting with Dobrynin and had already talked with him. Bobby later told me that Dobrynin called this message 'very important information.'" Rusk's account allowed for the possibility that it was Robert Kennedy, and not he, who crossed the barely perceptible line between the reciprocal deal and the unrelated removal of missiles from Turkey. In actual fact, all those involved must have known what they were doing—making a secret swap without acknowledging it not only publicly but even privately.[11]

The conspirators were supposed to return to the ExCom session in an hour or so and discuss the options for the solution of the crisis while keeping Robert's mission secret from any interlocutors. The president had already decided on the trade. At that point, of course, few believed that the mission would succeed. After all, secret diplomatic deals were normally struck by allies or allies-to-be, not by adversaries on the verge of a major military conflict. The new atomic weapons turned both sides into hostages of possible nuclear annihilation. The two parties had to find some way of trusting each other. They had managed to do that in Berlin one year earlier. Maybe they would get lucky once again.

◊◊◊

ROBERT KENNEDY MET WITH ANATOLY DOBRYNIN IN HIS office at the Department of Justice soon after the president's secret gathering in the White House. "I told him first that we knew that work was continuing on the missile bases in Cuba and that in the last few days it had been expedited," wrote Robert Kennedy in *Thirteen Days*, recalling the message that he delivered to Dobrynin. "I said that in the last few hours we had learned that our reconnaissance planes flying over Cuba had been fired upon and that one of our U-2s had been shot down and the pilot killed. That for us was a most serious turn of events. President Kennedy did not want a military conflict. He had done everything possible to avoid a military engagement with Cuba and with the Soviet Union, but now they had forced our hand."[12]

In his own memoirs, Dobrynin recalled that Robert Kennedy had been much more explicit in speaking of the urgency of the situation. "The American military was demanding permission from the president to retaliate," Robert allegedly told the ambassador. In the report on the meeting that Dobrynin filed later that night, he expanded on Kennedy's explanation of the dangers posed by the new situation. "The USA government is determined to get rid of those bases—up to, in the extreme case, of bombing them, since, I repeat, they pose a great threat to the security of the USA," read Dobrynin's cable to Moscow recapitulating Robert Kennedy's words. "But in response to the bombing of these bases, in the course of which Soviet specialists might suffer, the Soviet government will undoubtedly respond with the same against us, somewhere in Europe. A real war will begin, in which millions of Americans and Russians will die."[13]

According to Dobrynin's report, he was the first to raise the issue of American missiles in Turkey after Kennedy explained his brother's official proposal to dismantle the Soviet missile bases and remove nuclear weapons from Cuba in exchange for an American pledge of noninvasion. As Dobrynin recalled decades later, at that moment he still had no instructions from Moscow on how to deal with the Americans, nor even a complete copy of Khrushchev's letter proposing a Cuban-Turkish swap—he had to rely on Western broadcasts. Still, now that Moscow's official backing of such a deal was clear to him, he decided to address the issue.[14]

According to Dobrynin, "Robert Kennedy was ready with an answer" to his question about Turkey. What we know today is that Kennedy was in fact waiting for an opportunity to discuss the missiles in Turkey. "If that is the only obstacle to achieving the regulation I mentioned earlier, then the president doesn't see any insurmountable difficulties in resolving this issue," Robert told Dobrynin. "The greatest difficulty for the president is the public discussion of the issue of Turkey," he continued, explaining to Dobrynin how his brother proposed to resolve the issue. "Formally the deployment of missile bases in Turkey was done by a special decision of the NATO Council. To announce now a unilateral decision by the president of the USA to withdraw missile bases from Turkey—this would damage the entire structure of NATO and the US position as the leader of NATO, where, as the Soviet government knows very well, there are many arguments. In short, if such a decision were announced now it would seriously tear apart NATO. However, President Kennedy is ready to come to agree[ment] on that question with N. S. Khrushchev, too. I think that in order to withdraw these bases from Turkey, we need 4–5 months."

Robert Kennedy had successfully delivered the "additional message" to Dobrynin with which he had been entrusted by his brother. But that was not the end of his mission: its sine qua non was to assure the secrecy of the deal. He told Dobrynin: "The president can't say anything public in this regard about Turkey." According to Dobrynin, Robert added that John Kennedy's "comments about Turkey are extremely confidential; besides him and his brother, only 2–3 people know about it in Washington." Kennedy could not swear Dobrynin and, through him, Khrushchev to secrecy, but he indicated very clearly that the deal would be honored only if it remained secret. Robert Kennedy requested an answer from Khrushchev by the following day: a "clear answer in principle, not to get into a wordy discussion, which might drag things out. The current serious situation, unfortunately, is such that there is very little time to resolve this whole issue."

Robert Kennedy bade goodbye to Dobrynin, leaving him the number of a direct telephone line to the White House through which he was asked to deliver Khrushchev's response as soon as he got it. Kennedy also told the ambassador that he was going to see his brother, with whom he was spending "almost all his time now." Dobrynin fully understood the seriousness of the situation as communicated not only by the content of Robert's message but also by his overall appearance and demeanor. "I should say that during our meeting R. Kennedy was very upset," reads the final paragraph of Dobrynin's report to Moscow, "in any case, I've never seen him like this before. True, about twice he tried to return to the topic of 'deception' (that he talked about so persistently during our previous meeting), but he did so in passing and without any edge to it. He didn't even try to get into fights on various subjects, as he usually does, and only persistently returned to one topic: time is of the essence and we shouldn't miss the chance."[15]

The concluding portion of the conversation is known to us only through Dobrynin's recollections as recorded in the report he filed that night and the memoirs he wrote decades later. Robert Kennedy's recollections are of little use. Both in the report to Rusk that he filed three days later, on October 30, when the most acute phase of the crisis was already over, and in *Thirteen Days*, which he cowrote years later, he remained silent about the Turkish deal. Only one sentence in Kennedy's memorandum on the meeting, three and a quarter pages in length, dealt with the secret part of his negotiations with Dobrynin. It concerned the time period after which the missiles should be withdrawn. Robert informed Rusk: "If some time elapsed—and per your instructions, I mentioned four to five months—I said I was sure that these matters could be resolved satisfactorily." In the copy of the memo available today, even that sentence has been crossed out.[16]

◊◊◊

ROBERT KENNEDY WAS BACK AT THE WHITE HOUSE AROUND 8:40 p.m., where he found his elder brother talking on the phone with his four-year-old daughter, Caroline. Together with her younger brother, John, and their mother, Jacqueline, Caroline was at the family estate of Glen Ora in Virginia. With a nuclear strike on DC and the White House becoming a distinct possibility, John Kennedy wanted his family to be outside the possible zone of destruction. Members of the administration would be evacuated in case of nuclear attack, but the wives and children of his aides would have to get out of DC on their own. Although he could take his family with him into evacuation, Kennedy wanted to save them the ordeal. Jacqueline's pleas to allow them to stay in DC that weekend were to no avail.[17]

Robert briefed John Kennedy on his rendezvous with the Soviet ambassador while sharing a meal with his brother and John's confidant and special assistant, David Powers. Powers was present at some of the ExCom meetings but always remained silent, having been charged by the president with the task of observing the scene and reporting his thoughts about Kennedy's performance and the dynamics in the room. Now Powers was eating a warmed-up chicken left by the kitchen staff for the president and drinking wine, while John and Robert Kennedy conversed. "God, Dave," said John Kennedy jokingly to his aide. "The way you're eating up all that chicken and drinking up all my wine, anybody would think it was your last meal." Powers was quick to respond: "The way Bobby's been talking, I thought it was my last meal."[18]

Given the grim situation, there was a grain of truth in that exchange. "The President was not optimistic, nor was I," wrote Robert in his memoir. With two ExCom sessions in one day behind him, John Kennedy was getting ready to resume the meeting at 9:00 p.m. to continue discussion. Military confrontation and possibly all-out war were closer at that point than ever before. Discussion resumed as planned but led to no new policy decisions. Kennedy was playing for time. So were Rusk, Bundy, and other members of ExCom who knew of Robert's secret approach to Dobrynin. The president was waiting for a response from Khrushchev both to his official letter and to his private proposal. He also had an alternative plan ready. On his instructions, Rusk had approached Andrew Cordier, an American diplomat who had served as U Thant's special representative, with a request to persuade U Thant to propose the Cuba-Turkey swap. But first he had to hear the word from Moscow.[19]

Before going to bed that night, John Kennedy and Dave Powers entertained themselves by watching *Roman Holiday*, a 1953 romantic comedy with Gregory Peck and Audrey Hepburn. In the next room, if one believes her recollections, the nineteen-year-old Mimi Alford, a student at Wheaton College in Norton, Massachusetts, and one of Kennedy's lovers, lay sleeping peacefully. Allegedly, Powers had brought her to the White House earlier that day, knowing of the president's affinity for Mimi and deciding to take advantage of Mrs. Kennedy's absence. No romantic encounter happened that evening—Kennedy was too concerned, remembered Mimi, about the prospects of war. "His mind was elsewhere," she recalled. "His expression was grave. Normally, he would have put his presidential duties behind him, had a drink and done his best to light up the room and put everyone at ease. But not on this night. Even his quips had a halfhearted, funereal tone."[20]

John Kennedy had a lot on his mind that night. He had at least two secrets to hide: his extramarital affair and his brother's mission to Dobrynin. It was a desperate measure undertaken in secret from the full membership of ExCom. If rejected and made public by Khrushchev, the offer would not only endanger prospects for peace but also put Kennedy in an impossible political situation. The fate of the proposed secret deal would determine his future.

As he went to bed, the US Army, Navy, and Air Force were getting ready for war. At 22:10 the Air Force chief of staff, General Curtis LeMay, paid a visit to the chief of naval operations, Admiral George Anderson, apparently to discuss the president's order to call in twenty-four air reserve squadrons, altogether fourteen thousand reservists. At 23:03 the commander in chief of the Continental Air Defense Command (CINCONAD) specified new rules of engagement for his units. "No nuclear weapons only for engagement with Cuba alone," read the new instruction, before stating: "If Sino/Soviet Cuban attacks nuclear weapons can be used." How to distinguish Cuban forces from Sino/Soviet units in Cuba was not explained.[21]

21

BERMUDA TRIANGLE

In the late hours of October 27, as Anatoly Dobrynin was busy in his Soviet embassy office completing his report to Moscow on the secret deal offered by Robert Kennedy, Gary Slaughter, a twenty-three-year-old Navy ensign, and his fellow seamen on the USS *Cony* finally set eyes on the prey they had been tracking for the past few days. From the waters of the Sargasso Sea, known to sailors throughout the world for its Bermuda Triangle (its other names include the Devil's Triangle and Hurricane Alley), a Soviet submarine was emerging.

The vessel was almost 90 meters (295 feet) long, painted black above the waterline and red below. Known to the Americans as Foxtrot, it was one of the most recent additions to the Soviet fleet of attack submarines in the Zulu class. Its turbines were powered by three diesel engines and three electric motors. It had ten torpedo tubes, six at the bow and four astern, and carried twenty-two torpedoes. With a regular crew of up to eighty officers, warrant officers, and seamen, it could dive more than 200 meters and stay submerged for days. But with the batteries for its electric motors running low, it had no choice but to surface in order to start its diesel engines and recharge its batteries.[1]

As the sub "broached the surface, we bathed her in blue-white light," recalled Slaughter decades later. He watched as "the sub's crewmen streamed out and stripped off their sweat-soaked uniforms," with "expressions of joy and relief" on their faces as they breathed the fresh night air. The difference between the temperature within the sub and outside was at least thirty degrees Celsius. Before coming to the surface, the submariners had been drenched in sweat produced by high temperatures and the short supply of oxygen.

A group of Soviet navy officers appeared on the sub's bridge and the red flag was raised above it. "My lead signalman and I used our flashing light to interrogate the submarine by use of the Cyrillic Transliteration Table, the International Signals Book, and Morse Code," recalled Slaughter, whose specialty was communications. "I asked the submarine to identify itself." The sub's captain, "using his flashing-light operator . . . replied the sub was Soviet ship X [Korabl' X]." To Slaughter's other question, "Do you require any assistance?" the captain answered "No [Nyet]."

Meanwhile the sub got its diesels running and began to recharge its batteries, clearly using every available minute to do so before diving and leading the Americans on a wild chase once again. But recharging batteries was a slow process that took hours, so the pursuers—besides the USS *Cony*, they included ships belonging to a group led by the aircraft carrier USS *Randolph*—and the prey engaged in something of a staring contest. They moved slowly in the warm waters—a lone Soviet submarine surrounded by a flotilla of US Navy destroyers and auxiliary ships.

"Suddenly, a Navy pilot disrupted our serenity," recalled Slaughter, describing an episode that occurred approximately an hour and a half after the submarine came to the surface. "His gigantic P2V Neptune roared over the scene. He dropped several incendiary devices to activate his photoelectric camera lenses. Bam! Bam! Bam! The light flashes were blinding." Slaughter saw the officers on the bridge getting back into the submarine, which turned around minutes later. "Believing he was under attack," wrote Slaughter, the captain of the submarine brought "his forward torpedo tubes to bear on *Cony*."

It was a panicky moment on board the destroyer, but the captain, Commander William Morgan, kept his cool. "*Cony*'s captain," recalled Slaughter, "directed me to apologize for the P2V's aggressive behavior." He returned to his flashing light and began transmitting the message. Luckily, it was a short one. Slaughter could hardly have imagined that he was not just clearing up a minor misunderstanding but preventing a nuclear war. The torpedo aimed at the *Cony* and the rest of the US Navy group surrounding the submarine was armed with a nuclear warhead.[2]

◊◊◊

THE SOVIET OFFICERS WHOM GARY SLAUGHTER HAD SEEN ON the bridge of the submarine on the night of October 27 were its captain, Valentin Savitsky, and the commander of a task force of four Foxtrot-class submarines lurking in the warm waters of the Atlantic on the approaches to Cuba, Vasilii Arkhipov. They were of equal rank, with their parade uniforms displaying the shoulder boards of captain second grade, equivalent to lieutenant colonel in the army. Savitsky was in charge of the submarine, but Arkhipov was his superior. Two captains on one ship was an arrangement that might cause trouble if their relations did not remain on an even keel.

Arkhipov was an experienced officer who had taken command of the Foxtrot group after a period of service on the first Soviet nuclear-armed and nuclear-powered submarines, which belonged to the Hotel class, according to American specifications. In July 1961, Arkhipov had been on board a Hotel-class sub designated K-19 when on its return from military exercises off the shores of Greenland one of its nuclear reactors developed a huge leak in the cooling system. The vessel had no backup system, as its construction had been rushed through, and was dogged with technical problems.

Crew members were sent into the reactor compartment to build a new cooling system in order to prevent a meltdown of the reactor. Following orders would cost them their lives. The captain of the sub, backed by Arkhipov, who was a reserve commander of the vessel, prevented a mutiny by taking guns from the seamen and throwing them into the sea. Eight members of the crew died within three weeks of the accident; more deaths would follow later. The incident became the basis for the plot of the 2002 Hollywood movie *K-19: The Widowmaker*, starring Harrison Ford.[3]

Captain Arkhipov survived the ordeal and was appointed chief of staff of the 69th Submarine Brigade. In the fall of 1962 he assumed command of the four Foxtrots, named B-4, B-10, B-36, and B-59, that were dispatched to Cuba. Originally they were to be part of a large flotilla of Soviet ships and submarines that the navy was planning to send to Cuba to establish a Soviet naval base. The flotilla was supposed to include two cruisers, two missile ships, two destroyers, and two submarine tenders. Besides the four Foxtrots there were to be seven Project 629 submarines, known to NATO as Golf-class subs, powered by diesel engines and equipped with missile launchers capable of delivering nuclear charges.

But on September 25, 1962, the navy changed its plans, considering that the dispatch of such an armada to Cuban ports "would attract the attention of the whole world and would not be to the advantage of the Soviet Union," as stated in the report. It was decided to send only the torpedo-armed Foxtrots, leaving the missile-armed Golfs at home. The navy was no longer planning to build a base in Cuba or to threaten the United States with submarine-based nuclear missiles but limiting itself to submarines with torpedoes that had a range of 19 kilometers. If anything, they would be there to protect cargoes going to Cuba.[4]

Arkhipov was well aware that the Foxtrots had weaknesses as well as strengths. Built at the Admiralty Shipyard of Leningrad (now St. Petersburg) as part of Project 641, they were relatively new additions to the Soviet navy, the first Foxtrot submarine having been commissioned in 1958. But they were designed to perform in the cold waters of the North Sea and ill-equipped for long transatlantic voyages in which Soviet submarines had never engaged. Their operating range was 20,000 kilometers above water and 11,000 kilometers if snorkeling, but their speed was relatively slow. The Foxtrots could not remain submerged and move quickly at the same time. They could develop a speed up to 16 knots (30 kilometers) per hour surfaced, proceeding at 15 knots while submerged and 9 knots snorkeling.

Theoretically, the vessels could remain submerged up to ten days, but their speed would then be reduced to no more than 2 knots. The problem was the lack of electrical battery capacity. In order to recharge its batteries, the submarine had to surface. The designers tried to deal with the problem as best they could by increasing battery space to take up two decks of the submarine, making the Foxtrot extremely crowded for the crew, even by the standards of the time. The nuclear-powered Hotel-class submarines were much better suited to transatlantic crossings, as they could attain higher speeds and, most important, did not need to surface in order to recharge their batteries. But as Arkhipov could attest personally, the Hotel-class vessels had numerous problems with their nuclear reactors and were not ready yet to undertake long voyages.[5]

◇◇◇

THE FOXTROTS LEFT THEIR SUPERSECRET ADVANCE BASE IN Saida Bay near Murmansk at 4:00 a.m. local time on October 1. One day before departure, the commanding officers of the navy removed the commander of submarine B-59, which would become the lead vessel of the group, and replaced him with Valentin Savitsky. Arkhipov, the commander of the group, also came on board.

Like the personnel of Soviet cargo ships bound for Cuba, the captains and crews of the submarines did not know their final destination. Special envelopes with directions would be opened only when they reached the Barents Sea, and their contents would be revealed to the crews only after the vessels had passed through the Greenland–Iceland–United Kingdom Gap, which served as one of the antisubmarine defense bar-riers of the NATO countries. One of the captains of Arkhipov's Foxtrot group, Captain Second Grade Aleksei Dubivko, recalled a meeting with the senior commanders of the Soviet Northern Fleet: "We did not receive answers to the following questions: 'Where are our vessels going?' 'Our sailing areas?' 'What is the general situation in the areas to which we will be sailing?'"

Arkhipov had questions of his own. The commanders of each of his submarines took an unusual weapon on board: one of their twenty-two torpedoes was nuclear-tipped with a charge equal to ten kilotons of TNT, two-thirds of the destructive power of the Hiroshima bomb. According to the commander of another of Arkhipov's four submarines, Captain Second Grade Riurik Ketov, Arkhipov asked one of the senior commanders of the Northern Fleet at the meeting: "It's not clear to us why we are taking atomic weapons along." "That's the directive," came the answer. "You should familiarize yourself with it [i.e., the weapon]." Arkhipov was not satisfied with that reply. "Fine," he continued, "but when and how should we use it?" The question was met with silence. The senior commanders had no clear answers. The captains of Arkhipov's submarines were confused, at least when it came to their memories of the orders they had received concerning nuclear weapons.

Captain Ketov later recalled an oral order from the chief of staff of the Northern Fleet, Admiral Anatoly Rassokho: "Use the special weapon in the following cases. First, if you are bombed and there is a breach in the pressure hull. Second, if you surface and come under fire and, again, if there is a breach. And third, on orders from Moscow!" Captain Dubivko recalled a written order that read: "Use standard weapons on orders from the Commander in Chief of the Soviet Navy or in case of an armed attack on the vessel. Torpedos with nuclear warheads are to be used only on special orders from the USSR Ministry of Defense or the Commander in Chief of the Soviet Navy." It would appear that every captain had his own understanding of what he could do with his single nuclear torpedo.[6]

While Arkhipov had many questions regarding the mission, he also had some answers. He was one of the very few people to be told immediately the final destination of the submarines—Mariel Bay on the northwestern shore of Cuba. Arkhipov and his group of submarines followed a course from the Barents Sea to the Norwegian Sea and then through the North Atlantic toward the Azores, and from there toward the Bahamas.

The submarines were supposed to reach Cuba covertly, without being detected, but the Moscow planners had little idea of how that could be accomplished. Some believed that Moscow did not fully realize that the submarines dispatched to Cuba were powered by diesel engines, not nuclear reactors. Maintaining the speed ordered by Moscow was impossible without surfacing and thus potentially disclosing the presence and location of the submarines. Arkhipov and Savitsky had no choice but to take the risks. According to the recollections of the lead submarine's navigator, Viktor Mikhailov, they "made a decision: proceed by day in RDP mode or using the electric motors at a speed of 6 to 8 knots, and by night under power of three diesel engines at a speed of 14 to 15 knots while recharging the accumulator battery."[7]

While on the surface they could also maintain radio contact with headquarters, but as they moved farther away from the Barents Sea it turned out that the time allocated to them for radio contact, night hours Moscow time, was daytime in the Atlantic. They could communicate with Moscow only while remaining on the surface, in full view of any vessels and planes that happened to be in the area. The Soviet Navy had never undertaken transatlantic submarine raids: Arkhipov's group was pioneering in that regard.

Upon approaching the Sargasso Sea, the submarines encountered a major storm that made surfacing more difficult and slowed down their progress toward Cuba. But the storm also made it easier for them to avoid surveillance, as patrol planes were not flying and the sonar systems of antisubmarine ships could not penetrate the mixed cold and warm layers of ocean water produced by the storm. The subs managed to remain undetected in the Sargasso Sea until October 13, by which time the storm had subsided and water temperature stabilized. On that day sailors on the US Navy tanker *Yukon* observed a surfaced submarine 130 miles north of Caracas. That sighting took place one day before the discovery of medium-range Soviet ballistic missiles in Cuba. Two days later, the submarines would change course.[8]

◊◊◊

ON OCTOBER 15, THE CAPTAINS OF THE SUBMARINES RECEIVED an order from Moscow to abort their movement toward Mariel and take positions in the Sargasso Sea, adopting a condition of four-hour combat readiness. The decision was made at the insistence of the Kremlin "dove" Anastas Mikoyan, who convinced Nikita Khrushchev to stop the submarines even before Kennedy announced the discovery of Soviet missiles in Cuba.

"Given all that, I proceeded from the premise that the missiles deployed in Cuba had seriously complicated the situation, and that would lead to new complications," recalled Mikoyan, referring to the surface-to-air missiles—the ballistic missiles were still a secret at the time. "We do not want to fight over that issue," said Mikoyan, continuing his line of argument. "If our submarines remain at three days' sailing distance, that does not impair their combat-readiness, but those are not Cuban waters and can have nothing to do with Cuba, and the Americans can undertake nothing against them at that distance." He indicated the dire consequences of the opposite scenario: "But if they proceed to Cuba under water, then they may be discovered by American submarines, and then there would be a clash between our navy and the American navy, which, given prevailing conditions, would worsen the situation even more and produce a serious conflict."

Khrushchev was prepared to listen, but Marshal Malinovsky wanted the submarines to remain on course. Two or three members of the Presidium supported Malinovsky, and Mikoyan's proposal was voted down. He convinced Khrushchev to put it back on the agenda but lost again. "I said that the shores there were shallow and winding, with many islands, and that it would be very difficult to pass unnoticed," wrote Mikoyan, noting how he had used his firsthand knowledge of

Cuban geography in discussion. "Malinovsky maintained his position, although it was apparent that he was incompetent on that question." Not until Admiral Sergei Gorshkov, the commander in chief of the Soviet Navy, joined the meeting did Mikoyan get his way.

"I asked Gorshkov," recalled Mikoyan, " 'Couldn't you say where our submarines are, and can they proceed farther?' Gorshkov showed very clearly on the map where our submarines were located and explained their forward movement. He noted that in one place the submarines would have to make their way through a narrow strait near a small island on which an American base was located. There were locators and other equipment there, and it would be impossible to pass undetected through that strait. He therefore found it expedient to keep the fleet at a distance of two or three days' sailing. Malinovsky could make no objection. All agreed."[9]

The Presidium decided to lie low and keep the Americans unaware of the presence of nuclear-armed submarines on the approaches to Cuba. The decision proved unavailing. On October 14, the day after the first sighting of the Soviet submarines, a U-2 plane discovered the Soviet ballistic missiles on the island. On October 22, the Soviet submarine captains learned from American radio broadcasts that President Kennedy had announced the imposition of a naval blockade. By that time, the number of Soviet submarines and their approximate locations were already known to the US Navy, and John McCone of the CIA had informed Kennedy and his advisers of the threat presented by the submarines to American ships enforcing the blockade. On the following day the chief of naval operations, Admiral George Anderson, informed McNamara about the formation of a Hunter/Killer group consisting of ships and airplanes whose task was to locate the Soviet submarines.[10]

The members of ExCom discussed the Soviet submarines at their morning meeting on October 24. Their main concern was that the submarines would prevent the US Navy from inspecting Soviet ships crossing the quarantine line. "If this submarine should sink our destroyer, then what is our proposed reply?" Kennedy asked his aides. General Taylor assured him that the submarines would be "covered by our anti-

submarine warfare patrols." He also told the president about procedures of signaling submarines to surface. They had been passed to the
Soviet side, added Alexis Johnson, who had telegraphed the arrangements to Moscow the previous night. McNamara also described the
new procedure that had been developed the previous day. It included
the dropping of practice depth charges—a tactic to be used in combina-
tion with sonar signals.

Kennedy pushed on with his line of questioning: "If he does not
surface or he takes some action . . . ? At what point are we going to
attack him?" He added that he did not want the submarine to be the
first Soviet vessel attacked by the US Navy. He preferred a merchant
ship. "Well, we won't get to that unless the submarine is really in a position to attack our ship in the course of an intercept," responded General Taylor. McNamara proposed sending "antisubmarine helicopters
to harass the submarine." "[The plan, therefore, is]," he concluded his
proposal, "to put pressure on the submarine, move it out of the area by
pressure, by the pressure of potential destruction, and then make the
intercept." "OK. Let's proceed," replied the president.[11]

And proceed they did. Between October 22 and 26, US Navy patrol
planes and the operators of the SOSUS (Sound Surveillance System),
which utilized long acoustic sensors or hydrophones installed on the
ocean floor, managed to pick up locations and establish numerous
sonar contacts with the submerged submarines. The destroyers and
patrol aircraft of the two Hunter/Killer groups led by the aircraft car-
riers *Randolph* and *Sussex* recorded numerous cases of submarines
surfacing on the approaches to the blockade line. Until October 27,
however, no submarine was forced to the surface by the US Navy.[12]

◊◊◊

SUBMARINE B-59, WITH SAVITSKY AND ARKHIPOV ON BOARD,
was first spotted by the US Navy off Bermuda on the evening of October
25. It would be registered under the code name C-19. Next evening a
patrol aircraft spotted it again. The hunt for B-59 had begun. The sub's

navigator, Viktor Mikhailov, recalled those days decades later: "The anti-submarine defense ships fastened onto us with their hydrolocators and started 'beating' on the hull of the vessel. Their ringing pulses could be heard perfectly in the first compartment and made it hard to breathe. The crew of the B-59 was summoned to battle stations, and maneuvers began to evade detection by changing depth of submersion, course, and speed, and engaging interference equipment. That continued for more than two days."[13]

But the real hunt for Savitsky and Arkhipov's vessel began at midday on Saturday, October 27. Three US Navy destroyers, the USS *Cony*, *Beale*, and *Murray* from the *Randolph* group, took on the task of hunting down the submarine. Close to 5:00 p.m. local time, the USS *Beale* tried to establish contact with the submarine, first by sonar signal and then by dropping practice depth charges. There was no response from the depths. Half an hour later the *Cony* dropped five hand grenades but again received no response, raising the question of whether the submarine's officers had received the identification and surfacing procedures transmitted to Moscow on the evening of October 23. In fact Savitsky and Arkhipov had received the procedures but had trouble distinguishing the practice charges from the real ones. As far as they were concerned, they were most probably under attack.[14]

Lieutenant Vadim Orlov, the commander of the eavesdropping team on board the submarine, recalled the effect of the practice charges and grenades on his fellow seamen: "They exploded next to the deck. It was as if you were sitting in an iron barrel that was being beaten with a sledgehammer." The officers and sailors on the submarine, already hunted by the US Navy for two days, felt ever more desperate. "The accumulators on the B-59 discharged to 'water' [as water and sulfuric acid in the electrolyte got separated], and only the emergency lights stayed on. The temperature in the compartments was as high as 45–50 degrees [Celsius], and in the electrical motor compartment and generally it was more than 60. The stuffy atmosphere was insufferable. The level of carbon dioxide reached a critical level, almost deadly for human beings," wrote Orlov, recalling the situation in the overheated interior of a submarine designed for the North Sea but now sailing in waters whose temperatures approached 30 degrees Celsius. "One of the men standing guard lost consciousness and fell. Following him, a second and a third . . . fell over like dominoes. But we still held on, trying to make our way out."[15]

Captain Savitsky maneuvered for close to four hours, trying to shake off his pursuers, but to no avail. Then, to the best of Orlov's recollection, there came a major blast that shook the vessel: "The Americans slammed us with something stronger than a grenade—obviously, it was practically a depth charge. . . . We thought: this is it, it's all over!" recalled Orlov. "After that attack Savitsky, totally exhausted and, furthermore, unable to make contact with the General Staff, flew into a rage. He summoned the officer in charge of the atomic torpedo and ordered him to make it combat-ready." Orlov recalled the captain's words: "Perhaps war has already started up above, and we're going nuts here. . . . Now we'll hit them with everything we've got! We'll die and drown everyone [on board], but we won't disgrace the fleet."[16]

According to Orlov, the order to prepare the nuclear-armed torpedo was rescinded after Savitsky calmed down and discussed the situation with Arkhipov and the political officer, Maslennikov. The three of them decided to bring the submarine to the surface. Orlov's story about Savitsky's order to make the torpedo combat-ready gained currency in the literature on the Cuban missile crisis in the early 2000s and served as the basis for numerous academic and popular accounts about the B-59's ordeal. They also helped to burnish the image of Vasilii Arkhipov as the man who saved the world from nuclear catastrophe by dissuading Savitsky from firing an atomic weapon. This turned out to be just one of many accounts. The recollections of other officers on board the B-59 that have appeared subsequently paint a somewhat different though no less dramatic picture of what happened beneath the surface of the Sargasso Sea during those fateful hours and minutes of October 27.

The sub's navigator, Viktor Mikhailov, and the officer responsible for the torpedo launchers, Anatoly Leonenko, agree that the decision to surface was prompted not by the American practice charges and grenades, which the vessel could withstand, but by the simple fact that its batteries had run down and it could no longer remain underwater. According to the same accounts, however, Savitsky indeed gave the order to prepare the atomic torpedo for firing and only then agreed to have the vessel surface. Leonenko recalls that Savitsky ordered him to get the torpedoes in the seventh stern compartment of the submarine ready to fire.

"Prepare the equipment for firing!" ordered Leonenko on reaching the stern compartment, but his order was met with bewilderment by his subordinates. "The commander of the torpedo group, Senior Lieutenant V. Liashetsky, stood mutely rooted to the spot, a look of astonishment in his eyes," recalled Leonenko. "After a brief pause the commander of the torpedo unit, Petty Officer Second Class Kalita, told me that war had broken out and that we ought to be at home; our fiancées were waiting for us." Leonenko was faced with something close to insubordination. He used every term of abuse he could think of, and the lieutenant and petty officer fell into line. Leonenko reported to Savitsky that his order had been carried out. They began to surface.[17]

This was the moment that Gary Slaughter, the communications officer on the USS *Cony*, recalled so vividly decades later. The Soviet naval officers he saw on the bridge were Savitsky and Arkhipov. Savitsky ordered that the red state flag, not that of the Soviet Navy, be raised to indicate that the submarine belonged to the USSR. The Soviets remembered their first direct encounter with the Americans more or less the same way as Slaughter. "When the vessel came up and took its position, the chief of staff of the brigade [Arkhipov], the commander of the submarine [Savitsky], and the signals officer with his searchlight came onto the bridge," wrote Mikhailov decades later. "In spite of the dark southern night, it was as bright as day on the bridge because of the searchlights trained on it by the anti-submarine defense planes," wrote Leonenko, echoing him.[18]

But the Soviets also remembered something that Slaughter did not: the American airplanes were threatening and harassing the slow-moving Soviet submarine. "They flew low down the length of the submarine and, illuminating it with their searchlights, fired tracer bullets ahead of it," recalled Mikhailov. "The US anti-submarine defense planes, their searchlights on, circled the submarine from the right in hedge-hopping maneuver and, approaching the deck, opened fire with such force that voice communications at the central post were drowned out by the roar of the cannonade," wrote Leonenko.[19]

It was after the episode described by Slaughter, with a US Navy plane dropping flares to get a better photo of the submarine, that Savitsky and the others on the bridge panicked and decided that they were under attack. "Emergency dive! Prepare torpedo tubes 1 and 2 for firing!" Leonenko, who was in charge of the torpedoes, wrote, recalling the order that Savitsky gave after climbing down from the bridge. This time Savitsky was ready to use his nuclear torpedo. His previous order had concerned regular torpedoes, but this one referred to the nuclear weapon. "This order was intended for the first compartment, and tube no. 1 contained the nuclear-armed torpedo," remembered Leonenko. The forward torpedo tubes that Slaughter recalled being turned toward the USS *Cony* included tube no. 1.

◊◊◊

NEITHER JOHN KENNEDY NOR HIS ADVISERS IMAGINED AT the time that dropping pyrotechnic devices on submarines could be as dangerous as releasing depth charges. But pyrotechnic devices were Vice President Lyndon Johnson's prime concern at the ExCom meeting on the afternoon of October 27, just as the B-59 drama was unfolding in the Caribbean. "I have been afraid of those damned flares ever since they mentioned them," he told the ExCom members who were discussing the possibility of night surveillance flights over Cuba. "Imagine some crazy Russian captain doing it. The damn thing goes 'blooey' and lights up the skies. He might just pull a trigger. Looks like we are playing Fourth of July over there or something." Johnson drew on his political experience: "Psychologically you scare them. Well, hell, it's always like the fellow telling me in Congress, 'Go on and put the monkey on his back.' Every time I tried to put a monkey on somebody else's back, I got one. If you are going to try to psychologically scare them with flares, you're liable to get your bottom shot at."[20]

Johnson's view prevailed, and the proposed surveillance flights over Cuba were not authorized. He had no idea that at the time he intervened in the debate a proverbial monkey on the back of Captain Savitsky almost caused him to fire a nuclear torpedo at the American "bottom." Triggered by unintended consequences of air photography in the night skies over the Caribbean and stopped from further escalation by a stuck searchlight in the silo of the Soviet submarine, the most dangerous episode of the sea hunt faded away almost as soon as it occurred.

It was Slaughter's searchlight and the message he was transmitting that saved the situation. But that required a stroke of good luck. Savitsky descended from the bridge and gave his order to prepare the nuclear torpedo immediately after a US Navy plane dropped flares above the submarine. The others, including the communications officer with a searchlight and Arkhipov, began to descend as well, but, as Leonenko recalled, "coming down, the signals officer got stuck with his searchlight in the shaft of the upper hatch of the conning tower, thereby delaying the commander." Arkhipov, who remained on the bridge, noticed Slaughter's searchlight and read the message. It was an apology. As Leonenko recalled, Arkhipov, realizing that the "American frigate had begun signaling us by searchlight to respond, gave the order to stop preparations for firing." Although the torpedo was ready to be fired, it remained in its tube.[21]

"Savitsky," wrote Slaughter long afterward, when he had learned the Soviet commander's name, "acknowledged my apology and closed his torpedo-tube doors. He wheeled to port and returned to his easterly heading. I was greatly relieved not to be staring down the barrel of B-59's torpedo tubes." "When things settled down, Morgan gave me my standing orders in the language of a sailor: 'Keep that Russian bastard happy,'" recalled Slaughter. "I did just that. I nodded my thanks for Savitsky's patience. The Russian even nodded back. Our relationship appeared slightly more cordial."[22]

Although they did not know it at the time, the seamen of the USS *Cony* and other ships of the *Randolph* group were moments away from being killed or shipwrecked by the tremendous waves that a nuclear explosion would produce. Savitsky's torpedo carried a warhead with 10 kilotons of explosive power. If dropped on a city, that would suffice to kill everyone within a half-mile radius. Moreover, the torpedoes' nuclear warheads were designed to create shock waves that would topple or incapacitate ships. The 20-kiloton load tried by the US Navy in the Baker underwater test in 1946 produced waves up to 94 feet high. The Soviets tested their T-5 torpedoes near Novaia Zemlia in the Arctic in 1957 but never released the results. Any ship hit by the torpedo would almost certainly have been destroyed, while the rest of the *Randolph* group would have suffered significant damage.[23]

The political consequences of a nuclear attack in the Sargasso Sea would have been even more significant. "It shall be the policy of this nation to regard any nuclear missile launched from Cuba against any nation in the Western Hemisphere as an attack on the United States, requiring a full retaliatory response upon the Soviet Union," declared Kennedy in his television address on October 22. In response to a nuclear attack on the US Navy, the president would have had little choice but to order an air strike against Soviet targets. The Soviets would have had little choice but to retaliate, whether they wanted to do so or not.[24]

VI

RISING

from the

DEAD

22

SUNDAY SCARE

October 28, 1962, happened to be a Sunday. In Russian that day of the week is called *voskresenie*, meaning "resurrection." The Bolsheviks, who came to power in 1917 with the goal of building communism and eradicating religion, were uneasy about keeping a Christian name for a day of rest. Accordingly, in the middle of an antireligious campaign in 1929, they switched from a seven-day week to a five-day cycle with no place for a "resurrection" day. The new calendar added some days free of labor, but the population resisted the change, remaining loyal to the old calendar. In 1940, as Stalin prepared the country for war and became concerned about the loyalty of Soviet citizens, he reversed the policy, switching back to a seven-day week and reestablishing Sunday.[1]

With few churches open, people no longer attended services as a matter of course. Instead they slept in on the only free day of the week—Saturdays would not become work-free until the late 1960s. For those concerned about the rapidly worsening international situation, Sunday morning presented a chance to catch up on the news. Most Soviet newspapers did not publish on Sundays, with the notable exception of the leading party daily, *Pravda*, which appeared seven days a week. That morning its front page featured the text of Khrushchev's letter to President Kennedy offering the Turkey-Cuba missile swap. A quotation from a recent appeal by Bertrand Russell indicated the guilty party. The famous philosopher had written that if Kennedy proved unwilling to come to an agreement with the Soviet Union, the result might be an unprecedented disaster for humanity.[2]

Judging by *Pravda*, the Soviet people were fully supportive of their wise leader and his policies. The foreman of a communist shock brigade in Leningrad, S. Vitchenko, allegedly told a *Pravda* reporter: "N. S. Khrushchev is right, a thousand times right, in calling on the president of the USA at this bleak and alarming hour to show prudence and negotiate. Good sense, and not the psychosis of nuclear war, should triumph." The quotation continued: "You think, Mr. President, that Cuba is a threat to you! But are the nuclear installations in Turkey not menacingly directed against our land? So stop your saber-rattling at last, sit down at the negotiating table, and do not bring humanity to the verge of military catastrophe!" Such was the key message that Khrushchev's propaganda machine was now delivering at home and abroad.[3]

As always, the Soviet papers were reporting yesterday's news. Reports arriving in Moscow from Washington and Havana after 1:00 a.m. local time indicated that things were spinning out of control. Not only was Castro directly confronting the Americans by ordering his troops to fire at their aircraft without asking Moscow's opinion, but Moscow's own commanders were joining in, having shot down an American plane. The shooting war in the Caribbean had already broken out, and Khrushchev had to react without delay. But it was Sunday. He would not see his minister of defense until late morning.[4]

◊◊◊

MARSHAL RODION MALINOVSKY REPORTED TO KHRUSHCHEV on the latest developments in Cuba sometime after 10:45 a.m.—the time indicated on his memo to the Soviet leader on the downing of the U-2 plane. He knew that he had fouled up: his troops had shot down the plane in spite of direct orders not to open fire unless attacked. In a terse report, Malinovsky laid out the facts. He began with information about the U-2 overflight, which photographed the "combat disposition of the troops" for one hour and twenty-one minutes. He continued: "With the aim of not permitting the photographs to fall into US hands, at 18:20 Moscow time this aircraft was shot down by two anti-aircraft missiles of the 507th Anti-aircraft Missile Regiment at an altitude of 21,000 meters. The aircraft fell in the vicinity of Antilla; a search has been organized."[5]

Malinovsky unequivocally stated that it was his troops who had shot down the plane but gave no assessment of their actions and named no names. In lieu of explanation if not excuse for what had happened, Malinovsky added: "On the same day there were 8 violations of Cuban airspace by U.S. aircraft." The report offered no reason why the downing of the plane at 6:20 p.m. Moscow time the previous day had not been reported to the supreme commander until the next day, ten and a half hours later. We do not know what Malinovsky told Khrushchev in private, but the Soviet military literally managed to get away with murder. Malinovsky's message to General Pliev, who had lost control of his own deputies and allowed the incident to take place, contained scant criticism despite the gravity of the situation. The minister of defense kept his calm and shielded his subordinates. Pliev was reproached for acting "too hasty" in shooting down the American airplane.[6]

"Khrushchev was seriously alarmed by the news that an antiaircraft missile had been fired on the orders of a middle-rank Soviet commander," recalled his aide Oleg Troianovsky. "He was keenly aware, as were all of us, that in the situation that had arisen, when nerves were strained to the breaking point, a single spark might cause an explosion." Khrushchev sensed the danger: he was losing control over his own men. Instead of blaming his military, though, he decided to blame Castro. At the start of the crisis, he had already considered claiming that the Soviet missiles were under Cuban control and thereby reformatting the conflict as Cuban-American rather than Soviet-American. Now he probably decided to prepare the ground for the same maneuver. "You shot down one such plane yesterday," wrote Khrushchev to Castro later that day.[7]

Khrushchev knew that was not the case and admitted it later, in his memoirs. "American planes were constantly flying over the island," recalled Khrushchev years later. "That drove Castro out of his mind. Castro gave the order to fire, and our soldiers brought down the American reconnaissance U-2 plane with a missile." Khrushchev the memoirist, as opposed to Khrushchev the politician, was right for the most part. It was Castro's fear of imminent invasion and his decision to open fire on American airplanes that created a situation in which the Soviet military believed that if they were not yet under attack, it might come any minute, and thus felt justified in using antiaircraft missiles.[8]

◊◊◊

KHRUSHCHEV HAD CLEARLY LOST CONTROL OVER THE SITUAtion in Cuba. But not everything was bleak and gloomy for him on that Sunday morning. If his military and his client in Cuba were sources of bad news, there was unexpected good news from the White House. John Kennedy's letter of the previous night, which had been delivered to Khrushchev, offered hope that the looming nuclear conflict could be avoided.

"1. You would agree to remove these weapons systems from Cuba under appropriate United Nations observation and supervision; and undertake, with suitable safeguards, to halt the further introduction of such weapons systems into Cuba," was Kennedy's first condition. "2. We, on our part, would agree—upon the establishment of adequate arrangements through the United Nations to ensure the carrying out and continuation of these commitments—(a) to remove promptly the quarantine measures now in effect and (b) to give assurances against an invasion of Cuba. I am confident that other nations of the Western Hemisphere would be prepared to do likewise."[9]

True, the letter made no reference to Khrushchev's latest proposal for the Cuba-Turkey missile swap, but Khrushchev had come up with that idea relatively late in the game, almost as an afterthought, and it certainly was not his key condition for a settlement. It was Kennedy, not Khrushchev, who believed that giving up the American missiles in Turkey was the sine qua non for a peaceful resolution of the crisis, and it was not the Soviet but the American media—Walter Lippmann—that discussed such a proposal first. That particular issue aside, Kennedy was de facto accepting Khrushchev's proposal of October 26. He wrote about "weapons" rather than about the "Soviet specialists" who serviced them, but that was what Khrushchev had in mind anyway.

There was, however, one caveat that did not appear in Khrushchev's offer—the United Nations' supervision of the withdrawal of the missiles. Khrushchev already knew about that proposal from the report of his KGB chief in Washington, Aleksandr Feklisov, who had allegedly received it from John A. Scali, an ABC correspondent with direct connection to the State Department and the White House. Khrushchev did not know, however, that in an apparent attempt to upstage Dobrynin as a confidential channel to the White House, Feklisov proposed a deal to Scali that no one in the Soviet leadership ever authorized him to offer, namely, to agree to the removal of the missiles under UN supervision. Kennedy considered that to be Khrushchev's position, and Khrushchev now had no choice but to believe that it was Kennedy's.[10]

Khrushchev was ready for action. After the shooting down of the U-2, he did not think that he was in a position to reject UN supervision of the withdrawal process. With reports from Havana suggesting that Cuba and the world in general were moving rapidly toward war, and Kennedy's letter offering a way out, he was prepared to accept Kennedy's official offer. He seemed as frightened of impending war as the US president. They were both eager to accept whatever they believed to be the other side's latest offer. Now it was Khrushchev's turn.

◊◊◊

Khrushchev called a meeting of the party Presidium for noon at a villa in Novo-Ogarevo outside Moscow. Anatoly Dobrynin later recalled that Khrushchev had moved the venue from the Kremlin to Novo-Ogarevo once he learned that Western journalists were reporting on how late the lights were burning in the Kremlin. Mikoyan told Dobrynin that the Presidium went into session in Novo-Ogarevo on the evening of October 27 and "remained there until Sunday."

Originally an estate of Grand Prince Sergei Romanov, a son of Tsar Alexander II, Novo-Ogarevo was turned into a government residence by Khrushchev's ally and later nemesis, Georgii Malenkov. The site would become world-famous when George H. W. Bush met there with Gorbachev in July 1991, and Gorbachev held court there in the dying days of the Soviet Union. It would later become the living and working quarters of Vladimir Putin, who hosted scores of foreign dignitaries, including George W. Bush, at the residence. In the fall of 1962 Novo-Ogarevo was a secluded location where Khrushchev could meet with his aides out of the public eye.[11]

As always, it was Khrushchev who opened the discussion. Present that afternoon were the key members of the ruling elite, including the second most powerful figure in the Soviet hierarchy, the Central Committee secretary Frol Kozlov; the head of the Soviet parliament, Leonid Brezhnev; Minister of Defense Malinovsky, accompanied by the secretary of the Defense Council, General Ivanov; Minister of Foreign Affairs Gromyko; chairman of the KGB, Aleksandr Shelepin; and, last but not least, the country's main expert on Cuba, Anastas Mikoyan. "From the very beginning, those taking part in the meeting were in a highly electrified state," recalled Khrushchev's aide Oleg Troianovsky decades later. "It was practically Khrushchev alone who expressed himself, while Mikoyan and Gromyko gave individual responses. The others preferred to remain silent, as if giving to understand that it was you who got us into this mess; now get yourself out of it."[12]

Khrushchev's meeting with the members of the Presidium was nothing like the meetings of ExCom. All Kennedy's advisers, with the exception of Vice President Lyndon Johnson, were his appointees, serving to some degree or other at the pleasure of the president. Khrushchev's aides had been elected by party congresses or the Central Committee plenum and had the right not only to disagree with the first secretary but also to recommend that the Central Committee remove him from office—an option that they exercised two years later, in October 1964, when they dismissed Khrushchev and sent him into retirement. It would be only later that Leonid Brezhnev ridiculed Khrushchev for declaring at the Presidium meeting: "We can hit a fly in Washington with our missiles!" For now, he was silent. Khrushchev's aides, probably with the sole exception of Mikoyan, were there either to approve and endorse Khrushchev's decisions or to remain silent. Khrushchev called in his peers not to seek their opinions and collectively formulate a policy but to get their approval and thereby legitimize his actions in case things went wrong. And at this point they were truly going wrong.

Khrushchev's goal was to sell his colleagues-turned-clients another abrupt turn of his policy. The previous day he had convinced them to add the missiles in Turkey to his offer to Kennedy; now he wanted them to agree to remove that element. He began with an appeal to party history, recalling Lenin's tactics during the revolution and civil war: "There was a time when we advanced, as in October 1917. But in March 1918 we had to retreat, having signed the Treaty of Brest-Litovsk with Germany. That decision was dictated by our interests: we had to save Soviet rule. Now we find ourselves face to face with the threat of war and nuclear catastrophe, as a result of which human civilization may perish. To save humanity, we should retreat." To hear Khrushchev tell it, he was now saving not only Soviet rule but humankind as a whole.[13]

"I have called you all together to take counsel and consider whether you agree with such a decision," said Khrushchev, concluding his opening remarks. The "decision" was already there: he was simply asking for approval. He had a two-pronged strategy: "If an attack is provoked, we have issued an order to inflict a retaliatory strike." Then came his "peace" proposal. "We agree to dismantle the missile installations," he said, according to the terse protocol of the meeting. No dissent was recorded. Troianovsky recalled Gromyko and Mikoyan expressing their opinions: since neither was a hawk, they probably approved Khrushchev's de facto decision. With the rest remaining silent and taking the attitude "Whatever you say," Khrushchev got his authorization.[14]

It was in the middle of the discussion of Khrushchev's proposal that Troianovsky interrupted the meeting: he had an urgent message for the Presidium. "During the session I was called to the telephone. Vladimir Suslov, the senior assistant to the minister of foreign affairs, was calling. He said that a coded telegram had arrived from Dobrynin about a new conversation with Robert Kennedy," recalled Troianovsky. Decades later he remembered Kennedy's message as an ultimatum in all but form: the Americans were determined to get rid of the Soviet missile bases; the military was putting pressure on the president; time was running out; and a clear Soviet response was expected within one day. Troianovsky returned to the meeting room and read from his notes. Robert Kennedy was offering Khrushchev the Turkish missiles.[15]

In his memoirs, Khrushchev refers to the arrival of Dobrynin's cable as the climax of the crisis. If Troianovsky recalled Robert Kennedy's message as a form of ultimatum, Khrushchev remembered it as an appeal for mercy. In Khrushchev's retelling, Robert Kennedy begged Dobrynin to understand the peculiarities of the American political system and help the president find a way out of the crisis. "The president himself does not know how to get out of that situation, and the military is exerting strong pressure on him, insisting that he take military action with regard to Cuba, and the president's situation is becoming highly complicated," wrote Khrushchev, recalling the main points of the message years later. He was trying to prove that his retreat was in fact a maneuver in response to a plea from the Kennedy brothers. But that interpretation would come later. On the afternoon of October 28, he was eager to take the new deal as quickly as possible.[16]

Troianovsky remembered that in the middle of the discussions General Ivanov, the secretary of the Defense Council, was called to the telephone and reported to the Presidium that according to information picked up by the military, President Kennedy was to address the nation at 5:00 p.m. Moscow time. "[At] that moment those taking part in the meeting believed the worst, deciding that Kennedy would announce either an attack on Cuba or, what seemed more probable, the bombing of missile installations." They had to react promptly. The letter to Kennedy was not yet ready, but Khrushchev ordered Andrei Gromyko to cable Dobrynin right away with instructions to tell Robert Kennedy that Moscow was prepared to accept his brother's conditions. "Comrade Gromyko, we don't have the right to take risks. Once the president announces there will be an invasion, he won't be able to reverse himself. We have to let Kennedy know that we want to help him," Khrushchev told his minister of foreign affairs.[17]

Gromyko immediately instructed Dobrynin to contact Robert Kennedy. The message he forwarded to Washington read as follows: "The views expressed by Robert Kennedy at the president's request are met with understanding in Moscow. The reply to the president will be broadcast on radio today, and the reply will be most positive. The main problem troubling the president, that is, the dismantling of missile bases on Cuba under international supervision, arouses no objections and will be covered in detail in a message from N. S. Khrushchev."[18]

Khrushchev dictated a draft of his official letter to Kennedy to be edited and polished by his aides (Troianovsky later wrote that these were his colleagues from the Ministry of Foreign Affairs) as soon as possible. "I respect and trust your statement, set forth in your message of October 27, 1962, that there will be no attack on Cuba; that there will be no invasion not only on the part of the United States but also on the part of other countries of the Western Hemisphere, as stated in your message," read the letter. "In that case, the motives that prompted us to provide such assistance to Cuba become invalid. We have therefore instructed our officers (and those resources, as I have already informed you, are in the hands of Soviet officers) to take appropriate measures to stop building the aforementioned installations, to dismantle them, and return them to the Soviet Union. As I have already informed you in my letter of October 27, we agree to arrange with you that UN representatives be able to verify the dismantling of those resources."[19]

That was it. Khrushchev accepted all Kennedy's conditions, including an immediate halt to the construction of new missile sites, the removal of the missiles, and UN supervision of their withdrawal. Robert Kennedy asked Dobrynin for a short and nonverbose answer. But Khrushchev would not have been Khrushchev if his letter were short and to the point. In a message of more than 1,500 words, he wrote at length on the peace-loving intentions of the Soviet people. Nor did he miss the opportunity to condemn unfriendly American actions: the shelling of Havana from an unidentified vessel and a U-2 flight over Soviet territory the previous day. "Your airplane violates our border, and at such an alarming time that we are undergoing together with you, when everything has been made combat-ready," wrote Khrushchev. "After all, the American airplane committing the violation might very well be taken for a nuclear-armed bomber, and that might prompt us to take a fateful step."

That was a stretch: confusing a U-2 with a bomber was a virtual impossibility, but the recent flight of Captain Charles Maultsby had caused Kennedy and McNamara themselves to consider that the Soviets might have taken his inadvertent violation of their airspace as a last prestrike reconnaissance flight. Khrushchev never mentioned the downing of Anderson's U-2 over Cuba, but the passages of his letter on the American violation of Cuban airspace following his description of the Maultsby episode were clearly intended to provide justification for the Soviet action. "I would ask you, Mr. President, to consider that the violation of Cuban airspace by American airplanes may also have unfortunate consequences. And if you do not want this, then it would be best to avoid causing occasions for a dangerous situation to arise," wrote Khrushchev.[20]

The letter to Kennedy was accompanied by two additional messages. The first was cabled by Gromyko to Dobrynin, as discussed above, instructing him to inform the Kennedys that a positive response was coming. The second, prepared either at the same time as the main letter or soon thereafter, was supposed to be passed secretly by Dobrynin to Robert Kennedy. It concerned the confidential proposal to swap Soviet missiles in Cuba for American ones in Turkey. Khrushchev wrote: "I agree that our discussion of this subject be pursued confidentially through Robert Kennedy and the Soviet Ambassador in Washington. You may have noticed that in my message to you on October 28, which was to be published immediately, I did not raise this question—precisely because I was mindful of your wish conveyed through Robert Kennedy. But all the proposals that I presented in that message took into account the fact that you had agreed to resolve the matter of your missile bases in Turkey consistent with what I had said in my message of October 27 and what you stated through Robert Kennedy in his meeting with Ambassador Dobrynin on the same day."[21]

◊◊◊

KHRUSHCHEV HAD SEALED HIS SECRET DEAL WITH KENNEDY. Next on the agenda were a letter to Castro, instructions to Pliev, and a letter to U Thant. With the decision made to retreat from his public position on the missile swap announced less than twenty-four hours earlier, Khrushchev had to do some explaining and pacify his unhappy ally, instruct his military commander, and ensure the cooperation of the United Nations, which was now included in his deal with Kennedy.

"No sooner had I dictated that telegram," remembered Khrushchev, recalling the fateful meeting of the Presidium and one of the letters he sent Kennedy that day, "than we received a telegram from our ambassador transmitting a message from Castro. Fidel informed us that according to reliable information he had received, the USA would invade Cuba in a few hours." According to Khrushchev, this was the first time that he either saw the message or comprehended its sense. "What was most important in Fidel's message," recalled Khrushchev, "was not what he had been told but his conclusion: he considered that if attack was inevitable, then it had to be counteracted, and he proposed that we immediately make a first strike on the USA with nuclear missiles so that our missiles not be put out of action." According to Khrushchev, the proposal came as a shock not only to him but also to the others around the table. "When this was read to us, we, sitting in silence, looked at one another for a long time," he recalled.[22]

After some discussion, Khrushchev began dictating a letter to Castro. It was much shorter and more to the point than the official letter to Kennedy. Addressing his unruly client, Khrushchev told him: "We would like to offer the following friendly advice to you: show patience, restraint, and more restraint. Of course, if there is an invasion, then it will be necessary to repel it with all the forces at your disposal. But do not let yourselves be provoked, since the frenzied military men in the Pentagon now, at the very moment when an elimination of the conflict is taking shape to your advantage, by including a guarantee against the invasion of Cuba, seem to want to undermine the agreement and provoke you to actions which could then be used against you."[23]

It was then decided to inform U Thant immediately about the Soviet decision to dismantle the missile sites. Indeed, he was all but invited to visit missile installations during his planned trip to Cuba, and representatives of the Red Cross were welcome on board Soviet ships heading for Cuba to make sure that they were carrying no weapons. "You must inform U Thant, for his personal information, that on those Soviet ships which at the present time are bound for Cuba, there are no weapons at all," read Gromyko's cable to the Soviet representative at the UN, Valerian Zorin. The instructions to Zorin mentioned nothing about U Thant visiting missile sites, but the Presidium decided to instruct Pliev "on admitting U Thant and those accompanying him to the sites." Khrushchev was determined to have U Thant in his corner as he sought ways of making his deal with Kennedy stick.[24]

General Pliev received two cables that day, at least one of them dictated by Khrushchev. Unlike the verbose letter to Kennedy and the shorter but still substantial message to Castro, the instructions to Pliev, transmitted to him by Marshal Malinovsky, were curt and precise. "We believe that you were too hasty in shooting down the US U-2 reconnaissance plane; at the time an agreement was emerging to avert, by peaceful means, an attack on Cuba," read the message, conveying Khrushchev's displeasure with Pliev's loss of control on the ground and putting him on the defensive. Then came an order: "We have made the decision to dismantle the R-12s and remove them. Begin to implement this measure. Confirm receipt." The telegram was sent at 4:00 p.m. Moscow time. At 6:30 p.m., Malinovsky sent additional instructions: "In addition to the order not to use S-75s, you are ordered not to dispatch fighter aircraft in order to avoid collisions with US reconnaissance planes." The Americans would be able to fly unobstructed over Cuban territory. Khrushchev was trying not to give any pretext to the "warmongers" in the Pentagon to undo his bargain with Kennedy.[25]

◊◊◊

THE LETTER TO KENNEDY COULD NOT BE SENT BY DIPLOMATIC channels, as Khrushchev was afraid of being late to accept the president's offer and prevent war. He had the recourse of broadcasting it via radio, as he had done only two days earlier. Of course, a private message would have been preferable to avoid publicizing Khrushchev's reversal of position about the missiles in Turkey, but he no longer seemed to care. The Central Committee secretary in charge of ideology, Leonid Ilichev, was personally tasked by Khrushchev with hand-delivering the letter to the Soviet Radio Committee. Ilichev recalled that his driver violated all speed limits and traffic rules as he sped from Novo-Ogarevo to the center of Moscow to deliver the letter. He made it on time. At 5:00 p.m. Moscow time, an announcer began reading Khrushchev's message to Kennedy.

In Washington, DC, it was 9:00 a.m. It was Sunday morning, and Kennedy had no intention of delivering a new address to the nation. The address that had so frightened Khrushchev and his colleagues and made them speed up the delivery of their letter to Kennedy was never planned. Soviet military spies had picked up information about a rebroadcast of Kennedy's speech of October 22. Like many other episodes of the Cuban crisis, it was a mistake—a case of one side completely unable to understand the other. Not only did the Soviets confuse what they heard on television and radio, perhaps because of poor knowledge of English, but they also had little understanding of American politics and culture. Had Kennedy intended to deliver a televised address on Sunday, October 29, he would not have scheduled it for 9:00 a.m., when he and his fellow citizens were heading for church services. That did not occur to operatives of the officially atheist Soviet Union. It was a double mistake, but a lucky one. By now, not only was war off the table, but a proposed solution to the crisis was on the air.[26]

23

WINNERS AND LOSERS

October 28 arrived in Washington eight hours later than it did in Moscow. That night they switched the clock from Eastern Daylight Time to Eastern Standard Time. By 9:00 a.m., which was 5:00 p.m. Moscow time, a good half of Americans were either already in church or on their way there.

The director of the CIA, John McCone, was attending a 9:00 a.m. Mass precisely when news of Khrushchev's imminent address was announced on American television and radio networks. McCone had no clear idea of what the address could entail. His fellow Catholic and Irishman John Kennedy was in a much better position to know. At 10:00 a.m. Kennedy, in the company of Dave Powers, attended Mass at the St. Stephen Martyr Catholic Church on Pennsylvania Avenue. As he was getting ready to leave for the service, McGeorge Bundy read him a short summary of Khrushchev's speech on the phone: Khrushchev had accepted his proposal and was dismantling the missile sites. "I feel like a new man now," the president told Powers. "Do you realize that we had an air strike all arranged for Tuesday? Thank God it's all over."[1]

One can make an educated guess about what Kennedy was praying for during the service at St. Stephen's. The previous afternoon he had called John Scali, whom he knew quite well, and thanked him for the service he had performed for Rusk and the administration by maintaining informal negotiations with Aleksandr Feklisov, the KGB man in Washington. "Do you go to church, John?" asked Kennedy. "Yes, I do, Mr. President," came the answer. "Well, this afternoon or this evening," continued Kennedy, "most of us should go to church and pray that we have not misunderstood and that we have correctly read what the Soviets are preparing to do, because there could be a very long tomorrow."[2]

But not everyone was in church that morning. Robert McNamara spent his Sunday morning at the Pentagon, trying to calm down General Curtis LeMay and his colleagues in the Joint Chiefs Committee, who had their own reading of Khrushchev's recently received letter to the president. Their meeting in the "tank," the Pentagon conference room, began at 9:00 a.m. with LeMay demanding an assault on Cuba the next day. "I want to see the president later today, and I hope all of you will come with me," he told the chiefs. "Monday will be the last day to attack the missiles before they become fully operational," continued LeMay. When the ticker tape of Khrushchev's speech was presented to the chiefs about 9:30 a.m., LeMay was anything but happy. "The Soviets may make a charade of withdrawal and keep some weapons in Cuba," he told the gathering. McNamara and Paul Nitze, who joined the meeting, tried their best to calm down LeMay and the others, stating that the deal would leave the Americans in a much stronger position in the Caribbean than the Soviets. The generals, perplexed by Khrushchev's sudden acquiescence to Kennedy's offer, had to retreat.[3]

◊◊◊

KENNEDY RETURNED FROM MASS A WINNER. WHEN, SOON after 11:00 a.m., he entered the White House Cabinet Room, he felt the atmosphere of jubilation. His aides had just finished reading the translation of Khrushchev's letter. Dean Rusk was speaking to the group, declaring the news a victory for everyone, irrespective of the position they had taken during the negotiations. "I think there is some gratification of everyone's line of action," Rusk told the gathering. Bundy, less than completely satisfied with Rusk's "feel good" speech, said that it was the "day of the doves." Undoubtedly it was Kennedy's day—a reluctant hawk at the start of the crisis, he had become a committed "dove."

Kennedy, who had turned on the tape recorder at first, turned it off after listening for a few minutes to his aides' self-congratulatory remarks. He was also dismissive of their compliments. One of them had suggested, while Kennedy was chatting with Ted Sorensen outside the Cabinet Room, that he was now in a position to do almost anything, including ending the ongoing war between China and India. As Kennedy denied that possibility, the aide told him: "But Mr. President, today you're more than ten feet tall." "That will last about a couple of weeks," responded Kennedy, laughing.[4]

The peacemaker in the White House had yet to explain his unexpected and stunning success to his generals and most of his aides. But his standing at home and in the international arena had just been transformed in a matter of hours, if not minutes. After having been accused of weakness by his predecessor, and then of losing one confrontation after another with Khrushchev, he had suddenly become a hero who was capable of standing his ground and forcing a powerful enemy to retreat. If up to that point he had been reacting to Khrushchev, who held the initiative, he would now consistently maintain the upper hand. Nevertheless, Kennedy's laurel wreath was full of thorns, since he had one more skeleton to hide in his closet—the Cuba-Turkey missile swap.

◊◊◊

THE EXCOM SESSION THAT FOLLOWED BECAME ONE OF THE shortest in the committee's history, lasting from 11:10 a.m. to 12:15 p.m. The participants canceled reconnaissance flights that day to avoid possible accidents and decided what UN inspection of the withdrawal of Soviet missiles would mean in practice. The United States would be prepared to monitor the dismantling and removal of the missiles on behalf of the UN or through it and provide the United Nations with intelligence information on the location and status of the sites.

Kennedy wanted the IL-28 Soviet airplanes out of Cuba as well. They were old and outdated but still capable of delivering nuclear bombs to US territory and thus constituted a threat. As such, they could be included in the "offensive weapons" category established in Kennedy's statement on the discovery of the SAM missiles in early September. During a meeting with his advisers on October 20, Kennedy had declared that he did not care about Soviet airplanes on the island, and that they all "must be prepared to live with the Soviet threat as represented by Soviet bombers." But now things had changed. No longer being hunted by Khrushchev, he had become a hunter in his own right, and Khrushchev was on the run. Bombers reentered the picture, but Kennedy decided not to raise the question immediately lest the issue derail his missile deal with Khrushchev. Everyone was in agreement. Kennedy asked the members of ExCom to avoid exuberant public comments—the crisis was not yet over.[5]

The letter to Khrushchev that Kennedy signed later that day was nothing like those he had previously sent to Moscow. They had been prepared after long discussions with aides, agonizing over what to say and which of Khrushchev's arguments to address. Nor were there any references to past deceptions or misdeeds, but there was an apology for Captain Maultsby's inadvertent foray into Soviet airspace. "I think that you and I, with our heavy responsibilities for the maintenance of peace, were aware that developments were approaching a point where events could have become unmanageable," wrote Kennedy.

The president continued, expressing his understanding of what constituted a deal and indicating his commitment to it: "I consider my letter to you of October twenty-seventh and your reply of today as firm undertakings on the part of both governments which should be promptly carried out." Finally, he responded positively to Khrushchev's offer to continue discussions on nuclear disarmament. "I think we should give priority to questions relating to the proliferation of nuclear weapons, on earth and in outer space, and to the great effort for a nuclear test ban," wrote Kennedy. He was ready to move beyond the Cuban crisis by returning to the discussions they had had before it exploded about the prohibition of nuclear tests.[6]

Kennedy's letter dealt with the open or public side of the deal. He would probably have preferred to forget about the offer he had passed through Robert to Dobrynin the previous evening, but Khrushchev was there to remind him about it. Dobrynin called Robert that morning, requesting a meeting. Robert Kennedy recalled that instead of going to church that morning, he had taken his three daughters to a horse show at the Washington Armory. It was there, around 10:00 a.m., that he received a phone call from Dean Rusk informing him about Khrushchev's acceptance of President Kennedy's offer. Robert rushed to the White House, where he took the call from Dobrynin. They agreed to meet in Robert Kennedy's office at the Justice Department at 11:00 a.m.[7]

The Soviet ambassador was, as always, the last person to learn what was going on in Moscow. He complained to his bosses that their instructions had arrived approximately an hour and a half after American radio had broadcast the essence of Khrushchev's response. Dobrynin did not yet have either the text of the public letter to Kennedy or Khrushchev's private note to the president concerning the Turkey-Cuba deal. What he had to guide him instead was Gromyko's message, sent from Moscow about 4:00 p.m. local time, instructing him to get in touch with Robert Kennedy immediately and tell him that Moscow was appreciative of what he had had to say to Dobrynin the previous night, and that the response to his brother's offer would be positive. Consequently, the ambassador headed to the Justice Department with yesterday's news— a message telling Robert that a letter to his brother was in the making. By then, its substance was all over the airwaves.

When they met, Dobrynin explained the obsolescence of his message by problems at the telegraph station. Robert was happy nevertheless to receive confirmation of the news he had already learned at the White House. It was the first time in several weeks that Dobrynin saw him smiling. "This is a great relief," Kennedy told the ambassador, who noted in his subsequent report to Moscow that "it was evident that he expressed his words somehow involuntarily." Gromyko's message implied that the offer passed to Dobrynin by Robert the previous night was largely responsible for Khrushchev's positive response to President Kennedy's official offer. That was certainly how Robert Kennedy understood the purpose of his meeting with Dobrynin.

Before parting ways with the ambassador, Kennedy asked him to keep the Turkish part of the deal secret. "Especially so that the correspondents don't find out," he told Dobrynin, according to the latter's report to Moscow. "At our place for the time being even [Pierre] Salinger does not know about it." Dobrynin assured him that he was the only person in the entire embassy who had the information. Robert left, telling Dobrynin that he would finally be able to see his children, as he had been "entirely absent from home."[8]

"It was quite a different meeting from the night before," wrote Robert Kennedy in his memoir. He remembered going back to the White House to brief the president on his meeting with Dobrynin.[9]

◊◊◊

ROBERT KENNEDY ARRIVED IN THE OVAL OFFICE AS HIS brother placed calls to three of his predecessors—Herbert Hoover, Harry Truman, and Dwight Eisenhower. He was calling to report the victory and lie about the way it was achieved. All he relied on were the assurances given by Dobrynin that the Soviets would keep silent about the Turkish missiles.

John Kennedy placed his first telephone call to the predecessor who mattered most to him, General Eisenhower. "General, how are you?" began Kennedy before going into details of his exchange of messages with Khrushchev. He reminded Eisenhower that Khrushchev had issued a public message agreeing to remove the missiles from Cuba "if we withdrew our missiles from Turkey." Kennedy continued: "We then, as you know, issued a statement that we couldn't get into that deal. So we then got this message this morning." "But Mr. President, did he put any conditions . . . ?" asked Eisenhower. The president responded with a lie: "No, except that we're not going to invade Cuba." To Eisenhower's "Yes," Kennedy continued in the same vein: "That's the only one that we've got now."[10]

The next call was to President Truman. Kennedy continued with his deception tactics, although Truman never asked any explicit question about Turkey. "Then on Saturday morning, twelve hours after the other letter was received, we got this entirely different letter about the missile bases in Turkey," said Kennedy, recounting the letter drama. "That's the way they do things," responded Truman. "Then, well then we rejected that," continued Kennedy. "Then they came back . . . and accepted the earlier proposal." Truman told Kennedy that he was on the right track. Hoover, whom Kennedy got on the line next, was in agreement with Truman. He told Kennedy: "It seems to me these recent events are rather incredible." "They are incredible," responded Kennedy. "That represents a good triumph for you," remarked Hoover.[11]

From this point on, Kennedy had no way back in his concealment of the secret deal with Khrushchev, but one thing he decided not to do was to commit the deal to paper. Khrushchev, meanwhile, wanted Kennedy's promise in writing. On October 29, Dobrynin got in touch with Robert Kennedy once again, this time to pass a confidential letter from Khrushchev to the president. "Dear Mr. President," began the message, "Ambassador Dobrynin has apprised me of his conversation with Robert Kennedy which took place on October 27." Khrushchev thanked Kennedy for having his brother convey the offer to remove American missiles from Turkey and explained that his agreement to Kennedy's official terms had been influenced by the president's unofficial offer. Khrushchev had no problem in conducting secret negotiations and was ready to keep that channel open. "I feel I must state to you that I do understand the delicacy involved for you in an open consideration of the issue of eliminating the US missile bases in Turkey," wrote Khrushchev. "I take into account the complexity of this issue, and I believe you are right about not wishing to publicly discuss it."[12]

The next day, Robert Kennedy assured Dobrynin that the president would honor his word but could not sign any letters, even the most secret ones. "We . . . are not prepared," said Robert to Dobrynin, "to formulate such an understanding in the form of letters, even the most confidential letters, between the President and the head of the Soviet government when it concerns such a highly delicate issue. Speaking in all candor, I myself, for example, do not want to risk getting involved in the transmission of this sort of letter, since who knows where and when such letters can surface or be somehow published—not now, but in the future—and any changes in the course of events are possible. The appearance of such a document could cause irreparable harm to my political career in the future. This is why we request that you take this letter back."

Dobrynin, who reported Robert Kennedy's words to Moscow, found himself obliged to take the letter back. On November 1, the Soviet ambassador delivered another message from Khrushchev to the attorney general. The Soviet leader trusted the president's word. The possibility of an immediate public scandal over the missiles in Turkey was avoided.[13]

Khrushchev had a lot of his own explaining to do. If Kennedy had to keep his political concession secret, Khrushchev was in no position to explain to his own people and the world at large why he had abandoned his demand to remove the American missiles from Turkey. He had to lie in order to make his deal work. Khrushchev probably understood quite well that a leak would make it impossible for Kennedy to keep his word. Not surprisingly, given his style and temperament, Khrushchev declared himself the victor in the crisis. He had allegedly achieved his goal of saving Cuba and did not need his missiles on the island for geostrategic reasons, as he could hit the United States from the USSR. Last but not least, he had saved the world from the nuclear war that Castro was ready to ignite.

The first opportunity to explain himself came on October 29, the day after he accepted Kennedy's conditions, when a Czechoslovak delegation led by the country's communist leader, Antonín Novotný, visited Moscow. The master of the Kremlin remained true to the word he had given Kennedy and did not mention the Cuba-Turkey swap to Novotný and his colleagues, although he hinted that "[t]hrough certain persons who they knew were in contact with us, they made it clear they would be grateful if we helped them get out of this conflict." Khrushchev accepted Kennedy's argument about his political inability to make a public deal on Turkey. "We understood that these questions are too far removed from the concrete situation in the Caribbean and Cuba, that Kennedy could not answer them because he would have also to consult with other members of NATO, and the situation was too serious for us to postpone its solution."[14]

"Who won?" Khrushchev asked the delegation before answering the question himself and maintaining that he had achieved his principal goal. "I am of the opinion that we won. One must start from the final aims we set ourselves. What aim did the Americans have? To attack Cuba and get rid of the Cuban Republic, to establish a reactionary regime in Cuba. Things did not work out as they planned. Our main aim was to save Cuba, to save the Cuban revolution. That is why we sent missiles to Cuba. We achieved our objective—we wrenched the promise out of the Americans that they would not attack Cuba and that other countries on the American continent would also refrain from attacking Cuba."

Khrushchev took the opportunity to blame Castro for aggravating the conflict and suggesting a nuclear strike against the United States. He also made a larger point about nuclear war, an issue on which he disagreed passionately with his main communist rival, Mao Zedong. He was eager to prove the Chinese communists wrong. "This clash (and we were truly on the verge of war) demonstrated that war today is not inevitably destined by fate, that it can be avoided. The Chinese claim was therefore once again refuted, as well as their assessments of the current era, the current balance of forces. Imperialism, as can be seen, is no paper tiger; it is a tiger that can give you a nice bite in the backside."

Khrushchev presented himself not only as the savior of Cuba from imperialism but also of the whole world from nuclear war—a seasoned and reasonable politician who knew when and how to compromise, but also as a winner in the court of world public opinion, scoring points even with the capitalists. With his fellow communist Novotný, Khrushchev allowed himself to be open, if not cynical, in that regard. "One of the important consequences of the whole conflict and of our approach is the fact that the whole world now sees us as the ones who saved peace," he argued. "I now appear to the world as a lamb. That is not bad either. The pacifist [Bertrand] Russell writes me thank-you letters. I, of course, have nothing in common with him, except that we both want peace."[15]

To all appearances, Khrushchev's explanations and bravado were accepted by his colleagues, de facto underlings, without question. The same applied to the Soviet media. *Pravda* and other leading newspapers published not only Russell's letter to Khrushchev, praising him for his efforts to maintain peace, but also similar congratulatory letters and telegrams from heads of state of third-world countries, especially leaders of the nonaligned movement such as Premier Jawaharlal Nehru of India.

Not all of that was pure propaganda. Many around the world were indeed grateful to Khrushchev for backing away from the brink of nuclear war, and some saw the outcome of the crisis as an American defeat. On October 28, the day the world media reported on Khrushchev's acceptance of Kennedy's offer, the Brazilian ambassador Roberto de Oliveira Campos reported from Washington that because Cuba was being recognized as a country that had defended itself, "the moral posture of the United States suffered strain and that, in spite of having originated the crisis, Khrushchev appears in the eyes of neutralist world opinion as a peace-maker."[16]

But outside the Soviet-controlled and nonaligned world, Khrushchev was perceived more as a loser than as a winner. In the United States, Kennedy was judged the victor. "Russian Accedes: Tells President Work on Bases Is Halted—Invites Talks," ran the title of a *New York Times* article published on October 29. Oliveira Campos sensed the atmosphere of jubilation among American officials. "In Washington it is considered that the incident 1) demonstrates the truth of the North

American accusation of the existence of nuclear arms; 2) the judgment of the Pentagon to be correct that at this moment the Russians recognize North American nuclear superiority; 3) that after an extreme cost of efforts in the last four months, with expenses estimated at a million dollars per day, the Soviets have returned to the point of departure, extracting from the United States only a guarantee of non-invasion, a declaration that Washington had already made unilaterally."[17]

The same feeling was also spreading in Western Europe. The *New York Times* Moscow correspondent, Seymour Topping, based his assessment of the outcome on the opinions of Western diplomats and reporters in Moscow. They saw the "abrupt manner in which the proposal about Turkey was dropped after it had been rejected by President Kennedy as humiliating for Moscow." "Western observers here believe that Mr. Khrushchev's letter represents a retreat on the Cuban issues that may have profound reverberations," continued Topping. "The manner in which this question has been handled, from the clandestine installation of the missile bases to their withdrawal under United States pressure, was regarded as likely to damage Soviet prestige abroad and possibly to affect the internal political position of the present Soviet leadership." A report on media reaction to the resolution of the Cuban crisis prepared for the president and his advisers by the United States Information Agency stated that Cuban media had been silent for three hours, Peking (Beijing) was "sulking," and the West Europeans were discussing the shift in the balance of power toward the United States.[18]

Soviet reporters abroad found themselves on the defensive, obliged to comment on assertions that Khrushchev was no longer in charge in Moscow. The *Pravda* correspondent Yurii Zhukov, meeting with Llewellyn Thompson, denied Western reports to the effect that the abrupt change in Khrushchev's position in his letters to Kennedy suggested that he had been overruled by his colleagues. According to Thompson's report, Zhukov "immediately said that he was certain this wasn't the case and that Mr. Khrushchev was still the boss." Not everyone found that statement reassuring. A few days earlier, when Hervé

Alphand, the French ambassador in Washington, had asked Dean Rusk about Khrushchev's drastic changes of position and was shown his letter of October 26 to Kennedy, Alphand remarked that it "showed symptoms of hysteria and mental disequilibrium."[19]

John Kennedy tried to stay away from cheap psychoanalysis or manifestations of triumphalism, just as he had advised his aides to do at the end of the ExCom meeting on October 28. On the following day the *New York Times* published a piece by its prominent journalist James Reston, who was close to Kennedy. It began with the line: "President Kennedy is looking at the Cuban crisis not as a great victory but merely as an honorable accommodation in a single isolated area of the 'cold war.'" The article claimed that Kennedy was not yet drawing general conclusions from the crisis about future relations with the Soviet Union. On the same day, however, Kennedy's adviser Arthur Schlesinger Jr. wrote him a memo suggesting that he deliver a speech doing just that. "The speech should interpret the nature of the victory in such a way as to accustom the nation to the future use of limited force for limited purposes while at the same time pointing out that our success on Cuba does not prove that force can solve everything," wrote Schlesinger.[20]

Both Kennedy and Khrushchev claimed to have prevailed in the crisis. But if Kennedy was concerned about how to secure and make use of his victory, Khrushchev was more preoccupied with explaining his sudden changes of position and apparent capitulation on the issue of Turkey. He committed himself to fight that battle with one hand only; the second was busy concealing the "gift" that Kennedy had offered him—the Cuba-Turkey swap. Whatever he said to others and others told him, subsequent events showed that Khrushchev had dramatically changed his attitude toward Kennedy. The young president whom he had considered inexperienced and weak grew in his eyes into a formidable figure who could not be pushed around and had to be reckoned with. Khrushchev learned to respect Kennedy.

One leader who refused to claim victory was Fidel Castro. If one listened to Khrushchev, then Castro had benefited most from the deal that the Soviet leader had made with Kennedy, putting his own prestige and the security of his state on the line. Cuba had avoided not only American attack and occupation but almost certain annihilation in a nuclear conflict, and Castro's regime had received an American pledge of noninvasion. But Castro felt differently. He considered himself to have been robbed not only of the missiles and nuclear warheads that he already had on the island but also, and more importantly, of his dignity as head of an independent country. And he was not prepared to sacrifice his prestige on the altar of his newfound communist religion.

24

INDIGNATION

"The reaction of our nation was profound indignation, not relief," said Fidel Castro decades later, recalling his and his comrades' reaction to the Radio Moscow broadcast of Khrushchev's letter to Kennedy. He learned of the letter not from the Soviet ambassador, Aleksandr Alekseev, or from the Radio Moscow broadcast, but from the Associated Press teletype.[1]

It was about noon on October 28 that the editor of a Cuban newspaper called Castro, asking for guidance on how to handle the news. "What news?" asked Castro in surprise. When he realized what was going on, he flew into a rage, smashing the mirror in his home. "Son of a bitch," "bastard," and "asshole" were the expletives he addressed to his alleged savior, Nikita Khrushchev. His reaction was much more emotional than that of John Kennedy on learning twelve days earlier about Khrushchev's missiles in Cuba. "When this news reached us," recalled Castro in the early 1990s, using different vocabulary but still feeling the pain, "we felt that we had become some kind of bargaining chip." Castro was not only not consulted but not even informed about the deal by his Soviet ally.[2]

"Concessions on the part of the Soviet Union produced a sense of oppressiveness," said Castro to the visiting Soviet dignitary Anastas Mikoyan a few days later. "Psychologically our people were not prepared for that. A feeling of deep disappointment, bitterness and pain has appeared, as if we were deprived not only of the missiles but of the very symbol of solidarity. Reports of missile launchers being dismantled and returned to the USSR at first seemed to our people to be an insolent lie." Castro found Khrushchev's agreement to allow the UN to inspect the missile sites on Cuban territory even more offensive; again, the Cubans had not even been consulted. "The Soviet Union gave its consent for inspections also without sending a notification to the Cuban leadership," he told Mikoyan. "It is necessary to take into account the special delicacy of our people, which has been created as a result of several historic developments. The Platt Amendment, imposed by the Americans upon Cuba, played a particular role in this regard."[3]

It is not clear whether Mikoyan knew who Platt was, but Castro had in mind an amendment to the Army Appropriations Bill of 1901 passed by the US Congress in March of that year and named after Senator Orville Platt, who presented it. It allowed the United States to lease and buy lands in Cuba for its military bases (Guantánamo among them), prohibited the country from going into debt, and limited its sovereignty over its foreign affairs. All that was done without consulting the Cuban government. Castro implied that the Soviet Union was now acting in similar fashion. Castro was personally offended, but his grievances were more than a reflection of his own hurt pride. They expressed the feelings of the Cuban leadership and its revolutionary supporters, all of whom felt betrayed.[4]

While Kennedy spent many agonizing hours and whole days arguing with his aides on how to get the Turks on board with the removal of the Jupiter missiles and how to convince the NATO allies to go along with the decision, Khrushchev devoted little or no time to thinking about Castro and his possible reaction. He expected Castro to fall into line: as a client and junior member of the communist club, he was to follow the policy adopted by his protector and communist supreme leader. That was what the East European communist leaders used to do. Besides, Khrushchev truly believed that the deal he had made was in the best interests of Castro and Cuba. What Khrushchev failed to grasp was that Castro's revolution was more nationalist than communist. *Patria o muerte*, fatherland or death—the main slogan of the revolution was about nationalism, not communism—and being regarded or treated as puppets of another great power was the worst thing that Castro and his supporters could imagine.

A few days earlier, on the morning of October 26, Kennedy's ExCom had discussed instructions to the US ambassador in Brazil to use that country's diplomatic channels to drive a wedge between Castro and Khrushchev. This was to be accomplished by suggestions that Moscow's order for its ships to turn back from the quarantine line and rumors that the USSR was prepared to trade Cuba for concessions in Berlin were reducing Castro to a pawn in the hands of Khrushchev, who was about to betray him. The instructions were never sent to Brazil, and Castro was never approached by the Brazilians. But it now appeared that Castro was drawing a similar conclusion on his own—this at a time when the Americans found a split in the communist camp by no means desirable. Indignation became the driving force of Castro's new attitude toward Moscow, and Khrushchev had to find a way of dealing with a new crisis that he had failed not only to foresee but even fully to comprehend once it materialized.[5]

◊◊◊

ALEKSANDR ALEKSEEV, THE MAN CASTRO TRUSTED TO BE HIS direct channel to Khrushchev, found himself in the middle of the political hurricane that hit Soviet-Cuban relations on October 28. Like his Washington counterpart, Anatoly Dobrynin, Alekseev was at a loss when President Osvaldo Dorticós of Cuba asked him to explain the

news. Alekseev, who knew nothing about Khrushchev's letter, told Dorticós not to trust the American radio. Dorticós explained that what he
had in mind was the statement broadcast by Soviet radio. It was only a
few hours later that Alekseev received a copy of Khrushchev's letter to
Castro. He immediately tried to deliver it, but the Cuban leader refused
to see him.[6]

Khrushchev wrote to Castro to persuade him that the agreement
he had reached with Kennedy was in his own interest, as it provided "a
guarantee that the USA will refrain from invading Cuba not only with
its own forces, but with those of its allies as well." The main purpose
of the letter, however, was not to inform Castro but to calm him down
and stop him from acting in ways that might complicate Khrushchev's
deal with Kennedy. "We would like to recommend to you now, at this
critical moment, not to yield to your emotions, to show restraint," wrote
Khrushchev. "It must be said that we understand your indignation over
the US aggressions, and their violations of the basic guidelines of international law. But at present it is not so much the law at work as the
recklessness of certain military figures in the Pentagon. Now that an
agreement is beginning to take shape, the Pentagon is looking for an
opportunity to undermine that agreement." Khrushchev asked Castro
not to give in to these provocations.[7]

Shunned by Castro, Alekseev managed to arrange a meeting with
Dorticós and Carlos Rafael Rodríguez, the man responsible for Cuban
agricultural reform, to hand over the letter. "Unfortunately," said Dorticós to Alekseev, "the Cuban and Latin American peoples would perceive the decision to dismantle the special weaponry, relying only upon
Kennedy's assurances, as a defeat for the Soviet government." The
Cubans were disappointed, and Castro was struggling to find a way
of calming his loyalists, who believed that the entire Soviet contingent
was leaving Cuba. He wanted stronger guarantees and put forward his
own conditions for accepting the Khrushchev-Kennedy deal. "Confusion and bewilderment are reigning inside the Cuban leadership,"
reported Alekseev to Moscow on the results of the meeting.[8]

The five points enumerating the conditions on which Cuba would accept the American pledge of noninvasion were broadcast by Radio Havana on the afternoon of October 28. They included an end to overt and covert attacks on Cuba, the cessation of the American commercial blockade of the island, and American evacuation of the Guantánamo naval base. The points were accompanied by a statement to the effect that orders had been given to shoot down any airplanes violating Cuban airspace. The Kennedy-Khrushchev deal included as a crucial component the verification of the dismantling of missile sites on Cuban territory. That component now became Castro's leverage. His five points suggested that verification could be carried out only if the two superpowers, especially the United States, accepted Castro's demands.[9]

Although the five points were formally addressed to the United States, the Cuban minister of foreign affairs, Raúl Roa, told the Yugoslav ambassador in Havana, Boško Vidaković, they were "forwarded more to Khrushchev than to Kennedy." He added: "We have to say something when our skin is at stake." "We exist," wrote Vidaković in another cable, quoting Roa. "They have to know that—this side as well as the other side." The Polish ambassador Bolesław Jeleñ reported to Warsaw: "Cuban conditions may be calculated in order to show that Cuba participated in making the decision." He also pointed to a "very troublesome situation for Castro caused by Khrushchev's statement."[10]

Castro responded to Khrushchev's letter on the same day. "I want to inform you," he wrote, "that we are generally opposed to the inspection of our territory." But most of the letter was dedicated to an explanation of his decision to order antiaircraft fire against American airplanes—the development that had led, in Khrushchev's opinion, to the downing of the U-2. Castro advised Khrushchev to consult his own commanders: "The Soviet military leadership can provide you with additional information on how the plane was shot down." He did not rebuff Khrushchev's suggestion that it was he who had given the order to shoot down the U-2, and a few days later he told U Thant that "the plane was shot down by our anti-aircraft forces."[11]

Castro knew what had really happened but was not prepared to admit that the foreign troops on his territory were not under his jurisdiction. He had made a career in the international arena by protesting the presence of foreign bases in Latin America. Now it appeared that he had acquiesced to the establishment of a Soviet base in Cuba. Blaming the Soviets for shooting down the U-2 was tantamount to admitting that he had no control over foreign troops on his territory. Castro was not prepared to do that.

◊◊◊

CASTRO EVENTUALLY AGREED TO MEET WITH ALEKSANDR Alekseev on Monday, October 29, the day after Khrushchev's letter to Kennedy was broadcast. Alekseev had another letter for him, this one not from Khrushchev personally but from the entire Soviet leadership.

The Presidium wanted Castro to make a public statement supporting the Khrushchev-Kennedy deal: to "express in your own terms what we have already said." The idea had allegedly come from the Americans, a detail that Khrushchev expected to deflect Castro's wrath from him. To show that it was indeed the Americans and not Khrushchev who had proposed the idea, the Presidium sent Alekseev a transcript of a conversation between the KGB chief in Washington, Aleksandr Feklisov, and his American contact John Scali. Scali, whose name was not given in the transcript, had assured Feklisov, whose name was not there either, that such an initiative from Castro would be received positively in the United States. Khrushchev was trying to appease Castro and salve the wound to his pride by offering him a role in the settlement. But the role was that of endorsing a decision made without consulting him. Not surprisingly, Castro remained aloof, promising to study the proposal.[12]

"I have never yet encountered Castro so dispirited and irritable," reported Alekseev to Moscow. "We will not allow anyone to carry out any inspection in our land," Castro told the Soviet ambassador. He called the inspections a "humiliating procedure." He also attacked the Soviets where it hurt most, suggesting that they had caved in to the Americans: "an impression has been created that the Soviet Union yielded to pressure from the USA." To mollify Castro, Alekseev proposed to have Khrushchev send him a "warm" letter and make a public statement supporting Castro's five points.[13]

Khrushchev was now fully aware that he had a problem, and that it was getting worse. "Castro did not understand the full depth of the undertaking embodied in our action; he did not understand the political maneuver," recalled Khrushchev later. "He was highly nervous and lambasted us every which way, if one can put it like that. Castro's 'revolutionism,' his extremism was intensely fired up by the Chinese. And we suffered moral detriment. Instead of our stock rising in Cuba, it fell. Castro considered that we had betrayed Cuba while the Chinese were supporting it." At stake was not only the realization of the Soviet-American agreement but also Soviet leadership of the communist world.[14]

Khrushchev's first reaction was to ignore Alekseev's advice and, instead of sending Castro a "warm" letter, resort to his usual bullying. In the letter he sent Castro on October 30, Khrushchev began on a warm note: "We understand your situation and are taking your difficulties into account." But he then went on the offensive, castigating Castro for his suggestion of October 27 to use nuclear arms against the United States. "Dear Comrade Fidel Castro," wrote Khrushchev, "I find your proposal to be wrong, even though I understand your reasons." He continued: "We have lived through a very grave moment; a global thermonuclear war could have broken out. Of course, the United States would have suffered enormous losses, but the Soviet Union and the whole socialist bloc would also have suffered greatly. It is even difficult to say how things would have ended for the Cuban people. . . . We struggle against imperialism not in order to die but to draw on all our potential, to lose as little as possible, and later to win more, so as to be a victor and make communism triumph."[15]

But neither Khrushchev's bullying tactics nor his logical suppositions produced the desired result. Castro responded next day, as defiant as ever. "I do not see how you can state that we were consulted in the decision you took," he wrote, responding to a condescending line in Khrushchev's letter that read: "[W]e consider that consultation took place, my dear Commander Fidel Castro, given that we received your wires, each one more alarming than the last." Castro did not conceal his disapproval of the Khrushchev-Kennedy deal and would not trust Kennedy's assurances. "The imperialists," wrote Castro, "are talking once again of invading our country, which is proof of how ephemeral and untrustworthy their promises are." Alekseev advised Moscow not to respond to Castro's letter, and this time Khrushchev listened. He had to come up with different tactics but could not change the strategy: without Castro's consent to inspections, the Khrushchev-Kennedy deal could not be implemented.[16]

◊◊◊

CASTRO DUG IN HIS HEELS. HE WAS DETERMINED TO CONDUCT his own foreign policy and establish himself as an independent actor in the international arena. He demonstrated his full independence not only from the United States but also from the Soviet Union when, on the afternoon of October 30, he welcomed to the presidential palace in Havana a distinguished guest from New York, Secretary General of the United Nations U Thant.

The United Nations was a major battleground in the struggle for public support between the Soviet Union and Cuba on the one hand and the United States and its allies on the other. Adlai Stevenson's presentation of U-2 photos of Soviet missile sites and his confrontation with the Soviet ambassador, Valerian Zorin, was the most spectacular episode of that struggle, but the struggle itself was not limited to dramas of that kind. The acting secretary general of the United Nations, the Burmese diplomat U Thant, played an important role in keeping the crisis from escalating into an open confrontation. U Thant was the first to publicly suggest a solution to the crisis—withdrawal of the Soviet missiles in exchange for an American pledge not to attack Cuba—which he promoted both publicly and privately.[17]

For quite some time, the Americans encouraged U Thant to propose UN inspection of the Cuban missile sites, but Khrushchev never consulted with the secretary general on whether he would assume that role before accepting Kennedy's proposal that the missiles be withdrawn under UN supervision. Once he had accepted the proposal, however, Khrushchev instructed Gromyko to deliver the news not only to Robert Kennedy via Dobrynin but also to U Thant through the Soviet representative at the UN, Valerian Zorin. On the same day, October 28, U Thant wrote to Khrushchev expressing his "extreme satisfaction" with the Soviet leader's decision to dismantle the missile sites and his readiness "to reach an agreement about the possibility of UN representatives checking on the dismantling of these bases."[18]

Fidel Castro invited U Thant to visit Cuba on October 27, in the middle of the war scare that engulfed both him and the Soviet commanders on the island. He needed the secretary general not only as an intermediary, writing that he was prepared to discuss his differences with the United States, but also as a shield against invasion. By the time U Thant accepted the invitation and landed on the tarmac of Havana airport, the Cuban situation had changed dramatically. The American media were suggesting that U Thant was going to Cuba to convince Castro to accept the inspections agreed upon by Kennedy and Khrushchev. The secretary general announced that he was open to discussing a broad range of issues but never contradicted media reports about inspections being one of the main goals of his visit. Indeed they were.[19]

U Thant raised the question of inspections during his very first meeting with Castro on the afternoon of October 30. He laid out the American proposal for inspections without directly associating himself with it. The Cuban leader showed no inclination to change his position on the issue. "What we do not understand is precisely why this is asked of us. We have not violated any law. . . . To the contrary, we have been the victims, in the first place, of a blockade, which is an illegal act. And secondly, we have been victims of another country's claim to determine what we have the right to do or not to do within our own borders. It is our understanding that Cuba is a sovereign state, no more and no less than any other member state of the United Nations. . . . As I see it, all this talk about inspection is one more attempt to humiliate our country. We do not accept it."

When U Thant tried to counter his host's national sovereignty argument by citing the example of the government of the Congo, which had invited UN personnel into its territory, the infuriated Castro shot back: "In the Congo the government that made that request is now dead and buried!" The reference was to the former prime minister of the Republic of the Congo, Patrice Lumumba, who was killed in January 1961 by his Western-backed opponents despite the presence of UN troops in the country. Castro refused to accommodate U Thant's request for the inspection not only of missile sites but also of Soviet ships taking weapons back to the USSR as long as they were in Cuban ports. The meeting, in which Castro kept talking about national sovereignty and humiliation and U Thant about the threat to international peace, ended without agreement.[20]

When U Thant and Castro met the next day, the secretary general tried a different tactic. Instead of presenting the American proposal, he gently put forward the Soviet one. He asked Castro what he thought of Khrushchev's letter accepting Kennedy's proposal for UN inspection of missile sites on Cuban territory. This overture hit Castro in his most painful spot: Khrushchev's proposal questioned not only Castro's control over the Soviet missiles but also over Cuban territory. But the Cuban leader had his answer ready. "It is our understanding," said Castro, "that . . . they were referring to some kind of inspection outside Cuba's national territory—inasmuch as the premier of the Soviet Union could not talk about verification on Cuban territory, since that is something that concerns only the revolutionary government of Cuba."

Castro was prepared to repeat the same statement publicly in a speech that he was to deliver the same evening. U Thant asked him not to do so: "[T]his could create some division or some misunderstanding between the Soviet Union and Cuba." Ironically, it was U Thant and not Castro who was worried about possible misunderstandings between Moscow and Havana.[21]

◊◊◊

CASTRO COULD PREVENT UN PERSONNEL FROM INSPECTING the missile sites, and indeed barred U Thant from visiting them, but he could not prevent the secretary general from meeting with Soviet officials in Cuba. Khrushchev was ready to offer the secretary general such meetings in an attempt to satisfy the Americans and meet their demand for UN inspection at least halfway. The meeting that took place on the afternoon of October 31 included not only the Soviet ambassador to Cuba, Aleksandr Alekseev, but also the commander of the missile division on the island, General Igor Statsenko.

The meeting was a substitute for U Thant's request to visit the Soviet missile installations, which Castro's protests rendered impossible. U Thant first raised the possibility of visiting the installations on October 29, one day before he departed for Cuba, in a meeting with Vasilii Kuznetsov, the Soviet first deputy foreign minister, who had been dispatched to New York by Khrushchev to enhance Soviet diplomacy at the UN during the crisis. U Thant asked Kuznetsov whether it would be possible for him to see missiles being removed while he was in Cuba. Kuznetsov, who believed that inspectors should verify the absence of missiles, not monitor the process of their removal, demurred.

On the same day Kuznetsov wrote to Moscow, asking his government to speed up the dismantling of the missile sites. "If the dismantling is carried out in a short time, then the issue of inspection during the dismantling process will not arise at all," he cabled his boss in Moscow, Andrei Gromyko. But Kuznetsov was also in favor of accommodating U Thant's request by showing him already dismantled launchers. "We propose," wrote Kuznetsov, "that it would be appropriate to show U Thant himself the dismantling of certain installations during his stay in Cuba on 30 and 31 October. In such an event he would take a firmer stance, and it would be more difficult for the Americans to renew their 'quarantine' of Cuba. If this is recognized as expedient, I request urgently to give corresponding instructions to Havana."[22]

Khrushchev found Kuznetsov's suggestions attractive, and on October 31, with U Thant already in Cuba, Gromyko issued urgent instructions to the Soviet ambassador in Havana, Alekseev. "In Moscow," wrote Gromyko, "we consider it necessary to satisfy U Thant's desire that the launchers, which are being dismantled, be shown to him and persons accompanying him." Alekseev's other task was to inform Pliev about the decision to show the launchers to U Thant and his people. "We proceed from the assumption that the Cuban government and Comrade Pavlov [Pliev] would undertake all necessary measures on site," read the cable.[23]

The task entrusted to Alekseev turned out to be impossible to fulfill, since Castro and his government refused to allow U Thant to visit the missile sites. Alekseev therefore decided to accommodate the request of General Indar Jit Rikhye, who served as a military adviser to U Thant and accompanied him on the trip, to meet with the Soviet commander in Cuba. General Issa Pliev apparently refused to meet with Rikhye and volunteered instead General Igor Statsenko, the commander of the missile division on the island.

The meeting took place at U Thant's temporary residence in the presence of Alekseev. Statsenko later recalled that U Thant was the only participant who asked questions, while General Rikhye remained silent, making notes. For Statsenko, the last-minute request to meet with U Thant came as a complete surprise, especially because he was requested to demonstrate openness at the meeting. "They notified us that the presentation should be complete, including data on the status of the division and its organization, the number of missile launchers and missiles brought in, and plans for dismantling the missiles and taking them back to the Soviet Union," recalled Anatoly Gribkov, one of the planners of Operation Anadyr, who was then the representative of the General Staff in Cuba. Statsenko followed Pliev's order and made as complete a report as possible.[24]

As the Americans later learned, Statsenko told U Thant that the dismantling of the missiles was underway and would be finished soon. "We started the dismantling on Sunday at 5:00 p.m.," Statsenko told

U Thant. "It will be all over by tomorrow night, or at the latest on Friday [November 2], when we will have finished the bulldozing of the sites. . . . We have asked for ships. We don't know when they will be in the ports. But the equipment will be in the ports Thursday night or Friday morning. We are crating the equipment at the ports for the sea voyage. Most of it will not have to be crated because of deck loading. The bases no longer exist. Even the pads will be gone, but no Cuban observation of the dismantling is permitted."[25]

Statsenko was telling the truth. Upon his return to the Soviet Union a few months later, he filed a report providing essentially the same information on the dismantling of the missiles that he had given U Thant. He reported to his commanders that the whole task of dismantling the sites was accomplished in less than three days. "At 1500 hours on October 28, 1962, the Commander of the Group of Soviet Forces in Cuba gave me directive No. 7665, dated October 28th, 1962, in which the USSR Minister of Defense, on the basis of a decision of the Soviet government, ordered the dismantling of the launching sites and the relocation of the division to the Soviet Union in full," wrote Statsenko. "In the period from October 29th through October 31st, 1962, division units completed the dismantling of the launch sites in full."

General Gribkov recalled that what he had witnessed during those days was not "dismantling" but "the breaking down of the positional structures that had taken so much of the soldiers' labor to build." Statsenko was clearly unhappy. He complained to Gribkov: "It was you who pressed me with the building of the positional installations, but now you reproach me for dismantling them too slowly." It seemed that Kuznetsov's suggestion to dismantle the missiles before they could be inspected was fully implemented even before U Thant left Cuba on the evening of October 31. Khrushchev was eager to carry out his part of the bargain, no matter what. But he had a problem, and the name of that problem was Fidel Castro.[26]

In a major speech given on October 31, Castro rejected inspections and stated, as he had done in negotiations with U Thant, that the American insistence on inspections was meant to humiliate the

Cuban government. He also mentioned "certain discrepancies" that
had arisen between the Soviet and Cuban governments but said that
he was not going to discuss them further so as not to give ammunition to enemies. The "discrepancies," continued Castro, should be discussed on the party and government levels, "because above all we must
state that we are Marxists and Leninists and that we are friends of the
Soviet Union." Those words were met with an ovation. In all but form,
however, the speech was less a challenge to the Americans than to the
Soviets and to Nikita Khrushchev personally.[27]

VII

SETTLEMENT

25

MISSION IMPOSSIBLE

Khrushchev's letters to Castro failed to produce the result that the Soviet leader hoped for. The stubborn Castro stuck to his guns and refused to sanction the Khrushchev-Kennedy deal. Khrushchev, who so far had been playing bad cop, decided that he needed a good cop as well. He found one in Anastas Mikoyan, the only Presidium member who had objected to the deployment of nuclear arms on Cuba and who tried to stop the nuclear-armed Soviet submarines from coming to the island. Khrushchev wanted Mikoyan to go to Cuba and improve Soviet-Cuban relations. "I proposed that Mikoyan be dispatched to Cuba," recalled Khrushchev later. "Having known Mikoyan for many years, I considered that his diplomatic qualities would be useful in this case. His nerves are good; he is calm and can repeat one and the same argumentation without raising his voice. That is very important, especially in negotiations with such a fiery man as Fidel."[1]

Mikoyan remembered Khrushchev approaching him after receiving Alekseev's report on his meeting with Castro on October 29. "Look, he doesn't understand that we saved them from invasion; we saved them, but he doesn't understand our policy," said Khrushchev, referring to Castro. "You can't explain it by letter, but it has to be explained, otherwise they won't understand anything; someone has to go and explain it all properly." Mikoyan remained silent. His wife, the sixty-five-year-old Ashkhen Mikoyan, was mortally ill. Khrushchev knew of her condition but said that one couldn't help Ashken any longer. "You need to go," he told his closest ally and critic. "Anastas, if the worst comes to pass, we'll take care of everything—no need to worry." As Mikoyan remembered the conversation a few months later, "He began saying that they know me there; I've been there and spoken with them; it would be easier for me to explain the situation to them and make the right arguments." He eventually agreed: "I said that I was ready."[2]

Khrushchev once said about Mikoyan's diplomatic skills: "Not everyone understands what Mikoyan is saying when he talks, but he is a reasonable man." Mikoyan, the "reasonable man," became Khrushchev's best bet to solve two Cuban crises in one—the first in relations between Moscow and Washington, and the second in relations between Moscow and Havana. He had to keep the Americans out of Cuba and the Soviets in, and the way to achieve that was by convincing Castro to accept UN inspection on his territory. For the Kremlin, the stakes were enormous. From Khrushchev's perspective, he had saved Cuba from Kennedy by taking a huge risk but was about to lose it again, either to Kennedy or to Mao Zedong. The war that seemed to have been avoided could once again be on the doorsteps of Washington and Moscow, and Mikoyan was supposed to carry out what looked like mission impossible. By mid-October Cuba found itself in the middle of a new international crisis, bringing the possibility of nuclear war back into the picture.[3]

◊◊◊

KHRUSHCHEV PRESSED MIKOYAN TO GO TO CUBA ON THE evening of October 30. On the following night Mikoyan bade farewell to his dying wife and took a special Aeroflot flight to New York. If the commanders of the Soviet missile detachments had made their way to Cuba secretly, via Conakry and Bermuda, Mikoyan traveled openly, with the Americans hoping no less than the Soviets for the success of his diplomatic skills. On November 1, the day he landed in New York, Mikoyan met with U Thant and had dinner with two Americans directly dealing with the Cuban crisis, the US representative to the UN, Adlai Stevenson, and the chairman of the Council on Foreign Relations and Kennedy's point man for Cuba, John McCloy.[4]

The Americans knew Mikoyan from his visit to the United States in 1960, and the meeting around the dinner table lasted for four hours, from 7:00 to 11:00 p.m. A number of Soviet officials took part, including the deputy foreign minister, Vasilii Kuznetsov, and the Soviet ambassadors to the US, Anatoly Dobrynin, and to the UN, Valerian Zorin. "Mikoyan started in [an] aggressive mood, insisting on suspending quarantine now," reported Stevenson to Washington. Khrushchev's envoy was following the latest instructions he had just received from Moscow but did not get very far, as Stevenson and McCloy told him that there would be no lifting of the quarantine until the Red Cross could inspect Soviet ships. "Meeting became more cordial and friendly as it proceeded and was exclusively dominated by Mikoyan," wrote Stevenson in his report.[5]

According to Mikoyan, who filed his own report about the dinner, Stevenson and McCloy were largely interested in verifying the withdrawal of Soviet missiles from Cuba. They made it clear that the United States would not sign a joint protocol guaranteeing not to invade Cuba if Cuba was also a signatory of such a document, but they were allegedly open to the idea that guarantees would be given as part of a package of documents including American, Soviet, and even Cuban official statements. In his report, Stevenson denied ever agreeing to Cuba's participation. But that was something that Mikoyan wanted to take with him to Havana to appease Castro. Stevenson and McCloy, wrote Mikoyan in his report to Moscow, "stated that the US refused pointblank to discuss the question of liquidating the American base in Guantánamo." That was one of Castro's five points for the resolution of the crisis, and the

American refusal to discuss it even as a possibility promised nothing good for Mikoyan's mission in Havana.

On the issue of verifying the withdrawal of Soviet missiles, which was paramount for Stevenson and McCloy, both men fully realized the difficulties that Castro's unyielding position on inspections was creating for the Soviets. They were therefore prepared to be flexible. Perhaps verification could be achieved by continuing flights over Cuba, or by Soviet agreement to supply lists of the weapons they were removing from the island. They wanted those weapons to include the ground-to-air SAM missiles, one of which had shot down the U-2 plane on October 28. Mikoyan refused to discuss the SAM missiles, as they were not covered by the Khrushchev-Kennedy exchange. He also rejected the suggestion of overflights as a tool of verification. "McCloy," Mikoyan telegraphed Moscow, "received a very firm response that the US has no right to overfly Cuba, and nobody can guarantee security of such unlawful flights."[6]

◊◊◊

MIKOYAN FLEW FROM NEW YORK TO HAVANA ON THE AFTERnoon of November 2. At the last moment, before leaving for the airport, he saw the list of weapons that Stevenson and McCloy considered offensive and expected the Soviet Union to remove from Cuba. It did not include SAM missiles but specified Soviet IL-28 bombers capable of carrying nuclear payloads and therefore considered offensive.

The list and covering letter were addressed to Vasilii Kuznetsov, the Soviet deputy foreign minister, who had accompanied Mikoyan to dinner the previous night. It turned out that Stevenson had forgotten to give the list to Mikoyan at dinner. Mikoyan suspected foul play and an attempt to slip in at the last minute one more requirement that was not part of the original deal. A few days later he would call the two Americans "pilferers," but for the moment he did not think much about what had happened. Ahead was the trying task of convincing Castro to go along with Khrushchev's proposal. The only trump card Mikoyan had in his pocket was Soviet willingness to endorse Castro's five points. Mikoyan made a statement to that effect before leaving New York. It turned out to be a smart diplomatic move.[7]

Fidel Castro hesitated until the last minute whether to honor Mikoyan by meeting him at the airport or to ignore him as a sign of displeasure with Khrushchev's actions. He eventually decided to meet Mikoyan at the airport, but only after learning that in New York the Soviet representative had gone on record supporting the five points. Castro and Mikoyan had a brief conversation that evening, and while Castro tried to be friendly, Mikoyan, as he later reported to Moscow, "could feel his acute dissatisfaction with our policy." Negotiations began on the following morning, November 3, at Castro's residence in Havana. Castro struck a friendly note at the outset, quoting Khrushchev, who apparently had said that "there is a Cuban in the CC CPSU, and that Cuban is A. I. Mikoyan." But after listening to Mikoyan's assurances that he had come to Cuba "to discuss in the most frank way all the unclear questions with the Cuban comrades," Castro vented all the frustration with Soviet actions that he had accumulated during the previous week.[8]

"Reports on 28 October that N. S. Khrushchev had given orders to dismantle missile launchers, that such instructions had been given to Soviet officers, and that there was not a word in the message about the consent of the Cuban government, that report shocked people," Castro told Mikoyan. "Cubans were consumed by a sense of disappointment, confusion and bitterness. In walking along the street, driving to armed units, I observed that people did not understand that decision." It was a long list of grievances in which Castro also mentioned the Platt Amendment, the American legal act that had deprived Cuba of its sovereignty back in 1901. It was assumed that the Soviets were now trying to do the same.[9]

Mikoyan tried to defend the Soviet position but was cut short by tragic news from Moscow: his wife of forty-one years had died. The negotiations were interrupted. Everyone left the room in complete silence. Mikoyan headed back to his residence to absorb the news.

Khrushchev offered his ally condolences and the option of returning to Moscow, but Mikoyan decided to stay. "I can't cut short such important business," he told his son, Sergo, who was accompanying him on the trip. He asked Sergo to return to Moscow alone to bury his mother. His only request was to be informed of the date and time of the funeral.

Ashkhen Mikoyan was buried at the Novodevichy Cemetery in Moscow on November 5, and Mikoyan would see the filmed funeral after returning home. Khrushchev, who had sent him to Cuba and promised to attend the funeral, was not in the film. "I don't like funerals," he told Sergo Mikoyan later. "After all, it's not like going to a wedding, right?" The young Mikoyan was shocked. Khrushchev's backhanded compliment to his father's diplomatic skills—"Only Anastas, with his oxlike perseverance, can withstand this. I would have put my foot down long ago and left!"—did nothing to alleviate the young man's shock at what he considered Khrushchev's cynicism. Anastas Mikoyan would never forgive Khrushchev his betrayal. For the time being, however, he remained in Havana and pushed as hard for the desired result as only he, with his "oxlike perseverance," could do.[10]

Next day Mikoyan was ready to continue negotiations. His main goal was to overcome the mistrust between the two parties, and he began by explaining the reasons for placing the missiles in Cuba. The point, he argued, was not to create a military base there but to save Cuba from an American invasion. "When Khrushchev visited Bulgaria," he began, sharing with the Cubans the official story about the origins of the idea, "he expressed many things to us; he said: 'Although I was in Bulgaria, I was always thinking of Cuba. I fear the Yankees will attack Cuba, directly or indirectly, and imagine the effect on us of the defeat of the Cuban revolution. We cannot allow this to happen. Although the plan is very risky for us, it is a big responsibility, for it exposes us to a war. Cuba must be saved." He also explained that Khrushchev did not have time to consult with Castro before sending his proposal to Kennedy: "Consultations would have been appropriate, but Cuba would not exist, and the world would be enveloped in a war."[11]

The Cubans asked questions about guarantees of no American

invasion, the Cuba-Turkey swap, and the existence of secret letters and agreements between Khrushchev and Kennedy. Mikoyan was prepared to share not only his recollections but also copies of Khrushchev's letter to Kennedy. The Cubans still had their doubts and were more skeptical than trusting, but in Mikoyan's opinion things were changing for the better. He decided to use that momentum at the meeting next day, November 5, to convince Castro to accept the inspection regime. With the Cubans adamantly opposed to any foreign inspection of their territory, Mikoyan came up with an ingenious proposal: to receive official American guarantees that they would not invade, the Cubans would have to meet U Thant halfway and allow UN inspection of Soviet ships in their ports. That would avoid any violation of Cuban sovereignty.

His strategy backfired. Apparently, Castro had had enough of Mikoyan's insistence on something that the Cubans had rejected again and again. In a calm tone, he told Mikoyan that they would not accept inspection of any kind: that was the will of the Cuban people. "If our position puts peace throughout the world at risk, then we would think it more correct to consider the Soviet side free of its obligations, and we will resist by ourselves. Come what may. We have the right to defend our dignity ourselves." The statement had the force of an exploding bomb. Mikoyan reported to Moscow that for a few minutes everyone was silent. Then Dorticós took the floor to say that Castro had expressed the position of the entire Cuban leadership. The earth seemed to shake under Mikoyan's feet. "I do not understand such a sharp reaction to my proposal," he told the gathering.[12]

In his report to Moscow, Mikoyan asked Khrushchev not to draw any final conclusions from the statement, suggesting that Castro did not mean what he had said and indicating his mercurial personality. "One should not forget the complicated personal qualities of Castro's character, his acute sensitivity. While in power, he made many thoughtless statements caused by a fleeting impressionability, which he later regretted." But he also concluded that if Castro accepted any form of inspection after his numerous statements opposing it, then his prestige in Cuba and Latin America generally would be undermined. What that meant in practice was that Moscow would have to forget about inspections involving Cuban territory or waters.[13]

◊◊◊

AFTER KHRUSHCHEV'S SURPRISE PUBLIC ANNOUNCEMENT OF the withdrawal of the Soviet missiles from Cuba the cracks in the edifice of the Soviet-Cuban alliance grew deeper and wider with every passing day. On November 7 the Soviets celebrated one of their major holidays, the anniversary of the Bolshevik Revolution. This time it was a special occasion—the forty-fifth anniversary of the coup d'état, called the October Revolution, in Petrograd, then the capital of the Russian Empire. Soviet embassies all over the world hosted special receptions, and Havana was no exception. Upset by the Soviets, Fidel Castro ignored Ambassador Alekseev's invitation to a festive dinner at the Soviet embassy, but other high-ranking Cuban officials, led by Raúl Castro, showed up.

The Soviets were prepared to forgive the absence of the chief Cuban communist and Marxist but were upset by the behavior of Cuban officials at the event. The chief of Cuban military intelligence, Pedro Luis Rodríguez, proposed a toast to Fidel Castro and Joseph Stalin. General Gribkov and other Soviet commanders at the table, who had drunk to the previous toast in honor of Khrushchev and Castro, refused to raise their glasses. "His words came down to the notion that if Stalin had been alive, then the missiles would have remained in Cuba," recalled General Anatoly Gribkov, the representative of the General Staff in Cuba, who was sitting at the same table as Rodríguez. Later that night he mentioned the Rodríguez episode in his report on the day's developments to Marshal Malinovsky. Malinovsky passed it to Khrushchev, who became furious and ordered an investigation. As far as he was concerned, the Cubans were in revolt.[14]

By the fall of 1962, Stalin had become anathema in the Soviet Union. In the official report on the anniversary of the October Revolution delivered that year in Moscow by the future prime minister of the

Soviet Union, Aleksei Kosygin, Stalin's name was not mentioned, and the report lauded Soviet economic achievements since 1953, the year of Stalin's death. The party congress held the previous autumn decided to remove Stalin's body from the mausoleum: the dictator was buried instead near the Kremlin wall. As far as the Soviet leaders were concerned, he did not exist. But it turned out that Stalin was very much on the mind of Khrushchev's Cuban allies, who were disappointed with his retreat in the face of world imperialism.[15]

Khrushchev's investigation of the Rodríguez episode was one more piece of bad news for Mikoyan. Not that he was an admirer of Stalin, but he knew nothing about Gribkov's report to Moscow and wrote nothing about Rodríguez to Moscow himself. Now it looked as if he were either unaware of what was going on under his nose at the Soviet embassy or, worse, as if he were covering up for his Cuban friends. Mikoyan called in General Gribkov and, in Pliev's presence, dressed him down for failing to report the incident to him. As Gribkov later recalled, Mikoyan "strictly reminded everyone, and me in the first instance, that he was representing the Central Committee of the CPSU there and had to know who was reporting what to Moscow." Mikoyan wanted to be the only channel of information between Moscow and Cuba.[16]

The Cubans were not the only ones to misbehave on October Revolution Day. Soviet officers and men caused trouble in a different way. On November 7, Private Veselovsky of the 181st Missile Regiment, posted at Los Palacios (San Cristóbal area), opened fire at a military patrol. Luckily, no one was killed or wounded, and the whole episode was covered up. The drunken soldier, a candidate member of the Communist Party, was denied the right to join it but never faced criminal charges. They would have reflected badly on his commanders as well.[17]

The news about the withdrawal caused a great deal of confusion and worsened the already low morale among the Soviet troops, who had first been ordered to construct the launch sites and then to dismantle or even destroy them. "Why did they send us to Cuba? Why take this equipment here and back?" Private Stoianov, who left Cuba on the *Metallurg Anosov*, asked his fellow soldiers. When his comrade Cherny tried to calm him down, saying, "If we hadn't come here, perhaps none of us would be alive today, as there could have been a thermonuclear war," Stoianov was anything but convinced. Not only was morale sinking, but the ideological indoctrination was in jeopardy.

The officers and men were leaving their Cuban posts without the expected thanks from the locals. "The procedure of withdrawal from Cuba inflicted a deep wound on the souls of our warriors," recalled Rafael Zakirov, the commander of the group handling the tactical nuclear warheads. "It was done in secret, and the vehicles were loaded at night, without the usual leave-taking of the Cuban comrades: the ships departed from empty docks. We left Cuba just as if we had been guilty of something, although everyone had honorably and selflessly done his martial duty and carried out the Motherland's command." Those who had a chance to say goodbye to their Cuban friends and acquaintances were also leaving sick at heart. The officers departing on the *Divnogorsk* told the KGB officer that some of the Cuban peasants had tears in their eyes when they learned about the departure of the Soviets. Colonel Ivan Sidorov remembered that some of the Cubans were disheartened by his men's departure, saying, "Our friends are leaving, but our enemies remain."[18]

What awaited the military at the ports did not lift their spirits either. With the ships still on their way to Cuba, they had to wait for days if not weeks to board. Lieutenant Polkovnikov of the 181st Missile Regiment recalled the utter chaos that he encountered upon arrival at the port of Mariel. "We unloaded our gear on the grounds of the port, which was completely full of our missile equipment, including some elements of R-14 rockets, disassembled IL-28 bombers, and so on." They had to wait a whole week to board a ship: "We slept out in the open, took shelter from downpours as best we could, fed the mosquitoes, recalled the moments of greatest tension, and ate dry rations."

It turned out that their ship, the *Pobeda* (Victory), which had brought the future Soviet defense minister Dmitry Yazov to Cuba, was waiting for them in Havana. It was only there that the tired and filthy soldiers were given an appropriate send-off, though not by the Cubans but by their own commanders. The commander of Polkovnikov's regiment, Colonel Kovalenko, addressed his men: "We stood on the cutting edge of history and honorably carried out the task assigned us—to defend revolutionary Cuba." Polkovnikov noticed the absence of Cuban officials or representatives of the armed forces of Cuba.[19]

◊◊◊

GENERAL IGOR STATSENKO RECEIVED HIS ORDER TO BEGIN dismantling the missile sites that he had spent so much time and effort constructing on the afternoon of October 28. He began to implement the order next morning. Three days later, on October 31, he reported to the visiting UN Secretary General, U Thant, that the work was all but finished. Indeed, the dismantling of the missiles was completed by the end of that day.

On the following day, November 1, Statsenko received another order: load the missiles on the ships first; everything else, including the servicemen, could wait. The missiles, which were to be out of Cuba by November 10, began their trip back to the seashore, now in daytime and without the escort of the Cuban police. They left their bases much faster than they had arrived. By November 2 the first R-12 ballistic missiles were already in the Cuban ports, waiting to be loaded onto the decks and into the ships' holds. There were at least a dozen Soviet ships stranded in Cuba after the introduction of the American blockade, but few of them were capable of carrying the missiles. Still, eight ships were designated for the task.

Loading began on November 3 and lasted until the 8th. "The dispatch of the missiles took place under particularly complicated and difficult conditions. Circumstances were such that there were old-model ships in Cuba at the time, their decks encumbered with various superstructures; cranes that could handle heavy cargoes were generally lacking, and the ports where the loading took place were poorly supplied with cranes," reported Statsenko after his return to the Soviet Union. "The loading of the ships went on nonstop, day and night."[20]

In parallel, the servicemen were loading the warheads for the R-15 missiles on the *Aleksandrovsk*, which had brought warheads for R-14 medium-range missiles to Cuba, although the missiles themselves never reached the island because of the blockade. The *Aleksandrovsk* had managed to make it to Cuba a few hours before the imposition of the blockade and was docked for the duration, its nuclear cargo never unloaded—a perfect target for a possible American air strike.

On October 27, the most dangerous day of the crisis, Malinovsky ordered Pliev to send the *Aleksandrovsk* home with its nuclear payload as soon as possible. But the ship's departure was delayed because on the next day Malinovsky issued another order to Pliev: "We have made the decision to dismantle the R-12s and remove them. Begin to implement this measure." The departure of the *Aleksandrovsk* was postponed, and two days later, on October 30, Malinovsky issued yet another order: "Load warheads for R-12 on the *Aleksandrovsk* and send the transport accompanied by the ready ship to the Soviet Union."[21]

Now the *Aleksandrovsk* was supposed to take the warheads for both the R-12 and R-14 missiles back to the USSR. The most dangerous ship in the world was about to become even more dangerous. They loaded the nuclear warheads for R-12 Desna missiles into its hold on the night of November 4 at Isabela de Sagua. Next day the *Aleksandrovsk* sailed to Mariel, where it joined the dry cargo ship *Divnogorsk*, the first vessel to be loaded with missiles for return to the USSR. A brand-new ship built in Poland in 1960, the *Divnogorsk* had arrived in Mariel on October 23, beating the blockade by a few hours. Statsenko's men began loading the *Divnogorsk* on November 2, taking on board four R-12 missiles and 310 officers and men. Since it was the first ship ready for departure, it was chosen as an escort for the *Aleksandrovsk* with its nuclear cargo.[22]

The *Divnogorsk* and the *Aleksandrovsk* began their voyage home on November 6, with the former trailing the latter at a distance of three to five miles and maintaining radio contact. In case of emergency the two ships were supposed to communicate with each other by means of light signals. Major Protasov, the KGB officer assigned to the *Divnogorsk*, ordered his agents to keep the communications with the *Aleksandrovsk* under surveillance. They were also ordered to be on the lookout for possible spies and saboteurs. Their own people were under suspicion: one of the soldiers who had arrived in Cuba in October on the *Divnogorsk* had been overheard asking questions about transportation between Cuba and the United States—a clear sign in the eyes of Major Protasov that there was a defector in the making. No one knew what to expect of the new military contingent now on its way back from Cuba.[23]

The two ships traveled together until November 10, before reaching the thirtieth meridian, and then parted ways, the *Aleksandrovsk* heading for the Baltic Sea, while the *Divnogorsk*, whose home port was Odesa, made its way to the Black Sea. Major Protasov wrote in his report that American airplanes followed the two ships throughout their joint voyage. Overflights during the first day of sailing were especially intensive: the KGB officer referred to them as psychological attacks. "Making shaving flights, disregarding all rules, without signal lights, they circled the ships [even] in bad weather or fog," wrote Protasov. Some of the planes flew ten to fifteen meters above the surface of the water— Protasov believed that they were searching for Soviet submarines. On November 6, about 6:00 p.m., an American submarine surfaced a mile away from the *Divnogorsk* and followed it for some ten minutes.

Despite numerous overflights, no one asked the captains of either the *Divnogorsk* or the *Aleksandrovsk* to show their cargo until the evening of November 9. After 7:00 p.m., the American destroyer *Blandy* (DD 943) approached the *Aleksandrovsk* and demanded by megaphone that the tween decks be opened. The demand was ignored. After a forty-five-minute pursuit of the *Aleksandrovsk*, the *Blandy* approached the *Divnogorsk* and asked, first in English and then in Russian, that the crew show the cargo on the decks and open the tween decks. "According to the agreement of your government and ours, please open the missiles and holds," went the message. "We are going to make a film." Those on board the *Divnogorsk* noticed photographers and camera operators on the deck of the *Blandy*. Major Protasov insisted that the soldiers, who were half-naked because of the heat, be sent to the tween decks, and that only officers remain on the main deck. The military commanders were not happy with that demand but followed KGB orders.[24]

The captain of the *Divnogorsk*, Myroshnichenko, knew nothing about the intergovernmental agreements and refused to communicate with the American vessel. Instead he radioed the minister of the Soviet Merchant Fleet, Viktor Bakaev, and the head of the Black Sea–Azov steamship company, Oleksii Danchenko, for instructions. Radio-telegrams from Odesa and Moscow soon arrived, instructing the captain to reveal the missiles. He was to show the cargo on deck but not to open the tween decks or allow anyone to board the ship. The *Aleksandrovsk*'s cargo, referred to in a KGB report as "particularly important cargo," had to remain secret, as far as the Soviet leadership was concerned. The *Divnogorsk* fared differently. Almost immediately after receiving messages from his superiors in Moscow and Odesa, Captain Myroshnichenko got a radio message from the *Blandy*: you just received instructions, show us the missiles. The Americans had intercepted the *Divnogorsk*'s communication with the ministry.

Captain Myroshnichenko was finally ready to accommodate the American request, but his authority was insufficient—he needed the cooperation of the military commanders on board. The commanding officer of the echelon, Lieutenant Colonel Baranov, and the political officer, Major Guleshov, refused to follow the instructions, claiming that they were responsible to the minister of defense, not the minister of the merchant fleet. It was only after the captain, backed by the KGB officer, insisted that the military men gave up and agreed to remove the canvas from the missiles on deck. The *Blandy* approached the *Divnogorsk* on the right side and then asked that the missiles on the left side be shown as well. Despite the protests of the military men, the captain complied once again.[25]

◊◊◊

THE INSPECTION OF SOVIET SHIPS CARRYING MISSILES BACK to the Soviet Union was first suggested by the Soviet foreign minister, Andrei Gromyko, in his instructions of November 1 to his deputy, Vasilii Kuznetsov, who was about to join Anastas Mikoyan at dinner with the American ambassador to the UN, Adlai Stevenson, and John McCloy. Kuznetsov was instructed, if need be, to offer the Americans photographs of the launch sites once the missiles were removed. "We also," read the instruction, "would have no objections to your ships being shown, at close distance, the missiles loaded on the Soviet ships." Gromyko, undoubtedly acting on behalf of Khrushchev, was looking for a way to make the Kennedy-Khrushchev agreement work, given Castro's refusal to allow inspections on Cuban territory.[26]

The Americans were initially less than enthusiastic. McCloy said that "the Soviet Union and Cuba must agree between each other on what would be the form of inspection," throwing the problem back to the Soviets. But Stevenson was more flexible. "If we fail to carry out ground inspection, let us seek other means which would assure us that the armaments are withdrawn," he told the dinner party. "Otherwise, the danger of conflict will be reborn." Mikoyan did not miss that remark in his report on the dinner discussion. "The American side," he wrote, "would be ready not to insist on verification methods foreseen in the message to N. S. Khrushchev and was ready to look for some new methods that would in essence give the Americans a possibility to be certain of carrying out our commitment to withdraw weapons."[27]

On November 7, John McCloy and Adlai Stevenson informed Vasilii Kuznetsov that the United States was indeed prepared to accept the earlier Soviet offer to allow *de visu* inspection in neutral waters of ships carrying missiles back to the Soviet Union. The problem of inspection was now removed from the list of American-Soviet difficulties, becoming a problem for the Soviets alone. From that point on, Khrushchev owned it. The dry cargo ship *Metallurg Anosov*, which left Cuba on November 6 with eight missiles on board, was instructed by telegram that day to show the missiles on demand to ships under the United Nations flag but not to ones flying the American flag. On the following day, the order was changed: the missiles were to be shown to American helicopters. On the day after that, November 9, the captains of Soviet ships were instructed to remove canvas covers and show the Americans missiles on deck without opening the tween decks.[28]

The *Divnogorsk* under Captain Myroshnichenko was among the first Soviet ships to comply with that request. But the Soviets did their best to complicate and slow down the process by filing protests against American actions that allegedly exceeded official agreements. On November 9, the day on which the USS *Blandy* inspected the *Divnogorsk* and approached the *Aleksandrovsk*, the Soviets protested the actions of American ships forcing inspections of Soviet cargoes. The *Aleksandrovsk*, the *Divnogorsk*, and another ship, the *Volgoles*, were mentioned in the diplomatic note. The *Volgoles*, with seven missiles on board, was approached by the American destroyer *Saufley* (DD 465) on the morning of November 8: confirming that it had missiles on board, its captain refused to show them to the Americans, as current instructions allowed him to show missiles only to ships under the UN flag. He complied with the American demand on the following day, November 9, after receiving orders to show the missiles.

Vice Admiral Charles Wellborn, the chairman of the American delegation to the United Nations Military Staff Committee, responded to the Soviet protest by pointing out that under no circumstances were any threats made against Soviet ships or inspections forced on them. If the *Volgoles* had shown the missiles immediately, it would not have been approached again. Regarding the *Divnogorsk*, Wellborn suggested that the inspection took so long because of the language barrier. He found it more difficult to explain what had occurred with the *Aleksandrovsk*, as that ship was not listed by the Soviets as one transporting missiles and was thus supposed to be exempt from inspection. It was approached, however, wrote Wellborn, because the number of missiles provided by the other ships was not exact, and the American commanders decided to check the *Aleksandrovsk* as well.[29]

During the first ten days of November, General Statsenko managed to ship forty-two missiles, 1,056 pieces of equipment, and 3,289 officers and men back to the Soviet Union. The last ship to carry R-12 missiles left Cuba from the port of Casilda on November 9, the day the new inspection regulations went into effect. It was the Soviet-built dry cargo ship *Leninskii Komsomol,* on its second trip to Cuba, that took a load of eight R-12 missiles and 320 officers and men under the command of Lieutenant Colonel Feliks Khachaturov, the deputy commander of Ivan Sidorov's regiment, whose missiles had been the first to arrive in Cuba. The missiles on board the *Leninskii Komsomol* were inspected and photographed on the same day as the USS *Norfolk.*[30]

Igor Statsenko later reported that during the second stage of the evacuation of his division from Cuba, which lasted from November 18 to December 12, 3,716 men and 985 pieces of weaponry and equipment were loaded on twelve ships and sent back to the Soviet Union. Colonel Sidorov, whose R-12 ballistic missile regiment was the first to reach Cuba in August, was among the last rocket men to leave the island. "I left Cuba with the last naval echelon in mid-December 1962," he recalled. "Our echelon boarded the *Atkarsk* in the port of Cienfuegos, but the destination port was no longer Sevastopol but Baltiisk." If on the way to Cuba the soldiers had sweltered in the heat of the tween decks, they now froze in the cold of the approaches to the Baltic Sea. They were going back to Baltiisk and not Sevastopol for one simple reason: all nuclear warheads were shipped out and then returned to the Soviet Union through that port, and the *Atkarsk* was full of them.[31]

On the Soviet side, for the next few decades the story of the Soviet withdrawal from Cuba would be a secret history, full of silence, confusion, conflicting memories, and, last but not least, humiliation.

26

BACK AT THE BARRICADE

The congressional elections that John Kennedy was so concerned about in the weeks leading up to the Cuban showdown with Khrushchev took place on November 6. Kennedy had every reason to be pleased with their outcome. The elections strengthened the Democrats' hold on the Senate, where they gained four seats. In the House of Representatives they lost one seat despite increasing the margin of their popular vote by 5 percent but retained their majority. In the gubernatorial elections neither party gained an advantage, cementing the status quo. By all accounts, it was a victory: four years earlier, in November 1959, with a Republican president in office, the Republican Party had suffered major losses on all three fronts. Now a young and inexperienced president had managed to hold his ground and even marginally improve his party's position.[1]

On Election Day, Kennedy sent Khrushchev a letter with an explicit demand to remove "the missiles and bombers, with their supporting equipment, under adequate verification, and with a proper system for continued safeguards" as the "first necessary step away from the crisis."

He explained to Khrushchev that he had mentioned IL-28 bombers as part of the offensive weapons arsenal in his address to the nation on October 22, and thus they were covered by his exchange with Khrushchev, in which the president had referred to offensive weapons of all kinds. He assured Khrushchev that he would not extend the meaning of the term any further, and that it was only the bombers that bothered him. "There is really only one major item on the list, beyond the missiles and their equipment, and that is the light bombers with their equipment," wrote Kennedy to Khrushchev. "This item is indeed of great importance to us."[2]

Khrushchev must have felt trapped. With his ballistic missiles dismantled, the American promise to lift the blockade yet to be fulfilled, and their promise not to invade Cuba not formalized through the UN Security Council, he had nothing to show for his Cuban adventure but spoiled relations with both the United States and Cuba. The other American promise, to remove missiles from Turkey, besides remaining secret, now seemed more remote than ever.

Faced with Kennedy's insistence that the entire deal on Cuba hung on the removal of the IL-28 bombers, and confronted with the revolt of Castro and the Cubans, Khrushchev paused to consider the matter. For the time being at least, he wanted not only his bombers but also his tactical nuclear weapons—the nuclear-armed Luna missiles, about which the Americans knew nothing—to stay in place. On Khrushchev's orders Marshal Malinovsky instructed General Pliev in Cuba: "With regard to warheads for 'Luna,' FKR [cruise missiles] and IL-28 airplanes, so far their withdrawal has not been discussed. They should be left in Cuba under your command."[3]

◊◊◊

THE KEY DISCUSSION ON WHAT TO DO ABOUT KENNEDY'S NEW demands took place at the party Presidium meeting on Saturday, November 10. Khrushchev, who had been in retreat ever since Kennedy announced the discovery of the ballistic missiles in Cuba, decided to pull back even further to secure the deal he had reached on October 28. "We discussed these issues before the full quorum of our collective leadership and our military, and all those present arrived at the unanimous conclusion that it would be reasonable to act as follows—to agree to the removal of all IL-28s from Cuba," wrote Khrushchev to Mikoyan one day later. For him, the choice was clear: "to leave the bombers, and consequently to undermine the fulfillment of the obligations that were given on condition of the removal of the missiles . . . or to remove the IL-28s as we removed the missiles, but to have an agreement on non-invasion." Khrushchev chose the latter. Now the main question was how to present his new concession to the Cubans.[4]

On Sunday, November 11, Khrushchev dictated a long letter to Mikoyan that was more a stream-of-consciousness ramble than a diplomatic instruction. Khrushchev was now much more concerned about Soviet interests and prestige than those of Cuba and the pursuit of world revolution. "What do we lose and what do we gain as a result of the removal of the IL-28s from Cuba?" he asked his long-suffering Cuban envoy. "There are no particular losses. There will only be moral losses for Cuba." By now he was clearly distinguishing the interests of Moscow from those of Havana. "We can imagine how difficult it would be to impress such an understanding on our friends," wrote Khrushchev in a tone sympathetic to Mikoyan before turning around and putting additional pressure on him: "But therein lies the art of politicians—when encountering difficulties, to show the ability to overcome such difficulties."[5]

The list of "offensive weapons" passed by Adlai Stevenson to the Soviets before Mikoyan's departure from New York on November 2 was now catching up with Mikoyan. "Half an hour before my departure from New York, those pilferers (now we are speaking about Stevenson) sent a letter to Comrade Kuznetsov, saying that they supposedly had forgotten to raise questions about some kinds of weapons," Mikoyan told the Cuban leaders a few days later, recalling the shock he had felt on receiving the letter. He instructed the Soviet diplomats not to discuss the list—nothing but ballistic missiles had been mentioned in the correspondence between Kennedy and Khrushchev. It turned out, however, that the problem had not disappeared with Mikoyan's departure from New York but had simply been passed on to a higher level.[6]

Khrushchev gave up hope of persuading Castro to allow any inspection on Cuban territory and with the bombers he was going to reach an agreement with the Americans to have ships inspected in neutral waters. But he wanted Mikoyan to get Castro's approval for the removal of the bombers. Khrushchev was counting on Mikoyan to deliver a miracle in Havana. "Received, read, considered. I consider the indicated decision on the IL-28s perfectly correct," responded the always loyal Mikoyan. He knew that he had no choice but to say yes. The decision that he diplomatically called "indicated" had been already made. Mikoyan could influence the decision-making process while in Moscow, but in Cuba, with Khrushchev saying that all Presidium members were already on board, he was little more than a high-ranking messenger with a salesman's task entrusted to him.

Mikoyan delivered the bad news to Castro at a private meeting on November 12. His sales pitch was that the removal of the bombers would help to secure a deal with the Americans. Castro was probably stunned, or perhaps triumphant, as he had predicted that making concessions to the Americans was a slippery slope. In any case, he refused to buy Mikoyan's argument. "Whatever position the Soviet Union settles on, regardless of whether you remove the bombers or not, the USA will insist on inspection and, on the pretext that Cuba will find this unacceptable, the US will maintain its blockade," he told the Soviet envoy. The experienced Mikoyan did not insist on an immediate response. In fact, he encouraged Castro to think things through and talk to his comrades.[7]

The Cuban reply to Mikoyan, and through him to Khrushchev, was delivered on the following day, November 13, at a meeting with the Cuban leadership in Mikoyan's temporary home in Havana. Castro interrupted the small talk that Mikoyan seemed to be enjoying at the start of the meeting to deliver his and his government's position on the bombers. "We basically did not agree with the removal of strategic missiles, just as we disagree with the removal of IL-28 bombers from Cuba," began Castro. He then explained the reason for Cuban disapproval: "These measures create a difficult situation for us. They undermine our sovereign right to determine for ourselves what type of weapons we can have, and what agreements we can make."

Castro knew that he could not stop the Soviets from doing what they wanted to do. His new strategy was to extract as many concessions from the Americans as possible for the removal. "Our position is as follows," Castro told the Soviet envoy: "tie the removal of the naval blockade and the cessation of the violation of Cuban airspace to the withdrawal of IL-28 bombers." He then concluded with a threat: "Without these requirements, we cannot give our consent."[8]

Withdrawing the bombers in exchange for lifting the blockade had been the Soviet position from the start, but stopping overflights of Cuban territory was a tricky proposition. The Americans insisted on them as a substitute for on-ground inspections, which Castro opposed. Mikoyan protested the overflights at his meeting with Stevenson in New York on November 1. He knew that there was no way of convincing the Americans to stop the overflights in exchange for removal of the bombers. Meanwhile, Castro was adamant about stopping the overflights. "The Americans are insolent," he argued. "They make shaving flights over Cuban territory, flying at 100 meters over our military bases and units. This is bad for the morale of our people and makes them resentful. Our position led to the point that now our enemy knows everything."

When Mikoyan pushed for the need to lift the naval blockade, Castro asked him a direct question: "Will this position include the requirement to cease the violation of our airspace?" Mikoyan refused to link the overflights with the removal of the bombers. "We consider such flights to be illegal," he told Castro. "You are planning to send your protest to the UN. It will be a serious warning to the Americans." In short, the answer was no.[9]

Castro took offense. There were no conversations with Mikoyan on the following day, November 14, and no plans for meetings on November 15. A top-ranking member of the Soviet Presidium was sitting in

Havana in an atmosphere of growing tension between Washington, Moscow, and Havana with nothing to do and no one to meet. Mikoyan was alarmed and felt spurred to action. He asked Ambassador Alekseev to invite the Cuban leadership to dinner at the Soviet embassy on the evening of November 16. Probably to Mikoyan's surprise, Castro accepted and, even more surprisingly, was all congeniality. He embraced his Soviet friend, diminutive in comparison to him, in a bear hug. In fact, he had a surprise "present" for Mikoyan, arriving at the embassy immediately after visiting a Cuban antiaircraft battery in Havana, where he gave the order to resume shooting at low-flying American airplanes.

The actual order was signed on November 17, the day after Castro attended Mikoyan's dinner, and it instructed the antiaircraft units to open fire on intruders starting at 6:00 a.m. on November 18. It was the first such order since October 27, when the Soviets had downed the U-2. Castro also sent U Thant a long letter rejecting any form of inspection on Cuban territory and protesting American overflights.

On hearing what Castro had just done, Mikoyan protested: why had he not been informed? Castro was defiant if not stubborn: they had discussed a letter to U Thant previously, and he was not going to cancel his order, which had already been given. Mikoyan's attempt to convince Castro, Che Guevara, and other Cuban leaders present at the dinner that the Americans would never pledge not to invade Cuba if they were shot at proved futile. With Castro's order in place, the threat of military conflict over Cuba that everyone believed to have passed returned with new force.[10]

◊◊◊

ON NOVEMBER 12, ANATOLY DOBRYNIN HANDED ROBERT Kennedy a missive from the Kremlin. In a typically lengthy letter, Khrushchev proposed what amounted to a Turkish-type solution to the bomber problem, offering the president his word that the bombers would be removed in the future. "We will not insist on permanently keeping those planes in Cuba," wrote Khrushchev. "We have our difficulties in this question. Therefore, we give a gentleman's word that we will remove the IL-28 planes with all the personnel and equipment related to those planes, although not now but later."[11]

Robert Kennedy, to whom Dobrynin passed Khrushchev's message along with Khrushchev's oral congratulations to Kennedy on his successful midterm elections, was skeptical about the Soviet leader's proposal. He wanted the Soviets to announce publicly the date on which they would remove the bombers; once the announcement was made, the naval blockade of the island would be lifted. Dobrynin protested that such a solution was a nonstarter with Khrushchev, who wanted to avoid publicity. Robert understood that very well. He promised to talk to his brother, and in an hour and a half he was back at the embassy, where Dobrynin was hosting a reception honoring the Bolshoi Theater troupe then visiting Washington. Robert passed Dobrynin an oral message from Kennedy to Khrushchev: the United States would announce the lifting of the blockade if Khrushchev agreed to remove the bombers within thirty days. Robert Kennedy was now in a much better mood than during his previous visits to Dobrynin. After speaking with the ambassador, he joined the crowd at the reception for the Bolshoi troupe and even kissed the famous prima ballerina Maia Plisetskaia when he learned that they shared birthdays.[12]

Khrushchev called a Presidium meeting to discuss Kennedy's new proposal on November 14 and dictated a letter to Kennedy on the same day. "The question of the withdrawal of the IL-28s within the 30 days mentioned does not constitute any complicated question," began Khrushchev on a positive note, switching to a rather negative one almost on the fly: "Yet this period will probably not be sufficient." He asked for two or three months to complete the withdrawal. More importantly, he tried to bargain not only for the lifting of the blockade but also for a halt to American overflights of Cuba and a guarantee of noninvasion. "If we attain all that now and if this were announced, then more favorable conditions would be created for our country to solve the question of timetable for the withdrawal of IL-28 planes," wrote Khrushchev, doing Castro's bidding more than his own.

Once again Dobrynin met with Robert Kennedy to pass on Khrushchev's letter. Kennedy did not hide his displeasure with the response. "The President," he told Dobrynin, "will be disappointed by the answer when he receives it." John Kennedy was disappointed indeed. "The IL-28's are still in Cuba and are of deep concern to the people of our entire Hemisphere," wrote Kennedy in response. "Thus, three major parts of the undertakings on your side—the removal of the IL-28's, the arrangements for verification, and safeguards against introduction— have not yet been carried out." He concluded the letter in a constructive tone, promising negotiations on the noninvasion pledge once the immediate problem was resolved: "[T]he first step is to get the bombers started out, and the quarantine lifted—for both are sources of tension. Meanwhile discussion can continue on other aspects of the problem." The letter was handed to Dobrynin the same day along with a warning that "this matter was reaching a turning point and that if progress cannot be made, we may soon find ourselves back in a position of increasing tension."[13]

Once again it was Kennedy, not Khrushchev, who was demanding and threatening. The two leaders had long switched roles. If earlier the agenda and pace of events had been set mainly by Khrushchev, even when he was in retreat, now it was Kennedy who was in charge and running the show. Kennedy and his advisers were in a winner-take-all mood, no longer expecting Khrushchev to start a nuclear war over Cuba and pushing for new concessions. If on October 20 Kennedy had told his advisers that they would have to learn to live with Soviet bombers in Cuba, there was now a conviction that such tolerance would be unnecessary.

With pressure from Kennedy growing and Khrushchev's readiness to use nuclear weapons diminishing by the day, Khrushchev had to choose between Castro and his youthful dream of world revolution on the one hand and the interests of his country, which did not want war with the United States, on the other. When he issued his letter of October 28 accepting Kennedy's deal, he thought that he could reconcile the two visions. But now Khrushchev the revolutionary had to confront Khrushchev the national leader and choose one course or the other.

◊◊◊

CASTRO'S THREAT TO RESUME SHOOTING AT AMERICAN PLANES over Cuba, first made in his letter of November 15 to U Thant, had brought the situation back to the brink of war. Almost immediately after learning of the letter, Adlai Stevenson protested to Vasilii Kuznetsov, the top Soviet diplomat at the UN, warning him that "this would be a very serious matter with predictable consequences." He told his Soviet counterpart that "aerial surveillance was the only means we had to assure ourselves in light of the Soviet failure [to] produce verification in Cuba." Kuznetsov did his best to distance himself and his country from Castro's actions, saying that "he had nothing to add to the previous Soviet position on overflights."[14]

On the next day, November 16, Khrushchev called another meeting of the Presidium to discuss the escalating situation in and around Cuba. Officially on the agenda was the Soviet response to Kennedy's latest demand to remove the bombers in exchange for lifting the blockade, but the focus of the discussion was on Castro, not Kennedy. Khrushchev and then Gromyko, as the main spokesman on international relations, were first to speak, followed by Leonid Brezhnev, Aleksei Kosygin, and Frol Kozlov—people responsible in the party and government for domestic matters and the economy. Then came the turn of the two ideologues, Mikhail Suslov and Boris Ponomarev. All three groups of state and party officials were in agreement: Castro's position was "unreasonable and screechy."

"Let this be a lesson to us," wrote the notetaker, recording words probably spoken by Khrushchev. "We are coming to the crunch point: either they will cooperate, or we will let our people go." The notion of a

Soviet withdrawal from Cuba, regarded a few days earlier as a manifestation of Castro's immaturity, emotionality, and eccentricity, was now being entertained by the Soviet leadership as a legitimate option if Castro refused to go along with their policy. They no longer saw any room for maneuver. Discussing Mikoyan's request to allow him to meet once again with Castro, the Presidium decided to inform him that whatever the talks he engaged in, the decision on removing the bombers had not only been made but already delivered to the Americans.[15]

Khrushchev personally dictated the instructions to Mikoyan. He stated that the Cuban ultimatum to stop American overflights and start shooting at their planes could lead to war: "To act in such a manner now would lead to a military conflict, and it could develop if one would follow such a course, it could not be justified by anything and would have no grounds." Khrushchev instructed Mikoyan to present the Cubans with an ultimatum of a different sort. "If the Cuban comrades do not want to cooperate with us on this issue and do not want to undertake measures which would help us resolve this issue and avoid being pulled into a war together with us, then apparently the conclusion that we see is that our presence in Cuba is not helpful for our friends now," dictated Khrushchev. "Then let them state that openly, and we will have to make conclusions for ourselves."

The message was clear. If Castro did not reverse his order and his soldiers actually began shooting at American airplanes, then not only would the Soviets not follow in his footsteps, as had happened inadvertently on October 28, but Khrushchev would withdraw his troops from the island, leaving Castro and his comrades to face Kennedy alone. A guarantee that there would be no American invasion remained Khrushchev's main goal in resolving the Cuban crisis, and he made one last attempt to convince Castro to fall into line. Mikoyan was instructed to remind Castro of three possible scenarios for inspection: through the UN, Latin American ambassadors, or representatives of ten neutral countries. Castro had earlier rejected all those options, but after the Presidium meeting ended, one of the participants convinced Khrushchev to reintroduce them. It was a long, long shot. Khrushchev advised Mikoyan to leave if he thought there was no hope of agreement but to stay if there was any possibility of progress.[16]

Khrushchev paused in his correspondence with Kennedy. He was playing for time, hoping that Mikoyan would convince Castro not only to agree to the withdrawal of the bombers in exchange for the lifting of the blockade but also to accept some form of UN inspection that would clear the way for an American pledge not to invade Cuba. Reports from Cuba suggested that there was still time to negotiate. Mikoyan informed him on November 18 that Castro's decision to open fire had been emotional, and that he had admitted to Mikoyan that all he wanted was to stop the low-level flights: he had resigned himself to the high-level ones. Since the Americans had put a stop to low-level flights as of November 16, Mikoyan saw no imminent danger of conflict and war.[17]

In Havana, Sunday, November 18, the day on which the Cubans were to start shooting at American airplanes, passed without antiaircraft fire: there were no more low-level flights, and Castro could do nothing about the continuing U-2 overflights. In his letter of November 15 to U Thant, he had written that the Cubans would destroy airplanes violating their airspace "to the extent of the firepower of our antiaircraft weapons." The limit appeared to have been reached very quickly. On November 17, Malinovsky reported to the Central Committee that he had prohibited Pliev from "opening fire on American airplanes violating Cuban airspace with Soviet weapons, even if there should be an order from Fidel Castro to that effect." A day after that, Gromyko instructed Mikoyan on how to answer Cuban queries about the Soviet refusal to fire at the Americans. He was to state the following: "In view of the fact that the decision on firing at American planes was not submitted for our approval, we do not consider it possible to take part in this. For this reason, we have given instructions to our military men not to open fire on American planes."[18]

When Castro and his aides met with Mikoyan on the afternoon of November 19, the Cuban leader was as angry about the American overflights as ever. "The U-2 flights are continuing," he told Mikoyan.

"They rove wherever they want." But he was no longer trying to obtain an end to overflights for the withdrawal of the bombers. He saw the writing on the wall. Speaking on his own behalf and not, as he pointed out, on behalf of the entire leadership, Castro told Mikoyan: "If we manage to obtain the lifting of the blockade at the price of withdrawing the IL-28s, that will be an important step." After a break of at least two hours for consultations with colleagues, sometime after 9:00 p.m. Castro returned to Mikoyan's residence to deliver the verdict of the entire Cuban leadership: they would consent to the withdrawal of the bombers under the terms of an agreement to be formalized in a letter to U Thant, which they discussed with Mikoyan late that night. Its key sentence read: "If the Soviet Government considers it desirable for the smooth conduct of the negotiations and the solution of the crisis to withdraw these planes, the Revolutionary Government of Cuba will not object to this decision."[19]

By the evening of November 19, Castro realized that he had lost the battle for the bombers. Over his protests, Khrushchev had decided to make a deal with the Americans. Castro was also losing the propaganda war: Latin American leaders and the world media were pointing to Cuba as the main obstacle to reaching an agreement between the two superpowers that would prevent a nuclear war. And there was one more reason for his growing concern: Kennedy's imminent press conference that was announced in the US media. He was concerned that Kennedy would attack and humiliate Cuba—"make a dirty rag out of us"—demoralizing the Cubans and probably driving them to abandon their leader. Castro played with the idea of making a speech of his own to counter Kennedy's. Mikoyan tried to prevent him from making any statements running counter to the Soviet position and wrote to Moscow asking that Dobrynin be instructed to warn Robert Kennedy and, through him, the president not to attack Castro, as that would complicate the conclusion of the agreement between Kennedy and Khrushchev.[20]

Castro was afraid of what Kennedy might say in his speech and yet had high hopes for it. Fearing a humiliating attack on Cuba, he hoped for such an attack on the Soviet Union. "I consider that you have already made the decision to withdraw the IL-28s," said Castro to Mikoyan, "but if Kennedy makes a threatening and arrogant announcement, he will thereby place the Soviet Union in an unpleasant and difficult position." He assured Mikoyan that the Cubans were prepared to withstand the blockade: "We should not fear the blockade. It will not break the revolution." Mikoyan remained impervious to Castro's revolutionary rhetoric. "I did not find it necessary, feeling Fidel's weariness, to explain the erroneousness of his judgments in that conversation," reported Mikoyan to Moscow. He decided to drop the issue, leaving Castro at least a glimmer of hope that if not Khrushchev through his actions, then Kennedy through his words might help him keep his bombers.[21]

Mikoyan's report was typed for distribution to the Presidium members on November 29 at 11:40 a.m. Moscow time. By that time Khrushchev had already made up his mind.

27

THANKSGIVING

While Khrushchev played for time, Kennedy and many of his advisers believed that they were running out of it. The White House announced a long-awaited presidential press conference for November 20, the first in more than two months consumed by the Cuban crisis. Everyone was expecting a presidential statement on what was coming next: had the crisis been resolved, or was a new and even more dangerous threat emerging on the horizon? Kennedy was eager to declare the crisis resolved, but he could do so only if there was a deal on the bombers, and Khrushchev had yet to give his consent for their removal within thirty days.

Some members of the administration considered the deal offered to Khrushchev an unwarranted concession on Kennedy's part. The CIA and the military were not satisfied with the president's proposal to the Soviet leader, whether Khrushchev agreed to the thirty-day withdrawal deadline or not. At the ExCom meeting on November 16, the CIA director, John McCone, expressed concern about the continuing presence of the Soviet military in Cuba. "He considered this a more important consideration than the IL-28 bombers," reads the summary of the meeting. McCone was particularly uneasy about SAM missiles that could shoot down U-2 planes and thereby allow the reintroduction of nuclear missiles to Cuba.

The Joint Chiefs of Staff, with whom Kennedy met that day, were of the same opinion, concerned not only about the remaining SAMs but also about Soviet MiG fighters. They reiterated their standard solution to the problem: invasion. The chiefs informed the president that the armed forces were "in an optimum posture to execute" the invasion. They added, knowing Kennedy's deep-seated concern about Berlin, "We are not only ready to take any action you may order in Cuba, we are also in an excellent condition world-wide to counter any Soviet military response to such action."[1]

The next ExCom meeting, on November 19, one day prior to the announced presidential press conference, showed that the ranks of the optimists regarding a possible deal with the Soviets were shrinking dramatically. Khrushchev remained silent on the thirty-day deadline. The note-taker recorded Dean Rusk as saying, "We have received no word yet from Khrushchev." Rusk reported on the continuing negotiations with Vasilii Kuznetsov in New York, but Kuznetsov was indicating no change in the Kremlin's usual position. Time, however, was becoming an ever more urgent issue not only because of the forthcoming press conference but also because the suspension of American overflights, now dangerous in view of Castro's threats, had left the Americans in the dark with regard to the latest developments in Cuba.

Kennedy authorized high-level U-2 missions over the island but ordered a delay in the resumption of low-level missions. "President reluctant to send in low level flights," scribbled Robert Kennedy on a sheet of White House letterhead. "Major prob[lem] what all this does in USSR-China conflict. How far can we push K[hrushchev]." Still, JFK could not postpone low-level flights indefinitely. He asked his military to get ready to resume such flights on Wednesday, November 24. With no positive response from Khrushchev and Castro's standing order to shoot at low-level reconnaissance planes, losses of the planes and pilots were to be expected. Kennedy wanted to look into "military actions to be taken in retaliation for a shootdown." The chairman of the Joint Chiefs, General Taylor, pointed out that "existing plans call for an armed air reconnaissance and then an attack on the offending anti-aircraft site." "We are heading down the road to a choice," remarked Kennedy. "Either the IL-28s will come out and we will continue to fly high-level missions, or if the Russians refuse to withdraw the bombers, we are heading for a new showdown on Thursday or Friday."

Undersecretary of Defense Paul Nitze was all for an attack. He believed that, given the problems that the Soviets were having with the Cubans, they wanted the Americans to attack Cuban antiaircraft batteries anyway. Undersecretary of State George Ball opted for a tighter blockade of the island. He shared his impressions from attending a meeting of the NATO Council in Paris, where, according to him, there had been a "unanimous reaction that we had let the Russians off too easily and had not demanded the elimination of the Soviet base in Cuba." He added: "Our European allies would support us in finishing the job and . . . there would be no objection to putting pressure on the Russians again via a blockade."

But Kennedy was skeptical. He doubted that a tighter blockade was "the right response to the shooting down of a plane or the refusal to pull out the IL-28 bombers." "How can Khrushchev submit a second time?" asked the president. Paul Nitze expected the threat of force to deliver the desired result, arguing that "under Communist doctrine a Communist state can back down in the face of the superior position of an enemy." Bundy seemed to be in agreement with Nitze, indicating the need to distinguish between Soviet and Cuban targets. "We would not be acting against the Soviets by hitting Cuba," remarked the national security adviser, clearly favoring an attack.

They were back to square one, as if the fateful exchange of October 27–28 between Kennedy and Khrushchev had never taken place. As in the first days of the crisis, the president was more with the hawks than with the doves. "He asked that a statement be prepared for his use on the assumption that we have no Russian response to our IL-28 bomber withdrawal demand," reads the summary of the conversation. "We should emphasize Castro's rejection of ground inspection, thus requiring the continuance of air surveillance. We should seek to get the OAS to re-enforce our right to continue air surveillance."[2]

As in the past, John Kennedy was relying on his younger brother to maintain a line of communication to Khrushchev. The one that had worked previously, via Dobrynin, was no longer effective: nothing was coming through, despite Robert's reminder to Dobrynin on the evening of November 18 that the president was waiting for a reply. On November 18 Robert went to see his other Soviet contact, the military intelligence officer Georgii Bolshakov. The message was short and clear: Kennedy needed a response from Khrushchev before the start of his press conference at 6:00 p.m. EST on November 20. If the bombers were not removed, low-level reconnaissance flights would resume. As in the past, Robert Kennedy was not bluffing.[3]

◊◊◊

In Moscow, Khrushchev decided that he could not wait any longer for Mikoyan to produce a Cuban miracle. Not knowing yet that Castro had already caved on the issue of the bombers, he sent Kennedy a letter accepting his conditions. It was delivered by Dobrynin to Robert Kennedy a few hours before the president went to his press conference.

The two key sentences in the letter—long and rambling, as usual— read: "We expressed our readiness to remove also the IL-28 planes from Cuba. I inform you that we intend to remove them within a month term and maybe even sooner since the term for the removal of these planes is not a matter of principle for us." Khrushchev no longer insisted on an end to overflights or a guarantee that there would be no invasion of Cuba, saving those issues for future negotiations. On the lifting of the blockade, he wrote: "Permit me to express the hope that with receipt of this communication of mine you will issue instructions to the effect that the quarantine be lifted immediately with the withdrawal of your naval and other military units from the Caribbean area."[4]

Unbeknownst to the Americans, Khrushchev's letter to Kennedy included two paragraphs that he had never written or dictated. They were apparently added by Dobrynin on instructions from Moscow or by someone in Moscow after the letter had already been written and cabled to the embassy. The key sentence of the addendum read: "N. S. Khrushchev believes that it would be good if the President in his statements at the news conference did not introduce elements of aggravation and did not make any statements hurting the national feelings of the Cubans."

The impetus to add these points came from Mikoyan, who had finally convinced Castro to bow to the inevitable withdrawal of the bombers but missed the boat by a few hours. He managed to secure the agreement late in the evening of November 19, which was early morning in Moscow. By the time his reports were printed for distribution to the members of the Presidium, Khrushchev's letter had already gone to the Soviet embassy in Washington. All they could do was amend the letter to take into account Castro's concerns about Kennedy's forthcoming statement.[5]

Unbeknownst to Kennedy and his advisers, there was at least one false statement in Khrushchev's letter to Kennedy. It read: "All the nuclear weapons have been taken away from Cuba." That statement was correct as it pertained to the ballistic missiles, but the nuclear bombs for IL-28s and the tactical nuclear weapons remained in Cuba. Americans knew nothing about them, but Khrushchev apparently decided not to play any more with nuclear fire. He was determined to remove the tactical nukes as well. On November 20, the same day he sent his letter to Kennedy, Marshal Malinovsky issued an order to General Pliev in Cuba: "Missiles with conventional loads for 'Luna' and FKR [cruise missiles] should be left in Cuba. Send 6 nuclear bombs, 12 warheads for 'Luna' and 80 warheads for FKR to the Soviet Union on steamship "Atkarsk.""[6]

Khrushchev was cleaning up his act; everything seemed to be

under control. But once again Castro spoiled the game. On November 22, an alarmed Mikoyan informed Khrushchev that the Cubans had sent word to their United Nations representative, Carlos Lechuga, that they were in possession of the tactical nuclear weapons. They let the Soviet ambassador, Alekseev, know of their instructions challenging the Soviet resolve to remove all nuclear weapons from the island. Mikoyan urged Khrushchev to prevent this Cuban maneuver, proposing that he deceitfully invoke a nonexistent Soviet law prohibiting the transfer of nuclear weapons to other countries.

Khrushchev was fully on board. He wanted the Cubans to withdraw their instructions. "It could seriously complicate matters if the Americans obtained information that does not correspond to reality," read his letter to Mikoyan. Khrushchev was facing another not just embarrassing but extremely dangerous moment of being caught lying to the US president. The whole deal with Kennedy depended on mutual trust, and could collapse if that trust was broken. The information about the tactical nukes still on Cuban soil could topple the deal and launch the word into a new, even deeper crisis.[7]

On the same day, Mikoyan met with Castro to discuss further action in light of Kennedy's statement. Castro was unhappy, and once again he did not hide his feelings from the senior Soviet official. "You feel bad that the blockade was lifted?" asked Mikoyan. Castro shot back: "No, that the blockade is lifted is not bad. It was bad that we lost the IL-28 planes." He then sought assurance that the Soviet Union had made no promises to the United States to remove its tactical nuclear weapons. Mikoyan denied any such promises, saying that the Americans did not know about the existence of such weapons on the island, or that they were under General Pliev's command. When Castro asked about the transfer of tactical nuclear weapons to other countries, Mikoyan cited the nonexistent law prohibiting such transfers. Mikoyan then declined Castro's proposal to leave the nuclear weapons under Soviet command, the reason being the absence of a Soviet base in Cuba—a matter symbolically important to Castro, given his efforts to eliminate the American base at Guantánamo.[8]

The discussion moved on to other subjects, with Castro remaining as unhappy as he had been at the start of the meeting. But Mikoyan managed to do what he had believed to be right from the very beginning of the crisis—keep nuclear weapons not only out of Castro's hands but out of Cuba altogether. This time he had Khrushchev's full backing. The Soviet leader had finally decided to put his country's interests above those of the communist utopia of world revolution.

◊◊◊

As planned, at 6:00 p.m. on November 20 Kennedy appeared in front of the State Department auditorium, packed to capacity, and read a statement that began with the information on Khrushchev's agreement to remove the IL-28 bombers within a thirty-day period.

"I have this afternoon instructed the Secretary of Defense to lift our naval quarantine," declared Kennedy. "The evidence to date indicates that all known offensive missile sites in Cuba have been dismantled," continued Kennedy. "The missiles and their associated equipment have been loaded on Soviet ships. And our inspection at sea of these departing ships has confirmed that the number of missiles reported by the Soviet Union as having been brought into Cuba, which closely corresponded to our information, has now been removed. In addition, the Soviet Government has stated that all nuclear weapons have been withdrawn from Cuba and no offensive weapons will be reintroduced."

Kennedy decided to drop a statement from an earlier draft withholding any formal guarantee of noninvasion of Cuba until an international inspection regime was established on the island. The president was speaking only two days before Thanksgiving, and he had good reason to end his statement on a high note. "In this week of Thanksgiving there is much for which we can be grateful as we look back to where we stood only four weeks ago." The crisis seemed to be over. Kennedy persevered. Khrushchev was in retreat.[9]

In Moscow, Nikita Khrushchev was doing his best to present what had happened in and around Cuba as his victory and that of the Soviet Union. "As a result of correspondence we wrung a statement out of the president of the USA that he also had no thought of invading," Khrushchev told the plenary session of the Central Committee, the party's supreme decision-making body, on November 23. "Then we found it possible to make a statement that in that case we also considered it possible to remove our missiles and IL-28s. Was that a concession? It was. We conceded. Was there a concession on America's part? Did they publicly give their word not to invade? They did. Then who conceded, and who did not concede?"[10]

Khrushchev was speaking to a friendly audience. His statement, "Our men fired two shots and brought down a U-2—those are our expenses, nothing more. Not bad," was met with lengthy applause, which continued after he added: "God grant that we concede in the future with such results." But he also found it necessary to counter the critique of his main opponents in the communist camp—the Chinese. His words, though never published in the Soviet press, were addressed not only to a domestic but also to an international audience. He was clearly on the defensive as he countered Chinese arguments: "Some wiseacres say that you can't believe the imperialists. What a discovery! So what do you do, kill him? Kill him! Those wiseacres, who teach others so well, have caught the scent of capitalist crap in their own home and tolerate Mac[ao] on their territory. . . . The Portuguese crap; they've built themselves outhouses and spend their nights in Hong Kong. And so it goes!"[11]

The party secretaries and industry managers who made up most of the audience met Khrushchev's bravado and crude jokes with laughter and applause. He was indeed an effective and entertaining speaker, but whatever they thought of his policies as distinct from his presentation of them, they were in no position to oppose the leader or express any doubts about his actions. Any manifestation or even suspicion of disloyalty to the leader would have cost them their lives under Stalin and their careers under Khrushchev. Even so, there was growing resentment of the recklessness with which he had brought his country and the world to the verge of nuclear war, as well as of the humiliation to which he had subjected the military.

When the same members of the Central Committee voted to remove Khrushchev from power two years later, in October 1964, they applauded with equal enthusiasm as Presidium members unleashed a devastating critique of their leader for his arrogance, adventurism, and mistakes committed at home and abroad. Among the foreign policy failures, Cuba received special attention from the deputy prime minister chosen to present the accumulated grievances of Khrushchev's underlings in the Presidium against their boss.

Deputy Premier Dmitrii Poliansky, who had kept silent during long sessions on Cuba and never previously dared to criticize Khrushchev, expressed his and his colleagues' frustration with Khrushchev's nuclear brinkmanship: "In one of his speeches Comrade Khrushchev stated that if the USA touched Cuba, we would strike against them. He insisted that our missiles be sent to Cuba. That produced a tremendous crisis, bringing the world to the verge of nuclear war, and terribly frightening the organizer of so dangerous a venture himself. Having no other recourse, we were forced to accept all the demands and conditions dictated by the USA, including the shameful inspection of our ships by the Americans. At the demand of the USA, the missiles, as well as most of the armed forces, were withdrawn from Cuba. . . . But, as you know, Comrade Khrushchev also represents the defeat in the Caribbean crisis as a victory."[12]

Poliansky went on to argue that the Cuban venture had diminished the standing and international reputation of the party, the Soviet state, and the armed forces, as well as Soviet-Cuban relations. But if the international prestige of the party and state and the worsening of Cuban-Soviet relations were things that only people at the very top of the Soviet hierarchy knew and cared about, the humiliation of the military was an experience shared by thousands of Soviet officers and soldiers on their way back across the Atlantic to their home bases.

Soviet ships leaving Cuba with missiles, equipment, and servicemen were chased by American airplanes and had to open their holds to show the missiles that they had so carefully hidden on the way to Cuba. It was the retreat of a defeated army that many believed to have been betrayed by its leader.

"Neither the Russian nor the Soviet army had ever suffered such humiliation as to allow the adversary to inspect weapons transports," said Khrushchev's right-hand man at the time of the crisis, Marshal Rodion Malinovsky, addressing his general staff in October 1964 on the occasion of Khrushchev's ouster. Anastas Mikoyan considered Malinovsky his nemesis, a hawk who had helped Khrushchev launch the Cuban debacle. But in addressing his top commanders, Malinovsky knew that he was expressing the feelings of many if not most of them.[13]

Nikita Khrushchev had achieved his goal: he saved Cuba from a probable American invasion, kept it communist, and prevented it from defecting to the Chinese camp. He did not get to keep his rockets in Cuba to make up for American superiority in long-range missiles, but he got Kennedy to remove his own medium-range missiles from Turkey. Except in his own statements and pronouncements, Khrushchev never got credit for what he had achieved. The price that everyone—Americans, Cubans, and Soviets—paid for his adventurism turned out to be too high to justify his alleged successes.

EPILOGUE

John Kennedy and Nikita Khrushchev managed to avoid nuclear war after making almost every mistake conceivable and every step imaginable to cause it. But they did not step into the traps so masterfully created by themselves because they did not believe they could win a nuclear war, nor were they prepared to pay a price for such a victory. It is hard to imagine what the outcome of the Cuban crisis might have been if the two leaders had a more cavalier attitude toward the nuclear arms.

Both men departed the political scene soon after the events described in this book. A year after the official end of the Cuban missile crisis, Kennedy was dead, assassinated on a trip to Dallas, not to any foreign land, on November 22, 1963. Khrushchev, who called his tragic death "a heavy blow to all people who hold dear the cause of peace and Soviet-American cooperation," was removed from power not by foreign troops, but by his formerly sycophantic underlings on October 14, 1964, two years to the day after the American U-2 discovered the Soviet missiles in Cuba.[1]

Whether winners or losers in the eyes of the world, the two leaders left an enduring common legacy not limited to the terror and hard lessons of the Cuban missile crisis. With the signing in August 1963 of the partial nuclear test-ban treaty, Kennedy and Khrushchev saved the world a second time by drastically limiting radioactive fallout, which threatened life on this planet as we know it. If humanity is lucky enough to survive the new nuclear age and live for another thirty to forty million years, geologists of the future studying ice cores, corals, and rocks will still be able to pinpoint the time when the Kennedy-Khrushchev treaty was signed.

That is what the research done by earth scientists has suggested. Deposits of carbon-14, plutonium-239, and iodine-129 (their half-life is close to 6,000, 24,000, and 16 million years, respectively) will point in the same direction: a series of nuclear explosions shook the planet in the 1950s and 1960s. Isotope deposits were so high during that period that present-day geologists regard them as a "golden spike"—a geological marker created by an event of global proportions that indicates the start of a new age in the earth's history. The "golden spike" period began in the early 1950s, most notably 1954, the year of the Castle Bravo test of an American hydrogen bomb in the Marshall Islands, which went out of control and yielded a destructive force of 15 megatons of TNT, 2.5 times that predicted by its creators. It was one thousand times more powerful than either the Nagasaki or the Hiroshima bomb. In 1961, the Soviets exploded the 58-megaton Tsar Bomba in the Novaia Zemlia archipelago of the Arctic Ocean. The yield exceeded the projected one by "only" 8 megatons.[2]

The 1963 treaty opened the door to subsequent negotiations to control and then reduce nuclear arsenals. In slightly more than twenty years, between May 1972 and January 1993, the American presidents Richard Nixon, Jimmy Carter, Ronald Reagan, and George H. W. Bush, and their Soviet and Russian counterparts, Leonid Brezhnev, Mikhail Gorbachev, and Boris Yeltsin, signed a number of agreements that not only limited but actually reduced missile capabilities and nuclear arsenals by a whopping 80 percent. Unfortunately, the era of nuclear arms control launched so dramatically by the Cuban missile crisis is coming to an end as we witness the unraveling of the old treaties that kept the world safe. A particularly troubling development is the American and Russian withdrawal in 2019 from the Intermediate-Range Nuclear Forces Treaty, negotiated at the end of the Cold War by Presidents Reagan and Gorbachev back in 1987. Both parties announced their final withdrawal from the treaty on August 2, 2019.[3]

With the United States and Russia abandoning the treaty, we are entering a new stage of nuclear rearmament in which old missiles and nuclear bombs are being replaced with new, more precise, and smaller ones. This suggests that tactical nuclear weapons may be used on the battlefield, plunging the world back into the 1960s, when such use was a key part of military doctrine on both sides of the Cold War divide. For all the dramatic changes that have occurred in the world since the fall of the Berlin Wall, the end of the Cold War, and the disintegration of the USSR, we still have two nuclear superpowers, the United States and Russia, which inherited the entire nuclear arsenal of the Soviet Union. Their relations have been growing more tense with every passing year.

There are many parallels between Moscow-Washington relations today and at the height of the Cold War. After the loss of the Soviet Union, its territories and international prestige, Russia is now a revisionist power, as it was in the 1950s and early 1960s, when it tried to change the world balance of power in the era of decolonization. Nor has ideology completely disappeared from the current stage of nuclear brinkmanship. The United States is still interested in the defense if not the advance of democracy. Russia is no longer communist, but it has replaced its communist expansionism with the self-proclaimed mission of defending conservative values and supporting authoritarian regimes. Cultural differences also persist between the nuclear powers, creating unlimited opportunities for misreading each other's intentions.[4]

But we also face a situation in which not only have old threats returned but new ones have appeared to make the situation even more unstable and dangerous. The unprecedented proliferation of nuclear weapons and missile technologies has dramatically increased the number of states that can launch a nuclear strike. Even extremely poor but determined regimes, such as the one that rules North Korea, can threaten a superpower with a nuclear war. Two rivals, India and Pakistan, both have nuclear capabilities, and Iran's acquisition of nuclear technology causes grave concern not only in the undeclared nuclear state of Israel but also in the non-nuclear regional hegemon Saudi Arabia. Cyberwarfare also makes the current situation more dangerous than that of the early 1960s, as it allows one power to seize control of another's nuclear arsenal without firing a shot.[5]

What remains largely the same is that control over nuclear weapons is still in the hands of a very few individuals, and the rest of the world depends on their leadership and political skills, the soundness of their judgment, and the strength of their nerves. What saved the world during the Cuban crisis was that both leaders considered a nuclear war unwinnable. This is now changing with the scrapping of the old arms-control treaties, the renewal of the nuclear arms race, and the development of new technology making possible the execution of extremely accurate nuclear strikes. These factors have lowered the psychological barrier for using nuclear arms, making nuclear confrontation more likely.

What can be done? Hoping that populist and nationalist politicians will stop being irresponsible in their statements and actions, that revisionist autocrats will mutate into defenders of the status quo, that leaders of all political stripes will start following the advice of their experts, or that those experts will free themselves completely of their political and cultural biases is a hopeless proposition. We cannot count on that in a world where the number of nuclear "drivers" on the unregulated highways of international politics is growing with frightening persistence. So is the fear of being attacked and wiped out by a nuclear strike. Such fear may prompt a first strike, with incalculable consequences. The old strategy of mutually assured destruction works only if fear of nuclear war prevails, but such fear has waned with the withdrawal from the Anti-Ballistic Missile Treaty, nuclear testing, the end of the Cold War, and the growing conviction that tactical nuclear weapons may be used without provoking a wider war.

Today we are back to a period resembling the one that preceded the Cuban missile crisis, when there is no generally recognized "balance of terror," to use Churchill's phrase of the 1950s, and various countries are competing in a race to improve and extend their nuclear arsenals. This is one of the most dangerous moments in the history of nuclear arms. Back in the Reagan era, another highly unstable period in the nuclear-arms saga, the United States outspent the Soviets. The U.S. can outspend the Russians once again, but what about the Chinese? Can Washington do so without borrowing from Beijing? This is a rhetorical question.

To avoid a nuclear war, we must free ourselves from the belief that nuclear weapons belong to the past, are no longer relevant, and will fade into nonexistence almost on their own—a post–Cold War view dominant until recently in academic and political circles. We should return to the negotiating table and renew the arms-control process that began in the wake of the Cuban missile crisis. We can't wait for another crisis of such proportions to bring leaders back to their senses, as the next crisis may prove much worse than the previous one.

At the height of the Cold War, public debate put arms control on the political agenda: governments alone would not have done so. Thus, as citizens, we must reeducate ourselves about the history of nuclear weapons and the dangers they present so that a new arms-control regime can be negotiated. Elected politicians eventually listen to their electorates. As participants in democratic politics, we must relearn the forgotten lessons of the past in order to make politicians act upon them. Looking back is an essential prerequisite for moving forward.

ACKNOWLEDGMENTS

I am glad to perform the pleasant duty of any author and thank those who helped me most to research and write this book. I would like to start with the Harvard University History Department for granting me a sabbatical in the fall of 2018 and the Fulbright Program for helping me to spend it in Ukraine. I used part of the sabbatical to work on this book.

When it comes to primary sources and illustrative material used in the book, I am especially grateful to Andriy Kohut and Maria Panova at the Archives of the Security Service of Ukraine for making available to me as yet untapped KGB sources on the history of the Cuban missile crisis; to Svitlana Kovtun at the Archives of the Ministry of Foreign Affairs of Ukraine for initiating the declassification of formerly classified files; to Charles Borsos of the John F. Kennedy Presidential Library and Museum for his advice and help in acquiring the photos I use in this book; and to the Arkhipov family and Sven Lilienström of the Faces of Democracy Initiative for providing me with a photo of Captain Vasilii Arkhipov, one of the key figures in the crisis.

Turning to the manuscript itself, my thanks go to my colleague Myroslav Yurkevich, formerly of the University of Alberta, for editing the first draft of the manuscript, and to my colleague at Harvard, Fred Logevall, for very useful comments on the first draft. I am also grateful to Fred Logevall and Mary Sarotte for their encouragement. Sarah Chalfant and her team made me feel welcome at the Wylie Agency and helped me find an excellent home for the book: W. W. Norton & Company has published more on the Cuban missile crisis and the key figures involved in it than any other publishing house in the world. At Norton, I am grateful to John Glusman, Helen Thomaides, and Nancy Green for their guidance, support, and very useful though nonintrusive editing of the text.

I would also like to thank my students at Harvard who have taken my courses "The History of the Cold War" and "Cold War Summits" over the last few years. Many of their questions led to the answers that I provide on the pages of this book. At my home institution at Harvard, the Ukrainian Research Institute, I would like to thank the executive director, Tymish Holowinsky, and my colleagues on the institute's "ExCom," Tim Colton, George Grabowicz, Michael Flier, and Terry Martin, for their support of my academic endeavors. My chairing of our little ExCom provided me with some valuable insights into how the ExCom of 1962 may actually have worked.

Like all my previous books, this one would have been impossible to research and write without the unwavering support of my wife, Olena, for which I am profoundly grateful.

NOTES

Epigraphs

1. John F. Kennedy, Address before the General Assembly of the United Nations, September 25, 1961, John F. Kennedy Presidential Library and Museum, https://www.jfklibrary.org/archives/other-resources/john-f-kennedy -speeches/united-nations-19610925.
2. Nikita Khrushchev quoted in Norman Cousins, *Improbable Triumvirate: John F. Kennedy, Pope John, Nikita Khrushchev* (New York, 1972), 46.

Preface

1. Nicole Tam, "A moment of panic in paradise. Some university students frantically looked for shelter fearing ballistic missile attack," *Ka Leo*, January 22, 2018, http://www.manoanow.org/kaleo/news/a-moment-of-panic-in -paradise/article_ab93266c-ff27-11e7-94fa-7342ef31d879.html; "False alert of ballistic missile threat to Hawaii sent by human error," Xinhua, January 14, 2018, http://www.xinhuanet.com/english/2018-01/14/c_136894618.htm.
2. Matt Stevens, "Trump and Kim Jong-un, and the Names They've Called Each Other," *New York Times*, March 9, 2018, https://www.nytimes .com/2018/03/09/world/asia/trump-kim-jong-un.html; David E. Sanger and William J. Broad, "Iran Challenges Trump, Announcing End of Nuclear Restrictions," *New York Times*, January 14, 2020, https://www.nytimes .com/2020/01/05/world/middleeast/trump-iran-nuclear-agreement.html.
3. "John Bolton: North Korea standoff comparable to Cuban Missile Crisis," Fox News, August 11, 2017, https://www.foxnews.com/politics/john-bolton-north -korea-standoff-comparable-to-cuban-missile-crisis; "Panetta: North Korea 'most serious crisis' involving nukes since Cuba," CNN, August 12, 2017, https://edition.cnn.com/2017/08/11/politics/leon-panetta-nuclear-war/index

.html; Andrew Osborn, "Putin to U.S.: I'm ready for another Cuban Missile-style crisis if you want one," Reuters, February 21, 2019, https://www.reuters .com/article/us-russia-putin/putin-to-u-s-im-ready-for-another-cuban -missile-style-crisis-if-you-want-one-idUSKCN1QA1A3; Ray Sanchez, "Putin boasts military might with animation of Florida nuke strike," CNN, March 2, 2019, https://www.cnn.com/2018/03/01/europe/putin-nuclear-missile-video -florida/index.html; Fred Kaplan, "The People around Trump Are Totally Unqualified to Stop the Iran Crisis," *Slate*, January 6, 2020, https://slate.com/ news-and-politics/2020/01/trump-team-iran-crisis-pompeo-esper.html; Larry Provost, "Trump Acted as Great as JFK in Missile Crisis," *Townhall*, January 9, 2020, https://townhall.com/columnists/larryprovost/2020/01/09/ trump-acted-as-great-as-jfk-in-missile-crisis-n2559201.

4. Robert F. Kennedy, *Thirteen Days: A Memoir of the Cuban Missile Crisis*, with a new foreword by Arthur Schlesinger Jr. (New York, 1999); cf. Sheldon M. Stern, *The Cuban Missile Crisis in American Memory: Myths versus Reality* (Stanford, CA, 2012), 32–39, 68–98, 148–54.

5. *The Kennedy Tapes: Inside the White House during the Cuban Missile Crisis*, ed. Ernest R. May and Philip D. Zelikow, concise ed. (New York and London, 2002); Graham Allison and Philip Zelikow, *Essence of Decision: Explaining the Cuban Missile Crisis*, 2nd ed. (New York, 1999); Aleksandr Fursenko and Timothy Naftali, *"One Hell of a Gamble": Khrushchev, Castro and Kennedy, 1958–1964* (New York and London, 1997); Michael Dobbs, *One Minute to Midnight: Kennedy, Khrushchev and Castro on the Brink of Nuclear War* (New York, 2008); Tomás Diez Acosta, *October 1962: The "Missile" Crisis as Seen from Cuba* (New York, 2002).

6. Barbara Tuchman, *The Guns of August* (New York, 2012; first ed. 1962).

7. Robert Kennedy, *Thirteen Days*, 97–98; Barbara Tuchman, *The March of Folly: From Troy to Vietnam* (New York, 1984).

8. C. Todd Lopez, "U.S. Withdraws from Intermediate-Range Nuclear Forces Treaty," August 2, 2019, US Department of Defense, https://www.defense .gov/explore/story/Article/1924779/us-withdraws-from-intermediate-range -nuclear-forces-treaty/; David E. Sanger and Andrew E. Kramer, "U.S. Officials Suspect New Nuclear Missile in Explosion That Killed 7 Russians," *New York Times*, August 12, 2019, https://www.nytimes.com/2019/08/12/world/ europe/russia-nuclear-accident-putin.html.

9. Simon Craine and Noel Ryan, *"Protection from the Cold": Cold War Protection in Preparedness for Nuclear War* (Sheffield, UK, 2010), 12; Joseph M. Siracusa, *Nuclear Weapons: A Very Short Introduction* (Oxford, 2015), 60–61, 107; Paul Bracken, *The Second Nuclear Age: Strategy, Danger, and the New Power Politics* (New York, 2012), 49–50.

Prologue

1. Juan O. Tamayo, "Secret Nukes: The Untold story of the Cuban Missile Crisis," *Miami Herald*, October 13, 2012, http://www.cubademocraciayvida.org/web/ print.asp?artID=18987; James G. Blight, Bruce J. Allyn, and David A. Welch, with the assistance of David Lewis, foreword by Jorge I. Dominguez, *Cuba on the Brink: Castro, the Missile Crisis, and the Soviet Collapse* (New York, 1993), 40, 56–65, 258–60; Don Oberdorfer, "Cuban Missile Crisis More Volatile Than Thought," *Washington Post*, January 14, 1992, https://www.washingtonpost .com/archive/politics/1992/01/14/cuban-missile-crisis-more-volatile-than -thought/359ba0c1-1e6b-48b5-a0f2-82ceafb4262f/?utm_term=.235cb732df89.
2. Arthur Schlesinger Jr., "Four Days with Fidel: A Havana Diary," *New York Review of Books*, March 25, 1992, https://www.nybooks.com/articles/1992/03/26/four -days-with-fidel-a-havana-diary/.
3. Blight et al., *Cuba on the Brink*, 40; Martin Tolchin, "U.S. Underestimated Soviet Force in Cuba During '62 Missile Crisis," *New York Times*, January 15, 1992, https://www.nytimes.com/1992/01/15/world/us-underestimated-soviet -force-in-cuba-during-62-missile-crisis.html.

1. Apprentice

1. "The Inauguration of John F. Kennedy, the 35th President of the United States," The Movietone Production, 1961, https://www.youtube.com/watch?v=syWo_ gzGSoY.
2. Cited in John Burnside, *The Music of Time: Poetry in the Twentieth Century* (Princeton and Oxford, 2020), 251.
3. "For John F. Kennedy Inauguration" by Robert Frost, John F. Kennedy Presiden-tial Library and Museum, https://www.jfklibrary.org/learn/about-jfk/life-of -john-f-kennedy/fast-facts-john-f-kennedy/for-john-f-kennedys-inauguration -by-robert-frost-undelivered-poem; "Poets and Power: Robert Frost's Inaugu-ral Reading," Poets.org: From the Academy of American Poets, https://web .archive.org/web/20140112072836/; http://www.poets.org/viewmedia.php/ prmMID/20540#sthash.TVpwYYIc.dpuf; Arthur M. Schlesinger Jr., *A Thou-sand Days: John F. Kennedy in the White House* (Boston, 1965), 1–3.
4. "Ask Not What Your Country Can Do for You . . . ," Elementary School Cur-riculum Resources, John F. Kennedy Presidential Library and Museum, https://www.jfklibrary.org/learn/education/teachers/curricular-resources/ elementary-school-curricular-resources/ask-not-what-your-country-can-do -for-you.
5. "Inaugural Address of President John F. Kennedy, Washington, DC, January 20, 1961," John F. Kennedy Presidential Library and Museum, https://www

.jfklibrary.org/archives/other-resources/john-f-kennedy-speeches/inaugural
-address-19610120.

6. Clifford L. Staten, *The History of Cuba* (New York, 2003), 11–44; Jay Sexton, *The Monroe Doctrine: Empire and Nation in 19th-Century America* (New York, 2011), 85–122.

7. Louis Pérez, *Cuba under the Platt Amendment, 1902–1934* (Pittsburgh, 1986).

8. Staten, *The History of Cuba*, 45–70.

9. Aviva Chomsky, *A History of the Cuban Revolution* (Chichester, West Sussex, UK, 2015), 28–44; Staten, *The History of Cuba*, 71–106; Schlesinger, *A Thousand Days*, 215–23.

10. Maurice Halperin, *The Rise and Decline of Fidel Castro: An Essay in Contemporary History* (Berkeley, Los Angeles, and London, 1972), 46–48; Stephen G. Rabe, *Eisenhower and Latin America: The Foreign Policy of Anticommunism* (Chapel Hill and London, 1988), 117–25.

11. Memorandum Prepared in the Central Intelligence Agency, Washington, January 26, 1961, Cuba, *Foreign Relations of the United States (FRUS)*, 1961–1963, vol. 10, *Cuba, January 1961–September 1962*, no. 27, https://history.state.gov/historicaldocuments/frus1961-63v10/d27.

12. Memorandum for Discussion on Cuba, Washington, January 28, 1961, *FRUS*, 1961–1963, vol. 10, *Cuba*, January 1961–September 1962, no. 30, https://history.state.gov/historicaldocuments/frus1961-63v10/d30.

13. Memorandum of Meeting with President Kennedy, Washington, February 8, 1961, *FRUS*, 1961–1963, vol. 10, *Cuba, January 1961–September 1962*, no. 40, https://history.state.gov/historicaldocuments/frus1961-63v10/d40; Paper Prepared in the Central Intelligence Agency, Washington, March 11, 1961, Proposed Operation against Cuba, *FRUS*, 1961–1963, vol. 10, *Cuba, January 1961–September 1962*, no. 58, https://history.state.gov/historicaldocuments/frus1961-63v10/d58.

14. Paper Prepared in the Central Intelligence Agency, Washington, March 15, 1961, Revised Cuban Operation, *FRUS*, 1961–1963, vol. 10, *Cuba, January 1961–September 1962*, no. 61, https://history.state.gov/historicaldocuments/frus1961-63v10/d61; Schlesinger, *A Thousand Days*, 223–68.

15. Jim Rasenberger, *The Brilliant Disaster: JFK, Castro, and America's Doomed Invasion of Cuba's Bay of Pigs* (New York, 2011), 180–88.

16. "Bay of Pigs. Forty Years After. Chronology," National Security Archive, https://nsarchive2.gwu.edu/bayofpigs/chron.html; Rasenberger, *The Brilliant Disaster*, 189–206.

17. "The Bay of Pigs Invasion," Central Intelligence Agency, https://www
.cia.gov/news-information/featured-story-archive/2016-featured-story

-archive/the-bay-of-pigs-invasion.html; Rasenberger, *The Brilliant Disaster*, 207–59.

18. Richard Bissell Jr. with Jonathan E. Lewis and Frances T. Pudlo, *Reflections of a Cold Warrior: From Yalta to the Bay of Pigs* (New Haven and London, 1996), 184–204; *Operation ZAPATA: The Ultrasensitive Report and Testimony of the Board of Inquiry on the Bay of Pigs*, introduction by Luis Aguilar (Frederick, MD, 1981), 20–21.

19. Peter Wyden, *Bay of Pigs: The Untold Story* (New York, 1979), 277–78; Rasenberger, *The Brilliant Disaster*, 260–312.

20. Rasenberger, *The Brilliant Disaster*, 313–18; "The Bay of Pigs Invasion," Central Intelligence Agency; "Bay of Pigs. Forty Years After. Chronology," National Security Archive.

21. Evan Thomas, *The Very Best Men: Four Who Dared: The Early Years of the CIA* (New York, 2006), 261–72.

2. Master of the Game

1. William Taubman, *Khrushchev: The Man and His Era* (New York, 2003).

2. Aleksandr Feklisov, *Priznanie razvedchika* (Moscow, 1999), 376.

3. Sergei Rogoza and Boris Achkasov, *Zasekrechennye voiny, 1950–2000* (Moscow, 2004), 195.

4. Fursenko and Naftali, *"One Hell of a Gamble,"* 81–82. Cf. idem, *Adskaia igra: Sekretnaia istoriia karibskogo krizisa, 1958–1964* (Moscow, 1999), 85.

5. Larry Tart and Robert Keefe, *The Price of Vigilance: Attacks on American Surveillance Flights* (New York, 2001), 100–12; Andrew Glass, "JFK Holds First Televised News Conference," January 25, 1961, *Politico*, January 25, 2018, https://www.politico.com/story/2018/01/25/jfk-holds-first-televised-news -conference-jan-25-1961-355093; Frederick Kempe, *Berlin 1961: Kennedy, Khrushchev and the Most Dangerous Place on Earth* (New York, 2011), 73–75.

6. Andrei Sakharov, *Vospominaniia* (Moscow, 1990), 288.

7. Memorandum of Conversation, Vienna, June 3, 1961, in *FRUS*, 1961–1963, vol. 5. *Soviet Union*, no. 83.

8. Telegram from the Department of State to Secretary of State Rusk at Geneva, Washington, May 16, 1961, in *FRUS*, vol. 6, *Kennedy-Khrushchev Exchanges*, no. 15.

9. David Reynolds, *Six Summits That Shaped the Twentieth Century* (New York, 2007), 185–94.

10. Roger G. Miller, *To Save a City: The Berlin Airlift, 1948–1949* (College Station, TX, 2000), 14–18, 36–86; Daniel F. Harrington, *Berlin on the Brink: The Blockade, the Airlift, and the Early Cold War* (Lexington, KY, 2012).

11. Kempe, *Berlin 1961*, 22–24; Richard Millington, *State, Society and Memories of the Uprising of 17 June 1953 in the GDR* (New York, 2014); Christian F. Ostermann and Malcolm Byrne, eds., *Uprising in East Germany, 1953* (Budapest, 2001).

12. Vladislav Zubok and Constantine Pleshakov, *Inside the Kremlin's Cold War: From Stalin to Khrushchev* (Cambridge, MA, 1997), 194–200.

13. Kempe, *Berlin 1961*, 25–38.

14. Memorandum of Conversation, Vienna, June 3, 1961, in *FRUS*, 1961–1963, vol. 5, *Soviet Union*, no. 83, https://history.state.gov/historicaldocuments/frus1961-63v05/d83.

15. Memorandum of Conversation, Vienna, June 4, 1961, in *FRUS*, 1961–1963, vol. 5, *Soviet Union*, no. 87, https://history.state.gov/historicaldocuments/frus1961-63v05/d87; Kempe, *Berlin, 1961*, 241–45; "Research Starters: Worldwide Deaths in World War II," The National World War II Museum, New Orleans, https://www.nationalww2museum.org/students-teachers/student-resources/research-starters/research-starters-worldwide-deaths-world-war.

16. Memorandum of Conversation, Vienna, 3:15 p.m., June 4, 1961, in *FRUS*, 1961–1963, vol. 5, *Soviet Union*, no. 89, https://history.state.gov/historicaldocuments/frus1961-63v05/d89; Schlesinger, *A Thousand Days*, 358–74; Reynolds, *Six Summits*, 210.

17. Becky Little, "JFK Was Completely Unprepared for His Summit with Khrushchev," *History*, https://www.history.com/news/kennedy-krushchev-vienna-summit-meeting-1961.

18. Michael R. Beschloss, *The Crisis Years: Kennedy and Khruschev, 1960–1963* (New York, 1991), 224–28; Reynolds, *Six Summits*, 210–13; Taubman, *Khrushchev*, 495–96.

19. Richard Reeves, *President Kennedy: Profile in Power* (New York, 1993), 175.

20. "Radio and Television Report to the American People on the Berlin Crisis, July 25, 1961," JFK Presidential Library and Museum, https://www.jfklibrary.org/archives/other-resources/john-f-kennedy-speeches/berlin-crisis-19610725; "Legislative Summary: Defense and Military, 1961," JFK Presidential Library and Museum, https://www.jfklibrary.org/archives/other-resources/legislative-summary/defense-military.

21. Taubman, *Khrushchev*, 501.

22. Andrei Sakharov, *Memoirs* (New York, 1992), 217.

23. Hope M. Harrison, *Driving the Soviets Up the Wall: Soviet-East German Relations, 1953–1961* (Princeton, NJ, 2003), 139–223; "Berlin Wall and Migration," The Business of Migration, https://www.business-of-migration.com/migration-processes/other-regions/berlin-wall-and-migration/.

24. Taubman, *Khrushchev*, 503–6.

25. August 1961, *Chronik der Mauer*, http://www.chronik-der-mauer.de/en/chronicle/_year1961/_month8/?language=en&month=8&moc=1&year=1961&opennid=180144&filter=1&dokument=0&audio=0&video=0&foto=0.

26. Letter from Chairman Khrushchev to President Kennedy, Moscow, September 29, 1961, *FRUS*, 1961–1963, vol. 6, *Kennedy-Khrushchev Exchanges*, no. 21; letter from President Kennedy to Chairman Khrushchev, Hyannis Port, October 16, 1961, *FRUS*, 1961–1963, vol. 6, *Kennedy-Khrushchev Exchanges*, no. 22.

27. Zubok and Pleshakov, *Inside the Kremlin's Cold War*, 256–57; Kempe, *Berlin, 1961*, 470–79.

28. Theodore Voorhees, *The Silent Guns of Two Octobers: Kennedy and Khrushchev Play the Double Game* (Ann Arbor, 2020), 42–45.

3. Triumph of Communism

1. *Materialy XXII s"ezda KPSS* (Moscow, 1961); Arkadii Minakov, *Konservatizm v Rossii i mire*, pt. 2 (Voronezh, 2004), 232.

2. "Tsar Bomba," Atomic Heritage Foundation, https://www.atomicheritage.org/history/tsar-bomba; Vitaly I. Khalturin, Tatiana G. Rautian, Paul G. Richards, and William S. Leith, "A Review of Nuclear Testing by the Soviet Union at Novaya Zemlya, 1955–1990," *Science and Global Security* 13, no. 1 (2002): 18–19.

3. Aleksandr Emelianenkov, *Arkhipelag Sredmash* (Moscow, 2000), 71.

4. Jeremy Friedman, *Shadow Cold War: The Sino-Soviet Competition for the Third World* (Chapel Hill, NC, 2015); "Current Intelligence Staff Study. The New Stage of the Sino-Soviet Dispute (October 1961–January 1962)," Central Intelligence Agency, https://www.cia.gov/library/readingroom/docs/esau-16.pdf.

5. "Doklad tovarishcha N. S. Khrushcheva," *Izvestiia*, October 18, 1961; "Vystuplenie tovarishcha Blas Roka," *Izvestiia*, October 23, 1961.

6. Peter Shearman, *The Soviet Union and Cuba* (London, 1987), 6; Fidel Castro, "May Day Celebration (1961): Cuba Is a Socialist Nation," Castro Internet Archive, https://www.marxists.org/history/cuba/archive/castro/1961/05/01.htm.

7. Fursenko and Naftali, *"One Hell of a Gamble,"* 139–40.

8. *Fidel Castro Speaks on Marxism-Leninism*, December 2, 1961 (New York, 1962), http://www.walterlippmann.com/fc-12-02-1961.html.

9. "Na poroge novogo goda," *Izvestiia*, December 30, 1961.

10. *Khrushchev Remembers*, with introduction, commentary, and notes by Edward Crankshaw. Trans. and ed. Strobe Talbott (Boston, 1971), 544–45.

11. Fursenko and Naftali, *"One Hell of a Gamble,"* 146.

12. Fursenko and Naftali, *"One Hell of a Gamble,"* 162.

13. Fursenko and Naftali, *"One Hell of a Gamble,"* 163–65; "Fidel Castro Denounces Bureaucracy and Sectarianism," March 26, 1962 (New York, 1962), http://www.walterlippmann.com/fc-03-26-1962.html.

14. "Fidel Castro Denounces Bureaucracy and Sectarianism," March 26, 1962, http://www.walterlippmann.com/fc-03-26-1962.html; Maurice Halperin, *The Rise and Decline of Fidel Castro: An Essay in Contemporary History* (Berkeley, Los Angeles, and London, 1972), 145–48.

15. Fursenko and Naftali, *"One Hell of a Gamble,"* 169; "Splochenie sil Kubinskoi revoliutsii," *Pravda*, April 11, 1962.

16. "Alexei Adzhubei's Account of His Visit to Washington to the Central Committee of the Communist Party of the Soviet Union," March 12, 1962, History and Public Policy Program Digital Archive, Archive of the President of the Russian Federation (APRF), Moscow, Special declassification, April 2002; translated by Adam Mayle (National Security Archive), http://digitalarchive .wilsoncenter.org/document/115124.

17. Fursenko and Naftali, *"One Hell of a Gamble,"* 170.

18. "Zapiska zamestitelia predsedatelia Goskomiteta Soveta Ministrov SSSR po vneshnim ėkonomicheskim sviaziam I. V. Arkhipova," May 7, 1962, *Khrushchev. K 120-letiiu so dnia rozhdeniia*, http://liders.rusarchives.ru/hruschev/ docs/zapiska-zamestitelya-predsedatelya-goskomiteta-soveta-ministrov-sssr -po-vneshnim-ekonomicheskim; Proekt rasporiazheniia Soveta ministrov SSSR o spisanii zadolzhennosti s Kuby: May 1962, http://liders.rusarchives .ru/hruschev/docs/proekt-rasporyazheniya-soveta-ministrov-sssr-o-spisanii -sovetskim-soyuzom-zadolzhennosti-s-kuby.

19. Aleksandr Alekseev, "Kak ėto bylo," in *Nikita Sergeevich Khrushchev: Materialy k biografii* (Moscow, 1989), 67. Cf. Fursenko and Naftali, *"One Hell of a Gamble,"* 172–75.

20. Fursenko and Naftali, *"One Hell of a Gamble,"* 175; "Postanovlenie Prezidiuma TsK KPSS ob utverzhdenii pis'ma N. S. Khrushcheva F. Kastro," *Khrushchev. K 120-letiiu so dnia rozhdeniia*, http://liders.rusarchives.ru/hruschev/docs/ postanovlenie-prezidiuma-tsk-kpcc-ob-utverzhdenii-pisma-ns-khrushcheva -f-kastro-ob-okazanii-pom.

21. Fursenko and Naftali, *"One Hell of a Gamble,"* 170; Nikita Khrushchev, "Tovarichshu Fideliu Kastro Rus," *Izvestiia*, April 19, 1962.

4. Rocket Man

1. Ivaila Vylkova, "Serdtse za sedtse, vernost' za vernost'," *Ogonek*, May 27, 1962.
2. "Rech' N. S. Khrushcheva na mitinge v sele Osnova," *Izvestiia*, May 20, 1962.
3. *Khrushchev Remembers*, 545–46.
4. Andrew Glass, "U.S. Resumes Testing Bombs in the Atmosphere, April 25, 1961," *Politico*, April 24, 2017, https://www.politico.com/story/2017/04/25/us-resumes-testing-bombs-in-the-atmosphere-april-25-1961-237478; "Nekotorye napravleniia v amerikanskoi propagande v sviazi s vozobnovleniem Soedinennymi Shtatami Ameriki iadernykh ispytanii v atmosfere," Archives of the Ministry of Foreign Affairs of Ukraine (Kyiv), fond 7, opys 11, no. 641, ark. 7.
5. "Postanovlenie TsK KPSS i Soveta ministrov SSSR 'O vazhneishikh razrabotkakh mezhkontinental'nykh ballisticheskikh i global'nykh raket i nositelei kosmicheskikh ob'ektov,' April 16, 1962, in *Sovetskaia kosmicheskaia initsiativa v gosudarstvennykh dokumentakh, 1946–1964 gg.*, ed. Iu. M. Baturin (Moscow, 2008), http://www.coldwar.ru/arms_race/iniciativa/o-vazhneyshih-razrabotkah.php.
6. "Minuteman Missile," National Historic Site, http://npshistory.com/publications/mimi/srs/history.htm; Gretchen Heefner, *The Missile Next Door: The Minuteman in the American Heartland* (Cambridge, MA, 2012).
7. Sergei Khrushchev, *Nikita Khrushchev: krizisy i rakety* (Moscow, 1994), 154; "Moskalenko, Kirill Semenovich," *Generals DK*, http://www.generals.dk/general/Moskalenko/Kirill_Semenovich/Soviet_Union.html; Taubman, *Khrushchev*, 253–56, 320, 362.
8. Ekaterina Sazhneva, "Katastrofa na Baikonure: pochemu pogibli 124 cheloveka vo glave s marshalom?" *Moskovskii komsomolets*, October 29, 2015, https://www.mk.ru/incident/2015/10/29/katastrofa-na-baykonure-pochemu-pogibli-124-cheloveka-vo-glave-s-marshalom.html; Aleksandr Zhelezniakov, "Baikonurskaia tragediia," *Ėntsiklopediia Kosmonavtika*, http://www.cosmoworld.ru/spaceencyclopedia/index.shtml?bay24.html.
9. Sergei Khrushchev, *Nikita Khrushchev: krizisy i rakety*, 159; "Mezhkontinental'naia ballisticheskaia raketa R-16," https://web.archive.org/web/20020117180901/; http://rau-rostov.narod.ru/01/rvsn-mbr/r-16.htm.
10. Sergei Khrushchev, *Nikita Khrushchev: krizisy i rakety*, 159.
11. "R-7," *Encyclopedia Astronautica*, http://www.astronautix.com/r/r-7.html; Steven J. Zaloga, *The Kremlin's Nuclear Sword: The Rise and Fall of Russia's Strategic Nuclear Forces, 1945–2000* (Washington, DC, 2002), chap. 3; Sergei Khrushchev, *Nikita Khrushchev: krizisy i rakety*, 159.

12. "Postanovlenie TsK KPSS i Soveta ministrov SSSR 'O vazhneishikh raz-rabotkakh mezhkontinental'nykh ballisticheskikh i global'nykh raket i nos-itelei kosmicheskikh ob'ektov,' April 16, 1962; Zaloga, *The Kremlin's Nuclear Sword*, chap. 3; Anton Trofimov, "Kak gensek Khrushchev vybral samuiu massovuiu raketu RVSN," *Voennoe obozrenie*, March 30, 2017, https:// topwar.ru/112160-ur-100-kak-gensek-hruschev-vybral-samuyu-massovuyu -raketu-rvsn.html; Fedor Novoselov, "Proton ot Chelomeia," *Nezavisimoe voennoe obozrenie*, July 9, 2004, http://nvo.ng.ru/history/2004-07-09/5_ chelomey.html; V. Petrakov and I. Afanas'ev, "Strasti po Protonu," *Aviatsiia i kosmonavtika*, no. 4 (1993), http://www.astronaut.ru/bookcase/article/ article42.htm?reload_coolmenus; "Moskalenko, Kirill Semenovich," *Generals DK*.

13. Taubman, *Khrushchev*, 537; Nikita Khrushchev, *Vremia, liudi, vlast'. Vospominaniia* (Moscow, 1999), 1: 651.

14. Fursenko and Naftali, *"One Hell of a Gamble,"* 176–77.

15. "Rech' tov. N. S. Khrushcheva [na mitinge v Sofii, 19 maia 1962]," *Izvestiia*, May 20, 1962, 3.

16. "Rech' tov. N. S. Khrushcheva v Varne," *Izvestiia*, May 17, 1962, 2.

17. Ed Kyle, "King of Gods: The Jupiter Missile Story," *Space Launch Report* (August 14, 2011); Nur Bilge Criss, "Strategic Nuclear Missiles in Turkey: The Jupiter Affair, 1959–1963," *Journal of Strategic Studies* 20, no. 3 (1997): 97–122, https://www.tandfonline.com/doi/abs/10.1080/01402399708437689?journ alCode=fjss20; "Kratkoe soderzhanie politicheskogo otcheta posol'stva SSSR v Turtsii za 1961 g.," Archives of the Ministry of Foreign Affairs of Ukraine (Kyiv), fond 7, opys 11, no. 635, ark. 67, 72.

18. Sergei Khrushchev, *Nikita Khrushchev: krizisy i rakety*, 173; *Khrushchev Remembers*, 546; Taubman, *Khrushchev*, 541; Beschloss, *The Crisis Years*, 380–93.

19. Zaloga, *The Kremlin's Nuclear Sword*, chap. 3; "R-12," *Encyclopedia Astronautica*, http://www.astronautix.com/r/r-12.html; "R-14," *Encyclopedia Astronautica*, http://www.astronautix.com/r/r-14u.html.

20. Andrei Gromyko, *Pamiatnoe. Novye gorizonty* (Moscow, 2015), 523–24.

5. Going Nuclear

1. *Khrushchev Remembers*, 547–48.

2. "Central Committee of the Communist Party of the Soviet Union Presidium Protocol 32," May 21, 1962, History and Public Policy Program Digital Archive, RGANI, F. 3, Op. 16, D. 947, Ll. 15–16, trans. and ed. Mark Kramer, with assistance from Timothy Naftali, http://digitalarchive.wilsoncenter.org/ document/115065. Cf. *Prezidium TsK KPSS, 1954–1964*, ed. Aleksandr Fur-

senko (Moscow, 2003), 556; Fursenko and Naftali, *"One Hell of a Gamble,"* 180; Sergo Mikoyan, *The Soviet Cuban Missile Crisis: Castro, Mikoyan, Kennedy, Khrushchev, and the Missiles of November* (Cold War International History Project) (Stanford, CA, 2014), 93.

3. Cited in Mikoyan, *The Soviet Missile Cuban Crisis,* 91–93.

4. Mikoyan, *The Soviet Cuban Missile Crisis,* 92; *Prezidium TsK KPSS, 1954–1964,* 556.

5. John Erickson, "Rodion Yakovlevich Malinovsky," in Harold Shukman, ed., *Stalin's Generals* (New York, 1993); "Malinovskii, R. Ya," in A. N. Kutsenko, *Marshaly i admiraly flota Sovetskogo Soiuza. Forma, nagrady, oruzhie* (Kyiv, 2007), 232–41; "Biriuzov, Sergei Semenovich," *Geroi strany,* http://www.warheroes.ru/hero/hero.asp?Hero_id=717.

6. Priscilla Roberts, ed., *Cuban Missile Crisis: The Essential Reference Guide* (Santa Barbara, CA, 2012), 72–74; Anatolii Gribkov, "Karibskii krizis," *Voenno-istoricheskii zhurnal,* 1992, no. 10: 41.

7. R. Malinovsky and M. Zakharov, "Memorandum on Deployment of Soviet Forces to Cuba," May 24, 1962, in Raymond L. Garthoff, "New Evidence on the Cuban Missile Crisis: Khrushchev, Nuclear Weapons, and the Cuban Missile Crisis," *Cold War International History Project,* Bulletin 11 (Winter 1998), 251–62, here 254–56, https://www.wilsoncenter.org/sites/default/files/CWIHP_Bulletin_11.pdf.

8. *Prezidium TsK KPSS, 1954–1964,* 556.

9. S. P. Ivanov, "Untitled notes on the back of the May 24 Memorandum to Khrushchev," in Garthoff, "New Evidence on the Cuban Missile Crisis," 256–57; *Prezidium TsK KPSS, 1954–1964,* 556.

10. Mikoyan, *The Soviet Missile Cuban Crisis,* 96–97.

11. Gribkov, "Karibskii krizis," 45; Fursenko and Naftali, *"One Hell of a Gamble,"* 179–80.

12. Gribkov, "Karibskii krizis," 45; Mikoyan, *The Soviet Missile Cuban Crisis,* 97.

13. A. I. Alekseev, "Karibskii krizis: kak ėto bylo," in *Otkryvaia novye stranitsy . . . Mezhdunarodnye voprosy: sobytiia i liudi,* comp. N. V. Popov (Moscow, 1989), 157–72, here 160.

14. Alekseev, "Karibskii krizis: kak ėto bylo," 160; Gribkov, "Karibskii krizis," 42.

15. Alekseev, "Karibskii krizis: kak ėto bylo," 160.

16. Fursenko and Naftali, *"One Hell of a Gamble,"* 181–82.

17. Acosta, *October 1962,* 100.

18. Fursenko and Naftali, *"One Hell of a Gamble,"* 187; Fidel Castro in Carlos Lechuga, *Cuba and the Missile Crisis,* trans. Mary Todd (Melbourne and New York, 2001), 24.

19. Castro in Lechuga, *Cuba and the Missile Crisis*, 24; Alekseev, "Karibskii krizis: kak èto bylo," 161.

20. Alekseev, "Karibskii krizis: kak èto bylo," 161; Castro in Lechuga, *Cuba and the Missile Crisis*, 24.

21. Alekseev, "Karibskii krizis: kak èto bylo," 161.

22. Castro in Lechuga, *Cuba and the Missile Crisis*, 25; Acosta, *October 1962*, 101–3.

23. Acosta, *October 1962*, 103.

24. Anatolii Gribkov, "Karibskii krizis," *Voenno-istoricheskii zhurnal*, 1992, no. 11: 37.

25. "Central Committee of the Communist Party of the Soviet Union Presidium Protocol, no. 35, June 10, 1962," trans. and ed. Mark Kramer, with assistance from Timothy Naftali, *Cold War International History Project* (CWIHP), http://digitalarchive.wilsoncenter.org/document/115066; Mikoyan, *The Soviet Missile Cuban Crisis*, 97; Fursenko and Naftali, *"One Hell of a Gamble,"* 189.

6. Operation Anadyr

1. Leonid Garbuz, "Zamestitel' komanduiushchego gruppy sovetskikh voisk na Kube vspominaet," *Strategicheskaia operatsiia "Anadyr'." Kak èto bylo*, Memuarno-spravochnoe izdanie, ed. V. I. Esin (Moscow, 2000), 80–89, here 80–82.

2. Acosta, *October 1962*, 103–4.

3. V. I. Esin, "Uchastie raketnykh voisk strategicheskogo naznacheniia v operatsii "Anadyr'," in *Strategicheskaia operatsiia "Anadyr',"* 55–64, here 56; A. M. Burlov, "Vospominaniia glavnogo inzhenera raketnogo polka," in *Strategicheskaia operatsiia "Anadyr',"* 99–108, here 100.

4. Igor Kurennoi, cited in Igor' Prokopenko, *Iadernyi shchit Rossii: kto pobedit v Tret'ei mirovoi voine?* (Moscow, 2016), 107–8.

5. "R. Malinovsky and M. Zakharov, 'Memorandum on Deployment of Soviet Forces to Cuba,'" May 24, 1962, in Garthoff, "New Evidence on the Cuban Missile Crisis," 254.

6. Andrei Grigor'ev and Igor' Podgurskii, "Dostoinyi syn otechestva. Iz vospominanii polkovnika N. I. Antipova o general-maiore Igore Demianoviche Statsenko," *Krasnaia zvezda*, October 3, 2008, http://old.redstar.ru/2008/10/03_10/6_01.html; A. I. Gribkov, "Razrabotka zamysla i osushchestvlenie operatsii "Anadyr'," in *Strategicheskaia operatsiia "Anadyr',"* 26–53, here 41.

7. V. Nikitchenko, Chairman, Committee of State Security attached to the Council of Ministers of the Ukrainian SSR, to N. V. Podgorny, First Secretary, Central Committee of the Communist Party of Ukraine, "Spetsial'noe soobshchenie," February 15, 1962, in the Archive of Security Service of Ukraine

(henceforth: SBU Archives), fond 16, opys 11, no. 2, vol. 1, fols. 39–40; "General maior Kobzar Dmitrii Aleksandrovich," Kto est' kto v RVSN, http://rvsn
.ruzhany.info/names/kobzarj_d_a.html.

8. "43-ia Krasnoznamennaia raketnaia armiia," in *Raketnye voiska strategicheskogo naznacheniia. Spravochnik,* https://rvsn.info/army/army_43.html; "43-ia gvardeiskaia raketnaia Smolenskaia ordenov Suvorova i Kutuzova diviziia," in *Raketnye voiska strategicheskogo naznacheniia.*

9. "Interview with General Leonid Garbuz by Sherry Jones," in *Mikoyan's "Mission Impossible" in Cuba: New Soviet Evidence on the Cuban Missile Crisis,* National Security Archive Electronic Briefing Book No. 400, https://nsarchive2.gwu.edu/NSAEBB/NSAEBB400/docs/Interview%20with%20General%20Garbuz.pdf.

10. Khrushchev, *Vremia, liudi, vlast',* 2: 510.

11. "Pliev Issa Aleksandrovich. Biografiia," *Ėntsiklopediia,* Minoborony Rossii, http://encyclopedia.mil.ru/encyclopedia/heroes/USSR/more.htm?id=11904755@morfHeroes; "Legendy armii. Issa Pliev," https://www.youtube.com/watch?v=9gGZGM2mHL8

12. Petr Siuda, "Novocherkassk, 1–3 iiunia 1962, zabastovka i rasstrel," *Voennoe obozrenie,* June 4, 2012, https://topwar.ru/15007-novocherkassk-1962.html; V. A. Kozlov, *Neizvestnyĭ SSSR: protivostoianie naroda i vlasti, 1953–1985* (Moscow, 2005), 333–45.

13. Aleksandr Solzhenitsyn, *Sobranie sochinenii,* vol. 6: *Arkhipelag Gulag,* chaps. 5–7 (Moscow, 2000), 547; Tatiana Bocharova, *Novocherkassk: krovavyi polden'* (Rostov na Donu, 2002), 73; Urusbii Batyrov, *Gordost' Osetii: Issa Pliev, Georgii Khetagurov, Khadzhi-Umar Mamsurov* (Moscow, 2005), 97–99.

14. Acosta, *October 1962,* 107–10; Khrushchev, *Vremia, liudi, vlast',* 2: 510.

15. Gribkov, "Razrabotka zamysla i osushchestvlenie operatsii "Anadyr'," in *Strategicheskaia operatsiia "Anadyr',"* 32–33. Cf. Gribkov, «Karibskii krizis," *Voenno- istoricheskii zhurnal,* 1992, no. 11: 35; "51-ia raketnaia diviziia," in *Raketnye voiska strategicheskogo naznacheniia,* https://rvsn.info/divisions/div_051.html; Esin, "Uchastie raketnykh voisk strategicheskogo naznacheniia v operatsii "Anadyr'," 56.

16. "Tochno po raspisaniiu," *Izvestiia,* July 11, 1962, 5; *40 let grazhdanskomu vozdushnomu flotu. Sbornik statei* (Moscow, 1963); Acosta, *October 1962,* 110.

17. Burlov, "Vospominaniia glavnogo inzhenera raketnogo polka," in *Strategicheskaia operatsiia "Anadyr',"* 99–108, here 100.

18. Burlov, "Vospominaniia glavnogo inzhenera raketnogo polka," 100; Gribkov, "Razrabotka zamysla i osushchestvlenie operatsii "Anadyr'," 41.

19. Burlov, "Vospominaniia glavnogo inzhenera raketnogo polka," 100–102.

20. "Interview with General Leonid Garbuz by Sherry Jones," 3.

21. Igor' Statsenko, "Doklad komandira 51-i raketnoi divizii o deistviiakh soediineniia v period s 12 iiulia po 1 dekabria 1962 goda na o. Kuba," in *Raketnye voiska strategicheskogo naznacheniia. Spravochnik. Dokumenty*, https://rvsn.info/library/docs/doc_1_1001.html; Gribkov, "Razrabotka zamysla i osushchestvlenie operatsii "Anadyr'," 33.

22. Esin, "Uchastie raketnykh voisk strategicheskogo naznacheniia v operatsii "Anadyr'," 58; Statsenko, "Doklad komandira 51-i raketnoi divizii o deistviiakh soediineniia v period s 12 iiulia po 1 dekabria 1962 goda na o. Kuba."

23. Khrushchev, *Vremia, liudi, vlast'*, 2: 512.

24. Gribkov, "Razrabotka zamysla i osushchestvlenie operatsii "Anadyr'," 33; Fursenko and Naftali, *"One Hell of a Gamble,"* 192; Acosta, *October 1962*, 109.

7. High Seas

1. Aleksandr Rogozin, "Sovetskii flot v voinakh i konfliktakh kholodnoi voiny," chap. 2: "SSSR v stroitel'stve VMS Kuby," http://alerozin.narod.ru/CubaNavy/CubaNavySoviet-2.htm; "Klass 'Sergei Borkin,'" *FleetPhoto*, https://fleetphoto.ru/projects/3306/; Robert Alden, "Israel Is Accused in U.N. of Sinking a Soviet Ship," *New York Times*, October 13, 1973; Iu. M. Vorontsov, ed., *SSSR i blizhnevostochnoe uregulirovanie, 1967–1988. Dokumenty i materialy* (Moscow, 1989), 175.

2. *Morskoi transport SSSR: k 60-letiiu otrasli* (Moscow, 1984), 209; Vladimir Alekseev, *Russkie i sovetskie moriaki na Sredizemnom more* (Moscow, 1976), 219; Rogozin, "Sovetskii flot," chap. 2, sec. 8: "Sovetskie suda, uchastvovavshie v perebroske voisk v khode operatsii 'Anadyr', " http://alerozin.narod.ru/Cuba62/Cuba1962-8.htm; "Nachal'niku upravleniia KGB pri Sovete ministrov USSR po Odesskoi oblasti general-maioru tov. Kuvarzinu. Raport. Starshii operupolnomochennyi KGB pri SM SSSR po Krasnodarskomu kraiu kapitan Zozulia," September 21, 1962, SBU Archives, fond 1, opys 1, no. 1532, fols. 112, 119.

3. Zozulia, "Raport," September 21, 1962, SBU Archives, fond 1, opys 1, no. 1532, fols. 115, 116.

4. Aleksei Lashkov, "Sovetskie VVS i PVO na Kube v period i posle Karibskogo krizisa," *Avia Panorama*, 2012, no. 9, https://www.aviapanorama.ru/2012/09/sovetskie-vvs-i-pvo-na-kube-v-period-i-posle-karibskogo-krizisa-2/.

5. "Klass 'Omsk,'" *FleetPhoto*, http://fleetphoto.ru/projects/2374/.

6. Ivan Sidorov, "Vypolniaia internatsional'nyi dolg," in *Strategicheskaia operatsiia "Anadyr'."* 125–33, here 125.

7. Esin, "Uchastie voisk strategicheskogo naznacheniia v operatsii 'Anadyr'," in

Strategicheskaia operatsiia "Anadyr'," 55–64, here 58–61; Sidorov, "Vypolniaia internatsional'nyi dolg," 126.

8. Aleksandr Voropaev, "Otshumeli pesni nashego polka, pt. 1: 1960–1963," http://cubanos.ru/texts/txt035.

9. Sidorov, "Vypolniaia internatsional'nyi dolg," 127.

10. Esin, "Uchastie voisk strategicheskogo naznacheniia v operatsii "Anadyr'," 60; Sidorov, "Vypolniaia internatsional'nyi dolg," 127; Valentin Polkovnikov, "Startovyi divizion raketnogo polka na Kube," in *Strategicheskaia operatsiia "Anadyr',"* 148–60, here 151.

11. Dmitrii Iazov, *Karibskii krizis. 50 let spustia* (Moscow, 2015), 196–97; idem, *Udary sud'by. Vospominaniia soldata i marshala* (Moscow, 2014), 118–20; "Pobeda," ShipStamps.co.uk, https://shipstamps.co.uk/forum/viewtopic .php?t=12834; Arkadii Shorokhov, "Motostrelkovye voiska na Kube," in *Strategicheskaia operatsiia "Anadyr',"* 142–47.

12. Iazov, *Karibskii krizis*, 196–97, idem; *Udary sud'by*, 129–35.

13. Iazov, *Udary sud'by*, 131–32.

14. Captain Fedorov, "Raport," September 20, 1962, SBU Archives, fond 1, opys 1, no. 1532, fols. 87–96, here fol. 88; Senior Lieutenant Sennikov, "Raport," September 18, 1962, SBU Archives, fond 1, opys 1, no. 1532, fols. 37–44, here fol. 41; Senior Lieutenant Nechitailo, "Raport, po spetsreisu parokhoda 'Nikolai Burdenko,'" September 22, 1962, SBU Archives, fond 1, opys 1, no. 1532, fols. 155–64, here fol. 160.

15. Aleksei Butskii, "Rabota Glavnogo shtaba RVSN v period podgotovki i provedeniia operatsii "Anadyr'," in *Strategicheskaia operatsiia "Anadyr',"* 65–70, here 66; Major Morozov, "Raport," September 29, 1962, SBU Archives, fond 1, opys 1, no. 1532, fols. 121–128, here fol. 124; Captain Fedorov, "Raport," September 20, 1962, SBU Archives, fond 1, opys 1, no. 1532, fols. 87–96, here fol. 88; Major Verbov, "Raport po reisu teplokhoda 'Admiral Nakhimov,'" September 8, 1962, SBU Archives, fond 1, opys 1, no. 1532, fols. 34–35.

16. Captain Fedorov, "Raport," September 20, 1962, SBU Archives, fond 1, opys 1, no. 1532, fols. 87–96, here fol. 88; Senior Lieutenant Sennikov, "Raport," September 18, 1962, SBU Archives, fond 1, opys 1, no. 1532, fols. 37–44, here fol. 41.

17. Senior Lieutenant Topilsky, "Raport o spetsreise teplokhoda 'Dolmatovo,'" September 25, 1962, SBU Archives, fond 1, opys 1, no. 1532, fol. 98–105, here fol. 102.

18. Senior Lieutenant Sennikov, "Raport," September 18, 1962, SBU Archives, fond 1, opys 1, no. 1532, fols. 1-8 37–44, here fol. 39.

19. Major Morozov, "Raport," September 29, 1962, SBU Archives, fond 1, opys 1, no. 1532, fols. 121–128, here fols. 125, 126, 128.

20. Zozulia, "Raport," September 21, 1962, SBU Archives, fond 1, opys 1, no. 1532, fol. 113; Major Morozov, "Raport," September 29, 1962, SBU Archives, fond 1, opys 1, no. 1532, fols. 125–128.

21. "Nachal'niku upravleniia KGB pri Sovete ministrov USSSR po Odesskoi oblasti general-maioru tov. Kuvarzinu. Raport. Starshii operupolnomochen-nyi KGB pri SM SSSR po Krasnodarskomu kraiu kapitan Zozulia," September 21, 1962, SBU Archives, fond 1, opys 1, no. 1532, fols. 116–117; Major Morozov, "Raport," September 29, 1962, SBU Archives, fond 1, opys 1, no. 1532, fols. 121; Captain Zozulia, "Raport," September 29, 1962, SBU Archives, fond 1, opys 1, no. 1532, fols, 116–117.

22. Fursenko and Naftali, *One Hell of a Gamble,* 193–94; Fedor Ladygin and Vladimir Lota, *GRU i Karibskii krizis* (Moscow, 2012), 62–63.

8. Prisoner of Berlin

1. Lyman B. Kirkpatrick, "Memorandum for the Director, 'Action Generated by DCI Cables Concerning Cuban Low-Level Photography of Offensive Weapons,'" [n/d], in *CIA Documents on the Missile Crisis, 1962,* ed. Mary McAuliffe (Washington, DC, 1992), no. 12, 39–44, here 39, https://www.cia.gov/library/center-for-the-study-of-intelligence/csi-publications/books-and-monographs/Cuban%20Missile%20Crisis1962.pdf.

2. For a photo of the SAM construction site at La Coloma, taken on August 29, 1962, see The Cuban Missile Crisis 1962: The Photographs, National Security Archive, https://nsarchive2.gwu.edu/nsa/cuba_mis_cri/4.jpg; Ray S. Cline, "Memorandum for Acting Director of Central Intelligence, 'Recent Soviet Military Activities in Cuba,'" September 3, 1962, in *CIA Documents on the Missile Crisis, 1962,* no. 11, 34–37.

3. "Speech by Senator Keating, 'Soviet Activities in Cuba,'" August 31, 1962, History and Public Policy Program Digital Archive, 87th Congress, 2nd session, *Congressional Record* 108, pt. 14 (August 31, 1962), 18358–18361, http://digitalarchive.wilsoncenter.org/document/134658.

4. "Speech by Senator Keating, 'Soviet Activities in Cuba,'" August 31, 1962; Thomas G. Paterson, "The Historian as Detective: Senator Kenneth Keating, the Missiles in Cuba, and His Mysterious Sources," *Diplomatic History* 11, no. 1 (1987): 67–71.

5. Kirkpatrick, "Memorandum for the Director, 'Action Generated by DCI Cables Concerning Cuban Low-Level Photography of Offensive Weapons.'"

6. Barbara Leaming, *Jack Kennedy: The Education of a Statesman* (New York, 2006), 394; William A. Tidwell, "Memorandum for the Record, 'Instructions

Concerning the Handling of Certain Information Concerning Cuba,'" September 1, 1962, in *CIA Documents on the Missile Crisis, 1962,* no. 10, 33.

7. Robert Dallek, *Camelot's Court: Inside the Kennedy White House* (New York, 2013).

8. "Letter from President Kennedy to Chairman Khrushchev," Washington, July 17, 1962, *FRUS,* 1961–1963, vol. 6, *Kennedy-Khrushchev Exchanges,* no. 51, Fursenko and Naftali, *"One Hell of a Gamble,"* 193-94.; Dobbs, *One Minute to Midnight,* 226–27.

9. "Message from Chairman Khrushchev to President Kennedy," *FRUS,* 1961–1963, vol. 15, *Berlin Crisis, 1962–1963,* no. 73, https://history.state.gov/historicaldocuments/frus1961-63v15/d73; "Editorial note," FRUS, vol. 15, no. 63, https://history.state.gov/historicaldocuments/frus1961-63v15/d63; "Memorandum from the President's Special Assistant for National Security Affairs (Bundy) to President Kennedy," Washington, July 20, 1962, *FRUS,* vol. 15, no. 80, https://history.state.gov/historicaldocuments/frus1961-63v15/d80; "Telegram from the Embassy in the Soviet Union to the Department of State," Moscow, July 25, 1962, *FRUS,* vol. 15, no. 87, https://history.state.gov/historicaldocuments/frus1961-63v15/d87; Leaming, *Jack Kennedy,* 390–91.

10. Hope Harrison, *Ulbricht and the Concrete "Rose": New Archival Evidence in the Dynamics of Soviet-East German Relations and the Berlin Crisis, 1958–61,* Cold War International History Project Working Papers Series, no. 5 (Washington, DC, May 1993), https://www.wilsoncenter.org/sites/default/files/ACFB81.pdf; A. M. Betmakaev, "Na puti k vostochnogermanskoi identichnosti: V. Ul'brikht i otnosheniia mezhdu GDR i SSSR v 1949–1964 gg.," in *Amerikanskje issledovaniia v Sibiri,* vyp. 7 (Tomsk, 2003), http://hist.asu.ru/aes/gdr/btmkv.htm.

11. Taubman, *Khrushchev,* 540; V. M. Zubok, *Khrushchev and the Berlin Crisis (1958–1962),* Cold War International History Project Working Papers Series, no. 6 (Washington, DC, May 1993), https://www.wilsoncenter.org/sites/default/files/ACFB7D.pdf; V. V. Mar'ina, "Iz istorii kholodnoi voiny, 1954–1964 gg. Dokumenty cheshskikh arkhivov," Document no. 3: "Chast' zapisi besedy chlenov chekhoslovatskoi delegatsii s N. S. Khrushchevym, posviashchennaia situatsii v GDR," June 8, 1962, *Novaia i noveshaia istoriia,* 2003, nos. 1–3: 139–59, here 153, https://dlib-eastview-com.ezp-prod1.hul.harvard.edu/browse/doc/4746660.

12. Dobbs, *One Minute to Midnight,* 215; "Memorandum from Secretary of State Rusk to President Kennedy," Washington, August 2, 1962, *FRUS,* vol. 15, no. 91, https://history.state.gov/historicaldocuments/frus1961-63v15/d91.

13. East Germans Kill Man Trying to Cross Berlin Wall," This Day in History: August 17, 1962, *History,* https://www.history.com/this-day-in-history/east

-germans-kill-man-trying-to-cross-berlin-wall; "Current Intelligence Weekly Review," Washington, August 24, 1962, *FRUS*, 1961–1963, vol. 5, *Soviet Union*, no. 226, https://history.state.gov/historicaldocuments/frus1961-63v05/d226; Fursenko and Naftali, *"One Hell of a Gamble,"* 202–3.

14. National Intelligence estimate, number 85-2-65, The Situation and Prospects in Cuba, August 1, 1962, in *CIA Documents on the Missile Crisis, 1962*, no. 3: 9–12, here 10–11; John McCone, Memorandum, "Soviet MRBM on Cuba," October 31, 1962, in *CIA Documents on the Missile Crisis, 1962*, no. 4: 13–17, here 13; "Memorandum from the President's Military Representative (Taylor) to President Kennedy," Washington, August 17, 1962, *FRUS*, 1961–1963, vol. 10, *Cuba, January 1961–September 1962*, no. 380, https://history.state.gov/historicaldocuments/frus1961-63v10/d380.

15. Leaming, *Jack Kennedy*, 391; [McCone,] Memorandum on Cuba, August 20, 1962, in *CIA Documents on the Missile Crisis, 1962*, no. 5: 19–20; John McCone, Memorandum for the File, "Discussion in Secretary Rusk's Office at 12 O'clock," August 21, 1962, in *CIA Documents on the Missile Crisis, 1962*, no. 6: 21–23.

16. McCone, Memorandum for the File, "Discussion in Secretary Rusk's Office at 12 O'clock," August 21, 1962, no. 6: 22; Memorandum for the File, Washington, August 21, 1962, "Discussion in Secretary Rusk's Office at 12 O'clock, August 21, 1962," *FRUS*, 1961–1963, vol. 10, *Cuba, January 1961–September 1962*, no. 382, https://history.state.gov/historicaldocuments/frus1961-63v10/d382.

17. McCone, Memorandum for the File, "Discussion in Secretary Rusk's Office at 12 O'clock," August 21, 1962, no. 6: 21–23; McCone, "Memorandum on the Meeting with the President at 6:00 p.m. on August 22, 1962," in *CIA Documents on the Missile Crisis, 1962*, no. 7: 25–26; August 1962," President Kennedy's Schedule, *History Central*, https://www.historycentral.com/JFK/Calendar/August1962.html.

18. McCone, Memorandum for the File, "Discussion in Secretary Rusk's Office at 12 O'clock," August 21, 1962, no. 6: 22; Memorandum for the File, Washington, August 21, 1962, "Discussion in Secretary Rusk's Office at 12 O'clock," August 21, 1962, *FRUS*, 1961–1963, vol. 10, *Cuba, January 1961–September 1962*, no. 382, https://history.state.gov/historicaldocuments/frus1961-63v10/d382; Schedules, President's daily, January 1961–August 1962, John F. Kennedy Presidential Library and Museum, Archives, https://www.jfklibrary.org/Asset-Viewer/Archives/JFKPOF-140-041.aspx; "National Security Action Memorandum," no. 181, August 23, 1962, *Federation of American Scientists*, Intelligence Resource Program, National Secu-

rity Action Memorandums (NSAM) [Kennedy Administration, 1961–63], https://fas.org/irp/offdocs/nsam-jfk/nsam181.htm.

19. President's News Conference, August 29, 1962, *The American Presidency Project,* http://www.presidency.ucsb.edu/ws/index.php?pid=8839.

20. August 1962, President Kennedy's Schedule, *HistoryCentral,* https://www.historycentral.com/JFK/Calendar/August1962.html; *The Kennedy Tapes,* 5.

21. U.S., Department of State, *Bulletin,* vol. 67, no. 1213 (September 24, 1962), 450. (Read to news correspondents on September 4, by Pierre Salinger, White House Press Secretary.) For earlier versions of the statement, see John F. Kennedy Presidential Library and Museum, Papers of Robert F. Kennedy, Attorney General Papers, Attorney General's Confidential File 6-4-1: Cuba: Cuban Crisis, 1962: *Kennedy–Khrushchev Letters,* 1962: September–November, 107–38.

22. *The Kennedy Tapes,* 12–17.

9. Tip-Off

1. For Nikita Khrushchev's itinerary in the summer of 1962, see the appendix to his *Vospominaniia: Vremia, liudi, vlast'* (Moscow, 2016), vol. 2, "N. S. Khrushchev. Khronologiia 1953–1964. Sostavlena po ofitsial'nym publikatsiiam. 1962 god."

2. "Torzhestvennala vstrecha v Moskve," *Pravda,* August 19, 1962, 1; "Vo imia druzhby i solidarnosti," *Izvestiia,* September 3, 1962, 1–2; "Bratskaia pomoshch' revoliutsionnoi Kube. K prebyvaniiu v SSSR delegatsii Natsional'nogo rukovodstva Ob'edinennykh revoliutsionnykh organizatsii Kuby," *Pravda,* September 3, 1962, 1; Fursenko and Naftali, *"One Hell of a Gamble,"* 196–97; Blight et al., *On the Brink,* 334.

3. "Informal Communication from Chairman Khrushchev to President Kennedy, Moscow, September 4, 1962," *FRUS,* 1961–1963, vol. 6, *Kennedy-Khrushchev Exchanges,* no. 53, https://history.state.gov/historical documents/frus1961-63v06/d53; John F. Kennedy, Joint Statement with Prime Minister Macmillan on Nuclear Testing, August 27, 1962, *American Presidency Project,* http://www.presidency.ucsb.edu/ws/index.php?pid=8834.

4. Fred Coleman, *The Decline and Fall of the Soviet Empire: Forty Years That Shook the World from Stalin to Yeltsin* (New York, 1996), 6.

5. "Priem N. S. Khrushchevym Stiuarta L. Iudolla," *Pravda,* September 7, 1962, 1; "Telegram from the Embassy in the Soviet Union to the Department of State," *FRUS,* 1961–1963, vol. 5, *Soviet Union,* no. 236, https://history.state.gov/historicaldocuments/frus1961-63v05/d236.

6. "Memorandum of Conversation between Secretary of the Interior Udall and

Chairman Khrushchev," Pitsunda, Georgia, Soviet Union, September 6, 1962, 1 p.m.," *FRUS*, 1961–1963, vol. 15, *Berlin Crisis, 1962–1963*, no. 112, https://history.state.gov/historicaldocuments/frus1961-63v15/d112.

7. Editorial Note, *FRUS*, 1961–1963, vol. 10, *Cuba, January 1961–September 1962*, no. 416, https://history.state.gov/historicaldocuments/frus1961-63v10/d416; Fursenko and Naftali, *"One Hell of a Gamble,"* 208–9; "Telegram from Soviet Ambassador to Cuba Alekseev to the USSR MFA, September 11, 1962," in Raymond L. Garthoff, "Russian Foreign Ministry Documents on the Cuban Missile Crisis," Cold War International History Project, *Bulletin*, no. 5, pt. 2: The Cuban Missile Crisis (Spring 1995), 65, https://www.wilsoncenter.org/sites/default/files/CWIHPBulletin5_p2.pdf.

8. Fursenko and Naftali, *"One Hell of a Gamble,"* 208–9; "Telegram from the Embassy in the Soviet Union to the Department of State," *FRUS*, 1961–1963, vol. 5, *Soviet Union*, no. 236, https://history.state.gov/historicaldocuments/frus1961-63v05/d236; "Priem N. S. Khrushchevym Stiuarta L. Iudolla," *Pravda*, September 7, 1962, 1; "Memorandum of Conversation between Castro and Mikoyan," November 4, 1962, History and Public Policy Program Digital Archive, Russian Foreign Ministry archives, obtained and translated by NHK television, copy provided by Philip Brenner, trans. Aleksandr Zaemsky, slightly revised, https://digitalarchive.wilsoncenter.org/document/110961.

9. "Minutes of Conversation between the Delegations of the CPCz and the CPSU, The Kremlin (excerpt)," October 30, 1962, History and Public Policy Program Digital Archive, National Archive, Archive of the CC CPCz (Prague); File: "Antonín Novotný, Kuba," Box 193, https://digitalarchive.wilsoncenter.org/document/115219.

10. "Memorandum from R. Malinovsky to N. S. Khrushchev on the Possibility of Reinforcing Cuba by Air, 6 September 1962," in Aleksandr Fursenko and Timothy Naftali, "The Pitsunda Decision: Khrushchev and Nuclear Weapons," *CWIHP Bulletin* 10: 223–27, here 226, https://www.wilsoncenter.org/sites/default/files/CWIHPBulletin10_p6.pdf.

11. Fursenko and Naftali, *"One Hell of a Gamble,"* 206–13; idem, "The Pitsunda Decision," 223–27, https://www.wilsoncenter.org/sites/default/files/CWIHPBulletin10_p6.pdf.

12. "Memorandum from R. Malinovsky and M. Zakharov to the Chief of the 12th Main Directorate of the Ministry of Defense," in "New Evidence on Tactical Nuclear Weapons - 59 Days in Cuba," document no. 6, National Security Archive Electronic Briefing Book No. 449, ed. Svetlana Savranskaya and Thomas Blanton with Anna Melyakova, https://nsarchive2.gwu.edu/NSAEBB/NSAEBB449/; "Memorandum from R. Malinovsky and M. Zakharov to Commander of Group of Soviet Forces in Cuba, 8 September

1962," in "New Evidence on Tactical Nuclear Weapons - 59 Days in Cuba," document no. 6, National Security Archive Electronic Briefing Book No. 449, document no. 5, https://nsarchive2.gwu.edu/NSAEBB/NSAEBB449/docs/; cf. Fursenko and Naftali, "The Pitsunda Decision," 226–27, https://www.wilsoncenter.org/sites/default/files/CWIHPBulletin10_p6.pdf, 227.

13. "[Draft] Memorandum from R. Malinovsky and M. Zakharov to Commander of Group of Soviet Forces in Cuba on Pre-delegation of Launch Authority, 8 September 1962," in "New Evidence on Tactical Nuclear Weapons - 59 Days in Cuba," document no. 6, National Security Archive Electronic Briefing Book No. 449, document no. 7, https://nsarchive2.gwu.edu/NSAEBB/NSAEBB449/docs/.

14. Seymour Topping, "Kennedy Assailed. Moscow Asserts Bid to Call Reserves Aggressive Step," *New York Times*, September 12, 1962, 1, 16, https://www.mtholyoke.edu/acad/intrel/cuba.htm.

15. "Message from Chairman Khrushchev to President Kennedy," Moscow, September 28, 1962, *FRUS*, 1961–1963, vol. 6, *Kennedy-Khrushchev Exchanges*, no. 56, https://history.state.gov/historicaldocuments/frus1961-63v06/d56.

16. *The Kennedy Tapes*, 20–29; "Message from President Kennedy to Chairman Khrushchev," Washington, October 8, 1962, *FRUS*, 1961–1963, vol. 6, *Kennedy-Khrushchev Exchanges*, no. 59, https://history.state.gov/historical documents/frus1961-63v06/d59.

17. "United States Reaffirms Policy on Prevention of Aggressive Actions on Cuba," Department of State Bulletin, vol. 47, no. 1213 (September 24, 1962), 450, https://teachingamericanhistory.org/library/document/statement-on-cuba/.

10. Honeymoon

1. "John A. McCone and Mrs. Pigott Marry in Seattle; Director of C.I.A. Weds University Regent at Sacred Heart Villa," *New York Times*, August 30, 1962; David Robarge, *John McCone as Director of Central Intelligence, 1961–1965* (Washington, DC, 2005), 106.

2. Lyman B. Kirkpatrick, Memorandum for the Director, "Action Generated by DCI Cables Concerning Cuban Low-Level Photography and Offensive Weapons," in *CIA Documents on the Cuban Missile Crisis, 1962*, ed. Mary S. McAuliffe (Washington, DC, 1992), 39–44, here 41–42; McCone to Carter and Elder, September 10, 1962, *CIA Documents*, 59; McCone to Carter, September 16, 1962, *CIA Documents*, 78–79; Editorial Note in *FRUS*, 1961–1963, vol. 10, *Cuba, January 1961–September 1962*, no. 420, https://history.state.gov/historicaldocuments/frus1961-63v10/d420.

3. M. Mikhailov, "Snova U-2, snova naglaia provokatsiia," *Izvestiia*, September 5, 1962, 1; "Memorandum of Conversation Between Secretary of the Interior

Udall and Chairman Khrushchev," Pitsunda, Georgia, Soviet Union, September 6, 1962, 1 p.m.," *FRUS*, 1961–1963, vol. 15, *Berlin Crisis, 1962–1963*, no. 112, https://history.state.gov/historicaldocuments/frus1961-63v15/d112; Gregory W. Pedlow and Donald E. Welzenbach, *The CIA and the U-2 Program, 1954–1974* (Washington, DC, 1998), 229.

4. Lyman B. Kirkpatrick, Memorandum for the Director, "White House Meeting on September 10, 1962, on Cuban Overflights," in *CIA Documents on the Cuban Missile Crisis, 1962*, 61–62.

5. "Memorandum Prepared in the Central Intelligence Agency for the Executive Director," Washington, September 10, 1962, *FRUS*, 1961–1963, vol. 10, *Cuba, January 1961–September 1962*, no. 421, https://history.state.gov/historicaldocuments/frus1961-63v10/d421.

6. "Memorandum Prepared in the Central Intelligence Agency for the Executive Director," Washington, September 10, 1962; Kirkpatrick, Memorandum for the Director, "White House Meeting on September 10, 1962, on Cuban Overflights," 62.

7. Pedlow and Welzenbach, *The CIA and the U-2 Program*, 205–6.

8. "Special National Intelligence Estimate," Washington, September 19, 1962, *FRUS*, 1961–1963, vol. 10, *Cuba, January 1961–September 1962*, no. 433, https://history.state.gov/historicaldocuments/frus1961-63v10/d433.

9. "Special National Intelligence Estimate," Washington, September 19, 1962.

10. "R. Malinovsky and M. Zakharov, 'Memorandum on Deployment of Soviet Forces to Cuba, 24 May 1962,'" in Garthoff, "New Evidence on the Cuban Missile Crisis," 254–55; "Timetable of Soviet Military Buildup in Cuba, July–October 1962," in *CIA Documents on the Cuban Missile Crisis, 1962*, 7.

11. E. N. Evdokimov, "Karibskii krizis. Operatsiia Anadyr'," Sait veteranov GSVSK, http://www.gsvsk.ru/content/0/read103.html.

12. "Tokarenko, Mikhail Kuz'mich," *Geroi strany*, http://www.warheroes.ru/hero/hero.asp?Hero_id=6786; Anatolii Dmitriev, *Voenno-strategicheskaia operatsiia Anadyr' polveka spustia v vospominaniiakh ee uchastnikov* (Bishkek, 2014), pt. 2, 47.

13. Ivan Sidorov, "Vypolniaia internatsional'nyi dolg," in *Strategicheskaia operatsiia "Anadyr'." Kak èto bylo*. Memuarno-spravochnoe izdanie, ed. V. I. Esin (Moscow, 2000), 125–33, here 127; Statsenko, "Doklad komandira 51-i raketnoi divizii o deistviiakh soedineniia v period s 12 iiulia po 1 dekabria 1962 goda na o. Kuba."

14. Sidorov, "Vypolniaia internatsional'nyi dolg," 127; A. I. Gribkov, "Razrabotka zamysla i osushchestvlenie operatsii 'Anadyr'," in *Strategicheskaia operatsiia "Anadyr'*," 26–53, here 41.

15. Statsenko, "Doklad komandira 51-i raketnoi divizii."

16. "Memorandum from R. Malinovsky and M. Zakharov to Commander of Group of Soviet Forces in Cuba, 8 September 1962," in "New Evidence on Tactical Nuclear Weapons - 59 Days in Cuba," document no. 6, National Security Archive Electronic Briefing Book No. 449, document no. 5, https://nsarchive2.gwu .edu/NSAEBB/NSAEBB449/docs/; V. I. Esin, "Uchastie raketnykh voisk stra-tegicheskogo naznacheniia v operatsii 'Anadyr'," in *Strategicheskaia operatsiia "Anadyr'*," 55–64, here 61.

17. Statsenko, "Doklad komandira 51-i raketnoi divizii."

18. Sidorov, "Vypolniaia internatsional'nyi dolg," 128.

19. Gribkov, "Razrabotka zamysla," 41.

20. Sidorov, "Vypolniaia internatsional'nyi dolg," 131.

21. Fursenko and Naftali, *"One Hell of a Gamble,"* 217.

22. Robarge, *John McCone,* 107.

23. Robarge, *John McCone,* 107; Servando Gonzalez, *The Nuclear Deception: Nikita Khrushchev and the Cuban Missile Crisis* (Oakland, CA, 2002), 139.

24. "October 1962 - President Kennedy's Schedule," *History Central,* https://www .historycentral.com/JFK/Calendar/October1962.html; Pedlow and Welzen-bach, *The CIA and the U-2 Program,* 205–7.

25. "14 October 1962," in *This Day in Aviation. Important Dates in Aviation History,* https://www.thisdayinaviation.com/tag/4080th-strategic-reconnaissance -wing/; *Dino Brugioni's "Eyeball to Eyeball: The Inside Story of The Cuban Missile Crisis,"* ed. Robert F. McCort (New York, 1991), 182; Fursenko and Naftali, *"One Hell of a Gamble,"* 221–22.

11. "Wipe Them Out"

1. Peter Braestrup, "Colorful Ceremony Greets Ben Bella at the White House," *New York Times,* October 15, 1962, 1, 3; "White House Residents Watch Welcome for Ben Bella," *New York Times,* October 15, 1962, 3.

2. Warren W. Unna, "Kennedy-Ben Bella Talk Is 'Fine'," *Washington Post,* October 16, 1962, A1; Jeffrey James Byrne, "Our Own Special Brand of Socialism: Algeria and the Contest of Modernities in the 1960s," *Diplomatic History* 33, no. 3 (June 2009): 427–47; Fursenko and Naftali, *"One Hell of a Gamble,"* 221–22.

3. Tom Wicker, "Eisenhower Calls President Weak on Foreign Policy," *New York Times,* October 16, 1962, 1, 30.

4. Wicker, "Eisenhower Calls President Weak on Foreign Policy."

5. Reeves, *President Kennedy,* 368.

6. Dobbs, *One Minute to Midnight,* 6; Taubman, *Khrushchev,* 556; "Informal

Communication from Chairman Khrushchev to President Kennedy, Moscow, September 4, 1962," https://history.state.gov/historicaldocuments/frus1961 -63v06/d53; "John F. Kennedy, Joint Statement with Prime Minister Macmillan on Nuclear Testing. August 27, 1962," http://www.presidency.ucsb.edu/ws/index.php?pid=8834; Ted (Theodore) Sorensen, "Memorandum for the Files, September 6, 1962," https://history.state.gov/historicaldocuments/frus1961-63v10/d415; Anatoly Dobrynin, *In Confidence. Moscow's Ambassador to America's Six Cold War Presidents (1962–1986)* (New York, 1995), 67–68.

7. Kenneth P. O'Donnell and David F. Powers with Joe McCarthy, *"Johnny, We Hardly Knew Ye!" Memories of John Fitzgerald Kennedy* (New York, 1976), 359.

8. "Meeting on the Cuban Missile Crisis, 11:50 A.M.," *The Kennedy Tapes*, 32–72; Robarge, *John McCone as Director of Central Intelligence*, 110.

9. "Meeting on the Cuban Missile Crisis, 11:50 A.M.," 32–33; Bruce Lambert, "Arthur Lundahl, 77, C.I.A. Aide Who Found Missile Sites in Cuba," *New York Times*, June 26, 1992; interview with Dino Brugioni, "Oral Histories of the Cuban Missile Crisis," George Washington University National Security Archive (1998), https://web.archive.org/web/20071010134841/; http://www.gwu.edu/~nsarchiv/coldwar/interviews/episode-10/brugioni1.html.

10. "Meeting on the Cuban Missile Crisis, 11:50 A.M.," 32–35; "Hon. Sidney N. Graybeal," Smithsonian National Air and Space Museum, https://airandspace.si.edu/support/wall-of-honor/hon-sidney-n-graybeal.

11. "Meeting on the Cuban Missile Crisis, 11:50 A.M.," 36–38.

12. "Meeting on the Cuban Missile Crisis, 11:50 A.M.," 44–45.

13. Kempe, *Berlin 1961*, 256. Cf. Reeves, *President Kennedy*, 172.

14. "Meeting on the Cuban Missile Crisis, 11:50 A.M.," 47.

15. "Meeting on the Cuban Missile Crisis, 11:50 A.M.," 50; Sheldon M. Stern, *The Week the World Stood Still: Inside the Secret Cuban Missile Crisis* (Stanford, CA, 2005), 43–44.

16. "Meeting on the Cuban Missile Crisis, 11:50 A.M.," 53; "Crown Prince of Libya Starts Washington Visit," *New York Times*, October 17, 1962, 22.

17. Graham T. Allison, *Essence of Decision: Explaining the Cuban Missile Crisis* (New York, 1991), 202; Ernest R. May and Philip D. Zelikow, Commentary in *The Kennedy Tapes*, 53–54.

18. "Meeting on the Cuban Missile Crisis, 6:30 P.M.," in *The Kennedy Tapes*, 60–62; "Maxwell Davenport Taylor, 1 October 1962–1 July 1964," in *The Chairmanship of the Joint Chiefs of Staff, 1949–2012* (Washington, DC, 2012), 107–12.

19. "Meeting on the Cuban Missile Crisis, 6:30 P.M.," 67.

20. "Meeting on the Cuban Missile Crisis, 11:50 A.M.," 38; "Meeting on the

Cuban Missile Crisis, 6:30 P.M.," 57; Fursenko and Naftali, *"One Hell of a Gamble,"* 226.

21. "Meeting on the Cuban Missile Crisis, 6:30 P.M.," 58.
22. "Meeting on the Cuban Missile Crisis, 6:30 P.M.," 58–60.
23. "Meeting on the Cuban Missile Crisis, 6:30 P.M.," 70–71.
24. "Meeting on the Cuban Missile Crisis, 6:30 P.M.," 62.
25. "Meeting on the Cuban Missile Crisis, 6:30 P.M.," 66.
26. "RFK Notes Taken at First Meeting on Cuba, 10/16/62," 31, Papers of Robert F. Kennedy, Attorney General Papers, Attorney General's Confidential File 6-2-10: Cuba: Executive committee meetings: RFK notes and memos, 1962: October–December (2 of 2 folders). RFKAG-215-012. John F. Kennedy Presidential Library and Museum; Stern, *The Week the World Stood Still*, 53–54.

12. Quarantine

1. Marjorie Hunter, "President Cuts His Trip Short, Flies to Capital," *New York Times*, October 21, 1962, 1; Pierre Salinger, *John Kennedy, Commander in Chief: A Profile in Leadership* (New York, 1997), 116.
2. Salinger, *John Kennedy, Commander in Chief*, 116; Robert Kennedy, *Thirteen Days*, 37.
3. Dobbs, *One Minute to Midnight*, 25–26.
4. "Meeting on the Cuban Missile Crisis, 11:10 A.M., Thursday, October 18, 1962," *The Kennedy Tapes*, 76–77; John A. McCone, "Memorandum for the File," October 19, 1962, *FRUS, 1961–1963*, vol. 11, *Cuban Missile Crisis and Aftermath*, no. 28, https://history.state.gov/historicaldocuments/frus1961-63v11/d28.
5. John A. McCone, "Memorandum for the File," October 17, 1962, *FRUS, 1961–1963*, vol. 11, *Cuban Missile Crisis and Aftermath*, no. 23, https://history.state.gov/historicaldocuments/frus1961-63v11/d23.
6. "Meeting on the Cuban Missile Crisis, 11:10 AM, Thursday, October 18, 1962," *The Kennedy Tapes*, 79–82.
7. "Meeting on the Cuban Missile Crisis, 11:10 A.M., Thursday, October 18, 1962," *The Kennedy Tapes*, 92.
8. Fursenko and Naftali, *"One Hell of a Gamble,"* 229; McCone, "Memorandum for Discussion," October 17, 1962, *FRUS, 1961–1963*, vol. 11, *Cuban Missile Crisis and Aftermath*, no. 26.
9. "Memorandum of Conversation, Subject: Cuba, October 18, 1962," *FRUS, 1961–1963*, vol. 11, *Cuban Missile Crisis and Aftermath*, no. 29, https://history.state.gov/historicaldocuments/frus1961-63v11/d29; Robert Kennedy, *Thirteen Days*, 32–33; Andrei Gromyko, *Memories: From Stalin to Gorbachev*, trans. Harold Shukman (London, 1989), 226–32; Gromyko, *Pamiatnoe*, 528.
10. Dobrynin, *In Confidence*, 77; Fursenko and Naftali, *"One Hell of a Gamble,"* 232.

11. "Meeting on the Cuban Missile Crisis, 11:10 A.M., Thursday, October 18, 1962," *The Kennedy Tapes*, 93; "Kennedy Summarizes a Late-Night Meeting, Thursday, October 18, 1962," *The Kennedy Tapes*, 107–8.

12. "Meeting on the Cuban Missile Crisis, 11:10 AM, Thursday, October 18, 1962," *The Kennedy Tapes*, 84, 86.

13. "Meeting on the Cuban Missile Crisis, 11:10 A.M., Thursday, October 18, 1962," *The Kennedy Tapes*, 86, 88; "Kennedy Summarizes a Late-Night Meeting," 108.

14. "Meeting with the Joint Chiefs of Staff, 9:45 A.M., Friday, October 19, 1962," *The Kennedy Tapes*, 111–12.

15. "Meeting with the Joint Chiefs of Staff," 113–17.

16. Friday, October 19, 1962, JFK Appointment Books, September–October 1962, John F. Kennedy Presidential Library and Museum, https://jfklibrary.libguides.com/ld.php?content_id=26058008; "Meeting with the Joint Chiefs of Staff," 123.

17. "Meeting on the Cuban Missile Crisis, 6:30 P.M., Tuesday, October 16, 1962," 66.

18. Dobbs, *One Minute to Midnight*, 31.

19. "National Security Council Meeting, 2:30 PM, October 20, 1962," *The Kennedy Tapes*, 126–27.

20. Stern, *The Week the World Stood Still*, 72–74.

21. "National Security Council Meeting, 2:30 PM, October 20, 1962," *The Kennedy Tapes*, 126–27; Dobbs, *One Minute to Midnight*, 31.

22. "National Security Council Meeting, 2:30 PM, October 20, 1962," *The Kennedy Tapes*, 134.

23. "Conversation with Dwight Eisenhower, 10:40 a.m., October 22, 1962," *The Kennedy Tapes*, 142–46; "October 22, 1962: President Kennedy and Former President Eisenhower Discuss the Cuban Missile Crisis," Miller Center, University of Virginia, https://vimeo.com/237227689.

24. "Tentative Agenda for off-the-record NSC meeting, October 21, 1962, 2:30 pm," in Papers of Robert F. Kennedy, Attorney General Papers, Attorney General's Confidential File. 6-2-4: Cuba: Executive committee meetings: RFK notes and memos, October 22, 1962, RFKAG-215-005, John F. Kennedy Presidential Library and Museum; John F. Kennedy, "Radio and Television Report to the American People on the Soviet Arms Buildup in Cuba," The White House, October 22, 1962, John F. Kennedy Presidential Library and Museum, https://microsites.jfklibrary.org/cmc/oct22/doc5.html.

13. Moscow Night

1. Fursenko and Naftali, *"One Hell of a Gamble,"* 238–39.

2. "Top Aides Confer. U.S. Forces Maneuver off Puerto Rico—Link Is Denied," *New York Times*, October 22, 1962, 1, 16.

3. "Opasnye i bezotvetstvennye deistviia. Sekretnye soveshchaniia v Vashingtone. Kennedi otmeniaet poezdku po strane. Vblizi Kuby kontsentriruiutsia amerikanskie voiska," *Pravda*, October 23, 1962, 1; "Sosredotochenie amerikanskikh vooruzhennykh sil v Karibskom more," *Pravda*, October 23, 1962, 3.

4. Dobbs, *One Minute to Midnight*, 32; Sergo Mikoyan, *The Soviet Cuban Missile Crisis*, 156; Sergo Mikoian, *Anatomiia Karibskogo krizisa* (Moscow, 2006), 252, https://history.wikireading.ru/326580.

5. "Central Committee of the Communist Party of the Soviet Union Presidium Protocol 60," October 23, 1962, History and Public Policy Program Digital Archive, RGANI, f. 3, op. 16, d. 947, l. 36–41, trans. and ed. Mark Kramer, with assistance from Timothy Naftali, https://digitalarchive.wilsoncenter .org/document/115076; Anastas Mikoian, "Diktovka o poezdke na Kubu," January 19, 1963, in Aleksandr Lukashin and Mariia Aleksashina, "My voobshche ne khotim nikuda brosat' rakety, my za mir . . . ," *Rodina*, January 1, 2017, https://rg.ru/2017/04/24/rodina-karibskij-krizis.html.

6. Anastas Mikoian, "Diktovka o poezdke na Kubu," January 19, 1963; Sergo Mikoyan, *The Soviet Cuban Missile Crisis*, 156. Cf. Sergo Mikoian, *Anatomiia Karibskogo krizisa*, 252.

7. "Central Committee of the Communist Party of the Soviet Union Presidium Protocol 60," October 23, 1962.

8. "Central Committee of the Communist Party of the Soviet Union Presidium Protocol 60," October 23, 1962; cf. *Prezidium TsK KPSS, 1954–1964*, ed. Aleksandr Fursenko (Moscow, 2003), vol. 1, protocol no. 60, 617.

9. Sergo Mikoyan, *The Soviet Cuban Missile Crisis*, 148.

10. Anastas Mikoian, "Diktovka o poezdke na Kubu," January 19, 1963; Sergo Mikoyan, *The Soviet Cuban Missile Crisis*, 157; cf. Sergo Mikoian, *Anatomiia Karibskogo krizisa*, 252.

11. "Central Committee of the Communist Party of the Soviet Union Presidium Protocol 60," October 23, 1962; cf. *Prezidium TsK KPSS, 1954–1964*, ed. Aleksandr Fursenko (Moscow, 2003), vol. 1, protocol no. 60, 617.

12. Dobbs, *One Minute to Midnight*, 112.

13. Dobrynin, *In Confidence*, 78; "Letter from President Kennedy to Chairman Khrushchev," *FRUS*, 1961–1963, vol. 6, *Kennedy-Khrushchev Exchanges*, no. 60, https://history.state.gov/historicaldocuments/frus1961-63v06/d60.

14. Dean Rusk and Richard Rusk, *As I Saw It* (New York, 1990), 235; "Telegram from Soviet Ambassador to the USA Dobrynin to the USSR MFA," October 22, 1962, History and Public Policy Program Digital Archive, AVP RF, copy courtesy of NSA, trans. Vladislav M. Zubok, https://digitalarchive .wilsoncenter.org/document/111791.

15. Dobbs, *One Minute to Midnight*, 42; Anastas Mikoian, "Diktovka o poezdke

na Kubu," January 19, 1963; Sergo Mikoian, *Anatomiia Karibskogo krizisa*, 252.

16. "Central Committee of the Communist Party of the Soviet Union Presidium Protocol 60," October 23, 1962; cf. *Prezidium TsK KPSS, 1954–1964*, ed. Aleksandr Fursenko (Moscow, 2003), vol. 1, protocol no. 60, 617; Anastas Mikoian, "Diktovka o poezdke na Kubu," January 19, 1963; *Khrushchev Remembers*, 497; Dobbs, *One Minute to Midnight*, 45.

17. "Telegram from TROSTNIK (Soviet Defense Minister Rodion Malinovsky) to PAVLOV (General Issa Pliev)," October 22, 1962, History and Public Policy Program Digital Archive, Archive of the President of the Russian Federation, Special Declassification, April 2002, trans. Svetlana Savranskaya, https://digitalarchive.wilsoncenter.org/document/117316; "Telegram from TROSTNIK (Soviet Defense Minister Rodion Malinovsky) to PAVLOV (General Issa Pliev)," October 23, 1962, History and Public Policy Program Digital Archive, Archive of the President of the Russian Federation, Special Declassification, April 2002, trans. Svetlana Savranskaya, https://digitalarchive.wilsoncenter.org/document/117323.

18. Anastas Mikoian, "Diktovka o poezdke na Kubu," January 19, 1963, https://rg.ru/2017/04/24/rodina-karibskij-krizis.html; "Central Committee of the Communist Party of the Soviet Union Presidium Protocol 60," October 23, 1962; cf. *Prezidium TsK KPSS, 1954–1964*, ed. Aleksandr Fursenko (Moscow, 2003), vol. 1, protocol no. 60, 617.

19. "Central Committee of the Communist Party of the Soviet Union Presidium Protocol 60," October 23, 1962; cf. *Prezidium TsK KPSS, 1954–1964*, ed. Aleksandr Fursenko (Moscow, 2003), vol. 1, protocol no. 60, 617.

20. Anastas Mikoian, "Diktovka o poezdke na Kubu," January 19, 1963, https://rg.ru/2017/04/24/rodina-karibskij-krizis.html.

21. "Central Committee of the Communist Party of the Soviet Union Presidium Protocol 60," October 23, 1962; "Telegram from the Embassy in the Soviet Union to the Department of State Moscow," October 23, 1962, 5 p.m., *FRUS*, 1961–1963, vol. 6, *Kennedy-Khrushchev Exchanges*, no. 61, https://history.state.gov/historicaldocuments/frus1961-63v06/d61.

14. Blinking in the Dark

1. Robert Kennedy, "Memorandum for the President from the Attorney General," October 24, 1962, in John F. Kennedy Presidential Library and Museum, Papers of Robert F. Kennedy, Attorney General Papers, Attorney General's Confidential File 6-4-1: Cuba: Cuban Crisis, 1962: *Kennedy-Khrushchev Letters*, 1962: September–November, 34–37, 54–57; cf. Robert Kennedy, *Thirteen Days*, 50–51; "Telegram from Soviet Ambassador to the USA Dobrynin to the

USSR MFA," October 24, 1962, History and Public Policy Program Digital Archive, AVP RF, copy courtesy of NSA; transl. Mark H. Doctoroff, https:// digitalarchive.wilsoncenter.org/document/111625. Cf. Dobrynin, *In Confidence*, 74, 81–82.

2. Robert Kennedy, *Thirteen Days*, 45–46; "Executive Committee Meeting of the National Security Council, Tuesday, October 23, 1962, 10:00 A.M.," *The Kennedy Tapes*, 195–96.

3. "Executive Committee Meeting of the National Security Council, Tuesday, October 23, 1962, 10:00 A.M.," *The Kennedy Tapes*, 194–95, 202.

4. Robert Kennedy, *Thirteen Days*, 46–47; "Executive Committee Meeting of the National Security Council, Tuesday, October 23, 1962, 10:00 A.M.," *The Kennedy Tapes*, 196–204.

5. Robert Kennedy, *Thirteen Days*, 45; "Executive Committee Meeting of the National Security Council, Tuesday, October 23, 1962, 6:00 P.M.," *The Kennedy Tapes*, 207.

6. "Executive Committee Meeting of the National Security Council, Tuesday, October 23, 1962, 6:00 P.M.," *The Kennedy Tapes*, 208–13.

7. Executive Committee Meeting of the National Security Council, Tuesday, October 23, 1962, 6:00 P.M., 208–14; "Telegram from the Department of State to the Embassy in the Soviet Union," Washington, October 23, 1962, 6:51 p.m., in *FRUS, 1961–1963*, vol. 6, *Kennedy-Khrushchev Exchanges*, no. 62, https://history.state.gov/historicaldocuments/frus1961-63v06/d62.

8. "Executive Committee Meeting of the National Security Council, Tuesday, October 23, 1962, 6:00 P.M.," *The Kennedy Tapes*, 213–16; Robert Kennedy, *Thirteen Days*, 47–48.

9. "Discussion between President Kennedy and Robert Kennedy, Tuesday, October 23, 1962, 7:10 P.M.," *The Kennedy Tapes*, 219–21.

10. Robert Kennedy, *Thirteen Days*, 49. Cf. Robert Kennedy, "Draft, 10.24.62," 1962, in John F. Kennedy Presidential Library and Museum, Papers of Robert F. Kennedy, Attorney General Papers, Attorney General's Confidential File 6-4-1: Cuba: Cuban Crisis, 1962: *Kennedy-Khrushchev Letters*, 1962: September–November, 53.

11. Raport, Starshii upolnomochennyi 2ogo otdela KGB pri SM Azerbaidzhanskoi SSR maior Badalov nachal'niku upravleniia KGB USSR po Odesskoi oblasti general-maioru tov. Kuvarzinu A. I., Odessa, 31 oktiabria 1962 g., 5 pp, here 1–2, in SBU Archives, fond 1, opys 1, no. 1532: KGB USSR, 7-i otdel, 2-go upravleniia, Kontrol'no nabliudatel'noe delo no. 702. Po Azovsko-Chernomorskomu basseinu, vol. 8, January 1, 1962– December 31, 1962, fols. 332–36.

12. Raport, Starshii upolnomochennyi apparata upolnomochennogo UKGB pri SM UkSSR po Donetskoi oblasti maior Protasov nachal'niku upravleniia

KGB USSR po Odesskoi oblasti general-maioru tov. Kuvarzinu A. I., Odessa, 25 noiabria, 1962 g., 13 pp., here 4–5, in SBU Archives, fond 1, opys 1, no. 1532, fols. 339–50.

13. Fursenko and Naftali, *"One Hell of a Gamble,"* 247, 254–55. On Soviet plans for the departure of the *Aleksandrovsk, Indigirka,* and other ships, see "Report from General Zakharov and Admiral Fokin to the Defense Council and Premier Khrushchev on Initial Plans for Soviet Navy Activities in Support of Operation Anadyr, September 18, 1962," in "The Submarines of October: U.S. and Soviet Naval Encounters During the Cuban Missile Crisis," in *National Security Archive Electronic Briefing Book* No. 75, ed. William Burr and Thomas S. Blanton, October 31, 2002, https://nsarchive2.gwu .edu/NSAEBB/NSAEBB75/asw-I-1.pdf; "Report from General Zakharov and Admiral Fokin to the Presidium, Central Committee, Communist Party of the Soviet Union, September 25, 1962," in "The Submarines of October: U.S. and Soviet Naval Encounters During the Cuban Missile Crisis," https:// nsarchive2.gwu.edu/NSAEBB/NSAEBB75/asw-I-2.pdf; "Telegram from the Department of State to the Embassy in the Soviet Union," October 23, 1962.

14. "Executive Committee Meeting of the National Security Council, Wednesday, October 24, 1962, 10:00 A.M.," *The Kennedy Tapes,* 227.

15. "Raport, Starshii upolnomochennyi 2-go otdela UKGB pri SM USSR po Kirovogradskoi oblasti kapitan Gnida nachal'niku upravleniia KGB USSR po Odesskoi oblasti general-maioru tov. Kuvarzinu A. I., Odessa, 14 noiabria 1962 g.," 8 pp., here 4–5, in SBU Archives, fond 1, opys 1, no. 1532, fols. 325–30.

16. Aleksandr Rogozin, "Sovetskii flot v voinakh i konfliktakh kholodnoi voiny," chap. 2: "SSSR v stroitel'stve VMS Kuby," http://alerozin.narod.ru/CubaNavy/ CubaNavySoviet-2.htm.

17. "Executive Committee Meeting of the National Security Council, Wednesday, October 24, 1962, 10:00 A.M.," *The Kennedy Tapes,* 227–30.

18. Robert F. Kennedy, "Notes Taken at Meetings on the Cuban Crisis. Found at Home on October 30, 1962," Papers of Robert F. Kennedy, Attorney General Papers, Attorney General's Confidential File 6-2-10: Cuba: Executive committee meetings: RFK notes and memos, 1962: October–December (2 of 2 folders), RFKAG-215-012, John F. Kennedy Presidential Library and Museum; "Executive Committee Meeting of the National Security Council, Wednesday, October 24, 1962, 10:00 A.M.," *The Kennedy Tapes,* 230–31; Robert Kennedy, *Thirteen Days,* 54.

19. Robert Kennedy, *Thirteen Days,* 53–54.

20. "Executive Committee Meeting of the National Security Council, Wednesday, October 24, 1962, 10:00 A.M.," *The Kennedy Tapes,* 231–33.

21. Dobbs, *One Minute to Midnight*, 88–89.

22. Kapitan Gnida, "Raport," November 14, 1962, 4–5, fols. 325–30 [4719–24].

23. Arkadii Khasin, "Kapitan Golubenko," *Vecherniaia Odessa*, February 24, 2015, http://vo.od.ua/rubrics/odessa-gody-i-sudby/32520.php.

15. Wooden Knife

1. Ion Mihai Pacepa, *Programmed to Kill: Lee Harvey Oswald, the Soviet KGB and the Kennedy Assassination* (Lanham, MD, 2007), 184–85.

2. Khrushchev, *Vremia, liudi, vlast'*, 2: 518; Gromyko, *Pamiatnoe*, 489.

3. "V Bol'shom teatre SSSR," *Pravda*, October 24, 1962, 2; David G. Winter, "Khrushchev Visits the Bolshoi: [More Than] a Footnote to the Cuban Missile Crisis, Peace and Conflict," *Journal of Peace Psychology* 19 (2013), no. 3: 222–39.

4. Pacepa, *Programmed to Kill*, 185; Liu Yong, "Romania and Sino-Soviet Relations Moving Towards Split, 1960–1965," *Arhivele Totalitarismului* 22 (2014), nos. 82/83: 65–80.

5. G. M. Kornienko, *Kholodnaia voina. Svidetel'stvo ee uchastnika* (Moscow, 2001), 124; Dobrynin, *In Confidence*, 83.

6. Pacepa, *Programmed to Kill*, 185; "Rumynskaia pravitel'stvennaia delegatsiia otbyla na rodinu," *Izvestiia*, October 25, 1962, 1; *Pravda*, October 25, 1962, 2.

7. "Priem N. S. Khrushchevym Vil'iama E. Noksa," *Pravda*, October 25, 1.

8. Memorandum from Roger Hilsman to Rusk, October 26; Khrushchev's conversation with W. E. Knox, President of Westinghouse Electrical International, in Moscow on October 24. Secret. 2 pp. Kennedy Library, NSF, Cuba, General, vol. 6(A), 10/26–27/62, *FRUS, 1961–1963, American Republics; Cuba 1961–1962; Cuban Missile Crisis and Aftermath*, vols. 10/11/12, Microfiche Supplement, no. 419, https://history.state.gov/historicaldocuments/frus1961-63v10-12mSupp/d419; Dobbs, *One Minute to Midnight*, 85.

9. "Letter from Chairman Khrushchev to President Kennedy, Moscow, October 24, 1962," *FRUS, 1961–1963*, vol. 6, *Kennedy-Khrushchev Exchanges*, no. 63, https://history.state.gov/historicaldocuments/frus1961-63v06/d63; Fursenko and Naftali, *"One Hell of a Gamble,"* 254–55.

10. Georgii Bol'shakov, "Goriachaia liniia: Kak deistvoval sekretnyi kanal sviazi Dzhon Kennedi-Nikita Khrushchev," *Novoe vremia*, 1989, nos. 4–6; Georgii Bol'shakov, "Karibskii krizis: Kak èto bylo," *Komsomol'skaia pravda*, February 4, 1989, 3; Fursenko and Naftali, *"One Hell of a Gamble,"* 109–14, 197; Taubman, *Khrushchev*, 556.

11. "Proekt Postanovleniia TsK KPSS o konfidentsial'nom poslanii N. S. Khrushcheva prezidentu SShA Dzhonu Kennedi," October 25, 1962, Arkhiv prezidenta Rossiiskoi Federatsii, fond 3, op. 65, no. 904, fols. 131–40, in Rossiiskii

gosudarstvennyi arkhiv sotsial'no-politicheskoi istorii, "Khrushchev. K 120-letiiu so dnia rozhdeniia," http://liders.rusarchives.ru/hruschev/docs/proekt-postanovleniya-tsk-kpss-o-konfidentsialnom-poslanii-ns-khrushcheva-prezidentu-ssha-dzhon.

12. Nikolai Dorizo, "Solntse prorvet blokadu," *Izvestiia*, October 25, 1962, 1.

13. Telegram from the Department of State to the Embassy in the Soviet Union, Washington, October 25, 1962, 1:59 a.m., *FRUS*, 1961–1963, vol. 6, *Kennedy-Khrushchev Exchanges*, no. 64, https://history.state.gov/historicaldocuments/frus1961-63v06/d64.

14. Dobbs, *One Minute to Midnight*, 94–95.

15. Scott D. Sagan, *The Limits of Safety: Organizations, Accidents, and Nuclear Weapons* (Princeton, NJ, 1993), 68–69.

16. Kornienko, *Kholodnaia voina*, 129; Fursenko and Naftali, *"One Hell of a Gamble,"* 262; cf. Fursenko and Naftali, *Adskaia igra*, 386; Ladygin and Lota, *GRU i Karibskii krizis*, 112–13.

17. Sagan, *The Limits of Safety*, 67.

18. "Central Committee of the Communist Party of the Soviet Union Presidium Protocol 61," October 25, 1962; The Diary of Anatoly S. Chernyaev, 1976. Donated by A.S. Chernyaev to The National Security Archive. Translated by Anna Melyakova, 2, https://nsarchive2.gwu.edu//NSAEBB/NSAEBB550-Chernyaev-Diary-1976-gives-close-up-view-of-Soviet-system/Anatoly%20Chernyaev%20Diary,%201976.pdf; *Prezidium TsK KPSS, 1954–1964: Chernovye protokol'nye zapisi zasedanii. Stenogrammy* (Moscow, 2004), 621.

19. "Telegram from TROSTNIK (Soviet Defense Minister Rodion Malinovsky) to PAVLOV (General Issa Pliev)," October 25, 1962, History and Public Policy Program Digital Archive, Archive of the President of the Russian Federation, Special Declassification, April 2002. Trans. Svetlana Savranskaya, https://digitalarchive.wilsoncenter.org/document/117324.

20. "Excerpts from Debate on Cuba in the Security Council. Valerian A. Zorin, Soviet Union," *New York Times*, October 26, 1962, 16.

21. "Excerpts from Debate on Cuba in the Security Council. Stevenson-Zorin Exchange," *New York Times*, October 26, 1962, 16; Porter McKeever, *Adlai Stevenson: His Life and Legacy* (New York, 1989), 527.

22. Arnold H. Lubasch, "Stevenson Dares Russian to Deny Missiles Charge: Khrushchev Indicates Support for a Meeting with Kennedy," photo caption: "Stevenson Shows Photos of Cuban Bases," *New York Times*, October 26, 1962, 1; "Telegram from the Soviet Representative to the United Nations, Valerian Zorin, to the USSR MFA," October 25, 1962, History and Public Policy Program Digital Archive, AVP RF, copy courtesy of NSA, trans. Mark H. Doctoroff, http://digitalarchive.wilsoncenter.org/document/111833; Reeves, *President Kennedy*, 406.

16. The Americans Are Coming!

1. "Cable from Soviet Ambassador to the US Dobrynin to USSR Foreign Ministry (1)," October 25, 1962, History and Public Policy Program Digital Archive, Archive of Foreign Policy, Russian Federation (AVP RF), Moscow; copy obtained by NHK (Japanese Television), provided to CWIHP, and on file at National Security Archive, Washington, DC, trans. Vladimir Zaemsky, https://digitalarchive.wilsoncenter.org/document/111918; Fursenko and Naftali, *"One Hell of a Gamble,"* 257–61.

2. Kornienko, *Kholodnaia voina,* 129.

3. Telegram from the Embassy in the Soviet Union to the Department of State, Moscow, October 26, 1962, 7 p.m., *FRUS,* 1961–1963, vol. 6, *Kennedy-Khrushchev Exchanges,* n. 65, https://history.state.gov/historicaldocuments/frus1961-63v06/d65.

4. Telegram from the Embassy in the Soviet Union to the Department of State, Moscow, October 26, 1962.

5. Acosta, *October 1962,* 157–61; "Fidel Castro's 23 October Interview, Havana ,in Spanish to the Americas 0135 GMT 24 October 1962," Castro Speech Data Base, LANIC: Latin American Information Center, http://lanic.utexas.edu/project/castro/db/1962/19621024.html.

6. "Shifrotelegramma ot Alekseeva iz Gavanny o besede s Fidelem Kastro i Dortikosom," October 26, 1962, National Security Archive. George Washington University, Rosiiskie programmy Arkhiva natsional'noi bezopasnosti, Karibskii krizis: dokumenty, https://nsarchive2.gwu.edu/rus/CubanMissileCrisis.html; https://nsarchive2.gwu.edu/rus/text_files/CMCrisis/22.PDF; Fursenko and Naftali, *"One Hell of a Gamble,"* 268.

7. "Cable no. 323 from the Czechoslovak Embassy in Havana (Pavlíček)," October 25, 1962, History and Public Policy Program Digital Archive, National Archive, Archive of the CC CPCz (Prague), File: "Antonín Novotný, Kuba," Box 122, https://digitalarchive.wilsoncenter.org/document/115197; "Telegram from the Brazilian Embassy in Havana (Bastian Pinto), 6 p.m., Friday, October 26, 1962," History and Public Policy Program Digital Archive, "ANEXO Secreto—600.(24h)—SITUAÇÃO POLITICA—OUTUBRO DE 1962//," Ministry of External Relations Archives, Brasilia, Brazil, trans. from Portuguese by James G. Hershberg, https://digitalarchive.wilsoncenter.org/document/115303.

8. Fursenko and Naftali, *"One Hell of a Gamble,"* 268; Dobbs, *One Minute to Midnight,* 157; Jonathan Colman, *Cuban Missile Crisis: Origins, Course and Aftermath* (Edinburgh, 2016), 153.

9. Acosta, *October 1962,* 170–71; Fursenko and Naftali, *"One Hell of a Gamble,"* 268–69.

10. "Ciphered Telegram from Soviet Ambassador to Cuba Aleksandr Alekseev," October 27, 1962, History and Public Policy Program Digital Archive, obtained and translated by National Security Archive for the October 2002 conference in Havana on the 40th Anniversary of the Cuban Missile Crisis, https://digitalarchive.wilsoncenter.org/document/115063; "Interview with Alexander Alekseyev [Soviet Ambassador to Cuba]," in "Interviews with Soviet Veterans of the Cuban Missile Crisis," "Mikoyan's "Mission Impossible," in *Cuba: New Soviet Evidence on the Cuban Missile Crisis*, National Security Archive Electronic Briefing Book No. 400, eds. Svetlana Savranskaya, Anna Melyakova, and Amanda Conrad, https://nsarchive2.gwu.edu//NSAEBB/NSAEBB400/docs/Interview%20with%20Alekseev.pdf, 16; Fursenko and Naftali, *"One Hell of a Gamble,"* 272.

11. "Telegram from Fidel Castro to N. S. Khrushchev," October 26, 1962, History and Public Policy Program Digital Archive, Archive of Foreign Policy, Russian Federation (AVP RF), https://digitalarchive.wilsoncenter.org/document/114501.

12. "Interview with Alexander Alekseyev [Soviet Ambassador to Cuba]," 17; "Ciphered Telegram from Soviet Ambassador to Cuba Aleksandr Alekseev," October 27, 1962, History and Public Policy Program Digital Archive, obtained and translated by National Security Archive for the October 2002 conference in Havana on the 40th Anniversary of the Cuban Missile Crisis, https://digitalarchive.wilsoncenter.org/document/115063; Fursenko and Naftali, *"One Hell of a Gamble,"* 273.

13. "Telegramma t. Pavlova iz Gavanny ot 26 oktiabria 1962 g.," in "Vypiska iz protokola no. 62 zasedaniia Prezidiuma TsK KPSS ot 27 oktiabria 1962 goda," National Security Archive. George Washington University, Rossiiskie programmy Arkhiva natsional'noi bezopasnosti, Karibskii krizis: Dokumenty, https://nsarchive2.gwu.edu/rus/CubanMissileCrisis.html; Direktivy Prezidiuma TsK KPSS Plievu v otvet na ego shriftotelegrammu, https://nsarchive2.gwu.edu/rus/text_files/CMCrisis/23.PDF; cf. S Ia. Lavrenov and I. M. Popov, *Sovetskii Soiuz v lokal'nykh voinakh i konfliktakh* (Moscow, 2003), 258.

14. "Telegram from TROSTNIK (Soviet Defense Minister Rodion Malinovsky) to PAVLOV (General Issa Pliev)," October 27, 1962, History and Public Policy Program Digital Archive, Archive of the President of the Russian Federation, Special Declassification, April 2002, trans. Svetlana Savranskaya, https://digitalarchive.wilsoncenter.org/document/117326; "Telegram from TROSTNIK (Soviet Defense Minister Rodion Malinovsky) to PAVLOV (General Issa Pliev)," October 27, 1962, History and Public Policy Program Digital Archive, Archive of the President of the Russian Federation, Special Declassification, April 2002, trans. Svetlana Savranskaya, https://digitalarchive.wilsoncenter

.org/document/117325; "Telegram from TROSTNIK (Soviet Defense Minister Rodion Malinovsky) to PAVLOV (General Issa Pliev)," October 27, 1962, History and Public Policy Program Digital Archive, Archive of the President of the Russian Federation, Special Declassification, April 2002, trans. Svetlana Savranskaya, https://digitalarchive.wilsoncenter.org/document/117327.

15. "Central Committee of the Communist Party of the Soviet Union Presidium Protocol 62," October 27, 1962, History and Public Policy Program Digital Archive, RGANI, F. 3, Op. 16, D. 947, L. 43-44, trans. and ed. Mark Kramer, with assistance from Timothy Naftali, https://digitalarchive.wilsoncenter.org/document/115085.

16. "Central Committee of the Communist Party of the Soviet Union Presidium Protocol 62," October 27, 1962; "Telegramma t. Pavlova iz Gavanny ot 26 oktiabria 1962 g.," https://nsarchive2.gwu.edu/rus/text_files/CMCrisis/23 .PDF; "Memorandum of Conversation between Castro and Mikoyan," November 4, 1962, History and Public Policy Program Digital Archive, Russian Foreign Ministry archives, obtained and translated by NHK television, copy provided by Philip Brenner; trans. Aleksandr Zaemsky, slightly revised, https://digitalarchive.wilsoncenter.org/document/110961.

17. "Memorandum of Conversation between Castro and Mikoyan," November 4, 1962, History and Public Policy Program Digital Archive, Russian Foreign Ministry archives, obtained and translated by NHK television, copy provided by Philip Brenner; trans. Aleksandr Zaemsky, slightly revised, https:// digitalarchive.wilsoncenter.org/document/110961.

18. Letter from Chairman Khrushchev to President Kennedy, Moscow, October 27, 1962, *FRUS*, 1961–1963, vol. 6, *Kennedy-Khrushchev Exchanges*, no. 66, https://history.state.gov/historicaldocuments/frus1961-63v06/d66.

19. "Central Committee of the Communist Party of the Soviet Union Presidium Protocol 62," October 27, 1962.

17. Turkish Quagmire

1. "Executive Committee Meeting of the National Security Council, Saturday, October 27, 1962, 10:05 a.m.," *The Kennedy Tapes*, 303.

2. Leaming, *Jack Kennedy*, 402–4.

3. "Executive Committee Meeting of the National Security Council, Saturday, October 27, 1962, 10:05 a.m.," *The Kennedy Tapes*, 306.

4. "Meeting on the Cuban Missile Crisis, Tuesday, October 16, 1962, 11:50 a.m.," *The Kennedy Tapes*, 41–42.

5. Philip Nash, *The Other Missiles of October: Eisenhower, Kennedy, and the Jupiters, 1957–1963* (Chapel Hill, NC, 1997), 5–90.

6. "Meeting on the Cuban Missile Crisis, Tuesday, October 16, 1962, 6:30 p.m.," *The Kennedy Tapes*, 67.

7. "Meeting on the Cuban Missile Crisis," Thursday, October 18, 1962, 11:10 a.m.," *The Kennedy Tapes*, 95.

8. "Meeting on Diplomatic Plans, Monday, October 22, 1962, 11:00 a.m.," *The Kennedy Tapes*, 147–48.

9. Stern, *The Week the World Stood Still*, 78–79; Ernest R. May and Philip D. Zelikow, "Editorial Notes," *The Kennedy Tapes*, 140–41.

10. Walter Lippmann, "Today and Tomorrow," *Washington Post*, October 25, 1962; Thomas Risse-Kappen, *Cooperation Among Democracies: The European Influence on U.S. Foreign Policy* (Princeton, NJ, 1995), 165–67; "Cable from Soviet Ambassador to the US Dobrynin to Soviet Foreign Ministry (2)," October 25, 1962, History and Public Policy Program Digital Archive, Archive of Foreign Policy, Russian Federation (AVP RF), Moscow; copy obtained by NHK (Japanese Television), provided to CWIHP, and on file at National Security Archive, Washington, DC, trans. Vladimir Zaemsky, http://digitalarchive .wilsoncenter.org/document/110449; "Memorandum of Conversation between Castro and Mikoyan," November 4, 1962, History and Public Policy Program Digital Archive, Russian Foreign Ministry Archives, obtained and translated by NHK television, copy provided by Philip Brenner, trans. Aleksandr Zaemsky, slightly revised, https://digitalarchive.wilsoncenter.org/ document/110961.

11. "Executive Committee Meeting of the National Security Council, Saturday, October 27, 1962, 10:05 a.m.," *The Kennedy Tapes*, 307.

12. Executive Committee Meeting of the National Security Council, Saturday, October 27, 1962, 10:05 A.M., The Kennedy Tapes, 307–8.

13. Executive Committee Meeting of the National Security Council, Saturday, October 27, 1962, 10:05 A.M., *The Kennedy Tapes*, 308.

14. Executive Committee Meeting of the National Security Council, Saturday, October 27, 1962, 10:05 A.M., *The Kennedy Tapes*, 308–10, 321.

15. Walter S. Poole, *History of the Joint Chiefs of Staff: The Joint Chiefs of Staff and National Policy*, vol. 8: 1961–1964 (Washington, DC, 2011), 180, https://www .jcs.mil/Portals/36/Documents/History/Policy/Policy_Vo08.pdf.

16. "Press Release, Office of the White House Press Secretary, October 27, 1962," in *The Cuban Crisis of 1962: Selected Documents and Chronology*, ed. David L. Larson (Boston, 1963), 158.

18. Losing Control

1. Stephanie Ritter, AFGSC History Office, "SAC during the 13 Days of the Cuban Missile Crisis," Air Force Global Strike Command, October 19, 2012, https://www.afgsc.af.mil/News/Article-Display/Article/454741/sac-during -the-13-days-of-the-cuban-missile-crisis/.

2. "Memorandum from the President's Special Assistant for Science and Technology (Wiesner) to the President's Deputy Special Assistant for National Security Affairs (Kaysen)," Washington, September 25, 1962, Subject: Cuban Blockade Contingency Planning, FRUS, 1961–1963, vol. 10, *Cuba, January 1961–September 1962*, no. 439, https://history.state.gov/historicaldocuments/frus1961-63v10/d439.

3. "Notes from Transcripts of JCS Meetings," October 27, 1962, *FRUS*, 1961–1963, *American Republics*; Cuba 1961–1962; *Cuban Missile Crisis and Aftermath*, vols. 10/11/12, Microfiche Supplement, 21–22, https://static.history.state.gov/frus/frus1961-63v10-12mSupp/pdf/d428.pdf; Poole, *History of the Joint Chiefs of Staff*, 180.

4. Dobbs, *One Minute to Midnight*, 268–70; Robert Dallek, "JFK vs the Military," *The Atlantic*, August 2013, https://www.theatlantic.com/magazine/archive/2013/08/jfk-vs-the-military/309496/.

5. Dobbs, *One Minute to Midnight*, 258–65, 268–72, 288–89; cf. idem, "Lost in Enemy Airspace," *Vanity Fair*, June 1, 2008, https://www.vanityfair.com/news/2008/06/missile_crisis_excerpt200806; Amy Shira Teitel, "How the Aurora Borealis Nearly Started World War III," *Discover*, March 2103, http://blogs.discovermagazine.com/crux/2013/03/11/how-the-aurora-borealis-nearly-started-world-war-iii/#.XCk6zFxKjIV.

6. Nikolai Yakubovich, *Pervye sverkhzvukovye istrebiteli MIG 17 i MIG 19* (Moscow, 2014), 50.

7. David Donald, *Century Jets: USAF Frontline Fighters of the Cold War* (London, 2003), 68–70.

8. Dobbs, *One Minute to Midnight*, 258–65, 268–72, 288–89; cf. idem, "Lost in Enemy Airspace"; Teitel, "How the Aurora Borealis Nearly Started World War III."

9. "Executive Committee Meeting of the National Executive Council, Saturday, October 27, 1962, 4:00 p.m.," *The Kennedy Tapes*, 238, 326, 330, 338, 352.

10. For an earlier draft of Kennedy's letter to Khrushchev, see "The Handwritten Notes on White House Paper. Not Dated," 6–10, Papers of Robert F. Kennedy, Attorney General Papers, Attorney General's Confidential File 6-2-3: Cuba: Executive committee meetings: RFK notes and memos, October 16, 1962, RFKAG-215-004. John F. Kennedy Presidential Library and Museum; "Executive Committee Meeting of the National Executive Council, Saturday, October 27, 1962, 4:00 p.m.," *The Kennedy Tapes*, 348, 350.

11. "Executive Committee Meeting of the National Executive Council," Saturday, October 27, 1962, 4:00 p.m., *The Kennedy Tapes*, 327, 353–56.

12. "Executive Committee Meeting of the National Executive Council," Saturday, October 27, 1962, 4:00 p.m., 356–57.

13. Dobbs, *One Minute to Midnight*, 230–31.

14. "Executive Committee Meeting of the National Executive Council, Saturday, October 27, 1962, 4:00 p.m.," *The Kennedy Tapes*, 356–57.

19. "Target Destroyed"

1. Michael Dobbs, "The Photographs That Prevented World War III," *Smithsonian*, October 2012, https://www.smithsonianmag.com/history/the-photographs-that-prevented-world-war-iii-36910430/; "VFP-62 Operations over Cuba," Light Photographic Squadron 62, http://www.vfp62.com/index.html; William B. Ecker and Kenneth V. Jack, *Blue Moon over Cuba: Aerial Reconnaissance during the Cuban Missile Crisis. General Aviation* (Oxford, 2012).

2. Sergei Isaev, "Kamen' pretknoveniia. 759 mtab na Kube vo vremia Karibskogo krizisa 1962 goda," VVS Rossii: Liudi i samolety, http://www.airforce.ru/content/holodnaya-voina/1552-759-mtab-na-kube-vo-vremya-karibskogo-krizisa-1962-goda/.

3. Leonid Garbuz, "Zamestitel' komanduiushchego gruppy sovetskikh voisk na Kube vspominaet," *Strategicheskaia operatsiia "Anadyr'." Kak éto bylo. Memuarno-spravochnoe izdanie*, ed. V. I. Esin (Moscow, 2000), 80–89, here 84; Dobbs, *One Minute to Midnight*, 238.

4. "Interview with General Leonid Garbuz by Sherry Jones," "Cuban Missile Crisis: What the World Didn't Know," produced by Sherry Jones for Peter Jennings Reporting, ABC News (Washington Media Associates, 1992), in "Mikoyan's 'Mission Impossible' in Cuba: New Soviet Evidence on the Cuban Missile Crisis," National Security Archive Electronic Briefing Book No. 400, October 2012, eds. Svetlana Savranskaya, Anna Melyakova, and Amanda Conrad, https://nsarchive2.gwu.edu/NSAEBB/NSAEBB400/docs/Interview%20with%20General%20Garbuz.pdf; Fursenko and Naftali, *"One Hell of a Gamble,"* 271.

5. "Telegramma t. Pavlova iz Gavanny ot 26 oktiabria 1962 g.," in "Vypiska iz protokola no. 62 zasedaniia Prezidiuma TsK KPSS ot 27 oktiabria 1962 goda," National Security Archive. George Washington University, Rossiiskie programmy Arkhiva natsional'noi bezopasnosti, Karibskii krizis: Dokumenty, https://nsarchive2.gwu.edu/rus/CubanMissileCrisis.html; Anatolii Dokuchaev, "A Kennedi podozreval Khrushcheva . . . ," *Nezavisimoe voennoe obozrenie*, August 18, 2000, http://nvo.ng.ru/notes/2000-08-18/8_kennedy.html.

6. "Telegram from TROSTNIK (Soviet Defense Minister Rodion Malinovsky) to PAVLOV (General Issa Pliev)," October 22, 1962, History and Public Policy Program Digital Archive, Archive of the President of the Russian Federation,

Special Declassification, April 2002, trans. Svetlana Savranskaya, https://digitalarchive.wilsoncenter.org/document/117316.

7. Viktor Esin, "Uchastie raketnykh voisk strategicheskogo naznacheniia v operatsii "Anadyr'," in *Strategicheskaia operatsiia "Anadyr'*," 55–64, here 61.

8. Iazov, *Udary sud'by*, 137–40; idem. *Karibskii krizis*, 220–22.

9. Aleksandr Voropaev, "Otshumeli pesni nashego polka . . . ," pt. 1 (1960–1963), "Sovetskii chelovek na Kube, Karibskii krizis," http://cubanos.ru/texts/txt035.

10. Statsenko, "Doklad komandira 51-i raketnoi divizii o deistviiakh soediineniia v period s 12 iiulia po 1 dekabria 1962 goda na o. Kuba"; Ivan Sidorov, "Vypolniaia internatsional'nyi dolg," in *Strategicheskaia operatsiia "Anadyr'." Kak èto bylo. Memuarno-spravochnoe izdanie*, ed. V. I. Esin (Moscow, 2000), 125–33, here 131–32; Esin, "Uchastie raketnykh voisk strategicheskogo naznacheniia v operatsii "Anadyr'," 61–62.

11. Dokuchaev, "A Kennedi podozreval Khrushcheva. . . ."

12. Dobbs, *One Minute to Midnight*, 230–31, 236–37.

13. Dokuchaev, "A Kennedi podozreval Khrushcheva. . . ."

14. Dokuchaev, "A Kennedi podozreval Khrushcheva. . . ."

15. "Grechko, Stepan Naumovich," http://encyclopedia.mil.ru/encyclopedia/dictionary/details_rvsn.htm?id=12914@morfDictionary; Aleksandr Kochukov, "Beriia, vstat'! Vy arestovany," *Krasnaia Zvezda*, June 28, 2003, http://old.redstar.ru/2003/06/28_06/5_01.html.

16. "Interview with General Leonid Garbuz by Sherry Jones," 13; Garbuz, "Zamestitel' komanduiushchego gruppy sovetskikh voisk na Kube vspominaet," 85.

17. Dokuchaev, "A Kennedi podozreval Khrushcheva. . . ."

18. Artem Lokalov and Anna Romanova, "Aleksei Riapenko: Ia sbil U-2 i menia stali kachat'," *Rodina*, October 1, 2017, https://rg.ru/2017/10/16/rodina-aleksej-riapenko.html.

19. Gennadii Tolshchin, "Zhivut vo mne vospominaniia. Ili operatsiia "Anadyr'" glazami soldata," "Sovetskii chelovek na Kube, Karibskii krizis," http://cubanos.ru/texts/txt054.

20. Fursenko and Naftali, *"One Hell of a Gamble,"* 278; "Interview with General Leonid Garbuz by Sherry Jones," 13.

20. Secret Rendezvous

1. Robert Kennedy, *Thirteen Days*, 73.

2. "Executive Committee Meeting of the National Executive Council, Saturday, October 27, 1962, 4:00 p.m.," *The Kennedy Tapes*, 356–57.

3. "Executive Committee Meeting of the National Executive Council," Saturday, October 27, 1962, 4:00 p.m., 334–36.

4. "Executive Committee Meeting of the National Executive Council," Saturday, October 27, 1962, 4:00 p.m., 364–82; "Notes from Transcripts of JCS Meetings," October 27, 1962, 23. *FRUS, 1961–1963, American Republics; Cuba 1961–1962; Cuban Missile Crisis and Aftermath*, vols. 10/11/12, Microfiche Supplement, 23.

5. Robert Kennedy, *Thirteen Days*, 80–81.

6. "Notes from Transcripts of JCS Meetings," October 27, 1962.

7. "RFK Notes. Executive Committee Meeting. No dates," Papers of Robert F. Kennedy, Attorney General Papers, Attorney General's Confidential File 6-2-10: Cuba: Executive committee meetings: RFK notes and memos, 1962: October–December (1 of 2 folders), 1–4, RFKAG-215-011, John F. Kennedy Presidential Library and Museum; Robert Kennedy, *Thirteen Days*, 77–80; cf. "Telegram from the Department of State to the Embassy in the Soviet Union," Washington, October 27, 1962, 8:05 p.m, *FRUS, 1961–1963*, vol. 6, *Kennedy-Khrushchev Exchanges*, no. 67, https://history.state.gov/historicaldocuments/frus1961-63v06/d67.

8. Robert Kennedy, *Thirteen Days*, 81; McGeorge Bundy, *Danger and Survival: Choices about the Bomb in the First Fifty Years* (New York, 1988), 432; Jim Hershberg, "Anatomy of a Controversy: Anatoly F. Dobrynin's Meeting with Robert F. Kennedy, Saturday, October 27, 1962," *Cold War International History Project Electronic Bulletin* 5 (Spring 1995): 75–80.

9. "Cable received from U.S. Ambassador to Turkey Raymond Hare to State Department regarding Turkish missiles, October 26, 1962," Declassified Documents, *The Cuban Missile Crisis, 1962: A National Security Archive Documents Reader*, ed. Laurence Chang and Peter Kornbluh, https://nsarchive2.gwu.edu/nsa/cuba_mis_cri/19621026hare.pdf.

10. Bundy, *Danger and Survival*, 432.

11. Rusk and Rusk, *As I Saw It*, 238–40; cf. Ted Sorensen comments in *Back to the Brink: Proceedings of the Moscow Conference on the Cuban Missile Crisis, January 27–28, 1989*, ed. Bruce J. Allyn, James G. Blight, and David A. Welch (Lanham, MD, 1992), 92–93.

12. Robert Kennedy, *Thirteen Days*, 81–82.

13. Dobrynin, *In Confidence*, 87; "Dobrynin's Cable to the Soviet Foreign Ministry, October 27, 1962," in Hershberg, "Anatomy of a Controversy: Anatoly F. Dobrynin's Meeting with Robert F. Kennedy," 79–80, https://nsarchive2.gwu.edu/nsa/cuba_mis_cri/moment.htm.

14. Hershberg, "Anatomy of a Controversy: Anatoly F. Dobrynin's Meeting with Robert F. Kennedy"; Dobrynin, *In Confidence*, 87.

15. Hershberg, "Anatomy of a Controversy: Anatoly F. Dobrynin's Meeting with Robert F. Kennedy," 79–80; cf. "Dobrynin Cable to the USSR Foreign Ministry, 27 October 1962," Declassified Documents, *The Cuban Missile Crisis, 1962 A National Security Archive Documents Reader,* https://nsarchive2.gwu.edu/nsa/cuba_mis_cri/621027%20Dobrynin%20Cable%20to%20USSR.pdf.

16. Robert Kennedy, "Memorandum to the Secretary of State from Attorney General, October 23, 1962," 3, Declassified Documents, *The Cuban Missile Crisis, 1962: A National Security Archive Documents Reader,* https://nsarchive2.gwu.edu/nsa/cuba_mis_cri/621030%20Memorandum%20for%20Sec.%20of%20State.pdf.

17. Dobbs, *One Minute to Midnight,* 309–10; Leaming, *Jack Kennedy,* 406–7.

18. O'Donnell and Powers, *"Johnny, We Hardly Knew Ye,* 283, 394.

19. "Executive Committee Meeting of the National Security Council, Saturday, October 29, 1962, 9:00 PM," *The Kennedy Tapes,* 391–401; Rusk and Rusk, *As I Saw It,* 240–41; *An International History of the Cuban Missile Crisis: A 50-Year Retrospective,* ed. David Gioe, Len Scott, and Christopher Andrew (London and New York, 2014), 202–3; Beschloss, *The Crisis Years,* 537–38.

20. O'Donnell and Powers, *"Johnny, We Hardly Knew Ye,"* 395; Mimi Alford, *Once Upon a Secret: My Affair with President John F. Kennedy and Its Aftermath* (New York, 2013), 93–94.

21. The Flag Plot "Office Log" for October 27; Cuban Missile Crisis Day by Day: From the Pentagon's "Sensitive Records," National Security Archive, https://nsarchive2.gwu.edu/NSAEBB/NSAEBB398/docs/doc%2014E%20office%20log.pdf; Opnav [Chief of Naval Operations], "24 Hour Resume of Events 270000 to 280000," with "Intercept Items of Immediate Interest," and "Items of Significant Items [sic]" attached, n.d., Top Secret, Cuban Missile Crisis Day by Day: From the Pentagon's "Sensitive Records," National Security Archive, https://nsarchive2.gwu.edu/NSAEBB/NSAEBB398/docs/doc%2014F%20chronology.pdf.

21. Bermuda Triangle

1. Norman Polmar and Kenneth J. More, *Cold War Submarines: The Design and Construction of U.S. and Soviet Submarines* (Dulles, VA, 2003), 201–6, 218–19; "Pr. 641 Foxtrot," *Military Russia: Otechestvennaia voennaia tekhnika,* http://militaryrussia.ru/blog/topic-206.html.

2. Gary Slaughter, "A Soviet Nuclear Torpedo, an American Destroyer, and the Cuban Missile Crisis," *Task & Purpose,* September 4, 2016, https://taskandpurpose.com/cuban-missile-crisis-nuclear-torpedo; cf. Gary Slaugh-

ter and Joanne Slaughter, *The Journey of an Inquiring Mind: From Scholar, Naval Officer, and Entrepreneur to Novelist* (Nashville, 2019), 171–80.

3. "Memoriia: Vasilii Arkhipov," *Polit.ru*, January 30, 2016, http://www.submarines.narod.ru/Substory/6_658_19.html; https://polit.ru/news/2016/01/30/arhipov/.

4. "Report from General Zakharov and Admiral Fokin to the Defense Council and Premier Khrushchev on Initial Plans for Soviet Navy Activities in Support of Operation Anadyr, 18 September 1962," *The Submarines of October: U.S. and Soviet Naval Encounters during the Cuban Missile Crisis*, National Security Archive Electronic Briefing Book No. 75, ed. William Burr and Thomas S. Blanton, October 31, 2002, https://nsarchive2.gwu.edu/NSAEBB/NSAEBB75/asw-I-1.pdf; "Report from General Zakharov and Admiral Fokin to the Presidium, Central Committee, Communist Party of the Soviet Union, on the Progress of Operation Anadyr, 25 September 1962," *The Submarines of October*, https://nsarchive2.gwu.edu/NSAEBB/NSAEBB75/asw-I-2.pdf.

5. Polmar and More, *Cold War Submarines*, 201–6; "Pr. 641 Foxtrot," *Military Russia: Otechestvennaia voennaia tekhnika*, http://militaryrussia.ru/blog/topic-206.html.

6. Riurik Ketov, in Nikolai Cherkashin, *Povsednevnaia zhizn' rossiiskikh podvodnikov* (Moscow, 2000), 146; cf. idem, "The Cuban Missile Crisis as Seen Through a Periscope," *Journal of Strategic Studies* 28, no. 2 (2005): 217–31; Aleksei Dubivko, "V puchinakh Bermudskogo treugol'nika," in A. V. Batarshev, A. F. Dubivko, and V. S. Liubimov, *Rossiiskie podvodniki v Kholodnoi voine 1962 goda* (St. Petersburg, 2011), 13–62, here 20–23; Svetlana V. Savranskaya, "New Sources on the Role of Soviet Submarines in the Cuban Missile Crisis," *Journal of Strategic Studies* 28, no. 2 (2005): 233–59, here 240.

7. Dubivko, "V puchinakh Bermudskogo treugol'nika," 23–24; Viktor Mikhailov, "Vospominaniia byvshego komandira rulevoi gruppy shturmanskoi boevoi chasti podvodnoi lodki B-59," https://flot.com/blog/historyofNVMU/5705.php?print=Y.

8. Jeremy Robinson-Leon and William Burr, "Chronology of Submarine Contact during the Cuban Missile Crisis, October 1, 1962–November 14, 1962," *Submarines of October*, https://nsarchive2.gwu.edu/NSAEBB/NSAEBB75/subchron.htm.

9. Anastas Mikoian, "Diktovka o poezdke na Kubu," January 19, 1963, in Aleksandr Lukashin and Mariia Aleksashina, "My voobshche ne khotim nikuda brosit' rakety, my za mir . . . ," *Rodina*, January 1, 2017.

10. Robinson-Leon and Burr, "Chronology of Submarine Contact during the Cuban Missile Crisis, October 1, 1962–November 14, 1962."

11. "Executive Committee Meeting of the National Security Council," Wednesday, October 24, 1962, 10:00 a.m.," *The Kennedy Tapes*, 228–31.

12. Robinson-Leon and Burr, "Chronology of Submarine Contact during the Cuban Missile Crisis, October 1, 1962–November 14, 1962."

13. Robinson-Leon and Burr, "Chronology of Submarine Contact during the Cuban Missile Crisis, October 1, 1962–November 14, 1962"; Mikhailov, "Vospominaniia byvshego komandira rulevoi gruppy shturmanskoi boevoi chasti podvodnoi lodki B-59."

14. Robinson-Leon and Burr, "Chronology of Submarine Contact during the Cuban Missile Crisis, October 1, 1962–November 14, 1962"; "U.S. Navy, Charts/Deck Logs of Anti-Submarine Warfare Operations Related to USSR Submarine B-59, October 1962," *The Cuban Missile Crisis of 1962*. National Security Archive, Declassified Documents, https://nsarchive2.gwu.edu/nsa/cuba_mis_cri/621000%20Charts-deck%20logs.pdf.

15. Vadim Orlov, "Iz vospominanii komandira gruppy OSNAZ podvodnoi lodki B-59," in *Karibskii krizis. Protivostoianie. Sbornik vospominanii uchastnikov sobytii 1962 g.*, ed. V. V. Naumov (St. Petersburg, 2012).

16. Orlov, "Iz vospominanii komandira gruppy OSNAZ podvodnoi lodki B-59."

17. Anatolii Leonenko, "Vospominaniia byvshego komandira BCh-3 podvodnoi lodki B-59," in *Karibskii krizis, Protivostoianie*, https://flot.com/blog/historyofNVMU/5708.php?print=Y.

18. Gary Slaughter, "A Soviet Nuclear Torpedo, an American Destroyer, and the Cuban Missile Crisis."

19. Leonenko, "Vospominaniia byvshego komandira BCh-3 podvodnoi lodki B-59"; Mikhailov, "Vospominaniia byvshego komandira rulevoi gruppy shturmanskoi boevoi chasti podvodnoi lodki B-59."

20. "Executive Committee Meeting of the National Security Council, Saturday, October 27, 1962, 4:00 p.m.," *The Kennedy Tapes*, 372–73.

21. Slaughter, "A Soviet Nuclear Torpedo, an American Destroyer, and the Cuban Missile Crisis"; Leonenko, "Vospominaniia byvshego komandira BCh-3 podvodnoi lodki B-59."

22. Slaughter, "A Soviet Nuclear Torpedo, an American Destroyer, and the Cuban Missile Crisis."

23. "Russian nuclear torpedoes T-15 and T-5," *Encyclopedia of Safety*, http://survincity.com/2012/02/russian-nuclear-torpedoes-t-15-and-t-5/; Samuel Glasstone and Philip Dolan, *The Effects of Nuclear Weapons* (Washington, DC, 1977), 248–50.

24. John F. Kennedy, "Radio and Television Report to the American People on the Soviet Arms Buildup in Cuba," The White House, October 22, 1962, John F. Kennedy Presidential Library and Museum, https://microsites.jfklibrary.org/cmc/oct22/doc5.html.

22. Sunday Scare

1. Oleg Gerchikov, "Kalendarnaia revoliutsiia. Kak bol'sheviki vveli grigorian-skoe letoischislenie," *Argumenty i Fakty*, no. 4 (January 24, 2018), http://www .aif.ru/society/history/kalendarnaya_revolyuciya_kak_bolsheviki_vveli_ grigorianskoe_letoischislenie.

2. "Prezidentu SShA D. Kennedi, kopiia i. o. general'nogo sekretaria OON U Tanu," *Pravda*, October 28, 1962, 1; "Mudroe predlozhenie sovetskogo prem'era," ibid.

3. "Govoriat leningradtsy," *Pravda*, October 28, 1962, 1.

4. Fursenko and Naftali, *"One Hell of a Gamble,"* 283.

5. "Memorandum from S. P. Ivanov and R. Malinovsky to N. S. Khrushchev," October 28, 1962, History and Public Policy Program Digital Archive, Library of Congress, Manuscript Division, Dmitriĭ Antonovich Volkogonov papers, 1887–1995, mm97083838, reprinted in *Cold War International History Bulletin* 11, trans. Raymond Garthoff, https://digitalarchive.wilsoncenter .org/document/111757.

6. "Memorandum from S. P. Ivanov and R. Malinovsky to N. S. Khrushchev," October 28, 1962; "Telegram from TROSTNIK (Soviet Defense Minister Rodion Malinovsky) to PAVLOV (General Issa Pliev)," October 28, 1962, History and Public Policy Program Digital Archive, Archive of the President of the Russian Federation, Special Declassification, April 2002, trans. Svetlana Savranskaya, https://digitalarchive.wilsoncenter.org/document/117329.

7. Oleg Troianovskii, *Cherez gody i rasstoianiia: Istoriia odnoi sem'i* (Moscow, 1997), 249, "Letter from Khrushchev to Fidel Castro," October 28, 1962, History and Public Policy Program Digital Archive, Archive of Foreign Policy, Russian Federation (AVP RF), https://digitalarchive.wilsoncenter.org/ document/114504.

8. Khrushchev, *Vremia, liudi, vlast'*, 2: 518.

9. "Telegram from the Department of State to the Embassy in the Soviet Union," Washington, October 27, 1962, 8:05 p.m, *FRUS*, 1961–1963, vol. 6, *Kennedy-Khrushchev Exchanges*, no. 67, https://history.state.gov/historicaldocuments/ frus1961-63v06/d67.

10. "War and Peace in the Nuclear Age: At the Brink; Interview with John Scali, 1986," Open Vault from WGBH, http://openvault.wgbh.org/catalog/V_9F23 6717EB2649008E00E863CAAF296A; Aleksandr Feklisov, *Za okeanom i na ostrove: Zapiski razvedchika* (Moscow, 2001), 227–28; Fursenko and Naftali, *"One Hell of a Gamble,"* 264–65, 269–71.

11. Anatolii Dobrynin, *Sugubo doveritel'no: Posol v Vashingtone pri shesti prezidentakh SShA, 1962–1986* (Moscow, 1996), 74–75; Dobrynin, *In Confidence*, 88–89; Dobbs, *One Minute to Midnight*, 321–22; Fred Weir, "Vladimir Putin Joins

Pajama Workforce, Decides to Work from Home," *Christian Science Monitor*, October 18, 2012.

12. Troianovskii, *Cherez gody i rasstoianiia*, 250.

13. Boris Ponomarev, quoted in Fursenko and Naftali, *Adskaia igra*, 124; *The Diary of Anatoly S. Chernyaev*, 2.

14. Boris Ponomarev, quoted in Fursenko and Naftali, *Adskaia igra*, 424; "Central Committee of the Communist Party of the Soviet Union Presidium Protocol 63," October 28, 1962, History and Public Policy Program Digital Archive, RGANI, F. 3, Op. 16, D. 947, L. 45-46^v, trans. and ed. Mark Kramer, with assistance from Timothy Naftali, https://digitalarchive.wilsoncenter .org/document/115092.

15. Troianovskii, *Cherez gody i rasstoianiia*, 251.

16. Khrushchev, *Vremia, liudi, vlast'*, 2: 519.

17. Troianovskii, *Cherez gody i rasstoianiia: Istoriia odnoi sem'i*, 251; Sergei Khrushchev, *Nikita Khrushchev and the Creation of a Superpower* (University Park, PA, 2000), 630.

18. Dobrynin, *Sugubo doveritel'no*, 75; Dobrynin, *In Confidence*, 89; Fursenko and Naftali, *Bezumnyi risk: Sekretnaia istoriia kubinskogo raketnogo krizisa 1962 g.* (Moscow, 2006), 283.

19. "Poslanie Pervogo sekretaria TsK KPSS Nikity Sergeevicha Khrushcheva, prezidentu Soedinennykh Shtatov Ameriki, Dzhonu F. Kennedi," *Pravda*, October 29, 1962, 1; cf. *1000(0) kliuchevykh dokumentov po sovetskoi i rossiiskoi istorii*, https://www.1000dokumente.de/index.html?c=dokument_ru& dokument=0038_kub&object=translation&l=ru; cf. "Letter from Chairman Khrushchev to President Kennedy," Moscow, October 28, 1962, *FRUS*, 1961–1963, vol. 6, *Kennedy-Khrushchev Exchanges*, no. 68, https://history.state.gov/ historicaldocuments/frus1961-63v06/d68.

20. "Poslanie Pervogo sekretaria TsK KPSS Nikity Sergeevicha Khrushcheva"; "Letter from Chairman Khrushchev to President Kennedy," Moscow, October 28, 1962.

21. "Letter from Chairman Khrushchev to President Kennedy," Moscow, October 28, 1962, *FRUS*, 1961–1963, vol. 6, *Kennedy-Khrushchev Exchanges*, no. 70, https://history.state.gov/historicaldocuments/frus1961-63v06/d70.

22. Khrushchev, *Vremia, liudi, vlast'*, 2: 520-21.

23. "Letter from Khrushchev to Fidel Castro," October 28, 1962, History and Public Policy Program Digital Archive, Archive of Foreign Policy, Russian Federation (AVP RF), https://digitalarchive.wilsoncenter.org/document/114504.

24. "Central Committee of the Communist Party of the Soviet Union Presidium Protocol 63"; cf. *Prezidium TsK KPSS, 1954–1964: Postanovleniia*, 388; "Soviet Foreign Minister Gromyko's Instructions to the USSR Representative at the

United Nations," October 28, 1962, History and Public Policy Program Digital Archive, AVP RF, copy courtesy of NSA; trans. Mark H. Doctoroff, https://digitalarchive.wilsoncenter.org/document/111845.

25. "Telegram from TROSTNIK (Soviet Defense Minister Rodion Malinovsky) to PAVLOV (General Issa Pliev)," October 28, 1962, https://digitalarchive.wilsoncenter.org/document/117329; "Telegram from TROSTNIK (Soviet Defense Minister Rodion Malinovsky) to PAVLOV (General Issa Pliev)," October 28, 1962, History and Public Policy Program Digital Archive, Archive of the President of the Russian Federation, Special Declassification, April 2002, trans. Svetlana Savranskaya, https://digitalarchive.wilsoncenter.org/document/117330.

26. Troianovskii, *Cherez gody i rasstoianiia*, 252.

23. Winners and Losers

1. Dobbs, *One Minute to Midnight*, 334; O'Donnell and Powers, *"Johnny, We Hardly Knew Ye,"* 341.

2. "War and Peace in the Nuclear Age: At the Brink; Interview with John Scali, 1986," OpenVault from WGBH, http://openvault.wgbh.org/catalog/V_9F236 717EB2649008E00E863CAAF296A.

3. "Notes Taken from Transcripts of Meetings of the Joint Chiefs of Staff, October–November 1962, Dealing with the Cuban Crisis," October 27, 1962, *FRUS, 1961–1963, American Republics; Cuba 1961–1962; Cuban Missile Crisis and Aftermath*, vols. 10/11/12, Microfiche Supplement, 24–25, https://static .history.state.gov/frus/frus1961-63v10-12mSupp/pdf/d441.pdf.

4. "Executive Committee Meeting of the National Security Council, Sunday, October 28, 1962, 11:05 a.m.," *The Kennedy Tapes*, 404; "Summary Record of the Tenth Meeting of the Executive Committee of the National Security Council, Washington, October 28, 1962, 11:10 a.m.", *FRUS, 1961–1963*, vol. 11, *Cuban Missile Crisis and Aftermath*, no. 103, https://history.state.gov/ historicaldocuments/frus1961-63v11/d103; Ted Sorensen, *Counselor: A Life at the Edge of History* (New York, 2009), 9.

5. "National Security Council Meeting, Saturday, October 20, 1962, 2:30 p.m.," *The Kennedy Tapes*, 131; "Executive Committee Meeting of the National Security Council, Sunday, October 28, 1962, 11:05 a.m.," *The Kennedy Tapes*, 404–5; "Summary Record of the Tenth Meeting of the Executive Committee of the National Security Council, Washington, October 28, 1962, 11:10 a.m.," *FRUS, 1961–1963*, vol. 11, *Cuban Missile Crisis and Aftermath*, no. 103, https:// history.state.gov/historicaldocuments/frus1961-63v11/d103.

6. "Telegram from the Department of State to the Embassy in the Soviet Union, Washington, October 28, 1962, 5:03 p.m.," *FRUS, 1961–1963*, vol. 6, *Kennedy-*

Khrushchev Exchanges, no. 69, https://history.state.gov/historicaldocuments/frus1961-63v06/d69.

7. Robert Kennedy, *Thirteen Days*, 83–84.

8. "Telegram from Soviet Ambassador to the USA Dobrynin to USSR MFA, October 28, 1962," History and Public Policy Program Digital Archive, AVP RF, copy courtesy of NSA, trans. Mark H. Doctoroff, https://digitalarchive.wilsoncenter.org/document/111852; Dobrynin, *In Confidence*, 89.

9. Robert Kennedy, *Thirteen Days*, 84.

10. "Conversations with Dwight Eisenhower, Harry Truman and Herbert Hoover, Sunday, October 28, 1962, 12:08 p.m.," *The Kennedy Tapes*, 405–7.

11. "Conversations with Dwight Eisenhower, Harry Truman and Herbert Hoover, Sunday, October 28, 1962, 12:08 p.m.," *The Kennedy Tapes*, 407–9.

12. Dobrynin, *In Confidence*, 90; "Letter from Chairman Khrushchev to President Kennedy, Moscow, October 28, 1962," *FRUS*, 1961–1963, vol. 6, *Kennedy-Khrushchev Exchanges*, no. 70, https://history.state.gov/historicaldocuments/frus1961-63v06/d70; cf. Fursenko and Naftali *Adskaia igra*, 426.

13. "Telegram from Soviet Ambassador to the US Dobrynin to the USSR Foreign Ministry, October 30, 1962," History and Public Policy Program Digital Archive, Archive of Foreign Policy, Russian Federation (AVP RF), Moscow; copy obtained by NHK (Japanese Television), provided to CWIHP, and on file at National Security Archive, Washington, DC, trans. John Henriksen, Harvard University, https://digitalarchive.wilsoncenter.org/document/112633; Dobrynin, *In Confidence*, 90.

14. "Pribytie v Moskvu t. A. Novotnogo," *Pravda*, October 30, 1962, 1; "Priem v TsK KPSS," *Pravda*, October 31, 1962, 1.

15. "Minutes of Conversation between the Delegations of the CPCz and the CPSU, The Kremlin (excerpt), October 30, 1962," History and Public Policy Program Digital Archive, National Archive, Archive of the CC CPCz, (Prague); File: "Antonín Novotný, Kuba," Box 193, https://digitalarchive.wilsoncenter.org/document/115219.

16. "Mudrost' i muzhestvo v bor'be za mir. Vse progressivnoe chelovechestvo privetstvuet miroliubuvye deistviia sovetskogo pravitel'stva," *Pravda*, October 31, 1962, 1; "Telegram from Brazilian Embassy in Washington (Campos), 2 p.m., Sunday, October 28, 1962," History and Public Policy Program Digital Archive, Ministry of External Relations Archives, Brasilia, Brazil (copy courtesy of Roberto Baptista Junior, University of Brasilia), trans. James G. Hershberg, https://digitalarchive.wilsoncenter.org/document/115314.

17. Seymour Topping, "Russian Accedes: Tells President Work on Bases Is Halted—Invites Talks," *New York Times*, October 29, 1962, 1, 16; "Telegram

from Brazilian Embassy in Washington (Campos), 2 p.m., Sunday, October 28, 1962."

18. Topping, "Russian Accedes: Tells President Work on Bases Is Halted—Invites Talks"; "Overseas Reaction to the Cuban Situation as of 3:00 pm, October 29, 1962, 2–3, 16, 22, Papers of Robert F. Kennedy, Attorney General Papers, Attorney General's Confidential File 6-9: Cuba: Cuban Crisis, 1962: USIA.

19. "Llewellyn E. Thompson to the Secretary of State, Memorandum of Conversation—Yurii Zhukov and Mr. Bolshakov—Ambassador Thompson, Wednesday, October 31, 1962, 2:00 p.m.," *FRUS*, 1961–1963, *American Republics*; *Cuba 1961–1962*; *Cuban Missile Crisis and Aftermath*, vols. 10/11/12, Microfiche Supplement, https://static.history.state.gov/frus/frus1961-63v10-12mSupp/pdf/d468.pdf; "[Memorandum of Conversation], The Secretary, Hervé Alphand, Ambassador of France, and William R. Tyler, Assistant Secretary of State for European Affairs, Subject: Cuba, October 28, 1962," *FRUS*, 1961–1963, *American Republics*; *Cuba 1961–1962*; *Cuban Missile Crisis and Aftermath*, vols. 10/11/12, Microfiche Supplement, https://static.history.state.gov/frus/frus1961-63v10-12mSupp/pdf/d446.pdf.

20. James Reston, "The President's View. Kennedy Rejects Thesis That Outcome on Cuba Shows 'Tough Line' Is Best," *New York Times*, October 29, 1962, 1, 17; Arthur Schlesinger Jr., "Memorandum for the President: Post Mortem on Cuba, October 29, 1962," *FRUS*, 1961–1963, *American Republics*; *Cuba 1961–1962*; *Cuban Missile Crisis and Aftermath*, vols. 10/11/12, Microfiche Supplement, https://static.history.state.gov/frus/frus1961-63v10-12mSupp/pdf/d457.pdf.

24. Indignation

1. Fidel Castro's remarks at the Havana Conference, January 1992, in Blight, et al., *Cuba on the Brink*, 214.

2. Fidel Castro's remarks at the Havana Conference, January 1992, 214; Dobbs, *One Minute to Midnight*, 335–36.

3. "Notes of Conversation between A. I. Mikoyan and Fidel Castro," November 3, 1962, History and Public Policy Program Digital Archive, Russian Foreign Ministry Archives, obtained and translated by NHK television, copy provided by Philip Brenner, trans. Vladimir Zaemsky, https://digitalarchive.wilsoncenter.org/document/110955; "Memorandum of Conversation between Castro and Mikoyan," November 4, 1962, History and Public Policy Program Digital Archive, Russian Foreign Ministry Archives, obtained and translated by NHK television, copy provided by Philip Brenner, trans. Aleksandr Zaemsky, slightly revised, https://digitalarchive.wilsoncenter.org/document/110961.

4. Louis Pérez, *Cuba Under the Platt Amendment, 1902–1934* (Pittsburgh, 1986).

5. Secretary of State to White House, Bundy, October 26, 1962, in "Notes on Cuba Crisis," October 26, 1962, 25–27, in Papers of Robert F. Kennedy, Attorney General Papers, Attorney General's Confidential File 6-2-7: Cuba: Executive committee meetings: RFK notes and memos, October 26, 1962, RFKAG-215-008, John F. Kennedy Presidential Library and Museum.

6. Dobbs, *One Minute to Midnight*, 336.

7. "Letter from Khrushchev to Fidel Castro," October 28, 1962, History and Public Policy Program Digital Archive, Archive of Foreign Policy, Russian Federation (AVP RF), https://digitalarchive.wilsoncenter.org/document/114504.

8. "Cable from USSR Ambassador to Cuba Alekseev to Soviet Ministry of Foreign Affairs," October 28, 1962, History and Public Policy Program Digital Archive, Archive of Foreign Policy, Russian Federation (AVP RF), Moscow; copy obtained by NHK (Japanese Television), provided to CWIHP, and on file at National Security Archive, Washington, DC, trans. Vladimir Zaemsky, https://digitalarchive.wilsoncenter.org/document/111985.

9. Fidel Castro's remarks at the Havana Conference, January 1992, in Blight, et al., *Cuba on the Brink*, 214–15; David Coleman, "Castro's Five Points," Research: History in Pieces, https://historyinpieces.com/research/castro-five-points.

10. "Telegram from Yugoslav Embassy in Havana (Vidaković) to Yugoslav Foreign Ministry," October 28, 1962, History and Public Policy Program Digital Archive, Archive of the Ministry of Foreign Affairs (AMIP), Belgrade, Serbia, PA (Confidential Archive) 1962, Kuba, folder F-67. Obtained by Svetozar Rajak and Ljubomir Dimić, trans. Radina Vučetić-Mladenović, https://digitalarchive.wilsoncenter.org/document/115468; "Telegram from Polish Embassy in Havana (Jeleń)," October 28, 1962, History and Public Policy Program Digital Archive, Szyfrogramy from Hawana 1962, 6/77 w-82 t-1264, Polish Foreign Ministry Archive (AMSZ), Warsaw. Obtained by James G. Hershberg (George Washington University), trans. Margaret K. Gnoinska (Troy University), https://digitalarchive.wilsoncenter.org/document/115766.

11. "Letter from Fidel Castro to Khrushchev," October 28, 1962, History and Public Policy Program Digital Archive, Archive of Foreign Policy, Russian Federation (AVP RF), https://digitalarchive.wilsoncenter.org/document/114503; Acosta, *October 1962*, 279.

12. "Ukazanie sovposlu na Kube dlia besedy s F. Kastro," October 28, 1962, in *Karibskii krizis, dokumenty*, Rossiiskie programmy Arkhiva natsional'noi bezopasnosti, National Security Archive, George Washington University, https://nsarchive2.gwu.edu/rus/text_files/CMCrisis/30.PDF; Alekseev, "Shifrotelegramma," October 29, 1962, https://nsarchive2.gwu.edu/rus/text_files/CMCrisis/33.PDF.

13. Alekseev, "Shifrotelegramma," October 29, 1962, in *Karibskii krizis, dokumenty*, Rossiiskie programmy Arkhiva natsional'noi bezopasnosti, National Security Archive, George Washington University, https://nsarchive2.gwu.edu/rus/text_files/CMCrisis/33.PDF.

14. Khrushchev, *Vremia, ludi, vlast'*, 2: 522.

15. "Letter from Khrushchev to Castro," October 30, 1962, JFK, Primary Source, *American Experience*, https://www.pbs.org/wgbh/americanexperience/features/jfk-defendcuba/.

16. "Letter from Castro to Khrushchev," October 31, 1962, History of Cuba, http://www.historyofcuba.com/history/Crisis/Cltr-4.htm.

17. A. Walter Dorn and Robert Pauk, "50 Years Ago: The Cuban Missile Crisis and Its Underappreciated Hero," *Bulletin of the Atomic Scientists*, October 11, 2012, https://thebulletin.org/2012/10/50-years-ago-the-cuban-missile-crisis-and-its-underappreciated-hero/.

18. "Soviet Foreign Minister Gromyko's Instructions to the USSR Representative at the United Nations," October 28, 1962, History and Public Policy Program Digital Archive, AVP RF, copy courtesy of NSA, trans. Mark H. Doctoroff, https://digitalarchive.wilsoncenter.org/document/111845; "Telegram from Soviet Delegate to the UN Zorin to USSR Foreign Ministry on Meeting with Cuban Delegate to the UN Garcia-Inchaustegui," October 28, 1962, History and Public Policy Program Digital Archive, Archive of Foreign Policy, Russian Federation (AVP RF), Moscow; copy obtained by NHK (Japanese Television), provided to CWIHP, and on file at National Security Archive, Washington, DC, trans. John Henriksen, Harvard University, https://digitalarchive.wilsoncenter.org/document/111977; "U Thant's Message to Khrushchev," October 28, 1962, History and Public Policy Program Digital Archive, Archive of Foreign Policy, Russian Federation (AVP RF), https://digitalarchive.wilsoncenter.org/document/114505.

19. Lechuga, *Cuba and the Missile Crisis*, 100.

20. "Our Five Points Are Minimum Conditions to Guarantee Peace," Discussions with UN Secretary-General U Thant, October 30–31, 1962, in Acosta, *October 1962*, 262–63, 265.

21. "Our Five Points are Minimum Conditions to Guarantee Peace," Discussions with UN Secretary-General U Thant, October 30-31, 1962, in Acosta, *October 1962*, 272–73, 275.

22. "Telegram from Deputy Foreign Minister Kuznetsov to Soviet Foreign Ministry (1) On the Second Meeting with U Thant on October 29, 1962," October 30, 1962, History and Public Policy Program Digital Archive, Archive of Foreign Policy, Russian Federation (AVP RF), Moscow; copy obtained by NHK (Japanese Television), provided to CWIHP, and on file at National Secu-

rity Archive, Washington, DC, trans. John Henriksen, Harvard University, https://digitalarchive.wilsoncenter.org/document/112636.

23. "Cable from Soviet Foreign Minister Gromyko to USSR Ambassador to Cuba A. I. Alekseev," October 31, 1962, History and Public Policy Program Digital Archive, Archive of Foreign Policy, Russian Federation (AVP RF), Moscow; copy obtained by NHK (Japanese Television), provided to CWIHP, and on file at National Security Archive, Washington, DC; trans. Vladimir Zaemsky, https://digitalarchive.wilsoncenter.org/document/110461.

24. "Report of Major-General Igor Demyanovich Statsenko, Commander of the 51st Missile Division, about the Actions of the Division from 07.12.62 through 12.01.1962," The Documents, no. 1, p. 13, National Security Archive Electronic Briefing Book No. 449, ed. Svetlana Savranskaya and Thomas Blanton with Anna Melyakova, https://nsarchive2.gwu.edu/NSAEBB/NSAEBB449/docs/Doc%201%20Igor%20Statsenko%20After-action%20report.pdf; Anatolii Gribkov, "Karibskii krizis," *Voenno-istoricheskii zhurnal*, 1993, no. 1: 5, http://archive.redstar.ru/index.php/news-menu/vesti/v-voennyh-okrugah/iz -zapadnogo-voennogo-okruga/item/5959-operatsiya-anadyir.

25. "Memorandum of Telephone Conversation between Secretary of State Rusk and the Permanent Representative to the United Nations (Stevenson)," *FRUS, 1961–1963*, vol. 11, *Cuban Missile Crisis and Aftermath*, no. 124.

26. "Telegram from Alekseev to USSR Foreign Ministry," October 31, 1962, History and Public Policy Program Digital Archive, Archive of Foreign Policy, Russian Federation (AVP RF), Moscow; copy obtained by NHK (Japanese Television), provided to CWIHP, and on file at National Security Archive, Washington, DC, trans. John Henriksen, Harvard University, https://digitalarchive.wilsoncenter.org/document/112641; "Report of Major-General Igor Demyanovich Statsenko," 13; Gribkov, "Karibskii krizis," 5.

27. Fidel Castro's broadcast, October 31, 1962, United Nations Archives, https://search.archives.un.org/uploads/r/united-nations-archives/e/8/0/e80a7439 b558c1781c4d73157d944d9d0075f0540caf75804e730b138f29ef78/S-0872 -0003-10-00001.pdf.

25. Mission Impossible

1. Khrushchev, *Vremia, liudi, vlast'*, 2: 522; *Khrushchev Remembers*, 554.

2. Anastas Mikoian, "Diktovka A. Mikoiana o poezdke na Kubu," January 19, 1962, in "My voobshche ne khotim nikuda brosat' rakety. My za mir," *Rodina*, January 1, 2017; Taubman, *Khrushchev*, 580.

3. *Khrushchev Remembers*, 554.

4. "Cable of V. V. Kuznetsov on 1 November 1962 Conversation between CPSU CC Politburo Member A. I. Mikoyan and Acting UN Secretary Gen-

eral U Thant," November 2, 1962, History and Public Policy Program Digital Archive, AVPRF, obtained by NHK, provided to CWIHP, copy on file at National Security Archive, trans. Vladislav M. Zubok (National Security Archive), https://digitalarchive.wilsoncenter.org/document/110033.

5. "Telegram from the Mission to the United Nations to the Department of State," FRUS, 1961–1963, vol. 11, Cuban Missile Crisis and Aftermath, no. 133, https://history.state.gov/historicaldocuments/frus1961-63v11/d133; "Soviet Record of 1 November 1962 Dinner Conversation between CPSU CC Politburo Member A. I. Mikoyan and White House envoy John McCloy and US Ambassador to the UN Adlai Stevenson," November 1, 1962, History and Public Policy Program Digital Archive, AVP RF, obtained by NHK, provided to CWIHP, copy on file at National Security Archive, trans. Vladislav M. Zubok (National Security Archive), https://digitalarchive.wilsoncenter .org/document/112645; "Telegram from USSR Foreign Minister Gromyko to Soviet Mission in New York, for A. I. Mikoyan," November 1, 1962, History and Public Policy Program Digital Archive, AVP RF; copy obtained by NHK, provided to CWIHP, and on file at National Security Archive, Washington, DC, trans. John Henriksen, Harvard University, https://digitalarchive .wilsoncenter.org/document/112651.

6. "Mikoyan Cable to Central Committee of the CPSU about His Conversation with US Permanent Representative to the UN Stevenson," November 1, 1962, History and Public Policy Program Digital Archive, Archive of Foreign Policy, Russian Federation (AVP RF).

7. "Memorandum of Conversation between Castro and Mikoyan," November 5, 1962, History and Public Policy Program Digital Archive, Russian Foreign Ministry Archives, obtained and translated by NHK Television, copy provided by Philip Brenner, trans. by Aleksandr Zaemsky, slightly revised, https://digitalarchive.wilsoncenter.org/document/110980; cf. "Zapis' besedy Mikoiana s Fidelem Kastro et al.," November 5, 1962, 7–8, in Karibskii krizis, dokumenty, Rossiiskie programmy Arkhiva natsional'noi bezopasnosti, National Security Archive, George Washington University, https:// nsarchive2.gwu.edu/rus/text_files/CMCrisis/40.PDF.

8. "Ciphered Telegram from Anastas Mikoyan to CC CPSU," November 6, 1962, History and Public Policy Program Digital Archive, Archive of the President of the Russian Federation (APRF), Special Declassification, April 2002, trans. Svetlana Savranskaya and Andrea Hendrickson, https://digitalarchive .wilsoncenter.org/document/117334.

9. "Notes of Conversation between A. I. Mikoyan and Fidel Castro," November 3, 1962, History and Public Policy Program Digital Archive, Russian Foreign Ministry Archives, obtained and translated by NHK television, copy provided

by Philip Brenner, trans. Vladimir Zaemsky; Sergo Mikoyan, *The Soviet Cuban Missile Crisis*, 192.

10. Sergo Mikoyan, *The Soviet Cuban Missile Crisis*, 193; Fursenko and Naftali, *"One Hell of a Gamble,"* 295.

11. "Meeting of the Secretary of the Communist Party of Cuba with Mikoyan in the Presidential Palace," November 4, 1962, History and Public Policy Program Digital Archive, Institute of History, Cuba, obtained and provided by Philip Brenner (American University), trans. from Spanish by Carlos Osorio (National Security Archive), https://digitalarchive.wilsoncenter.org/document/110879; "Memorandum of Conversation between Castro and Mikoyan," November 4, 1962, History and Public Policy Program Digital Archive, Russian Foreign Ministry Archives, obtained and translated by NHK television, copy provided by Philip Brenner, trans. Aleksandr Zaemsky, slightly revised, https://digitalarchive.wilsoncenter.org/document/110961.

12. "Ciphered Telegram from Anastas Mikoyan to CC CPSU," November 6, 1962, History and Public Policy Program Digital Archive, Archive of the President of the Russian Federation (APRF), Special Declassification, April 2002, trans. Svetlana Savranskaya and Andrea Hendrickson, https://digitalarchive .wilsoncenter.org/document/117334; "Memorandum of Conversation between Castro and Mikoyan," November 5, 1962, History and Public Policy Program Digital Archive, Russian Foreign Ministry Archives, obtained and translated by NHK television, copy provided by Philip Brenner, trans. by Aleksandr Zaemsky, slightly revised, https://digitalarchive.wilsoncenter.org/document/110980.

13. "Ciphered Telegram from Anastas Mikoyan to CC CPSU," November 6, 1962, History and Public Policy Program Digital Archive, Archive of the President of the Russian Federation (APRF), Special Declassification, April 2002, trans. Svetlana Savranskaya and Andrea Hendrickson, https://digitalarchive .wilsoncenter.org/document/117334; "Zapis' besedy Mikoiana s Fidelem Kastro et al.," November 5, 1962, 12, https://nsarchive2.gwu.edu/rus/text_files/CMCrisis/40.PDF; cf. Anastas Mikoian, "Shifrotelegramma," November 6, 1962, 13–14, in *Karibskii krizis, dokumenty*, Rossiiskie programmy Arkhiva natsional'noi bezopasnosti, National Security Archive, George Washington University, https://nsarchive2.gwu.edu/rus/text_files/CMCrisis/42.PDF.

14. Anatolii Gribkov, "Razrabotka zamysla i osushchestvlenie operatsii 'Anadyr'," in *Strategicheskaia operatsiia "Anadyr',"* 26–53, here 51.

15. Aleksei Kosygin, "45-ia godovshchina Velikoi Oktiabrskoi sotsialisticheskoi revoliutsii," *Pravda*, November 7, 1962, 1–3.

16. Gribkov, "Razrabotka zamysla i osushchestvlenie operatsii 'Anadyr'," 51; Fursenko and Naftali, *"One Hell of a Gamble,"* 297–98.

17. "Raport. St. Oper-upolnomochennyi 2-go otdela UKGB pri SM SSSR po Iar-oslavskoi oblasti starshii leitenant Goncharov," November 2, 1962, in SBU Archives, fond 1, opys 1, no. 1532, fol. 12/363/4757; Valentin Polkovnikov, "Startovyi divizion raketnogo polka na Kube," in *Strategicheskaia operatsiia "Anadyr'*," 148–60, here 159.

18. Rafael Zakirov, "V dni Karibskogo krizisa," in *Strategicheskaia operatsiia "Anadyr'*," 179–85, here 184; "Raport. Starshii upolnomochennyi apparata upol-nomochennogo UKGB pri SM UkSSR po Donetskoi oblasti maior Protasov," Odessa, 25 noiabria 1962 g., in SBU Archives, fond 1, opys 1, no. 1532, fol. 345; Ivan Sidorov, "Vypolniaia internatsional'nyi dolg," in *Strategicheskaia operatsiia "Anadyr'." Kak èto bylo*. Memuarno-spravochnoe izdanie, ed. V. I. Esin (Moscow, 2000), 125–33, here 132.

19. Polkovnikov, "Startovyi divizion raketnogo polka na Kube," 159.

20. Statsenko, "Doklad komandira 51-i raketnoi divizii o deistviiakh soedineniia v period s 12 iiulia po 1 dekabria 1962 goda na o. Kuba."

21. "Telegram from TROSTNIK (Soviet Defense Minister Rodion Malinovsky) to PAVLOV (General Issa Pliev)," October 27, 1962, History and Public Policy Program Digital Archive, Archive of the President of the Russian Federation, Special Declassification, April 2002, trans. Svetlana Savranskaya, https://digitalarchive.wilsoncenter.org/document/117327; "Telegram from TROST-NIK (Soviet Defense Minister Rodion Malinovsky) to PAVLOV (General Issa Pliev)," October 28, 1962, History and Public Policy Program Digital Archive, Archive of the President of the Russian Federation, Special Declassification, April 2002, trans. Svetlana Savranskaya, https://digitalarchive.wilsoncenter.org/document/117329; "Telegram from TROSTNIK (Soviet Defense Minis-ter Rodion Malinovsky) to PAVLOV (General Issa Pliev)," October 30, 1962, History and Public Policy Program Digital Archive, Archive of the President of the Russian Federation, Special Declassification, April 2002, trans. Svet-lana Savranskaya, https://digitalarchive.wilsoncenter.org/document/117331.

22. Ivan Shyshchenko, "Raketnyi pokhod na Kubu," in *Strategicheskaia operatsiia "Anadyr'." Kak èto bylo*. Memuarno-spravochnoe izdanie, ed. V. I. Esin (Mos-cow, 2000), 134–41, here 140.

23. Shyshchenko, "Raketnyi pokhod na Kubu," 140; "Raport. Starshii upolno-mochennyi apparata upolnomochennogo UKGB pri SM UkSSR po Donets-koi oblasti maior Protasov," Odessa, 25 noiabria 1962 g., in SBU Archives, fond 1, opys 1, no. 1532, fols. 341, 345.

24. "Raport. Starshii upolnomochennyi apparata upolnomochennogo UKGB pri SM UkSSR po Donetskoi oblasti maior Protasov," fols. 346, 347.

25. "Raport. Starshii upolnomochennyi apparata upolnomochennogo UKGB pri SM UkSSR po Donetskoi oblasti maior Protasov," fols. 347, 348.

26. "Telegram from USSR Foreign Ministry to Soviet Deputy Foreign Minister V. V. Kuznetsov," October 31, 1962, History and Public Policy Program Digital Archive, Archive of Foreign Policy, Russian Federation (AVP RF), Moscow, copy obtained by NHK (Japanese Television), provided to CWIHP, and on file at National Security Archive, Washington, DC, trans. John Henriksen, Harvard University, https://digitalarchive.wilsoncenter.org/document/112642; "Telegram from USSR Foreign Minister A. Gromyko to Deputy Foreign Minister Kuznetsov at the Soviet Mission in New York," November 1, 1962, History and Public Policy Program Digital Archive, AVP RF, copy obtained by NHK, provided to CWIHP, and on file at National Security Archive, Washington, DC, trans. John Henriksen, Harvard University, https://digitalarchive.wilsoncenter.org/document/112650.

27. "Telegram from the Department of State to the Mission to the United Nations, Washington," October 31, 1962, 12:46 p.m., *FRUS, 1961–1963*, vol. 11, *Cuban Missile Crisis and Aftermath*, no. 125, https://history.state.gov/historicaldocuments/frus1961-63v11/d125; "Telegram from A. I. Mikoyan in New York to CC CPSU (2)," November 2, 1962, History and Public Policy Program Digital Archive, AVP RF, copy obtained by NHK, provided to CWIHP, and on file at National Security Archive, Washington, DC, trans. John Henriksen, Harvard University, https://digitalarchive.wilsoncenter.org/document/110425.

28. "Telegram from Soviet envoy in New York V. V. Kuznetsov to USSR Foreign Ministry," November 7, 1962, History and Public Policy Program Digital Archive, AVP RF, copy obtained by NHK, provided to CWIHP, and on file at National Security Archive, trans. John Henriksen, Harvard University, https://digitalarchive.wilsoncenter.org/document/110440; "Raport. St. Operupolnomochennyi 2-go otdela UKGB pri SM SSSR po Iaroslavskoi oblasti starshii leitenant Goncharov," November 2, 1962, in SBU Archives, fond 1, opys 1, no. 1532, fol. 365.

29. Aleksandr Rogozin, "Sovetskii flot v voinakh i konfliktakh kholodnoi voiny," chap. 2, "SSSR v stroitel'stve VMS Kuby," http://alerozin.narod.ru/CubaNavy/CubaNavySoviet-2.htm.

30. Statsenko, "Doklad komandira 51-i raketnoi divizii o deistviiakh soedineniia v period s 12 iiulia po 1 dekabria 1962 goda na o. Kuba"; "Nachal'niku upravleniia KGB pri Sovete ministrov USSR po Odesskoi oblasti general-maioru tov. Kuvarzinu. Raport. Starshii upolnomochennyi 2-go otdela UKGB pri SM SSSR po Iaroslavskoi oblasti starshii leitenant Goncharov," November 28, 1962, SBU Archives, fond 1, no. 1532, fols. 352–369, here fol. 365; "Nachal'niku upravleniia KGB pri Sovete ministrov USSR po Odesskoi oblasti general-maioru tov. Kuvarzinu. Raport. Starshii upolnomochennyi 2-

go otdela UKGB pri SM Adzharskoi SSR kapitan Dzhaparidze, December 8, 1962," SBU Archives, fond 1, opys 1, no. 1532, fols. 383–389, here fols. 386–387.

31. Statsenko, "Doklad komandira 51-i raketnoi divizii o deistviiakh soediineniia v period s 12 iiulia po 1 dekabria 1962 goda na o. Kuba"; Sidorov, "Vypolniaia internatsional'nyi dolg," 132–33; Rogozin, "Sovetskii flot v voinakh i konfliktakh kholodnoi voiny," chap. 2, "SSSR v stroitel'stve VMS Kuby; "Sovetskii Soiuz v lokal'nykh voinakh I konfliktakh," 280; "Telegram from TROSTNIK (Soviet Defense Minister Rodion Malinovsky) to PAVLOV (General Issa Pliev)," November 20, 1962, History and Public Policy Program Digital Archive, Archive of the President of the Russian Federation, Special Declassification, April 2002, trans. Svetlana Savranskaya, https://digitalarchive .wilsoncenter.org/document/117337.

26. Back at the Barricade

1. Rhodes Cook, "The Midterm Election of '62: A Real 'October Surprise,'" Sabato's Crystal Ball, University of Virginia Center for Politics, September 30, 2010, http://www.centerforpolitics.org/crystalball/articles/frc2010093001/.

2. "Letter from President Kennedy to Chairman Khrushchev," Washington, November 6, 1962, FRUS, 1961–1963, vol. 6, Kennedy-Khrushchev Exchanges, no. 74, https://history.state.gov/historicaldocuments/frus1961-63v06/d74; Beschloss, The Crisis Years, 555–57.

3. "Telegram from TROSTNIK (Soviet Defense Minister Rodion Malinovsky) to PAVLOV (General Issa Pliev)," November 5, 1962, History and Public Policy Program Digital Archive, Archive of the President of the Russian Federation, Special Declassification, April 2002, trans. Svetlana Savranskaya, https:// digitalarchive.wilsoncenter.org/document/117333.

4. "Telegram from Nikita Khrushchev to Anastas Mikoyan," November 11, 1962, History and Public Policy Program Digital Archive, From the personal papers of Dr. Sergo A. Mikoyan, donated to the National Security Archive, trans. Svetlana Savranskaya for the National Security Archive, https:// digitalarchive.wilsoncenter.org/document/11509.

5. "Telegram from Nikita Khrushchev to Anastas Mikoyan," November 11, 1962, History and Public Policy Program Digital Archive, From the personal papers of Dr. Sergo A. Mikoyan, donated to the National Security Archive, trans. Svetlana Savranskaya for the National Security Archive, https:// digitalarchive.wilsoncenter.org/document/115098.

6. "Memorandum of Conversation between Castro and Mikoyan," November 5, 1962; cf. "Zapis' besedy Mikoiana s Fidelem Kastro et al.," November 5, 1962, 7–8, https://nsarchive2.gwu.edu/rus/text_files/CMCrisis/40.PDF;

Raymond Garthoff, *Reflections on the Cuban Missile Crisis: Revised to Include New Revelations from Soviet and Cuban Sources* (Washington, DC, 1989), 108.

7. Nikita Khrushchev, "Telegram to Mikoian, November 11, 1962," in *Karib-skii krizis, dokumenty*, Rossiiskie programmy Arkhiva ntasionalnoi bezopas-nosti, National Security Archive, George Washington University, https://nsarchive2.gwu.edu/rus/text_files/CMCrisis/46.PDF; Fursenko and Naf-tali, *"One Hell of a Gamble,"* 302–3.

8. "Record of Conversation between Mikoyan and Fidel Castro, Havana," November 13, 1962, History and Public Policy Program Digital Archive, From the personal papers of Dr. Sergo A. Mikoyan, donated to the National Security Archive, trans. Anna Melyakova for the National Security Archive, https://digitalarchive.wilsoncenter.org/document/115099.

9. "Record of Conversation between Mikoyan and Fidel Castro, Havana," November 13, 1962, https://digitalarchive.wilsoncenter.org/document/115099.

10. Fursenko and Naftali, *"One Hell of a Gamble,"* 305–6; "Cuban Military Order Authorizing Anti-Aircraft Fire," November 17, 1962, in *Karibskii krizis, doku-menty*, Rossiiskie programmy Arkhiva natsional'noi bezopasnosti, National Security Archive, George Washington University, https://nsarchive2.gwu.edu/nsa/cuba_mis_cri/621117%20Authorizing%20Anti-aircraft%20Fire.pdf; *American Foreign Policy: Current Documents 1962* (Washington, DC, 1966), 459–60.

11. "Letter from President Kennedy to Chairman Khrushchev," Washington, November 6, 1962, *FRUS, 1961–1963*, vol. 6, *Kennedy-Khrushchev Exchanges*, no. 74, https://history.state.gov/historicaldocuments/frus1961-63v06/d74; "Let-ter from Chairman Khrushchev to President Kennedy," Moscow, Undated, *FRUS, 1961–1963*, vol. 6, *Kennedy-Khrushchev Exchanges*, no. 75, https://history.state.gov/historicaldocuments/frus1961-63v06/d75.

12. "Telegram from Soviet Ambassador to the USA A. F. Dobrynin to USSR Foreign Ministry," November 12, 1962, History and Public Policy Program Digital Archive, AVP RF, copy obtained by NHK, provided to CWIHP, and on file at National Security Archive, trans. J. Henriksen, https://digitalarchive.wilsoncenter.org/document/110442; "Editorial Note," *FRUS, 1961–1963*, vol. 6, *Kennedy-Khrushchev Exchanges*, no. 76, https://history.state.gov/historicaldocuments/frus1961-63v06/d76.

13. "Message from Chairman Khrushchev to President Kennedy," Moscow, November 14, 1962, *FRUS, 1961–1963*, vol. 6, *Kennedy-Khrushchev Exchanges*, no. 77, https://history.state.gov/historicaldocuments/frus1961-63v06/d77; "Telegram from Soviet Ambassador to the USA A. F. Dobrynin to USSR For-eign Ministry," November 14, 1962, History and Public Policy Program Digi-tal Archive, AVP RF, copy obtained by NHK, provided to CWIHP, and on file

424 NOTES (PAGES 344–346)

at National Security Archive, trans. John Henriksen, https://digitalarchive
.wilsoncenter.org/document/110443; "Message from President Kennedy to
Chairman Khrushchev," Washington, November 15, 1962, *FRUS*, 1961–
1963, vol. 6, *Kennedy-Khrushchev Exchanges*, no. 78, https://history.state.gov/
historicaldocuments/frus1961-63v06/d78; "Memorandum from the President's Special Assistant for National Security Affairs (Bundy) to the Executive Committee of the National Security Council," Washington, November
16, 1962, *FRUS*, 1961–1963, vol. 11, *Cuban Missile Crisis and Aftermath*, no.
184, https://history.state.gov/historicaldocuments/frus1961-63v11/d184.

14. "Telegram from the Mission to the United Nations to the Department of
State," New York, November 15, 1962, midnight, *FRUS*, 1961–1963, vol.
11, *Cuban Missile Crisis and Aftermath*, no. 183, https://history.state.gov/
historicaldocuments/frus1961-63v11/d183.

15. "Central Committee of the Communist Party of the Soviet Union Presidium
Protocol 66," November 16, 1962, History and Public Policy Program Digital Archive, RGANI, F. 3, Op. 16, D. 947, L. 49, trans. and ed. Mark Kramer,
with assistance from Timothy Naftali, https://digitalarchive.wilsoncenter
.org/document/115093.

16. "Excerpt from Protocol No. 66 of Session of CC CPSU Presidium, 'Instructions to Comrade A. I. Mikoyan,'" November 16, 1962, History and Public Policy Program Digital Archive, Personal Archive of Dr. Sergo A.
Mikoyan, trans. Svetlana Savranskaya, https://digitalarchive.wilsoncenter
.org/document/117335; cf. Nikita Khrushchev, "Ob ukazaniiakh tovarish-
chu Mikoianu," 10 pp., in *Karibskii krizis, dokumenty*, Rossiiskie programmy
Arkhiva natsional'noi bezopasnosti, National Security Archive, George Washington University, https://nsarchive2.gwu.edu/rus/text_files/CMCrisis/47
.PDF.

17. "Anastas Mikoian Nikite Khrushchevu," November 18, 1962, 3 pp., in *Karibskii krizis, dokumenty*, Rossiiskie programmy Arkhiva natsional'noi bezopasnosti, National Security Archive, George Washington University, https://
nsarchive2.gwu.edu/rus/text_files/CMCrisis/50.PDF.

18. "Rodion Malinovsky and Matvei Zakharov to the Central Committee," Novem-
ber 17, 1962, in *Karibskii krizis, dokumenty*, Rossiiskie programmy Arkhiva
natsional'noi bezopasnosti, National Security Archive, George Washington
University, https://nsarchive2.gwu.edu/rus/text_files/CMCrisis/48.PDF;
"Telegram from Soviet Foreign Minister A. A. Gromyko to A. I. Mikoyan,"
November 18, 1962, History and Public Policy Program Digital Archive, AVP
RF; copy obtained by NHK, provided to CWIHP, and on file at National Security Archive, Washington, DC, trans. John Henriksen, Harvard University,
https://digitalarchive.wilsoncenter.org/document/110445; "Anastas Mikoian

Nikite Khrushchevu," November 18, 1962, 3 pp., in *Karibskii krizis, dokumenty*, Rossiiskie programmy Arkhiva natsional'noi bezopasnosti, National Security Archive, George Washington University, https://nsarchive2.gwu.edu/rus/text_files/CMCrisis/50.PDF; "Anastas Mikoian to Nikita Khrushchev," November 19, 1962, 4 pp., in *Karibskii krizis, dokumenty*, Rossiiskie programmy Arkhiva natsional'noi bezopasnosti, National Security Archive, George Washington University, https://nsarchive2.gwu.edu/rus/text_files/CMCrisis/52.PDF.

19. "Zapis' besedy tovarishcha Anastasa Ivanovicha Mikoiana s tovarishchami Fidelem Kastro, Osval'do Dortikosom et al.," November 19, 1962, https://nsarchive2.gwu.edu/rus/text_files/CMCrisis/51.PDF; "Anastas Mikoian to Nikita Khrushchev," November 19, 1962; "Anastas Mikoian to the Central Committee," November 20, 1962, in *Karibskii krizis, dokumenty*, Rossiiskie programmy Arkhiva natsional'noi bezopasnosti, National Security Archive, George Washington University, https://nsarchive2.gwu.edu/rus/text_files/CMCrisis/53.PDF; "Text of Communication Dated 19 November 1962 from Prime Minister Fidel Castro of Cuba to Acting Secretary-General U Thant," Press Release SG/1379, 20 11 1962, 2, https://search.archives.un.org/uploads/r/united-nations-archives/7/e/e/7ee400f4f307d5d29bf66c5d1d0dcfdb5aa620d4117d73a7feaoeaa93d4964d3/S-0872-0002-06-00001.pdf.

20. Acosta, *October 1962*, 188–90; "Anastas Mikoian to Nikita Khrushchev," November 19, 1962, 2–4, https://nsarchive2.gwu.edu/rus/text_files/CMCrisis/52.PDF.

21. "Zapis' besedy tovarishcha Anastasa Ivanovicha Mikoiana s tovarishchami Fidelem Kastro, Osval'do Dortikosom et al.," November 19, 1962; "Anastas Mikoian to Nikita Khrushchev," November 19, 1962; "Anastas Mikoian to the Central Committee," November 20, 1962.

27. Thanksgiving

1. "Summary Record of the 26th Meeting of the Executive Committee of the National Security Council," Washington, November 16, 1962, 11 a.m., *FRUS*, 1961–1963, vol. 11, *Cuban Missile Crisis and Aftermath*, no. 185, https://history.state.gov/historicaldocuments/frus1961-63v11/d185; "Memorandum from the Joint Chiefs of Staff to President Kennedy," Washington, November 16, 1962. *FRUS*, 1961–1963, vol. 11, *Cuban Missile Crisis and Aftermath*, no. 186, https://history.state.gov/historicaldocuments/frus1961-63v11/d186; "Paper Prepared for the Chairman of the Joint Chiefs of Staff (Taylor) for a Meeting with President Kennedy," Washington, November 16, 1962, *FRUS*, 1961–1963, vol. 11, *Cuban Missile Crisis and Aftermath*, no. 187, https://history.state.gov/historicaldocuments/frus1961-63v11/d187; "Memorandum of a Conference with President Kennedy," Washington, November 16, 1962, 4 p.m.,

FRUS, 1961–1963, vol. 11, *Cuban Missile Crisis and Aftermath*, no. 188, https://history.state.gov/historicaldocuments/frus1961-63v11/d188.

2. "RFK Notes. Executive Committee Meetings." Papers of Robert F. Kennedy, Attorney General Papers, Attorney General's Confidential File 6-2-10: Cuba: Executive committee meetings: RFK notes and memos, 1962: October–December (1 of 2 folders), 29, RFKAG-215-011, John F. Kennedy Presidential Library and Museum; "Summary Record of the 27th Meeting of the Executive Committee of the National Security Council," Washington, November 19, 1962, 10 a.m., *FRUS*, 1961–1963, vol. 11, *Cuban Missile Crisis and Aftermath*, no. 192, https://history.state.gov/historicaldocuments/frus1961-63v11/d192.

3. Fursenko and Naftali, *"One Hell of a Gamble,"* 307; "Editorial Note," *FRUS*, 1961–1963, vol. 11, *Cuban Missile Crisis and Aftermath*, no. 194, https://history.state.gov/historicaldocuments/frus1961-63v11/d194; cf. Arthur M. Schlesinger Jr., *Robert Kennedy and His Times* (Boston and New York, 1978), 550.

4. "Message from Chairman Khrushchev to President Kennedy," Moscow, November 20, 1962, *FRUS*, 1961–1963, vol. 11, *Cuban Missile Crisis and Aftermath*, no. 196, https://history.state.gov/historicaldocuments/frus1961-63v11/d196.

5. "Message from Chairman Khrushchev to President Kennedy," Moscow, November 20, 1962.

6. Message from Chairman Khrushchev to President Kennedy, Moscow, November 20, 1962, *FRUS*, 1961–1963, vol. 11, *Cuban Missile Crisis and Aftermath*, no. 196, https://history.state.gov/historicaldocuments/frus1961-63v11/d196; "Telegram from TROSTNIK (Soviet Defense Minister Rodion Malinovsky) to PAVLOV (General Issa Pliev)," November 20, 1962, History and Public Policy Program Digital Archive, Archive of the President of the Russian Federation, Special Declassification, April 2002, trans. by Svetlana Savranskaya, https://digitalarchive.wilsoncenter.org/document/117337.

7. "On Additional Instructions to comrade A. I. Mikoian on the Cuban Issue, November 22, 1962," The Cuban Missile Crisis 1962: The 40th Anniversary, Documents, National Security Archive, George Washington University, https://nsarchive2.gwu.edu/nsa/cuba_mis_cri/621122%20CPSU%20Instructions%20to%20Mikoyan.pdf; cf. Mikoyan's report to the Central Committee on the Cuban instruction to Lechuga and Khrushchev's and Gromyko's instructions to him in that regard, in Sergo Mikoyan, *The Soviet Cuban Missile Crisis,* Documents nos. 35 and 36, 478–80.

8. "Memorandum of A. I. Mikoyan's Conversation with Comrades F. Castro, O. Dorticós, E. Guevara, E. Aragonés, and C. R. Rodríguez," in Sergo Mikoyan, *The Soviet Cuban Missile Crisis*, Document no. 37, 481–88.

9. John Fitzgerald Kennedy, President Kennedy's Statement on Cuba, November 20, 1962, American History, http://www.let.rug.nl/usa/presidents/john-fitzgerald-kennedy/president-kennedys-statement-on-cuba-november-20-1962.php. Cf. *"Third Draft,"* *11.20.62,* in John F. Kennedy Presidential Library and Museum, Papers of Robert F. Kennedy, Attorney General Papers, Attorney General's Confidential File 6-4-1: Cuba: Cuban Crisis, 1962: *Kennedy-Khrushchev Letters,* 1962: September–November, 24–27; Robert Kennedy, *Thirteen Days,* Documents, 172–74; President John F. Kennedy's 45th News Conference –November 20, 1962, https://www.youtube.com/watch?v=e7dB0AkhvgM.

10. "Ia vam ėkspromptom dolozhil," Iz zakliuchitel'nogo slova N. S. Khrushcheva na plenume TsK KPSS 23 noiabria 1962 goda," Stenogramma, *Ogonek,* October 22, 2012, https://www.kommersant.ru/doc/2049584.

11. "Ia vam ėkspromptom dolozhil," Iz zakliuchitel'nogo slova N. S. Khrushcheva na plenume TsK KPSS 23 noiabria 1962 goda," Stenogramma, *Ogonek,* October 22, 2012, https://www.kommersant.ru/doc/2049584.

12. Dmitrii Poliansky's address in *Nikita Khrushchev, 1964: Stenogrammy plenuma i drugie dokumenty,* comp. Andrei Artizov et al. (Moscow, 2007), 198, https://on-island.net/History/1964.htm.

13. Aleksei Butskii, "Rabota Glavnogo shtaba RVSN v period podgotovki i provedeniia operatsii "Anadyr'," in *Strategicheskaia operatsiia "Anadyr',"* 65–70, here 70.

Epilogue

1. "Khrushchev calls Kennedy death 'a heavy blow,'" UPI, November 23, 1963, https://www.upi.com/Archives/1963/11/23/Khrushchev-calls-Kennedy-death-a-heavy-blow/3503214243588/.

2. Simon L. Lewis and Mark A. Maslin, *The Human Planet: How We Created the Anthropocene* (London, 2018), 257–58; Odd Arne Westad, *The Cold War: A World History* (New York, 2017), 224–25, 303; Joseph M. Siracusa, *Nuclear Weapons: A Very Short Introduction* (Oxford, 2015), 39–79.

3. Thomas Graham Jr. and Damien J. LaVera, *Cornerstones of Security: Arms Control Treaties in the Nuclear Era* (Seattle and London, 2002); Ishaan Tharoor, "Trump Embraces a New Nuclear Arms Race," *Washington Post,* February 4, 2019, https://www.washingtonpost.com/world/2019/02/04/trump-embraces-new-nuclear-arms-race/?utm_term=.634a16c21ba1; "U.S. Withdrawal from the INF Treaty on August 2, 2019," Press Statement, Michael R. Pompeo, Secretary of State, August 2, 2019, https://www.state.gov/u-s-withdrawal-from-the-inf-treaty-on-august-2-2019/; "'Destructive U.S.': Russia Reacts to INF Treaty Withdrawal," *Moscow Times,* August 2, 2019, https://

428   NOTES (PAGES 361–362)

www.themoscowtimes.com/2019/08/02/destructive-us-russia-reacts-to-inf
-treaty-withdrawal-a66680.

4. Max Fisher, "The Cuban Missile Misunderstanding: How cultural misreadings almost led to global annihilation," *Washington Post*, October 16, 2012.

5. Paul Bracken, *The Second Nuclear Age: Strategy, Danger, and the New Power Politics* (New York, 2012), 93–214.

INDEX